INSIGHT GUIDES

Created and Directed by Hans Höfer

CHINA

Update Editor: Tim Larimer
Executive Editor: Scott Rutherford

Editorial Director: Brian Bell

Houghton Mifflin

With the collapse of Communism in the former Soviet Union, China was left as the world's foremost guardian of Marxist thought. Questions arose that have yet to be answered. Would the winds of change blow as decisively in Beijing as they had in Moscow and Eastern Europe? Clearly, events have suggested otherwise. The lingering unknowns regarding the succession of power after Deng Xiaoping made interpretations of China's actions dubious. Yet China is, in a measured way, changing.

China has always had an intoxicating effect on Westerners. A fifth of the world's people are Chinese citizens. China has a governmental bureaucracy of 40 million. It also has 4,000 years of continuous written history. No other contemporary society comes close.

Like all of the books in this 190-title series, Insight Guide: China is written and structured in the belief that ignorance is neither bliss nor recommended, especially when in strange lands. Indeed, since the first Insight Guide, on Bali, over a quarter of a century ago, it has been our editorial belief that unless the traveler understands the background of a destination, travel is a shallow experience and can actually narrow the mind.

The original edition of Insight Guide: China was produced out of Apa's editorial office in Munich. Project editor **Manfred Morgenstern** gathered together the authors and photographers, most of whom he had known during 15 years of work relating to China. Morgenstern first went to the country in early 1977, shortly after the death of Mao Zedong. Countless trips to China followed, in which Morgenstern, a sociologist by background and travel writer and tour organizer by profession, peeled back the layers of Chinese history, culture and politics.

Morgenstern

Rutherford

Revamping Insight Guide: China fell upon **Scott Rutherford**, Apa's executive editor in Singapore and responsible for the Asian and Pacific titles. Rutherford first came to Asia – Japan – in 1985 for a National Geographic assignment. He later returned to Tokyo to live, working on publishing and television projects before joining Apa in Singapore. Rutherford wrote several new essays and updated some of the chapters for this new edition.

Updating many of the Places chapters was Hanoi-based **Tim Larimer**, a frequent contributor and correspondent for international publications such as *Time, The Asian Wall Street Journal*, and *The Economist*. Larimer, an American, took off on an extended ramble through much of eastern and southern China. One highlight of his travels was the unexpected ease of traveling in China nowadays. Larimer was the update editor for a revamped *Insight Guide: Vietnam*.

Larimer

Helmut Forster-Latsch and **Marie-Luise Latsch** have spent many years studying and researching in China, specializing in Chinese culture and in the traditions of China's ethnic minorities. Both have written various textbooks, and have translated Chinese literature and fairy tales.

Marie-Luise Beppler-Lie is particularly knowledgeable about the interior regions of China. After studies in Frankfurt focusing on China, she taught for three years in Chongqing, and trained a number of interpreters in the use of German. Beppler-Lie also translates contemporary Chinese literature into German.

Northwestern China, especially along the ancient Silk Road, is the interest of **Karl Grobe-Hagel**. With a background as editor of foreign political news for a major German daily, he has been responsible for covering eastern Asia and China.

Eva Klapproth wrote about the eastern provinces of China, something for which she was well prepared. For several years she studied in Taiwan, and later in Shanghai. Together with Helmut Forster-Latsch, she has tried to publicize in the West the writings of critical Chinese intellectuals.

Klapproth

Elke Wandel wrote about Beijing, where she worked for several years as a teacher, and on surrounding areas. She has published a book about the role of women in China.

Tom Ots contributed the section on Chinese medicine. He studied – and also practiced – Chinese medicine for several years in Beijing and Nanjing.

The photographic contributions are the supporting pillar of every Insight Guide. Visually, China has changed in the past decade as have few other countries. Numerous new photographs were required for this new edition.

Pansegrau

Catherine Karnow, based in San Francisco and a frequent Apa contributor, including Insight Guides on Vietnam, Los Angeles and Tokyo, has made countless trips covering most of Asia and the world for numerous international publications. **Olivier Laude**,

Karnow

also based in California, undertakes special projects for a number of publications. **Patrick Lucero** works out of Manila to cover Asia and the Pacific. He was the primary contributor to *Insight Guide: Philippines*.

Jack Hollingsworth travels the world from his home in Texas for numerous corporate and editorial clients. A contributor to new Apa publications on Bali and Singapore, Hollingsworth's pictures have a delightful aesthetic.

Photographic contributors for the book's original edition – and we have retained many of those timeless photographs – included project editor Morgenstern and **Erhard Pansegrau**, who collaborated on the first edition of *Insight Guide: Beijing*. Other contributors were **Mike Theiler, Bodo Bondzio, Peter Hessel, Elke Wandel** and **Kosima Weber-Liu**. Providing rare photographs from the Cultural Revolution was **China Travel and Tourism Press**, in Beijing.

New maps for this revamped edition were created by **Suriyani Ahmad** and **Kathy Wee**, of Apa's Singapore office. **Caroline Low**, also of Singapore's editorial office, handled the editorial layout and DTP work, as well as the editor's compulsive obsession with never-ending changes.

CONTENTS

INTRODUCTION

The ancient Greeks wrote about the Serers, the bearers of silk. The name China as we use it in the West can presumably be traced back to the Qin dynasty (221–207 BC), which was described as Tschin, Tschina or Tzinistan in the Indo-Germanic languages. The Chinese of the Qin dynasty called the country Da Qin, thus giving the empire not only their own name, but a sense of size by preceding *qin* with *da*, which means big or great in size. (In pinyin, the modern transliteration of Chinese pronunciation, *qi* is pronounced *chi*.)

While official references nowadays refer to Zhonghua Renmin Gongheguo – the People's Republic of China – this land has always been, simply, Zhongguo – the Middle Kingdom. For Westerners, it is simply China, the third-largest nation in the world, and the largest in population. It has the world's longest continuously-recorded history and existence, and it has given the world some of the most significant scientific and technological inventions ever.

In Tiantan, the Temple of Heaven in Beijing, a marble altar signifies the center of the known ancient world, a place that only the emperor was allowed to enter in order to communicate with heaven. According to the worldview of ancient China – which extends back in written history, continuously, 4,000 years – the Middle Kingdom lay precisely below the center of the firmament. The further one was from the emperor's throne, the lower one was in the cosmic hierarchy. The unfortunate people and cultures living on the dark peripheries of the earth, especially to the gloomy north and the arid west, were necessarily barbarians.

Likewise, for centuries Europeans similarly regarded China as equally near the edge of the earth, admittedly an empire of magnificence and interest – but of little importance to the world.

Much later, especially during the 1960s and 1970s, Western analysts and pundits referred to China as a sleeping giant, or, if metaphorically-inclined, a sleeping tiger or even dragon. It's been a few years since one has heard such expressions in regards to China. No one doubts that China is now wide awake, and increasingly a power that will help define the next millennium.

Yet sculpting the world's contours is not something with which China is comfortable or experienced. For most of its existence, it has focused inward, like a *taijiquan* student seeking a centered stability. Consequently, China's emergence as a world-power candidate has been clumsy and awkward, sometimes seeming the regional bully and blind as to how its actions are perceived elsewhere. China will learn, no doubt, and adjust its behavior if it thinks it needs to do so – but only if China itself thinks it necessary.

More immediate, perhaps, is China's confounding domestic concern: population. Since the end of World War II, just 50 years ago and but a blink in China's history, the country's population has doubled to over a billion people. Only around ten percent of China

Preceding pages: Li Jiang and limestone spires, Guilin; multilingual inscriptions, Yonghegong, Beijing; watching traditional opera, Wenzhou; Nanjing Lu, Shanghai; ballet class, Hong Kong. **Left**, memorial for Dr Sun Yatsen, Guangzhou.

is suitable for agriculture, but a fifth of the world's people must subsist on that land. Yet experts in both China and elsewhere say that China can realistically support but 800 million people. Furthermore, although the rate of population increase is decreasing, the male-female ratio is rising. In another decade or so, there may be nearly 100 million more men than women.

Travelers to China's large cities (towns are anything less than 1 million people) will see the result of accommodating the explosive growth: monochromatic, concrete cities veiled with the smoke of pollution, and legions of men from the countryside looking for work, and perhaps a partner, if lucky. They will also see increasing affluence and leisure time, and the capitalist signs of people spending money and nurturing a consumer society. Things are getting better in China for the individual. A result of Communism, or the intrusion of capitalism? The question, and answer, is dialectical.

In the fifty years since the Communist revolution, the quality of life for the average Chinese has improved nearly beyond measure. Life expectancy is double that of 1949, and the standard of living, and quality of life, has improved exponentially. At the same time, Communism has faltered in monumental ways. Misdirected policies created what may have been the world's worst famine in the early 1960s, and the so-called Cultural Revolution, initially nurtured by Mao to increase his stature, spun out of control, destroying much of China's ancient heritage in the process, not to mention China's intellectual and creative talents.

Travel guides typically waste time gushing on and on about China as a land of contrasts or a land of superlatives. Maybe true, but the smart traveler ignores all that wordy fluff. There is no room for generalizations about China, nor the possibility of distilling its essence into a few brilliant quips or quotable catch-phrases.

"Seeing is easy, learning is hard" goes an old Chinese proverb. Indeed. The insightful traveler must necessarily realize, and acknowledge, that China simply Is.

Notes about spellings: For the past century, the most common way to romanize Chinese was the Wade-Giles method. Increasingly, however, pinyin is the modern standard, and this book uses pinyin. Travelers will encounter both forms, and so must make certain linguistic leaps of recognition at times. China's capital was Peking the old way, Beijing in pinyin. The founder of the Communist Party used to be Mao Tse-tung; now it's Mao Zedong. The only pinyin transliterations libel to induce indigestion are qi, pronounced *chi*, and xi, or *shi*. The Ch'in dynasty is now the Qin dynasty.

Mandarin often uses suffixes to indicate many proper nouns, such as river (*-jiang* or *-he*), temple (*-si* or *-ta*), mountain (*-shan*), or street (*-lu* or *-dajie*). In romanized form, the suffix is sometimes integral with the root, sometimes not. In the above examples, we have chosen to separate the suffix to clearly identify the subject. Thus, the Tian Mountains are Tian Shan, but never Tian Shan Mountains or Tianshan Mountains. The decision to separate the suffix is primarily one of utility, especially with geographical landmarks. (Insightful readers will learn to recognize those that we've left attached to the root.) Additionally, we use Chinese names as the primary reference.

<u>Right</u>, Kong Fuzi, or Confucius.

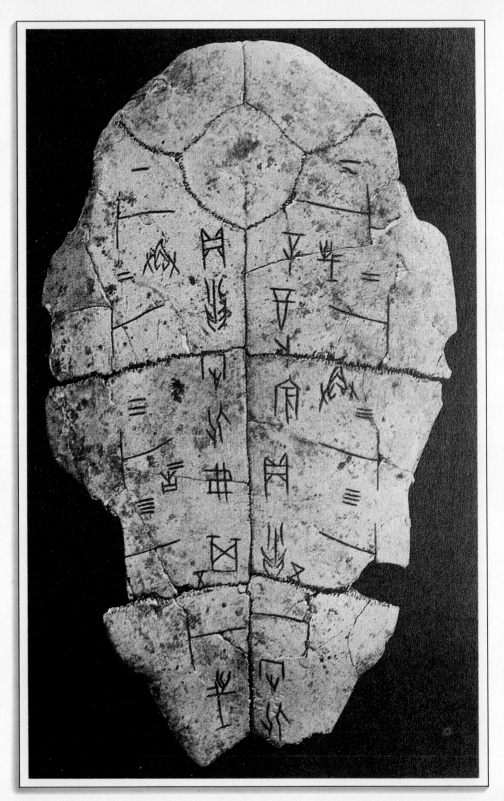

When the Chinese refer to their history, they might be speaking of times that are already legendary. After all, China's written history dates back approximately four thousand years. Archaeological findings indicate that people were already living in the territory of today's China one million years ago. In the 1920s, fossilized remains of human species were discovered in Yuanmou (Yunnan province) and in Lantian (Shaanxi province). More than 400,000 years ago, Peking Man (*Sinanthropus pekinensis*) lived in Zhoukoudian, near Beijing; he was able to walk upright, produced simple tools, and knew how to light fires.

Yet the Peking Man marks a point at which there is a break in development, and little is known from then on until around 3000 BC. The remains of various neolithic civilizations date from this time, especially the matriarchal Yangshao civilization and the patriarchal Longshan civilization.

When the prehistoric village of Banpo was discovered in what is today Xi'an, it seemed obvious to conclude that the bend in the Huanghe, or Yellow River, with its fertile loess landscape, had been the center of ancient Chinese culture and civilization. Discoveries made in recent years, however, suggest that neolithic civilizations were established in other areas – notably in Xinjiang, Manchuria, Sichuan and Guangdong.

It has not been proven conclusively that there really was an age of the Five Mythical Rulers. This is said to have been the time in which the foundations of Chinese culture, such as irrigation systems and rice plantations, were developed. The Yellow Emperor Huangdi, said to rule between 2490 and 2413 BC, is regarded as the forbearer of the Chinese nation. Huangdi is said to have overpowered the other tribes with weapons made of jade, and his wife Leizu is thought to have invented the breeding of silkworms. The wagon, boat and a precursor of the compass are all attributed to Huangdi. He is said to

have been knowledgeable in astronomy, and to have developed the first Chinese calendar. Under his rule, pictographic characters, the twelve-tone scale and various gauges were developed. To this day, there is a dispute as to the existence of the first dynasty noted in historical writings: the Xia dynasty (21st to 16th century BC).

Shang dynasty (16–11 cent. BC): If it existed, the Xia dynasty was followed by the Shang dynasty, which grew out of the plains of northern China, on the river Huanghe (Yellow River) and in the basin of the Wei River. The Shang were an aristocratically-minded society, with the family as the basis of their social structure. Small towns were surrounded by walls or ramparts; the ruler's residence and religious buildings anchored the center. The Shang had already mastered the breeding of silkworms and the technique of spinning and weaving silk. They produced bronze of very high quality and used it to make weapons, tools, utensils and artifacts. Written evidence, such as inscriptions on oracle bones or bronze receptacles used for religious rituals, have provided information on the Shang dynasty.

Zhou dynasty (11c–221 BC): The Zhou dynasty ruled from the eleventh century BC until 221 BC, when China was united under Qin Shi Huangdi. Originally, their settlements lay further west than those of the Shang (today, the provinces of Shanxi and Gansu). The rulers of the Zhou brutally overthrew the Shang, under the pretext that the Shang rulers had been corrupt and led a dissipated life, disregarding their duties and therefore forfeiting the mercy of the gods.

The Zhou took over the system that the Shang had developed and made many improvements. In order to administer their enormous territory, a system of fiefs, headed by a king, was established. He allocated land to the members of his clan, to the heads of tribes or to devout aristocrats. In exchange, they had to pay the king a tax or support him in wars. The first capital of the Zhou dynasty was Hao, situated near present-day Xi'an.

In matters of religion, the Zhou followed the tradition of the Shang, and combined this with their old heavenly religion. Heaven was the first among the gods, and the king was considered to be the son of heaven and acted as mediator between heaven and earth and the people. He alone was able to offer heaven the necessary ritualistic sacrifices. The Zhou banned human sacrifice, and it was no longer acceptable to consult oracle bones. The priests, who had been of great importance to the Shang and were the only people who knew how to read and write, had become superfluous. They became traveling teachers and earned their livelihood as advisers to the individual feifs. At the end of the seventh century and beginning of the eighth century BC, nomadic tribes and disgruntled feudal lords invaded the Wei valley, destroying the capital in 771 BC and murdering the king, ending the Western Zhou dynasty. The son of the murdered king founded the new capital of the Eastern Zhou dynasty in Luoyang.

From this time onwards, the role of the ruler was limited to being a high priest and carrying out important ritual sacrifices. The Eastern Zhou dynasty, which lasted until 221 BC, is divided into two main periods: the Spring and Autumn Period (771–471 BC) and the Warring States Period (476–221 BC).

In the Spring and Autumn Period, the feudal lords and the landed gentry gained power and soon considered the land to be their own property, which they felt at liberty to inherit, sell or lease to the farmers. The kingdom was replaced by a system of allied and competing noble states. In the sixth century, the aristocracy was hit by a serious institutional crisis and the Zhou empire disintegrated into small splinter states.

From the sixth century onwards, the stronger states imposed their will on the weaker ones. By the beginning of the Warring States Period, the number of states competing for supremacy had been reduced to seven. The Spring and Autumn Period, as well as the Warring States Period, was one of important changes in the social structure. New social classes and groups emerged, commerce and trade between the individual states increased, and unification of the empire became a source of conflict.

These arguments were also reflected in the debates of the great philosophical schools. Confucianism and Taoism developed. This period is often described as the one during which one hundred schools competed with each other. The most successful turned out to

be the legalistic. The legalists favored a highly codified, positive system of law; it contained generally binding norms designed to strengthen the state economically and militarily, and opposed feudal privileges.

Under the influence of the legalists, the feudal system in the state of Qin was replaced by administrative districts. The ruler of the belligerent border state of Qin was able to conquer the other states in the course of several campaigns, primarily because he had listened to his legalistic advisors and his troops were equipped with better weapons.

Qin dynasty (221–206 BC): The first emperor of the Qin dynasty, Qin Shi Huangdi, united the empire in 221 BC. Xianyang (west of the

present-day Xi'an) became the capital. The country was divided into prefectures and administered by specially chosen officials. To ward off the nomadic tribes, the Qin emperor launched a project to join together the already existing parts of a defensive wall into one continuous wall, the Great Wall. Some 300,000 people were supposed to have worked on its construction.

Members of the nobility were deprived of their power and forced to settle in the capital, where it was easier to control them. The Qin dynasty was in power for only a short time, yet its legacy was far-reaching. Measurements, weights and coins were standardized, and – most importantly – so was the Chinese script. Transport and communications were standardized, and all carriages had the same gauge. Qin Shi Huangdi was an extremely severe ruler. In 213 BC, all non-legalistic books were burned; to publish other books meant risking the death penalty. It is said that 460 Confucian scholars were buried alive. Everyone suffered under the despotic Qin Shi Huangdi. Because so many were forced to work on his countless construction projects – including the Great Wall and several palaces for the nobility – there was a shortage of labor in agriculture, resulting in numerous famines; after his death in 211 BC, his son was overthrown by a peasants' revolt.

Han dynasty (206 BC–AD 220): The leader of the revolt, Liu Bang, appointed himself first emperor of the Han dynasty in 206 BC. The Chinese derived their name from this dynasty, and up to this day still describe themselves as the people of Han. Chang'an (Xi'an) became the capital of the Western Han dynasty (206 BC–AD 8); this was followed by the Eastern Han dynasty (AD 23–220), with Luoyang as its capital. During the reign of the first emperors of the Han dynasty, which lasted 400 years, the strict laws were relaxed

Left, Qin Shi Huangdi, who created a uniform script. **Above**, old print of the imperial guards.

to some extent; those who fought for or were related to the emperor's clan were rewarded with fiefs; it became possible to acquire land by purchase. Not only the nobility, but also merchants and civil servants could now be landowners.

Essentially, the system of government developed by the Qin dynasty was absorbed, except that the civil servants gained executive power. State examinations for civil servants were introduced. Theoretically, anyone could take part in these tests; in practice, however, it was only possible for children of the wealthy classes, as learning to write the script was difficult and time-consuming. The Han rulers relied heavily on rich landowners, who made good profits and had the time to learn the script and study the cultural history. This class is often described as the gentry. Every clan aimed to have as many members of its family as possible placed in important government offices.

Confucianism became the state doctrine. The educated upper-class devoted itself to painting and the arts; new philosophical and historical works were also written. Paper was one of the most important inventions of the Han dynasty; until then, writing had been done on wood, bamboo or silk.

In 180 BC, a new group appeared at the imperial court for the first time: palace eunuchs, who were to play an important role until 1911. Originally, they were hired to look after the emperors' wives and concubines, but they soon advanced to the status of advisors, playing an important part in palace intrigues and power struggles.

The Han dynasty was in its prime under the rule of Han Wudi (140–87 BC). It had always been an important challenge for the Chinese empire to confront the nomadic tribes in the north and the west. Wudi succeeded in defeating the Huns, nomads who had established a strong empire in the north. Now Wudi's empire stretched all the way to the western region, to what is now Xinjiang. He conquered the Tarim Basin, southern Manchuria and the area that is now North Korea. During the reign of the Han, there were numerous contacts with other cultures, through traders coming from afar. Since the first century BC, caravans had traveled along the Silk Road, bringing horses and gold in exchange for silk.

The military expansion to the south was

also continued under the Han, and, as usual, the peasants had to carry the cost of the wars. Because of increases in taxation, land ownership was concentrated amongst fewer and fewer families during the last 70 years of the dynasty. More peasants left the land, intrigues at court and corruption amongst civil servants were everyday occurrences, and the eunuchs meddled in power struggles. There were also serious natural disasters.

A peasants' revolt in 184, which was led by the Yellow Turbans, a secret sect, weakened the rule of the Han. When the emperor formally abdicated in 220, the country was rundown and the population decimated.

Unsettled centuries: Amidst the chaos of war that followed the fall of the Han dynasty, Buddhism spread rapidly and gained followers amongst the ordinary people. The largest and most famous Buddhist caves (Dunhuang, Luoyang and Yungang) date from this time. From the end of the Han dynasty to the beginning of the Sui dynasty, in 581, various states fought each other. After the short period of the Three Empires, the Western and Eastern Jin dynasties, and the Dynasty of the Sixteen States, the time of the Southern and Northern dynasties followed. This turmoil brought the Sui dynasty to an end. It had only reigned for a short time, but had succeeded in uniting the country and establishing a new central government and consolidating agriculture. The division into North and South China, which had lasted 400 years, finally came to an end. Ambitious projects were set up, amongst them the building of the Grand Canal that connected the rivers Hai, Huang, Huai and Chang Jiang (Yangzi), enabling trade between north and south, especially for transporting rice from the south. As a result, the fertile regions of southern China gradually developed into an agricultural center. At that time, China's population was approaching 50 million people.

Projects for new buildings, wars and the great extravagance of the emperor proved too much for the country – the situation was similar to that under the reign of the first Qin emperor. The Sui were soon overthrown by a people's revolt.

The subsequent dynasties of the Tang (618–907) and the Song (960–1279), which were only briefly interrupted by a renewed breakup of political unity in China, are regarded as particularly rich times in Chinese history, with important military, economic, political and cultural concerns.

Tang dynasty (618–907): The first Tang emperors succeeded in reestablishing law and order. They practiced an expansive style of foreign politics and invaded central Asia, Korea and northern Vietnam. They subjugated the Turkic people and assumed supremacy over Tibet. (The Tibetans, however, through their military skills, briefly occupied the Chinese capital Chang'an.) In the first half of the eighth century, Chang'an (Xi'an) had approximately two million inhabitants, half of whom lived within the town walls. One tenth of the population was foreign. Based on the idea of squares as the

perfect universal form, the Tang capital was built like a chess board.

Under the rule of Emperor Taizong, there was an economic upswing. A new system of land distribution and improved irrigation methods led to a greater yield in agriculture. The state founded numerous manufacturing industries. Courier systems and postal coaches boosted commerce, and the Grand Canal was completed. The arts and sciences flourished; even today, poems dating from the Tang dynasty are regarded as unsurpassed. New administrative units, the *dao*, were created with structures similar to the provinces. The military administration was separated from the civilian. The imperial examination system for civil servants was reformed and reintroduced. Now the Confucian civil servants were able to stand up to regional and local nobility.

Certain symptoms of decay had already appeared during the rule of Taizong. After his death, the palace was riddled with intrigues. This was much to the advantage of Wu Zetian, the first and only enthroned empress of China. She ruled this enormous country for 20 years, until her son Xuanzong took over. He is alleged to have neglected his duties because of his infatuation with the beautiful concubine Yang Guifei. This led to the revolt of An Lushan, which was put

lute peak. Under the rule of the Song, there were impressive developments in agriculture, trade and commerce. There was gold, silver, copper and iron ore mining. The monetary system grew, and paper money came into circulation. Movable-type printing was invented (400 years before Gutenberg's press). Gunpowder had already been invented.

In southern China, the center of the Song rule, the town merchants attained a significantly higher status. Confucianism became the systematic political and ethical philosophy that it is today.

Repeated clashes with nomadic tribes continued throughout the Song era, until finally, in 1126, the Nuzhen conquered

down, but which left the country in ruins economically and militarily. Local governors and army officials exploited this power vacuum, while the eunuchs ruled in the emperor's palace. The country was shaken by peasants' revolts; nomadic tribes in the north gained strength. The Tang dynasty finally toppled and collapsed.

Song dynasty (960–1279): The Song dynasty followed after the short interlude of the Five Dynasties and Ten States. This was the time when Chinese civilization reached an abso-

Left, sculpture from Tang-period tomb. **Above**, ladies-in-waiting.

Kaifeng and founded the Jin dynasty. The Song court fled to the south and founded the Southern Song dynasty.

Yuan dynasty (1279–1368): Towards the end of the twelfth century, a new threat to the Song loomed in the north – the Mongols. Genghis Khan had united the Mongol tribes, and between 1218 and 1253 had succeeded in conquering all of central Asia, Russia and some parts of eastern Europe. In 1234, the Mongols overthrew the Jin dynasty, and in 1276, the Southern Song dynasty. Once the province of Guangdong had been conquered in 1279, the whole of China belonged to the enormous Mongol empire. For the first time, parts of Europe and Asia were united under one rule. Traffic along the Silk Road flourished. In 1275, the Venetian merchant Marco Polo took this route to Khanbalik (Beijing), which was then the capital of the Yuan dynasty. For 17 years, he served Genghis Khan; upon his return to Europe, he wrote the first comprehensive report on that legendary country in the East.

During the Mongol Yuan dynasty, the Han Chinese were discriminated against socially and politically. At the same time, however, the Mongols were dependent on the Chinese civil service for the administration of the Chinese part of their empire. Other nomadic groups had made attempts to assimilate with

Ming dynasty (1368–1644): After a long period of insurrections and disturbances, the Mongols were overthrown by Chinese troops under the leadership of Zhu Yuanzhang. He was enthroned as Emperor Taizu of the Ming dynasty, in 1386. Nanjing became the capital; he banished the Yuan Emperor Shundi and the Mongol nobility from Beijing. Now there was once again a true Chinese dynasty in China. The third Ming emperor later chose Beijing as the capital, and it retained this status until 1911.

The Ming were able to unify the economy once more; agriculture was subsidized, irrigation was improved and, for the first time, cotton was planted. Taxes were lowered, and

the Chinese, yet this was not the case with the Mongols. But the Mongol rulers were tolerant in religious matters, and encouraged Lamaism in particular.

During their rule, Tibet became part of China, which explains why China still claims the right to Tibet today.

But the peasants and the Chinese nobility were dispossessed of their land, which was distributed amongst the Mongol nobility and Lamaist monasteries. Taxes were increased, and the peasants were increasingly impoverished. Insurrection followed, with gangs of robbers often having entire areas under their control.

in some cases, land taxes were dropped altogether. As a result, the central government's position was strengthened. Chinese ships sailed far and wide. Under the command of the Moslem eunuch Zheng He, the fleet sailed to the Indian Ocean and the South Pacific. Trade links were established, and the first Chinese colonies abroad were set up. Trade and manufacture in particular experienced a significant upswing. In the fourteenth and fifteenth centuries, China was far ahead of Europe, in both economics and technology. Yet, in the sixteenth century, this relationship reversed – the reasons are still being debated amongst historians.

During the rule of the Ming, the first Christian missionaries came to China with the arrival at Canton, in 1516, of Portuguese ships. The danger to the Ming emperors' rule, however, continued to come from northern and central Asia. The Great Wall was once again reinforced to protect China from the nomads. The wars against the Mongols lasted into the sixteenth century.

Towards the end of the Ming dynasty, the peasants rapidly became impoverished, while land ownership was considerably concentrated. Moreover, the intrigues of the palace eunuchs paralyzed the imperial court, and the secret police attempted to suppress even the slightest signs of opposition. At the

established his own dynasty in the northeast of China. In the following years, he conquered vast areas of the northeast until finally – with the help of the Ming General Fu Lin – he succeeded in surmounting the Great Wall at Shanhaiguan and occupied Beijing.

By the end of the seventeenth century, the Qing occupied the entire Chinese heartland. In several big campaigns into central Asia and the south, the Qing managed to consolidate their power. They were also able to lay the groundwork for the greatest expansion the Chinese empire was to undergo. Taiwan was taken in 1683; Tibet and East Turkestan (Xinjiang) were securely annexed. The Qing reached the height of their power in the

beginning of the seventeenth century, there was another major peasant uprising.

Qing dynasty (1644–1911): The Manchus exploited this situation. In 1644, they toppled the Ming dynasty and established their own Qing dynasty, which was the last of the Chinese dynasties. The Manchus originated from the Nuzhen, a nomadic people who settled on the Songhua River. Towards the end of the sixteenth century, their ruler Nurhachi had already been successful in uniting various nomadic tribes. In 1616, he

Left, Kublai Khan, and the Ming emperors Hongwu and Wanli. **Above**, Kangxi at his calligraphy.

middle of the eighteenth century, at which time their territory covered more than 11 million square kilometers (4.3 million sq mi). In the northeast, the Qing empire reached beyond the river Heilong Jiang. The neighboring states in the south – Burma (Myanmar), Nepal and northern Vietnam – were forced to acknowledge Chinese supremacy and authority.

The first 150 years of Manchu rule – with important emperors like Kangxi (1662–1722) and Qianlong (1736–1796) – marked a period of expansion. Yet there were also signs of stabilization. The economy was reinvigorated with the help of lenient tax and agricultural policies. The areas for cultivation were increased, trade was boosted, industries such as mining and salt extraction were established, and foreign trade was strengthened. After all, the Qing were a minority ruling over this vast empire, hence they needed to exercise prudence. From the onset, the Qing emperors relied on the Confucian administration. Some of the Qing emperors – Qianlong in particular – were regarded as orthodox Confucians.

The Manchu clans, headed by the emperor, governed the Qing empire along strictly patriarchal lines. The Han Chinese were again discriminated against. One obvious sign of this was the plait that the Manchu forced

them to wear. Towards the end of the 1700s and the beginning of the 1800s, there were more and more revolts. One factor that contributed to the decay of the empire was a growing contradiction between the enormous population of China (in 1850, there were 430 million people in China, twice that of Europe) and the technological stagnation it had experienced since the late Ming and early Qing dynasties. The increasing population density soon exhausted the technical potential and the amount of land that could be cultivated. The Manchu had one solution to this problem – allow Chinese peasants to settle in northern China, in Manchuria.

The Qing empire had traditionally focused its foreign policies on areas of central Asia and thus was not able to withstand the increased threat from European forces. In the Opium War (1840–1842), the empire was weakened by its first defeat. The compensation payments that China was obliged to pay to foreign powers were simply passed on to the peasants and tradesmen in the form of higher taxes. More and more of them began to band together secretly. Finally, Hong Xiuquan, a village school teacher from the province of Guangdong, led the Taiping revolt. This shook the Chinese empire in the years between 1850 and 1864. With references to Christianity, the rebels demanded political and social equality, and justice. The Qing were able to suppress the Taiping rebellion, though only by taking advantage of internal wrangling at the Qing court, and by receiving military aid from abroad and from local military troops. In the second Opium War (1858–1860), the Qing had to grant the foreigners further concessions.

The Taiping unrests are said to have claimed between 20 and 30 million lives. The disturbances of the civil war caused severe famine and forced many Chinese to emigrate to the United States or to other Asiatic countries. Corruption and extravagance at the court increased, especially during the rule of the emperor's widow, Cixi. The court was unable to introduce any reforms. The so-called Boxer Rebellion, in 1900, which violently opposed the continuing humiliation of China by foreign colonial powers, was brutally suppressed by those same foreign powers. Thereafter, the imperial court was even more seriously weakened. One more desperate attempt to fight back was made with campaigns into central Asia. Yet the Qing dynasty was doomed, and it was overthrown in 1911 by the Republican Revolutionary League, led by Sun Yatsen.

In 1912, Puyi, who had taken the emperor's throne after the death of Cixi in 1908, was forced to sign a declaration of abdication. Puyi continued to live in the Imperial Palace, in Beijing, until 1924, but the rule of the sons of Heaven on the Dragon Throne, which had begun around 2000 BC, had already come to an end.

Left, the last emperor of China, Puyi. **Right**, the Empress Dowager Cixi.

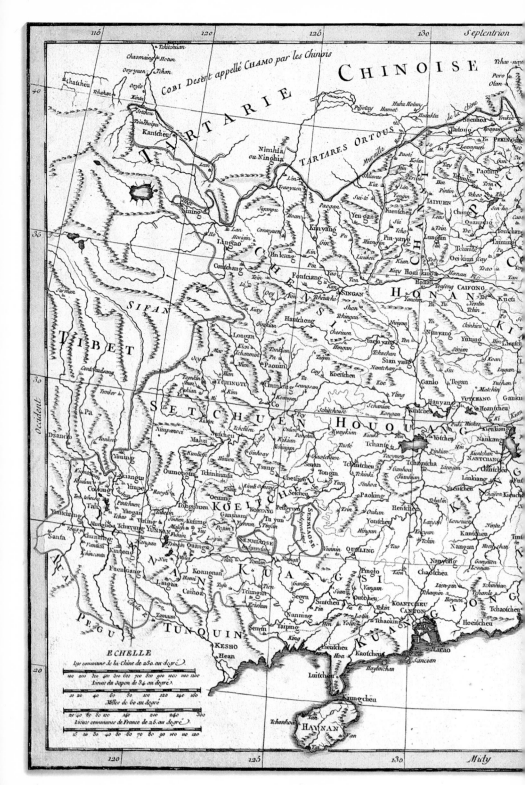

116   120   126   130

Tchitchuan

Chaomainq Hotun

oeyoyuen   Tchan

Chatcheu   Tchakan   ceylo   Kintu

40

Tchao-navi

Cobi Desert appellé CHAMO par les Chinois

CHINOISE

Pero
Olan

TARTARIE

Fotchen
TienThuipu

Kantcheu

Hubu Holan
Hamat

Peitotoy

de la chine

Ruluktu

Shenhoa   Yenkin
Tutong   Ropan

Nimhia
ou Ninohia

TARTARES ORTOUS

Muraille

Paoté
Kolan

In

Yu   PEKING
Tsewenyuen

Lin   Taoyuen

Paogan

Sui-té

Yen-gan

Hoan

Ohianu
Kia

Kinyang

Fuentcheu

Sie
Tcho

Lan
Yongin

Tching
Hin   Pintin
Tchao

Paoting

Quangpin
Touchuen
Taimin

SIFAN

Sining

Lan

Ho

Hoeujin

Liangao

Contchang

Connyuen

Bin Icane

Cin

Gin

Fu

Hiang-fu
Licuhei

Pin-yang

IAIYUEN
Leao

Trin

Lingan

Oei kun tay

Honan

Yo

Tchante
Honan

Trao

Han
Han-chong

Fontciang

Kan

Singan
Theutcho

Shan

Rhingan

Niuon

Tenfong CAIFONG

Yu

Yo

Kueti

TIBET

Couk-Gudsong

Pa

Timker

Kiay

Kiaky
Gingkien

Choruen

Hingan

Yueta yang

Nanchan

Nuian

Yu

Siam yang

Yentin
Tchin

Chinkieu

Longan

Kian
Tchammin

Tonkan
Pa
Mien

Paonin

Taipin

Sian yang

Siven

Koan

Ynming

Hin

Tehuteh

SETCHUEN

Dsancho
Tonkee

Yining

Mac

Han
Kim

Tcenkin
chan

Kia

Lcangsan

Cay

Koeitchen

Koc

Yling

Sau

Lugan

Yuchan

Matchin

Ganlo

Chumcin

Koanoan

Koe

Schitcheuse

Kongan

Kintches

Hanyang

VUTCHANG

Hoan tcheu

Ki

Gauki

Nimpanoci

Mahu

Kunlien

Outcheu

Ginhoay

HOUQUAN

Fey

Enlon

Nikiun

Pohchin

Kuaykim

Tarté

Tchant

Yotchen

Hoan tcheu

Pinkim

Kiankam

Nankang

Kiangor

Yinpel

Oumotertu

Tchinhumim

Tsung

Oxtoichuen

Senyan

Tchatcheu

Tchinki

Taoynen

Ganhou

Tchanhuen

Tchantcha

Licuyuen

Kuntchan

NANTCHENG

Linkiang

Tchutcheu

Fu

KOEICHEU

Penggu

Se

Yuen

Sinhoa

Paokin

Rhatin

Chaison Kienchai

Kiechai

Oumin

Ochiou

Gansham

Yinin

KOEYANG

Leyin

Paim

Tayin

Tsin

Oukan

Younchen

Hanyan

Tao

Trin

Hentche

Laiyen

Kieyan

Tchin

Lensruen

Kantchen

Nintu

Y U N N A N

Coldong

Patchhen

Tcheyune

Nie

Tulin

Numin

QUELING

Pinglo

Yangan

Chaotcheu

Nangan

Nanyong

Gauguen

Lienan

Santa

Chuming

Tsoin

Ouanga

Tchingoai

Segen

Sican

Outcheu

Lien-pin

Tchunian

Tchulo

Hoyuen

Tchanlo

Tchaotchen

KUANGTONG

Fuentiang

Koanonan

Homi

Tufa

Tchingoal

Tpin

Sintchai

Pin

Tekin

Losin

KOANTCHEU
CANTON

Hoeitcheu

Lingan

Caihoa

Keichan

Nanning

Taipin

Hen

Yolin

Tchaokin

Macao

Siancian

PEGU

TUNQUIN

Seun

KESHO

Hean

King

Hoa

Theatcheu

KUANGSI

Kaotcheu

Haydinchan

Hoeitcheu

Luitcheu

20

Kiumcheu

Tchonhoa

HAYNAN

Yan

Yai

Occident

40

36

30

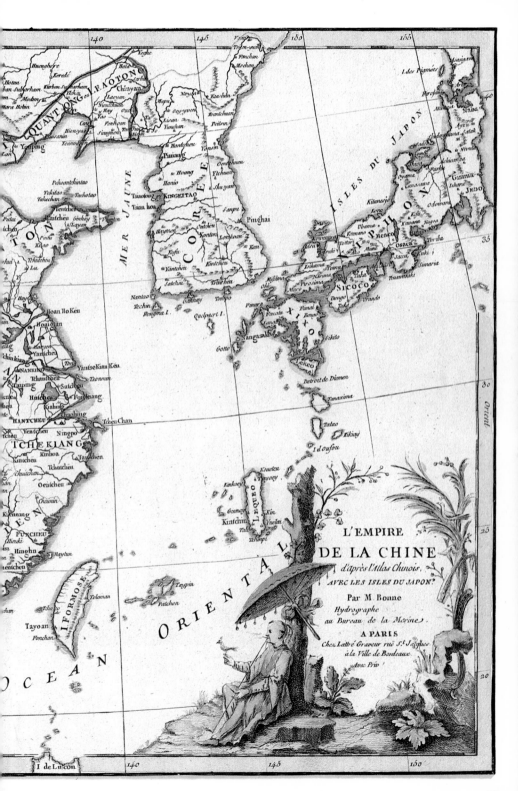

QUANTONG LEAOTONG

Huenghere   Ierede

Hotun   Kurban   Suibarham

ban   Subarham   Modun

Mara Holun

Youping

I des Pigmées

Liasianha

Pirofaise

Minbana

NABU

Aira

Piroufan

Ayzu

Dedayleana

Jatak

Nivulan

ISLES DU JAPON

Tsaolong   KINGKITAO

Tsan hoa

MER JAUNE

COREE

NIPHON

Kilanosjo

Kone

Osderara

O devara

JEDO

Pinyang

Hoang

Hanio

Sha yan

Omelhuen

Ychuen

Santi

Pimghai

Ubama

Kimano

Meaco

Kisu

Kiwama

Nagea

Tsuba

Mari

Osaca

Turiba

Jacco

Simaria

Sicoco

Kan

Yantcheu

Kintcheu

Trincheu

Dengo

Funai

Benuo

XIKO

Sikito

Vrando

Nantao   Techin

Bongma I.

Quelpaert I.

Pimura

Vacata

Yanaki

Nangasaki

Lekeo

Gotto

Detroit de Diemen

Tunaxima

Totao

Eikiaji

I d'Oufou

Kouclen

Tyngoey

Kinkoey

LEQUEO

Gonnay

Kintchin

Kin

Yuelai

Talbu

Whinpi

FORMOSE

Tayoan

Fonchan

OCEAN   ORIENTAL

I de Lucon

ICHEKIANG

HANTCHEU

NANKING

FUCHEU

L'EMPIRE
DE LA CHINE
d'Après l'Atlas Chinois,
AVEC LES ISLES DU JAPON.
Par M. Bonne
Hydrographe
au Bureau de la Marine.
A PARIS
Chez Lattré Graveur rüe St. Jacques
à la Ville de Bordeaux
avec Priv.

Marco Polo's reports about a legendary country in the East and the Mongol emperor's magnificent capital left many of his contemporaries amazed and in a state of disbelief. They even called him *il milione,* the braggart. During the rule of the Mongols in the thirteenth and fourteenth centuries, there were, for the first time, extended and organized contacts between east Asia and Europe.

This was a historical feat that many Chinese historians today continue to rate as a positive achievement. Some of the knowledge that the Europeans gained about China fell into oblivion later on, but, nevertheless, a basis for better understanding and closer contacts had been established.

At the height of its power, the Ming dynasty had sent its ships on expeditions as far afield as the Pacific and the coasts of Arabia. But the Ming emperor Yongle ordered the fleet to be destroyed, as he considered it unnecessary for the Chinese to travel to other parts of the earth.

This insularity was no doubt one of the main reasons why China did not recognize the significance of the slow but steady advance of the Europeans into Asia and China.

Until the Portuguese arrived in Guangzhou (Canton) in the sixteenth century, the Chinese had regarded their empire as the Middle Kingdom, the center of culture and civilization. According to Chinese ideas, the emperor ruled because of his superior moral qualities, and he could bestow these qualities upon all, Chinese as well as the non-Chinese barbarians hovering to the north.

When envoys from nomadic tribes or Southeast Asian regions came to China, the Chinese believed that they were doing so in order to ensure the emperor's goodwill and to learn from the Chinese culture. The delegations from these border areas usually arrived at the emperor's court with many gifts. They were lavishly entertained and often returned home with presents that were far superior to the ones they had brought with

them. This may have indicated condescending generosity or diplomatic considerations, but certainly not the meeting of equals. The first foreigners who arrived in the Middle Kingdom during the second half of the Ming dynasty were received with the same attitude and perception.

Arrival of Europeans: The first organized group of Europeans – Portuguese – landed in Guangzhou on the south coast in 1517. They were described as bearers of gifts from a foreign country, and the Chinese found their

long noses and deep-set eyes very conspicuous. Even today, foreigners are called "long noses" in colloquial Chinese.

When they arrived, the Portuguese fired a salute and created great concern among the Chinese, as weapons were prohibited in Guangzhou at the time and this custom was unknown. Thus, from the very first encounter, relations were marred by such misunderstandings, encouraging mutual disrespect and distrust. The damage was done, the effects of which are still felt today.

After the Portuguese, the Spanish, Dutch and English followed. In the sixteenth century, the first European missionaries came to

Preceding pages: old colonial French map depicting China. **Left,** the Jesuit priest Matteo Ricci. **Right,** the British negotiating for the purchase of tea from China.

China, notably Matteo Ricci, the founder of the Catholic mission in China, and Adam Schall von Bell.

They were not very successful in their missionary work, but thanks to their excellent knowledge of science, they were able to gain a foothold at court and became advisors to the emperor. They were captivated by Chinese culture, and fascinated with Confucianism so much so that the Pope in Rome finally decreed incompatibility between Catholicism and Confucianism.

The perceptions that Europeans had of China were strongly influenced by the Jesuit missionaries, an image of fascination on the one hand and disparaging rejection on the other. In the seventeenth and eighteenth centuries, *chinoiseries* were very fashionable at royal palaces in Europe, and in elegant homes there was often a Chinese room.

mained trapped in an endless cycle, like the Buddhist wheel of life.

Colonization of China: After a promising start, at the end of the eighteenth-century Christian missionary work was once more prohibited by the Chinese emperors. Even in 1793, the time of the industrial revolution in Great Britain, Emperor Qianlong informed a British envoy that China was economically well off and able to support itself, and that it had no need for goods from abroad. Foreign merchant ships were only allowed to use the port of Guangzhou, and business relations were subject to stringent regulations.

The Qing dynasty, which surpassed the prime of its power around 1800, did not

In the seventeenth and eighteenth centuries, *chinoiseries* were very fashionable at royal palaces in Europe, and in elegant homes there was often a Chinese room.

Many European scholars were fascinated by Chinese theories and concepts. Influenced by the system set out in the *Book of Changes,* Leibnitz developed a binary number theory that was to become the basis of computer technology.

Other academics and philosophers in Europe, notably Hegel and Marx, completely rejected China. They simply regarded it as a large empire of despotism and stagnation, a country that was not progressing, which re-

acknowledge the new and increasing threat that came from across the sea. They were preoccupied with the central Asian regions and belligerent nomads, thus underestimating the modern weapons of the "barbarians" from overseas: commodities, capital, cannons, and canons. In the end, it was these weapons that opened China to foreign traders and companies.

The British did not hesitate to use opium as a means of forcing China to its knees. For years, the Chinese had enjoyed the monopoly in the trading of tea, which was very popular in Great Britain. As a consequence, immense amounts of silver had been paid to China.

Yet – for the reasons mentioned earlier – they refused to import any goods. Around 1816, the British East India Company decided to smuggle more opium into China, and demanded to be paid for it in silver. In this unscrupulous way, they ruined the national budget of the Qing empire.

As a reaction, the smuggling of opium was stopped in 1839. The Chinese government intercepted 20,000 crates of opium in Guangzhou and made a public showing of their burning.

This provided a welcome opportunity for the British to demonstrate their "superiority" and, at the same time, to open China's gates to British business and military interests.

granting foreigners extraterritoriality, meaning that foreigners were no longer subject to Chinese jurisdiction. Most humiliating was that China was forced to cede Hong Kong to Great Britain.

It is doubtful whether the Qing court realized what far-reaching consequences these concessions would have. They were incapable of understanding the signs of the times and even tried to pass the costs of the war onto the population. (One of the consequences of this was the Taiping uprising.)

In the Second Opium War (1857–1860), British and French troops advanced as far as Beijing; the emperor was expelled and his summer palace was burnt to the ground. The

During the First Opium War, which lasted from 1839 to 1842, the British advanced as far as Nanjing.

According to the subsequent Treaty of Nanjing, the first of numerous "unequal" treaties (as they are still referred to in China today), the Middle Kingdom was forced to pay 21 million silver dollars in compensation. It was also obliged to open several ports – among them Shanghai and Guangzhou – and to agree to the import of opium and to

Left, in 1841, the British negotiated and enforced the opening of Chinese ports to trade. Above, the Qing emperor receives a foreign envoy.

unequal treaties that followed led to the final opening of China to foreigners. Now 43 ports were accessible to Western merchants. Adventurers, explorers, merchants and missionaries were allowed to move freely throughout China. The foreign enclaves in the ports from which "Chinese and dogs" were banned quickly developed into extraterritorial zones.

In the second half of the nineteenth century, xenophobia among the Chinese increased. These feelings were especially strong in the province of Shandong, where the Germans had taken the Bay of Jiaozhou on a lease, and where there was increasing opposition to the activities of missionaries. Moreover, Japanese interests in China threatened, and in 1895, China lost the Sino-Japanese War, ceding Korea and Taiwan to Japan. which was further followed by increased partitioning of the country. For decades, colonial powers had been following the British example; the Qing empire seemed unable to counter these challenges. China was threatened by the same fate as Africa: being split up between a number of colonial powers without regard to clan or tribal boundaries.

Chinese opposition coalesced into organized groups, the so-called Boxer Movement, or Boxer Rebellion. Sometimes secretly, sometimes openly, it was supported by the

imperial court. The Boxers, a strongly antiforeign movement, gained momentum by 1899. The following year, in June, nearly 150,000 Boxers occupied Beijing. For the next few months, they besieged Westerners of all nationalities, and many Chinese Christians, too. In August, an international military expedition of French, British, German, Russian, American and Japanese troops put down the Boxer Rebellion and lifted the siege of Beijing. The colonial powers leveled Beijing and then demanded reparation payments (US$333 million) from China, which were to be paid over the next 40 years. (The payments were discontinued in the 1930s.)

Paradigm shift: The Boxer Rebellion heralded a growing national consciousness. Under Sun Yatsen, a new political force grew that favored the unification of China as a republican nation-state. Sun Yatsen was influenced by Western and Christian ideas, and later by Marxism. He and many of his followers, who had studied abroad, had been forced to seek asylum outside of China for fear of repression and persecution.

The republicans did not play an important role after the fall of the imperial dynasty, yet their influence grew. They felt increasingly betrayed by the Western powers who, contrary to their promises, did not want to let go of their privileges in China. Instead, they used the war to make further territorial demands. At the Versailles Peace Conference, the former German territories were handed over to Japan, a further humiliation for China. The demands for unrestricted national sovereignty increased. The British sailed their gunboats up the Yangzi River one last time in 1927.

In the 1920s, the newly-formed Soviet Union approached Sun Yatsen's republic as an equal. The intellectuals who demanded a final end to imperialism had a lasting influence on opinions at the time. In 1928, Chiang Kaishek took over as president of China. Customs and the postal system were once again put under Chinese control, the abolition of extraterritorial rights was declared in 1930, and foreigners were to be subject to Chinese jurisdiction.

These measures were finally put into force after the end of World War II, in 1945, with China now accepted in the international community. After the successful revolution in 1949, all foreign privileges and ownership of foreign capital in China were abolished.

As the world's oldest continuous civilization, one that, for most of its existence, was more sophisticated than the powers that dominated the country in the 1800s, the colonial humiliation left deep scars in the Chinese mind. Indeed, for most of the twentieth century, the Chinese would be guided by the desire that never again would Chinese sovereignty be subjected to, much less humiliated by, any outside power.

Left, a member of the Boxer Movement, the murderer of the German ambassador, is executed. **Right**, Boxers fight German troops.

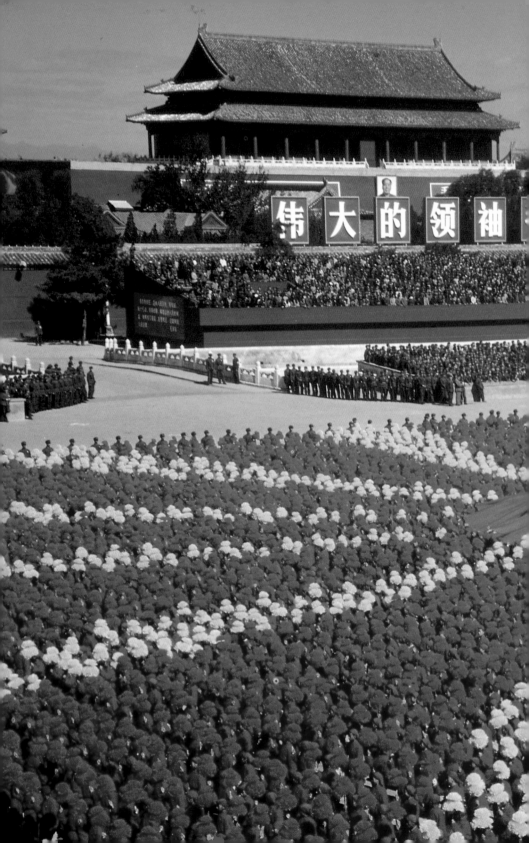

Since the middle of the last century, the dominant themes in China have been: How can the Western challenge be met, and how can China become strong enough to have equal rights among the world's nations? The decline of the old Confucian China was inevitable and all too obvious, but what would take its place? Were reforms possible, or was a revolutionary coup the only way towards modernizing the country?

The declaration of abdication by Puyi, the last emperor, says: "Yuan Shikai, who was recently elected president of the National Assembly in Beijing, will now be able to unify the North and South. He should therefore be given the power to do this and form a provisional government. This was done with the consent of the representatives of the People's Army in order to safeguard the peace and to allow the Chinese, Manchu, Mongols, Mohammedans and Tibetans to form one large state that would be named Republic of China."

The imperial dynasty had been overthrown, but no other stable political order replaced it, and the wish for peace was not fulfilled. The north was ravaged by feudal warlords who instigated wars and brutally exploited the power vacuum to their own advantage. After the death of Yuan Shikai in 1916, Sun Yatsen founded a republic in Guangzhou, used as a base from which to fight the warlords.

During World War I, a new left-wing intellectual movement emerged in China. This young political force manifested itself in a large student movement on 4 May 1919. The immediate cause for what came to be known as the May Fourth Movement was the Versailles Peace Treaty, which granted the former German territories in Shandong to Japan, and not to the Chinese. The patriotically-minded intellectuals were furious about this humiliation. They called for the boycott of Japanese goods and trading houses, while staging strikes in many cities. The immediate successes of the movement were mini-

mal: the warlords in the north remained in power, and the Western powers remained unimpressed. Nevertheless, the May Fourth Movement is regarded as the first significant national movement in China, and is considered to have been a decisive turning point in modern Chinese history.

The Communists: In the first half of the 1920s, the newly-formed Chinese Communist Party established itself surprisingly fast. Following the European example, attempts were made to instigate strikes among work-

ers in the cities, but they were usually unsuccessful. The Guomindang (National People's Party), which was led by Dr Sun Yatsen, also increasingly turned to the Soviet Union. They were disappointed by the lack of support from the West and were impressed by the Russian revolution.

There was an official coalition between the Guomindang and the Chinese Communists, and they set up a joint military academy near Guangzhou. Chiang Kaishek was in charge of the academy, while Communist party leader Zhou Enlai was his deputy. In a joint venture, the Southern Republic fought against the local military commanders in the

Preceding pages: the personality cult surrounding Mao ended with his death in 1976. Left, Red Guards on the march. Right, rural ingenuity in the use of wind power.

north. Chiang Kaishek, the commander-in-chief of the Nationalist forces, had, by 1928, succeeded in controlling the whole of China.

His main enemies were now the Communists, with whom he had broken off relations towards the end of the "northern expedition" the year before. The subsequent fight against the Communists consumed huge sums from the state budget.

The Communists were able to avoid directly engaging the Guomindang, retreating instead to the Jinggang Mountains in the southeast, where Mao Zedong developed a new strategy for the revolution in the late 1920s. Until then, influenced by Soviet advisers from the Communist International quarters. Only ten percent of the 130,000 people who began this grueling trek survived, but the march considerably improved the Communist Party's standing in China. In 1935, Mao established himself as leader of the Chinese Communists, remaining in this position until his death in 1976.

As early as 1931, Japan had annexed parts of northeastern China, where it founded a puppet state, Manchuguo, headed by Puyi, the last Manchu emperor who had abdicated the imperial throne.

The Japanese were planning further conquests in China. Faced by this threat, Chiang Kaishek was unable to use his troops against the Communists. Furthermore, criticism was

(Comintern), the main focus of attention was on the cities and the industrial proletariat. Mao realized that, in China, it was the peasants who would be the most important force for a revolution; promises of land reform, of course, would assure support of the impoverished peasants.

Between 1931 and 1935, Chiang Kaishek started five campaigns to eliminate the Communists. In turn, the Communists left southern China, where they were based, and began their legendary Long March, from 1934 to 1935. It led through 11 provinces, covering 12,000 kilometers (7,500 mi) before ending in Shaanxi, where they established their head-

being expressed within his own party. The critics wished to end the civil war and join forces with the Communists against the Japanese. They even "persuaded" Chiang Kaishek to agree to an alliance with the Communists: two Guomindang generals detained Chiang, in Xi'an, in 1937 and forced him to negotiate with the Communists. This alliance united both armies under one supreme command. The Communists agreed to abandon parts of their program, focusing on resistance to the Japanese aggression.

The Japanese provoked an incident at the Marco Polo Bridge, outside Beijing, on 7 July 1937, which led to war between China and Japan. In fact, the so-called incident was choreographed by the Japanese to justify their long-planned aggression in China. Shortly afterwards, Shanghai was bombarded and captured by the Japanese. Chiang Kaishek retreated to Chongqing, in the province of Sichuan. The Communists fought a guerilla war from their bases in the north, while Chiang's troops resisted the Japanese in the south. The Guomindang and Chinese Communists eventually stopped the Japanese advance. In part because of the drain on Japanese resources caused by the war in China, the Allies gained military superiority over the Japanese in the Pacific after 1942.

After Japan had capitulated in 1945, op-

they retreated to the island of Taiwan, along with nearly two million refugees.

Founding of a republic: With the declaration that "China has risen again!", Mao Zedong proclaimed the People's Republic of China from Tiananmen on 1 October 1949. At the time, China was considered the sick man of Asia. The population had suffered greatly. Only about one out of ten school-age children was able to read and write. The annual death rate was three percent of the population, and the average life expectancy was 36 years. Out of 1,000 children born, 160 to 170 died in infancy; only 84,000 hospital beds were available to half a billion people.

In addition, war and civil unrest had weak-

posing positions were clarified by civil war: on the one side was Chiang Kaishek, supported by the Americans; on the other side, Mao Zedong's Red Army. Soviet support was minimal. Looking back on the four-year civil war, it was an easy victory for the Communists, as the Guomindang had lost the support of most of the population.

After several campaigns into southern China, there was a decisive battle on Chang Jiang, the Yangzi River; the Guomindang troops were weakened to such an extent that

Left, Mao at Yan'an during the civil war. **Above**, the Red Army enters Beijing, January 1949.

ened China's economy and infrastructure. There was little modern industry, and China ranked as one of the poorest countries in the world. There was hardly any help coming from abroad; the Soviet Union was preoccupied with its own problems after World War II, and the Americans were very suspicious of this new socialist state. The Communists had taken on a difficult task. They had won the revolution, but now what?

In the early years of the People's Republic of China, the war damage was repaired, creating an environment for industrialization and modernization. Mao Zedong announced a "New Democracy," which meant working

20TH-CENTURY LEADERS

Almost without exception, it was the men who made history in China. This was the case in Confucian times and is still true today, and will perhaps be true for some time.

After the fall of the Qing dynasty, **Yuan Shikai**, born in 1859, made a futile attempt to establish himself as emperor. He came from a family of civil servants in the province of Henan, and had a brilliant military career and was a favorite of the emperor's widow, Cixi; she, however, dropped him as he held too many powerful offices. China's last reigning monarch, Puyi, reinstated him in 1911 to save the throne. But Yuan Shikai had understood the signs of the times and joined the republicans, only to betray them shortly afterwards, desiring as he did to become emperor of China. He died in 1916, shortly before the planned enthronement.

His direct opponent was **Dr. Sun Yatsen** (in Mandarin: **Sun Zhongshan**). Born in 1866 as Sun Wen, Sun lived near Macao, in the district of Guangdong. Influenced by Christian and Western ideas, he plotted the overthrow of the Qing dynasty and founded the republican Guomindang (National People's Party). Dismissed by Yuan Shikai, he founded a government in Guangzhou in 1920 that was to rival the military powers in the North; he then reorganized the Guomindang with the Soviet Union's help. He died in Beijing in 1925. He is honored as the father of modern China in both the People's Republic and Taiwan.

Chiang Kaishek (in Mandarin: **Chiang Zhongzheng**) was his successor. Born in 1887, he underwent military training, then joined the Guomindang and became Sun Yatsen's close friend. After defeat by the Communists in the civil war, he fled to Taiwan, where his autocratic government was able to boost the economy with the help of the United States. He died in 1975, without achieving his aim: overthrowing the Communists and recapturing the mainland.

The great opponent to Chiang Kaishek, as well as all other Chinese politicians, was **Mao Zedong**. No one else has had such an influence on China in this century. He was born in 1893, the son of a peasant family in the province of Hunan. In 1921, Mao became co-founder of the Chinese Communist Party. During the Long March, he established himself as leader of the party, retaining this position until his death in 1976. He led the country out of its post-war economic misery, only to let it sink into chaos twice: during the Great Leap Forward, then again during the Cultural Revolution. A personality cult around Mao emerged during the Cultural Revolution, turning him into a living monument. Mao had unlimited power, governing like an emperor.

The second-most important person after Mao Zedong was **Zhou Enlai**, Mao's closest ally since the Long March in 1925. Zhou was the son of a wealthy family of the gentry, born in Huai'an, province of Jiangsu, in 1898. After studying in Germany and France during the 1920s, Zhou joined the Communist movement and played a leading role soon after his return to China. His special skill, diplomacy, became apparent very soon. He was promoted to foreign minister in 1949, and then to prime minister. Some well-planned maneuvers and operations during the Cultural Revolution put him in a secure position. His successes in foreign policy are particularly significant; China emerged from isolation after becoming a member of the UN in 1971. He died in Beijing in 1976; in contrast to Mao Zedong, he died loved and honored by the people.

Deng Xiaoping, born in 1904, was Zhou Enlai's right-hand man and close friend. Hailing from a peasant family in Sichuan, Deng had an eventful past. In 1920, he first went to France as a student and worked his way through school. After his return, his career in the army and the party advanced rapidly; he took part in the Long March and was one of the most prominent politicians after 1949. In 1973, he was appointed by Zhou Enlai as deputy prime minister. He was responsible for opening China's economy to the world, the driving force behind the modernization program. Despite some setbacks – most notably the suppression of the Tiananmen Square democracy movement in 1989 – Deng displayed finesse by steering China back into the enclaves of the international community. ∎

together with patriotically-minded entrepreneurs who had not collaborated with foreign "imperialists" before 1949.

Initially, they were allowed to retain possession of their factories, but all enterprises controlled by foreign capital were soon nationalized. The most important event of this time was land reform, which began in 1952. Hundreds of millions of peasants were allocated land that had been expropriated from large landowners. Hundreds of thousands of wealthy landowners were brought before the so-called people's tribunals; most were sentenced to death.

One of the most important successes in China's internal politics involved those remote areas that, since the fall of the Qing dynasty in 1911, had only marginal connections with the Chinese empire. These included Tibet, Xinjiang, Inner Mongolia and the southern province of Yunnan. Beijing's control over these regions was strengthened. At the same time, the Soviet Union withdrew troops from Manchuria, now called Dongbei, and relinquished its rights over this area.

With support from the Soviet Union and East European states, the People's Republic initiated its first five-year plan (1953–1957),

which concentrated on developing heavy industry. By the end of this period, nearly all existing enterprises had been nationalized. Peasants were grouped in cooperatives.

In 1954, the People's Republic declared that the transitional period of the so-called New Democracy had ended. In its first constitution, it was defined as a socialist state, ruled by the proletariat, led by the Communist Party. A rigid centralist government was set up and any opposition from within was increasingly suppressed, with intellectuals usually the victims. In 1956, there was heavy criticism both from within and outside the party of its politics, which had been modeled on the Stalinist Soviet Union. This phase of liberal criticism was short-lived, ending in 1957 when critics were declared as rightwing radical bourgeois, and hundreds of thousands of them were interned in prisons or labor camps.

Great leap backward: The economic situation at the end of the first five-year plan was much improved. Mao Zedong, encouraged by this and supported by virtually all members of the party leadership, propagated the "Great Leap Forward" in 1958. In a period of just a few years, China wanted to be on an equal footing with economically-advanced countries, and to match their production rate. Communes, over 26,000 of them averaging

Left, Dr. Sun Yatsen. Above, class enemies were usually put on public trial.

5,000 households each, were to be the main means for achieving this aim.

By the end of 1958, virtually all peasants had been concentrated in large collectives, where they often took on several jobs. Collectives resembled military organizations and labor was often not compensated. The peasants, who had supported the Communists because they had been promised land allocations, now felt deceived by the party. Opposition against the policies that robbed them of their last patches of private land grew.

The Great Leap Forward ended in disaster; none of the goals were achieved. As a result of the massive deployment of labor, there was a shortage of workers in agriculture.

leader, the Dalai Lama, fled to India and has lived in exile ever since. Tibet continues to be an irritant to Beijing.

In 1960, a deep rift opened up between China and the Soviet Union. Both accused each other of betraying Marxism-Leninism. Furthermore, the Soviet Union refused to share atomic bomb secrets with the Chinese. The Soviet Union ceased all forms of economic aid, and recalled its advisers and their technical documentation.

Between 1961 and 1965, following the disastrous Great Leap Forward, internal politics were characterized by a pragmatic attitude encouraged by politicians like Liu Shaoqi and Deng Xiaoping. The institution

Workers and peasants reached the limits of their physical capabilities. Many large projects, such as the construction of dams, were carried out inadequately. Crop failures and natural disasters led to a dramatic aggravation of the situation, and between 20 and 40 million people died in what may have been the largest famine in world history.

In the settlement areas of the national minorities, the "great leap into Communism" meant that attempts were made to do away with customs and traditions. Latent national conflicts soon developed into armed insurrection. In 1959, the Tibetans started an unsuccessful revolt against the Chinese. Their

of the communes was retained, but attempts to gain alliance from several countries were partly withdrawn and private enterprise was again permitted to a limited extent. The economy began a slow recovery after the severe setbacks it had suffered during the years of the Great Leap. By 1965, it had regained the level of 1957.

Mao Zedong's image had suffered because of the failure of the Great Leap; in the following years, he made an attempt to re-establish his political credibility. He was of the opinion that a pragmatic approach could lead back to capitalism and thus undermine the power of the Communist Party. So he opposed most pragmatism, and was strongly supported by the defence minister, Lin Biao, who appeared to be Mao's successor.

Cultural Revolution: In 1966, discontent of young people culminated in massive protests at the universities. Mao exploited these protests in order to eliminate his opponents within the party. He initiated the Great Proletarian Cultural Revolution. Compliant cadres provoked a mass movement of the so-called Red Guards, pushing China again into chaos and close to a civil war.

Politicians, intellectuals and artists fell victim to the terror of these dogmatic Red Guards. One of these victims was Mao's main opponent, Liu Shaoqi, who had suc-

Mao was China's detonation of an atomic bomb in 1964, and the launching of its first satellite in 1970.

Lin Biao, who had been instrumental in creating the personality cult around Mao and had been designated as his successor in 1969, began to disagree with Mao's politics. After one failed attempt on his life, he died in 1971 in a plane crash over Mongolia while escaping, after an attempt to assassinate Mao.

In the following years, the debates between the moderate and radical political factions increased in intensity. One key figure was prime minister Zhou Enlai, who had always taken on the role of mediator between the two sides in any political clashes. In

ceeded him as president in 1959. Hundreds of thousands of people lost their lives during the revolutionary "excesses". Schools were closed for years, artistic life came to a standstill. Relics of traditional China – Buddhist temples and archeological sites, for example – were defaced and often destroyed.

While many of his opponents were being deprived of their positions and persecuted, Mao was worshipped nearly as a god in a personality cult unprecedented anywhere in the modern world. Buttressing the image of

Left, Mao's book of quotations. **Above**, students demonstrating in Tiananmen Square, 1989.

1973, he recalled Deng Xiaoping, who earlier had been publicly humiliated by the Red Guards, as his deputy and developed a more pragmatic approach in rebuilding the economic and educational systems of China.

Zhou Enlai also made great efforts to overcome China's international isolation. After China replaced Taiwan as a member of the United Nations in 1971, American president Richard Nixon visited the country in 1972 on the wave of the so-called ping-pong diplomacy. Relations with the Soviet Union, however, had reached an absolute low point, with several violent military clashes on the China–Soviet border.

Called the Gang of Four, the group around Mao's wife, Jiang Qing, showed increasing determination to put an end to the pragmatic politics of Zhou and Deng, and to take over the leadership of the party. Zhou Enlai died in 1976; on commemoration day for the dead in April of the same year, there were spontaneous mass demonstrations against the Gang of Four and in favor of Zhou Enlai and Deng Xiaoping.

Mao died on 9 September 1976. A month later, the leaders of radical groups – including the Gang of Four – were arrested. Once the radicals had been deprived of power, the conditions were set for a change. Changes only became concrete after Deng Xiaoping took over leadership of the Communist Party.

At the time of Mao's death, China had its own self-sustaining industry, but the country was now in a deep economic crisis as a result of the Cultural Revolution's excesses, and the reputation of the Communist Party reached a low point. In the mid 1970s, peasants had the same standard of living as they had 20 years before, and the same was true of the work force in the cities. The Communist Party estimated that between 150 and 200 million people were threatened by starvation at the end of the 1970s. There was a rapid increase in the number of beggars, and also outspoken complaints about the bureaucracy and the despotic rule of party cadres.

In 1978, a "Democratic Movement" began to form in Beijing and other major cities. In addition to the Four Modernizations that were being propagated officially, this movement demanded a fifth modernization: democracy. Although the movement was prohibited by the Communist Party and some of its leaders were imprisoned, it nevertheless made basic changes in internal as well as foreign politics.

In the same year, collectivism of agriculture ceased and the peasants were again allowed privately-held land. Free markets was once more permitted, and the establishment of light industry and service industries was strongly encouraged. These measures were accompanied by a cautious liberalization; religious freedom was granted again, and there were opportunities for literature and the arts to unfold. People who had been unjustly persecuted during the Cultural Revolution were reinstated to former positions.

In the years following, the ideology of the Communist Party was to overcome the Cultural Revolution's effects by introducing economic and political reforms, taking into account the country's real and immediate situation. The long-term aim was to create a mixture of both state and market economies. Private enterprises were again permitted, and special areas in the south were made into economic enterprise zones.

Deng Xiaoping's program of modernization and reform has not been without controversy, with opposition growing in conservative circles, especially in the army. At the end of 1983, a campaign was set in motion against "mental pollution", including intellectuals and artists, as well as against fashions like long hair and Western music.

Violent turning point: In the late 1980s, the Soviet Union underwent extensive changes in its power structure, with the Communist Party loosening its iron grip on society. Spearheading the Soviet reforms was Mikhail Gorbachev.

In 1989, Gorbachev visited Beijing to meet with Deng Xiaoping, the first summit between the two countries in three decades. Normalized relations soon followed.

Gorbachev's visit was preceded a month earlier by the beginning of student pro-democracy demonstrations in Beijing's Tiananmen Square, initiated in part to honor Party General Secretary Hu Yaobang, popular with liberals because he refused to halt student demonstrations two years earlier, and who had just died. By May, more than one million protestors filled central Beijing. The government warned the protestors to leave, but the peaceful protests – televised and broadcast live around the world by satellite – continued. Martial law was declared on 20 May. Protestors blocked most of the military convoys dispatched to Beijing. On 4 June, the army overran Tiananmen Square, pulling the plug on the world's media and squashing the protests. Chinese government figures range from 300 to 1,000 killed, mostly soldiers. Western estimates are that more than 3,000 were killed, mostly civilians. Arrests and executions followed.

A shake-up in the Communist Party brought Jiang Zemin, Deng's choice as successor, to power.

Right, Deng Xiaoping meets with Mikhail Gorbachev, 1989.

Events at Tiananmen in 1989 injected a bit of common sense – if not outright caution – into the regional and international communities. It was now clear that China's leadership would tolerate neither political changes nor challenges. Moreover, it appeared that Beijing cared little about world opinion regarding its internal affairs, or else it was simply naive in how the world would interpret events. It certainly seemed clear that Beijing had yet to grasp the power – and autonomy – of satellite television. Powerful were the transmitted images of authorities pulling the plug, literally, on foreign broadcasters.

The Tiananmen episode unnerved Hong Kong, the former British colony that, at the time, knew that it had less than a decade before Chinese rule. Demonstrations in Hong Kong's streets emphasized its residents' worries. Nor was the Chinese government's response to Tiananmen universally accepted by party cadres. Shortly afterwards, the Hong Kong bureau chief of Xinhua, China's official news agency and considered at the time to be the Communist Party's (banned in Hong Kong) unofficial representation in the then-British colony, defected to America.

In hindsight, Tiananmen Square was a marker ending what sometimes appeared a 1980s' love-fest between China and the world. In contrast, the 1990s would become a decade of tensions and awkwardness between China and other nations, regionally and elsewhere, as China grappled with its new influence and responsibilities in the international community.

The governing mechanism of China is anything but transparent, and analysts tripped over one another trying to rationalize China's increasing aggressiveness during the 1990s. Some pundits offered that the military was asserting itself as the aging Deng Xiaoping lost influence; others suggested that hard-liners, threatened by the collapse of Communism in the former Soviet Union and Eastern Europe, were consolidating both their positions and their influence.

Perhaps even more threatening, in the long run, to the Chinese leadership was the unanticipated intrusion across China's borders of the so-called information highway. First, it

was fax machines – which came into their own during 1989 – and then computer links through the ubiquitous Internet. In 1996, China announced that all economic news would have to be funneled through Xinhua. Later the same year, it banned access to the Internet sites of all Western media.

Throughout the 1990s, there were significant economic advances in China, and cities such as Shanghai were literally being recast and restructured to challenge Hong Kong and Singapore as regional financial centers.

Had it not been for China's continuing assertiveness – indeed perhaps a defensiveness to outside forces – these changes would have been the news stories of the decade.

Instead, actions by China – or perhaps interpretations of them by others – threatened not only smooth trade relations with neighbors and the world, but regional security. China claimed territorial sovereignty, for example, over islands far from its borders and closer to Vietnam, the Philippines and Indonesia. It offered two arguments: "historical" rights from centuries ago, when imperial ships sailed the South China Sea, and archipelagic rights, in fact applicable under international law only to true archipelagoes like Indonesia and the Philippines. The islands involved – the Paracels and Spratlys, among others – sit on petroleum reserves.

China's actions were difficult for others to interpret. Was China's agenda substantial and something about which to fret over, or were they simply symptomatic of internal power struggles that would resolve themselves when the aging leaders were replaced? Indeed, the question of China after Deng Xiaoping obsessed China watchers.

renegade province, not an independent state. When the People's Republic of China replaced Taiwan in the United Nations in 1971, and when the United States extended official recognition of the PRC (and removed same from Taiwan) in 1979, Taiwan's future appeared to be one of international pariah. But through various "trade" commissions and "special" representatives, Taiwan retained its political and diplomatic contacts.

Nevertheless, trade and communication links between the two Chinas expanded,

中國人民銀行

WU YUAN

Taiwan: Since 1949, a banner of the Chinese Communist Party has been to reunite Taiwan and China. It's thought that the leadership's internal deadline for such is 2010. (Likewise, the Nationalists on Taiwan have carried the same banner, but of differing terms.) Now that China has resolved the issue of Hong Kong, returned by Britain in 1997, and that of Macau, to be returned by Portugal in 1999, China can focus on Taiwan, which China claims is nothing but a

with Taiwanese tourists and investments flooding the mainland, especially the southeastern provinces, ancestral home of many Taiwanese. The first official talks between China and Taiwan took place in Singapore, in 1993. But hard-liners in both China and Taiwan melted any possibility of a substantial thaw. Indeed, Taiwanese politicians talked of officially declaring independence (which it has never done, claiming instead to be the rightful government of mainland China, from which the Nationalist forces fled nearly half a century earlier). China, meanwhile, rattled its missiles and threaten to invade the island if such were, in fact, declared.

Preceding pages: Mao's mausoleum. **Left,** pro-democracy demonstration, Hong Kong. **Above,** China's money in Taiwan one day?

China's admittedly clumsy attempt to influence Taiwan's first direct presidential elections in 1996 – by conducting "missile tests" directly into Taiwan's two primary shipping lanes – cost it considerable regional and global political capital. Afterwards, Taiwan's political and commercial contacts actually increased, with several regional governments warming up to Taiwanese interests.

But the question of Taiwan needs to answered. Confident after the elections, Taiwan's new and freely-elected president, Lee Teng-hui, offered to visit the mainland and meet with China's president, Jiang Zemin. Beijing responded with silence.

Such a visit would involve delicate questions of protocol. Would the meeting be as president to president, party leader to party leader, or in some other linguistically- and politically-safe environment?

Domestic changes: No doubt the implosion of Communism in the Soviet Union and Eastern Europe shook the Chinese leadership. It is true that, for decades, China and the former Soviet Union had sparred over the true path of Communism – they didn't speak to one another for nearly 30 years, until 1989. But for a developing Marxist superpower to see *the* Marxist superpower change its spots certainly must have been unsettling.

What may also be giving the Communist leadership indigestion is the changing role of the party in daily Chinese life.

During the industrialization of China in the 1950s and 1960s, the Communist Party was the paramount touchstone in work and society, not only assuring ideological consistency amongst workers, but dictating industrial policy itself.

Now, China's blossoming market economy discourages intellectual conformity and rigid industrial policy. And the expanding sector of the economy dominated by non-industrial entities – banks, securities and trading firms, information services – is virtually free of party influence. Those working in these areas are young, urban and affluent.

Communist officials privately acknowledge that establishing party cells within free-market enterprises is an unwinnable fight. Nevertheless, for now, the party is far from disappearing. In 1995, 54 percent of new party members were under 35 years old; in Shanghai, with a population of 14 million, there are 1.14 million members of the Communist Party, eight percent of the people. (Out of China's 1.2 billion people, less than five percent are members.)

The weakening of party influence is not the only variable that's redefining Chinese life, especially in the country's urban centers. Crime doesn't thrive amidst a proletariat equality; it is nurtured by economic class differences. With the exponential rise of personal wealth and the expansion of consumerism in China, crime has mushroomed 10 percent annually since the early 1980s.

The government's response to crime has been swift and direct. Between April and July of 1996, for example, in a campaign dubbed Strike Hard, more than 1,000 convicted thieves, murderers and rapists throughout China were executed.

In the past, citizens could rely on party functionaries to settle both criminal and civil problems. But with the waning of the party's influence, approximately 15 percent of Beijing residents, according to newspaper polls, would go to the media – a confrontational television news show called *Beijing Express* is a popular venue – rather than to local Communist cadres.

Minority groups continue to present Beijing with issues that compound its rule of this immense country. Buddhists in Inner Mongolia and Muslims in Xinjian, not to mention Tibetans, remain under pressure from Beijing to mind themselves. How China handles minority-group activism – and human rights questions – in the future may be a barometer of the leadership's self-confidence, and of China's direction.

Contemporary Chinese history since World War II has been defined, not by quiet progression, but by radical shifts, which are often unexpected. China's actions and resistance to foreign criticism often seem out of touch. Critics might remember, however, that China is an ancient institution and the world's oldest existing state. Any contemporary civilization with a written history over 4,000 years old – and with a government bureaucracy of 40 million – necessarily has inertia. Moreover, an undercurrent of Chinese policy this century is that China would never again suffer the 19th-century colonial humiliation and subjugation.

Right, the China of Mao's years is that of statues and strong memories.

If one were to transpose the frontiers of China onto the European continent, the northern border would be at the height of the North Sea and the southern border would run through the African Sahel; from east to west, the territory would reach from Portugal to the Ural Mountains of Russia. The Pacific Ocean defines the eastern and southeastern border – more than 18,000 kilometers (11,000 mi) long – while the northwestern part of the country extends deep into Central Asia; Heilongjiang in the northeast (what used to be Manchuria) is part of Siberia.

As a consequence, there are extreme climatic differences in China. On the southeastern islands, winter is warm and people enjoy tropical fruits, while at the same time, the northeast is paralyzed by Siberian frosts and people seek shelter from the icy winds. Some parts of Tibet endure perpetual frost, while crops grow year-round in Guangdong and southern Yunnan.

China is the third-largest country in the world – after Russia and Canada – and roughly the same size as the whole of Europe. China covers an area of 9,560,900 square kilometers (3,691,500 sq mi). The distance from the northern town of Mohe, on the Heilongjiang, which forms the border with Russia, to the Zhengmu Reef, on the Nansha Islands in the South China Sea, is 5,500 kilometers (3,420 mi). From the eastern border in the Pamir Mountains to the confluence of the Heilong Jiang and the Wusuli Jiang, the distance is 5,200 kilometers (3,230 mi).

China's border is 20,000 kilometers (12,500 mi) long; its neighboring countries are Korea, Mongolia, Russia, Kazakhstan, Kyrgyzstan, Tajikistan, Afghanistan, Pakistan, India, Nepal, Sikkim, Bhutan, Burma (Myanmar), Laos and Vietnam.

China has deserts and fertile loess plains, pine forests and tropical rain forests, rivers that are amongst the longest in the world, and most definitely the highest mountains and deepest valleys in the world. Almost a continent in itself, China is without doubt a country of extremes and superlatives.

Topography: With good reason, China is occasionally called the land of mountains. Two-thirds of its territory is mountainous, hilly or high plateau. China's topography is characterised by its terraced structure, with the land sloping downwards towards the northeast, east and southeast. The highest terrace is the Tibet-Qinghai Plateau – Tibet, Qinghai and western Sichuan – which is 4,000 meters (13,000 ft) above sea level.

All the major rivers of China and Southeast Asia rise in the Tibet-Qinghai Plateau. The Huang He (Yellow River) and the Chang Jiang (Yangzi River) flow eastwards through China, while the Zangbo Jiang (Bramaputra), the Nu Jiang (Salween) and the Lancang (Mekong) flow south and southeast; in doing so, they pass through some of China's neighboring countries.

The second terrace is formed by plateaus of heights averaging between 1,000 and 2,000 meters (3,000–6,500 ft); from north to south they are the Tarim Basin, the Mongolian Plateau, the Central Chinese Loess Plateau, the Red Basin of Sichuan and the Yunnan-

Preceding pages: a dusty evening light over the Summer Palace, Beijing; snow-covered peaks in the Himalaya. **Left**, limestone karst formations, Guilin. **Right**, bamboo message.

Guizhou Plateau. The third terrace is formed by the plains and lowlands on the lower reaches of the large rivers; in fact, it is a large and wide strip of land, barely rising more than 500 meters (1,600 ft) above sea level, running along the coast from the north of China right down to the south. More than two-thirds of the population lives here, and it is China's agricultural and industrial core heartland.

This terraced structure is the result of massive tectonic movements beneath the Chinese land mass, which remains unsettled. As a result, earthquakes continue to strike in many regions of China, such as the 1976 earthquake in Tangshan, which claimed sev-

of one centimeter higher every year. North of the Himalaya, the Kunlun mountains separate the Tibet-Qinghai Plateau from the Tarim Basin and the Taklamakan Desert. Its western-most point is in the Pamir Plateau, and from there it extends eastwards for 2,500 kilometers (1,500 mi). Muztag (7,723 m/25,338 ft), Muztagata (7,546 m/24,758 ft) and Kongur (7,719 m/25,326 ft) are the highest peaks in the Kunlun range.

In summer, the rivers that spring from the Qinghai Plateau are fed with water from the melting glaciers.

Farther north, again reaching from west to east, is the Tian Shan range; in English it means Heavenly Mountains (7,000 m/23,000

eral hundred thousand lives. Above those terraces are the mountains, and China has many of the highest mountains in the world; nine of the 14 peaks that are higher than 8,000 meters (26,000 ft) are found in the Himalaya. Shengmufeng (Mount Everest), on the border of Nepal, is of course the highest mountain in the world at 8,848 meters (29,028 ft).

More than one hundred peaks in China are higher than 7,000 meters (23,000 ft), and more than a thousand reach a height of more than 6,000 meters (20,000 ft). The Himalaya range is one of the youngest mountain ranges in the world; even today, it grows an average

ft). Between the Kunlun and Tian Shan ranges lies the Turpan depression, 154 meters (505 ft) below sea level. Only the Dead Sea depression is lower. The two ranges enclose China's largest desert, the Taklamakan, which means "the desert one enters but never comes out of again".

The Greater Xingan range in the northeast of China forms a natural border between the Manchurian lowland and the Mongolian steppe. It is also China's largest wooded area, and therefore it is an important watershed. The range, which is between 200 and 300 kilometers (120–190 mi) wide, reaches southwest from the banks of the Heilong

Jiang and is 1,200 kilometers (750 mi) long. The highest elevation is only 2,100 meters (6,800 ft), but this mountain range has a great influence on the climate. The southeastern summer monsoons pass here, so that the lowlands east of the mountains are very fertile, while the steppe west of the range remains dry year-round.

A similarly important climatic divide is the Qinling range, which is 1,500 kilometers (900 mi) long and reaches from the Gansu-Qinghai border through the Shaanxi province all the way to Henan. In summer, it acts as a barrier to the heavy masses of humid air caused by the monsoon; in winter, it stops the cold winds streaming down from the north

ters (10,000–13,000 ft); the highest peak, Gongga, is 7,556 meters (24,790 ft). The peaks are covered in snow, dense forests line the lower edges of the slope, and tropical fruits and plants grow in the valleys.

Great rivers: In historical terms, Huang He, or Yellow River, is no doubt the most important river in China. It rises in the Qinghai province, makes a sharp bend to the north near Lanzhou and then farther on, near Baotou in Mongolia, it turns south again, forming the famous Huang He knee. Along its course, it passes through the fertile loess plateau, creating favorable conditions for the development of human civilization. It is not surprising that it was here in the valleys of the

from entering too far into central China.

The group of mountain ranges running through eastern Tibet, west Sichuan and Yunnan are called the Hengduan, which means "barrier". It is a fact that these ranges have, even in modern times, formed an insurmountable barrier between east and west. Large rivers – the Jinsha (source river of the Chang Jiang), Lancang, Nu Jiang and others – flow through the deep valleys that run from north to south. The average height of the mountains is between 3,000 and 4,000 me-

Left, Xinjiang. **Above**, vast steppes of Inner Mongolia.

Huang He and its main tributary, the Wei He, that the first Chinese states were formed. The loess, which was constantly threatened by erosion, as well as the wild Huang He, called for large communities to work together in order to deal with the immense task of irrigating the land. It is because of this river that Chinese civilization began. So it may not be a coincidence that the Chinese describe the loess as *huangtu*, yellow earth, and that the most important mythological emperor is called Huangdi, the Yellow Emperor.

In the upper reaches of the river, which is 5,464 kilometers (3,395 mi) long, the water is crystal clear. Only as it passes through the

Central Chinese Loess Plateau does it fill up with the yellow earth that erodes very easily, as it is insufficiently vegetated. With 20 kilograms (44 lbs) of silt per cubic centimeter of water, the Huang He transports more than one billion tons of sediments into its lower reaches every year. As the river bed widens in the northern China lowland plain, the river deposits more than four million tons. Here, the river bed grows by about ten centimeters (4 in) every year. In order to prevent floods, dikes are constantly being constructed or repaired; at some points, the silt is dug from the river bed and used to fertilize the fields. The water level in the estuary is so low that there is no shipping route to the sea.

familiar and which, as a result, became established in Europe.

It geographically divides the Middle Kingdom into north and south, a border that is also significant in cultural terms. Even in this century, the river formed a barrier that was hard to overcome. In the north, there is predominantly the cultivation of grain and sweet potatoes, while the south is dominated by rice fields. Three large bridges across the Chang Jiang, constructed in the last decade at Chongqing, Wuhan and Nanjing, have contributed to the economic growth of China.

Along a stretch of 200 kilometers (130 mi), the river passes through Sanxia, the Three Gorges of the Chang Jiang. In the

The longest river in China, and the third-longest in the world, is the 6,300-kilometer (3,900-mi) long Chang Jiang (Yangzi River).

The Chang Jiang rises at the foot of Geladondong (6,621 m/21,724 ft high) in the Tanggula Mountains, in Qinghai province. In its upper reaches, its name is Tuotuo, then it is called Tongian He, and from Yibin in Qinghai all the way to Sichuan it is called Jinsha Jiang, the River of Golden Sand. Chang Jiang is the name commonly used for the middle reaches, while the locals call the lower reaches of the river, from Yangzhou to the estuary, Yangzi. This is the name with which missionaries and colonialists were

Qutang Gorge, the river is only 100 meters wide. At this point, the difference between deep and shallow water can be up to 60 meters (200 ft).

In the Wu Gorge, which is the next one, the mountains rise from the banks and tower over the river at a height of 500 to 1,000 meters (1,600 to 3,300 ft).

Climate: Given the size of China, it is not unusual to find a variety of climatic conditions and extreme differences in temperature. The horizontal gradient – between the northern and southern borders of the country are 49 degrees of latitude – and the vertical slope between the high plateaus in the west and the low plains in the east and southeast affect the climate, but the main determining factor is its position at the edge of the Asian continent and the vast Pacific Ocean. In winter, cold-air masses form over the high pressure zones of the Asian continent and then move southwards; this causes the dry climate typical of the Chinese winter. The only unpleasant aspect of this is the high dust content as the air blows the loess in from the Gobi Desert. In summer, the climate is a maritime one. The summer monsoons bring the rains from the Pacific, so that the rainy season lasts from May until September, the rain zones moving from south to north.

The northeast of China and northern Mongolia have short and warm summers, while the winters are long and cold. The growing season lasts for only three or four months. Immediately to the west lie the desert regions of Inner Mongolia and Xinjiang; they have hot and dry summers with occasional strong winds, and the winters are cold and dry. In the Tibet-Qinghai Plateau, which is, on average, 4,000 meters (13,000 ft) high, the winters are extremely cold and the short summers only moderately warm.

In central China, summers are without exception hot, and rainfall is high. North of the Chang Jiang, the main rainfall is in July and August. In the low plains of the Chang Jiang, the winters are somewhat milder than in the loess plains north of the Qinling mountains. Here, the growing period lasts for eight or nine months. One exception is the naturally-sheltered Red Basin in Sichuan, with a growing period of up to 11 months.

The Chinese have designated the land according to the color of its soil. There is black earth in northeast China; the desert and steppe soil is described as white; the loess earth in central China is yellow; red earth is found south of the Chang Jiang; and the fertile marshlands in the south are described as blue or green soil. This short list alone indicates that the fertile soil is to be found in the south and east of the country, while in the north and the west, there are pastures or steppes, deserts and high plateaus. Only 40 percent of the total area of the country can be used for agriculture or forestry, and only 11 percent of the total land is suitable for farming; the remaining 60 percent is barren land. In order to feed a population that has exceeded one billion, agriculture needs to be constantly intensified. Herein lies one of the most serious problems of the Chinese economy: providing enough food for the population without causing serious ecological damage.

Left, Huang He. **Above**, Geladandong Glacier; autumn in Tian Shan.

Ninety percent of China's population lives on just one-fifth of China's land, mostly in the east and south. In contrast, the vast empty areas in the north and west are sparsely populated, and often hardly habitable.

The Chinese consider themselves as Han, descended from the Han dynasty that was a pivotal point in Chinese history. Although over 90 percent of Chinese are ethnically Han, the distinction between Han and other racial groups is not black and white. The notion of being Chinese – Han Chinese – is to some degree a cultural concept, an acceptance of Chinese values. The Han Chinese are, of course, derived from a distinctive racial background, but over the centuries, the Han absorbed racial minorities.

The Han Chinese have traditionally populated the eastern part of the country, leaving the empty spaces to the west and north, at least up until modern times, to the minority ethnic groups. (Within China, only in Tibet is a national minority group actually the majority, with 98 percent of the population.)

Population headaches: China's population was counted for the first time about 2,000 years ago, in 4 AD. By 742 AD, during the Tang dynasty, China's population was just over 50 million people.

At around the same time as the invasion of Genghis Khan and the Mongols, around AD 1250, the 100 million mark was probably exceeded for the first time. By the middle of the 18th century, the number had doubled; a century later, in 1850, a population of 400 million people had been reached.

Shortly after World War II, there were half a billion people in China. Between the mid 1960s and the early 1980s, China's population increased by over 300 million, more than the total population of either the United States or the former Soviet Union. Today's population is over 1.2 billion people, nearly 20 percent of humanity. In recent years, China's population has increased annually by about 15 million people.

The governing and administrative chal-

lenges of such an immense population are mind-boggling. Gathering statistics for over a billion people, much less analyzing it, defies the imagination. Nevertheless, the statistics reveal much about China's options. The numbers are chilling, considering that less than ten percent of the world's agrarian areas are in China. For every 1,000 people, there are 21 births but just six deaths.

The government, in 1978, began a one-child-per-family program. Opportunities and incentives for those who have but one child

are considerable. In urban areas, the program has been mostly successful. In the countryside, where traditions die hard and larger families are needed for farming, the one-child family has had limited success.

Skewing any population statistics, however, is the preference for male heirs. In China, family lines are passed on through the male child. Partly because of this, and because – especially in rural areas – male offspring are more likely to support aging parents, sons are preferred to daughters. Female infants in the countryside have fallen victim to infanticide. From 1953 through 1964, the sex ratios at birth were a little under

Preceding pages: Guangzhou youth at disco. **Left,** old companions, Wenzhou. **Right,** department store in Shenzen.

105 males for every 100 female infants. Ultrasound scanners, which allow the determination of the sex of fetuses, were first introduced to China in 1979. As their use became widespread, especially amongst the middle and upper classes, the ratio climbed: 108 in 1982, 114 in 1990, and roughly 119 in 1992. Doctors are officially banned from disclosing the results of ultrasound scans, but they can usually be persuaded to tell. Also, private businessmen now offer the service, which can turn in handsome profits.

China's population is hard to sustain; most Chinese experts have said China can comfortably support a population of only 800 million. This is a major reason for the great

still provide the only security for old age. Second, sex education is still a taboo topic, especially in conservative rural areas where the grandmother educates her grandchildren according to her own beliefs.

In the cities, on the other hand, families actually prefer to have one child, as living space is restricted. Considering that living space in Shanghai or Beijing is, on average, 3.5 square meters, population-control measures are accepted.

Given the diverging sex ratio, many males will find themselves without female partners. The government has predicted that, if trends continued, there would be a 50- to 70-million-strong army of bachelors by 2000.

emphasis China has placed on birth control.

Although its original targets have proven excessively optimistic, the one-child policy has greatly reduced the rate of population increase. According to a 1993 estimate – comparing the average Chinese woman bearing five to six children in the 1950s, but only two in 1993 – the one-child policy had prevented 200 million births by 1993.

Yet problems still remain. Thirty percent of births are not planned, despite widespread use of condoms. The State Family Planning Commission, a government agency, suggests several reasons. First, attitudes have not changed in rural areas; to a farmer, sons

Little emperors: With so many hopes riding on them, particularly if they are male, children with no siblings are usually spoiled by doting parents and, especially, grandparents. These kids have been dubbed, literally, "little emperors". A Western equivalent might be "exceedingly spoiled brat". Even the Chinese consider them to be rude and spoiled.

Consider an episode in the mid 1990s, in Guangdong Province. It is an extreme case, certainly, but not unique. An electrical failure prevented a mother from preparing dinner for her teenage son. Enraged, he left the house, returning much later to find that, yes, dinner was still not ready. He stuck a meat cleaver into his mother's head ten times, then committed suicide by hanging himself. The fact that the government-controlled news media gave it extensive coverage reveals the wide-ranging concern regarding the self-absorbed younger generation, whose values ignore the centuries-old ideals of Confucianism, which emphasize social hierarchy and group responsibility.

The demographic shift to single-child families may have profound effects on Chinese society. Parents, growing up during the Cultural Revolution, excessively dote on their children amidst a limbo in values. Says an anthropologist at the Chinese University, in Hong Kong, in the *New York Times*: "You

family – and traditional Confucian values – remains Chinese society's most important unit. In rural areas, common surnames identify an extended clan.

Land, that icon of family wealth, was passed on, equally, to a family's sons by the father. Over generations, the amount of land being passed on to each individual grew less and less, until family plots became exceedingly small; average family wealth decreased.

At the turn of the century, and for the decades until the Communists took control in 1949, conditions for rural families were dismal, with scarce food, minimal health care and a continuing civil war. Rural conditions stabilized after 1949, with the quality

could either raise a generation of rebels against the controls of the Communist Party, or you could raise a generation that would feel more nationalistic and assertive as Chinese... I can see a whole generation perhaps more independent and willing to challenge authority, or simply more authoritative because of their intensified relationships with their parents, and the symbol of parents is government."

Traditional family values: Despite despotic little emperors dominating family life, the

of life gradually improving. In 1949, average life expectancy at birth was 35 years; by 1982, it was more than 65 years. Likewise, annual death rates fell from 23 to 6 for every 1,000 people. Literacy jumped from 20 percent to nearly 80 percent. (This is not to disregard, however, some central-government blunders, such as a colossal famine that killed 20 to 40 million people in the early 1960s because of poor planning.)

Although increasingly a rare occurrence in the cities, three generations may be living together in a rural family, with responsibility for elders falling to the sons. (Daughters, on the other hand, become members of her

Left, young children, Guilin. **Above**, hard-rock musicians, Shanghai.

husband's family after marriage.) Families in the cities, however, are increasingly small and self-contained, like families in most of the world's modern cities.

"Women hold up half the sky", proclaimed Mao, but even under his rule, women rarely achieved high positions. The years since have seen further official affirmations of sexual equality, but surveys comparing the real status of women in the world rank China in the bottom third.

Age-old beliefs are largely to blame. According to Confucius, a woman without talent is virtuous. Besides regarding women as problematic and less innovative, employers are also concerned that if a woman becomes

of an instructor who commands them to bend, twist and stretch in unison.

Such group activities start young for the Chinese. Before their lessons begin, schoolchildren may "exercise" together. Taped music and a voice blare out from speakers. *Yi er san. One two three.* The children massage their eyes, in a routine to counteract eyestrain resulting from too much studying.

Morning streets are crowded with commuters. Armadas of cyclists pour through cycle lanes and scatter across junctions. Buses lurch along the streets, sometimes slowing to a snail's pace as they encounter traffic jams. Buses are always packed – people pushing their way on into the throng, standing crushed

pregnant, she will be legally entitled to nine months' maternity leave. Adding to the woes of working women is the fact that they are victims of increasing sexual harassment.

Social life: Early morning, in a park in a Chinese city, men and women seem locked in solemn, slow-motion combat with invisible adversaries, swaying and turning and pushing into the air as they work through *taijiquan* routines. Some thrust swords into the air, while others inhale deep breaths and tighten muscles as they practice qong-fu.

Old folks may jog by in a soft-shoe shuffle that barely beats a walking pace. Or they join a group exercise session, gathering in front

against their neighbors, watching in case a seat becomes free, then pushing their way out when they reach their destinations. Queuing is a foreign concept.

As their rich and varied cuisine reflects, the Chinese love to eat, and China's rise in living standards is apparent at meal times. City residents, to whom even pork was once special, now regularly consume beef, fish, and shrimp.

While meals in the home may be relatively simple, with a small selection of dishes from which to choose, restaurant meals can be veritable banquets. This is especially the case if the meal is accounted to entertainment expenses, or is being paid for by a businessman who wants to impress – the Chinese do not usually split the tab. For a banquet to really impress, it should include rare delicacies such as exotic fungi or, sadly and illegally, endangered wildlife, such as tiger. One restaurant in Guangzhou has a banquet that includes a substance most of us do not even think of as food: gold sprinkled on delicacies such as abalone, sharks fin, crocodile and clam.

But whatever the offering, there should always be more food than the diners can eat. Otherwise, the host loses face. Sometimes banquets end with tables still piled with food. By one estimate, the Chinese waste

China's national and regional television stations are improving, but even though they feature foreign as well as domestic programs, their efforts rarely grip viewers. "There is too much garbage on television," wrote propaganda supremo Li Ruihuan in 1992. "The task of television stations is to liven things up (but) in every respect, television programs are far too dull and serious; there is not enough action." Because programs that have proven to be winners with the masses have often drawn flak from ideologues, the stations remain cautious, and are unlikely to rush to follow Li's exhortations to be more "open" and "courageous".

However, increasing numbers of people

enough food each year to adequately feed 100 million people.

Until recently, dinner was the chief evening event. It may remain so for many people, who, after eating, leave claustrophobic homes for the street outside, to meet neighbors or read under street lights. With little or no privacy at home, young couples may head for parks in search of romance. (While there are still arranged marriages in China, single people are increasingly free to marry as they please, particularly in urban areas.)

Left, home life, Xiamen. **Above**, some prefer traditional Chinese opera to television.

are no longer limited to watching domestic stations. The masses may be officially banned from receiving foreign satellite television – with its Western bourgeoise influences – but state-run factories have been enthusiastically producing satellite dishes, which now dot city rooftops and often serve many households. Numerous satellite channels – Star TV, MTV, Disney Channel – can be received throughout China, often in Mandarin.

Domestically-produced films are rare, since, like television, the movie industry is stymied by ideologues. Even so, the Chinese film industry is creative and gaining greater international respect, not to mention audiences. Some films, however, are approved for release in China only after achieving critical acclaim in the West.

Karaoke, that vain Japanese-invented sing-along addiction, has swept China as elsewhere in Asia, joining the discos, bars, and other social venues.

Karaoke bars range from the modestly priced to those that are costly even by Western standards. A few are fronts for prostitution and risk the ire of the authorities, who may close them down to "eliminate the social evils and purify the air of society". Overwhelmingly, the songs patrons prefer are from Hong Kong and Taiwan; there is also material from the decadent West.

when the distinction between rural and urban workers was quite clear and obvious. Rural life meant on the farm, urban life, the factory or office.

Two-thirds of China's people live in rural areas. Yet they are not all farmers. Increasingly, light industries are peppering the countryside, owned and operated by villages and towns in what the *Washington Post* called an industrial revolution more profound than that in the coastal urban areas.

Typically called township-and-village enterprises, these small industries blend private-style management with government ownership. For a decade and a half, annual growth rates of these enterprises has ex-

Working life: "To get rich is glorious", announced Deng Xiaoping in 1978. The people responded with gusto.

Despite increases in urban wages, China's current income levels are still very low compared to the West. The figures are, however, deceptive. This is partly because rents for most workers are still heavily subsidized, with apartments costing perhaps the equivalent of just a few dollars, literally, per month. The cost of living, too, is invariably lower in comparison with the West. (Urban life is rapidly becoming expensive, however, especially in Beijing, Shanghai, and Guangzhou.)

There was a time – until recently, in fact –

ceeded 20 percent, twice as high as China's economic growth. Employing over 100 million people, more than to be found in notoriously-inefficient state-owned industries, town-and-village enterprises are easing the problem of rural people migrating to the cities in search of work. Moreover, as agriculture becomes mechanized and automated, there are more people available to work in these small industries.

Many of these enterprises began as workshops in the commune system established in the 1960s. After Deng Xiaoping took power in 1978 and liberalized both agriculture and industry, rural incomes rapidly increased, as did buying power. These communal leftovers, at least those that survived, shifted to meet demand. Some are sweatshops, to be sure, and there is a conflict of interest for local governments, who are both owners and regulators of the enterprises.

While these township-and-village enterprises have offered new opportunities for the rural population and thus lessened the burden on cities somewhat, migrant workers seeking employment in the cities remains a city planner's headache.

The problem is especially acute in the south. In Guangzhou, a quarter of the population consists of migrant workers, the "floating population". It is estimated by the offi-

once called, has proven over the years to be ineffectual, whether in industry or the civil service (which is the world's largest at nearly 40 million bureaucrats).

Not surprisingly, most state-run firms have proved to be uneconomical and unresponsive to China's increasing demand for commodities and services.

China has moved to stem the losses, cutting hundreds of thousands of jobs in state-run companies during the early 1990s. But the job cuts have met with resistance; sacked workers have assaulted managers. By contrast, the flourishing private sector is characterized by vitality and vigor; lunch breaks are short. Time is, after all, money.

cial press that China's floating population may exceed 100 million, nearly equivalent to the population of Japan and greater than that of France.

What drives the floating population are urban incomes that are twice that to be found in the countryside; moreover, one-third of the rural population is underemployed, if not actually unemployed.

The "iron rice bowl", as the system of permanent jobs and guaranteed wages was

Left, with more time and money, youth seek the inspired life. **Above**, rural people seek work in Guangzhou.

Nationalities: There are over 50 officially-recognized minority groups in China, including those in Tibet and Xinjiang. Most minority groups live along China's strategic, sometimes troubled and usually sparsely-populated international borders.

Thus, when one of the minority groups needles Beijing, such as happens with Tibetans, the central government takes such deviations quite seriously. The minorities have often maintained close relationships with those of their group living on the other side of those borders. As a result, the central government cannot retain absolute control over some of these frontier peoples.

The defining elements of a minority are language, homeland, and social values. Perhaps eight percent of China's population is part of a minority group, with the largest being the 12-million-strong Zhuang, in southwestern China.

Given China's population of 1.2 billion, over 70 million people are non-Han Chinese. The constitution guarantees them certain national rights and privileges. One of the most important is the right to use their own language. To grant these minorities the right to live according to their own beliefs and traditions is, in the eyes of the Chinese, a sign of goodwill, and the renunciation of the expansionism of the old regime.

However, spoken and written fluency in standard Mandarin is the only way of becoming educated and improving social status. Schools for members of national minorities are not found everywhere, and universities teaching a minority language hardly exist.

This reflects an ancient concept, based on historical experience, that there is no other developed culture apart from the Chinese.

In reality, actually, the slow expansion of the Chinese nation from the original area on the Yellow River and its tributaries up to the South China Sea is linked to an equally slow assimilation of non-Chinese peoples into the Han Chinese society, considered culturally and technically more advanced than the surrounding cultures.

The small minorities that continue to live in less easily-accessible areas (known as "areas one flees to") have resisted the attraction of Chinese culture and civilization, and so have paid the price of slow progress within their own cultures. At the same time, over the past century, Han Chinese have moved to the outlying regions in great numbers, usually becoming the majority group.

In the autonomous region of Xinjiang, Uighurs remain the largest existing ethnic group, but make up only 45 percent of the population.

Only when grouped together with the Kazakhs, Kirghiz and others do Uighurs constitute an Islamic, Turkic-speaking majority. Forty years ago, 80 percent of the population fulfilled these criteria. But now, the large cities have a majority of Han Chinese (except for Kashi); Urümqi, a city with over one million people and the capital of Xinjiang, is made up of 80 percent Han Chinese.

The Muslim Hui only make up one-third of the population in their autonomous region of Ningxia, and they usually live in the economically less-privileged parts of the country, in the south.

In regards to Islam, most Hui can only satisfy the criteria used to classify a Hui (Chinese-speaking Muslim) with great difficulty. One often encounters a Hui to whom the city of Mecca means nothing.

In Inner Mongolia, the Han have predominated for decades, and now represent 80 percent of the population. On the other hand, more Mongols live in this region than in the neighboring country to the north, Mongolia. It is mainly the nomadic population who are Mongolians; almost all settled farmers and people living in towns are Han Chinese.

Although the Zhuang have given their name and the status of an autonomous region to Guangxi, they are nevertheless a minority In fact, the Zhuang are the largest non-Han nationality within modern China today. They are also more assimilated within mainstream society than any of the other minority groups. These changes are, of course, inevitable, as they are in all of the world's minority areas.

Left, Kazakh woman, Xinjiang Province. **Right**, roadside card gambling, Wenzhou.

For centuries before the Communists took power, several religious and philosophical beliefs were prominent in China. Two systems that originated in China, Daoism (or Taoism) and Confucianism, were not so much religions as ethical and pragmatic standards of behavior, especially for the educated classes. Buddhism was imported, coming to China from India in the first century AD.

When the Communists came into power, religion, of course, was deemed incompatible with Communism. In recent years, however, religious beliefs have gained wider acceptance, or at least are now more openly practiced. Confucianism, Daoism and Buddhism are practiced in varying degrees of mixing. Islam is also practiced, especially in the western parts of China, and there is a small Christian minority.

Ancestor worship: The ancestor worship of the Chinese is based upon the assumption that a person has two souls. One of them is created at the time of conception, and when the person has died, the soul stays in the grave with the corpse and lives on the sacrificial offerings. As the corpse decomposes, the strength of the soul dwindles, until it eventually leads a shadow existence by the Yellow Springs in the underworld. However, it will return to earth as an ill-willed spirit and create damage if no more sacrifices are offered. The second soul only emerges at birth. During its heavenly voyage, it is threatened by evil forces, and is also dependent upon the sacrifices and prayers of the living descendants. If the sacrifices cease, then this soul, too, turns into an evil spirit. But if the descendants continue to make sacrificial offerings and look into the maintenance of graves, the soul of the deceased ancestor may offer them help and protection.

Inscriptions on oracle bones from the Shang dynasty (16–11th century BC) and inscriptions on bronze, dating from the Zhou period (11th century–221 BC), reveal that an ancestor worship of high nobility, a cult of a high god called *Di,* and an animistic belief in numerous gods of nature had existed early in Chinese history. Originally, ancestor worship had been exclusive to the king. Only later did peasants too begin to honor their

ancestors. At first, people believed that the soul of the ancestor would search for a human substitute and create an abode for the soul during the sacrificial ritual. It was usually the grandson of the honored ancestor who took on the role of substitute. About 2,000 years ago, genealogical tables were introduced as homes for the soul during sacrificial acts. Up until that time, the king and noblemen had used human sacrifices for ancestral worship. Even today, the Chinese worship their ancestors and offer the deities

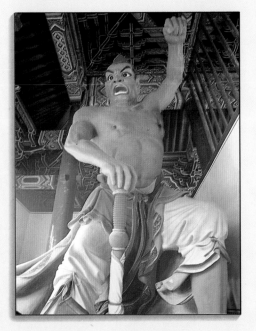

sacrifices of food. This is widely practised, for example, during the Qingming Festival.

The original religion of the people actually focused on the worship of natural forces. Later, the people began to worship the Jade Emperor, a figure from Daoism who became the highest god in the popular religion after the fourteenth century. Guanyin, the goddess of mercy, originated in Mahayana (Great Wheel) Buddhism. Among the many gods in popular Chinese religion, there were also earth deities. Every town worshipped its own unique god. Demons of illness, spirits of the house, and even the god of latrines had to be remembered. The deities of streams and rivers were considered to be particularly dangerous and unpredictable. Apart from Confucianism, Daoism and Buddhism, there was also a working-class religion known as Daoist Buddhism.

China had been divided into numerous small states. Only after the Qin dynasty had won over its rivals in 221 BC did the first emperor over a united China come to power. At the time, there were a number of schools of philosophical thought. Only Confucianism and Daoism gained wide acceptance.

ness, activity and heaven are considered to be yang forces; the feminine, weak, dark and passive elements are seen as yin forces.

Laozi was the founder of Daoism. He lived at a time of crises and upheavals. The Daoists were opposed to feudal society, yet they did not fight actively for a new social structure, preferring instead to live in a pre-feudalistic tribal society.

Laozi, it is said, was born in a village in the province of Henan in 604 BC, the son of a distinguished family. For a time, he held the

Daoism: Central concepts of Daoism are the *dao*, which basically means way or path, but it also has a second meaning of method and principle; the other concept is *wuwei*, which is sometimes simply defined as passivity, or "swimming with the stream". The concept of *de* (virtue) is closely linked to this, not in the sense of moral honesty, but as a virtue that manifests itself in daily life when dao is put into practice. The course of events in the world is determined by the forces *yang* and *yin*. The masculine, bright-

office of archivist in Luoyang, which was then the capital. But he later retreated into solitude and died in his village in 517. According to a famous legend, he wanted to leave China on a black ox when he foresaw the decline of the empire. Experts today are still arguing about Laozi's historical existence. Since the second century AD, many legends have been told about the figure of Laozi. One of them, for instance, says that he was conceived by a beam of light, and that his mother was pregnant with him for 72 years and then gave birth to him through her left armpit. His hair was white when he was born; he prolonged his life with magic.

Preceding pages: temple incense. Left, demonic tutelary god. Above, ancestor worship.

The classic work of Daoism is the *Daodejing*. It now seems certain that this work was not written by a single author. The earliest, and also most significant, followers of Laozi were Liezi and Zhuangzi. Liezi (fifth century BC) was particularly concerned with the relativity of experiences, and he strived to comprehend the dao with the help of meditation. Zhuangzi (fourth century BC) is especially famous for his poetic allegories.

The ordinary people were not particularly attracted by the abstract concepts and metaphysical reflections of Daoism. Even at the beginning of the Han period (206 BC–AD 220), there were signs of both a popular and religious Daoism. As Buddhism also be-

came more and more popular, it borrowed ideas from Daoism, and vice versa, to the point where one might speak of a fusion between the two.

The Daoists and Buddhists both believed that the great paradise was in the far west of China, hence the name, Western Paradise. It was believed to be governed by the queen mother of the West (Xiwangmu) and her husband, the royal count of the East (Dongwanggong). Without making any changes to it, the Daoists also took over the idea of hell from Buddhism.

Religious Daoism developed in various directions and schools. The ascetics retreat-

ed to the mountains and devoted all their time to meditation, or else they lived in monasteries. In the Daoist world, priests had important functions as medicine men and interpreters of oracles. They carried out exorcism and funeral rites, and read mass for the dead or for sacrificial offerings.

Historical and legendary figures were added to the Daoist pantheon. At the head were the Three Commendables. The highest of the three deities, the heavenly god, is identical to the Jade Emperor, worshipped by the common people. There is hardly a temple without Shouxinggong (the god of longevity), a friendly-looking old man with a long white beard and an extremely elongated, bald head. There are also the god of wealth (Caishen), the god of fire (Huoshen), the kitchen god (Zaoshen), the god of literature (Wendi), the god of medicine (Huatou) and others. Only the Eight Immortals are truly popular and well-known. Some of them are derived from historical personalities, some are fanciful figures. They are believed to have the ability to make themselves invisible, bring the dead back to life, and do other miraculous deeds.

Confucius: While Laozi was active in the south of China, Confucius lived in the north of the country. For him, too, dao and de are central concepts. For more than 2,000 years, the ideas of Confucius (551–479 BC) have influenced Chinese culture, which in turn sculpted the worldview of neighboring lands such as Korea, Japan and Southeast Asia. It is debatable whether Confucianism is a religion in the strictest sense. But Confucius was worshipped as a deity, although he was only officially made equal to the heavenly god by an imperial edict in 1906. (Up until 1927, many Chinese offered him sacrifices.)

Mencius, a Confucian scholar, describes the poverty at the time Confucius was born as follows: "There are no wise rulers, the lords of the states are driven by their desires. In their farms are fat animals, in their royal stables fat horses, but the people look hungry and on their fields there are people who are dying of starvation."

Confucius himself came from an impoverished family of the nobility who lived in the state of Lu (near the village of Qufu, in the west of Shandong Province). For years, Confucius – or Kong Fuzi (Master Kong) – tried to gain office with one of the feudal lords, but he was dismissed again and again. So he traveled around with his disciples and instructed them in his ideas. All in all, he is said to have had 3,000 disciples, 72 of them highly-gifted ones who are still worshipped today. Confucius taught mainly traditional literature, rites and music, and is thus regarded as the founder of scholarly life in China. The Chinese word *ru*, which as a rule is translated as Confucian, actually means "someone of a gentle nature" – a trait that was attributed to a cultured person. Confucius did not publish his philosophical thoughts in a book. They have, therefore, to be reconstructed from fragments of the comments he made on various occasions. The thoughts of Confucius were collected in the *Lunyu* (Con-

based upon the assumption that man can be educated. Ethical principles were turned into central issues. Confucius was a very conservative reformer, yet he significantly reinterpreted the idea of the *junzi*, a nobleman, to that of a noble man, whose life is morally sound and who is, therefore, legitimately entitled to reign.

Confucius believed that he would create an ideal social order if he reinstated the culture and rites of the early Zhou period (1100–700 BC). Humanity (*ren*) was a central concept at the time, its basis being the love of children and brotherly love. Accordingly, the rulers would only be successful in their efforts if they can govern the whole of

versations) by his loyal disciples. Some of the classic works on Confucianism are: *Shijing*, the book of songs; *Shujing*, the book of charters; *Liji*, the book of rites; *Chunqiu*, the spring and autumn annals; and *Yijing*, the book of changes.

Confucianism is, in a sense, a religion of law and order. Just as the universe is dictated by the world order, and the sun, moon and stars move according to the laws of nature, so a person, too, should live within the framework of world order. This idea, in turn, is

society according to these principles. Confucius defined the social positions and hierarchies very clearly and precisely. Only if and when every member of society takes full responsibility for his or her position will society as a whole function smoothly.

Family and social ties – and hierarchy – were considered to be of fundamental importance: between father and son (the son has to obey the father without reservations); man and woman (women have few individual rights); older brother and younger brother; friend and friend; and ruler and subordinate.

In the twelfth century, Zhu Xi (1130–1200 BC) succeeded in combining the metaphysical

Left, statue of Laozi, who spread Daoism. **Above**, Chen family temple, Guangzhou.

tendencies of Buddhism and Daoism with the pragmatism of Confucianism.

His systematic work includes teachings about the creation of the microcosm and macrocosm, as well as the metaphysical basis of Chinese ethics. This system, known as Neo-Confucianism, reached canonical status in China; it was the basis of all state examinations, a determining factor for Chinese officialdom until this century.

Buddhism: The Chinese initially encountered Buddhism at the beginning of the first century, when merchants and monks came to China over the Silk Road. The type of Buddhism that is prevalent in China today is the *Mahayana* (Great Wheel), which – as op-

posed to *Hinayana* (Small Wheel) – promises all creatures redemption through the so-called *bodhisattva* (redemption deities). There were two aspects that were particularly attractive to the Chinese: the teachings of *karma* provided a better explanation for individual misfortune, and there was a hopeful promise for existence after death. Nevertheless, there was considerable opposition to Buddhism, which contrasted sharply with Confucian ethics and ancestor worship.

At the time of the Three Kingdoms (AD 220–280), the religion spread in each of the three states. The trading towns along the Silk Road as far as Luoyang became centers of the new religion. After tribes of foreign origin had founded states in the north, and the gentry from the north had sought refuge in the eastern Jin dynasty (317–420), Buddhism developed along very different lines in the north and south of China for about two centuries. During the rule of Emperor Wudi (502–549), rejection and hostility towards Buddhism spread among Confucians. And during the relatively short-lived northern Zhou dynasty (557–581), Buddhism was officially banned (from 574 to 577).

Buddhism was most influential in Chinese history during the Tang dynasty (618–907). Several emperors officially supported the religion; the Tang empress Wu Zetian, in particular, surrounded herself with Buddhist advisors. During the years 842 to 845, however, Chinese Buddhists also experienced the most severe persecutions in their entire history: a total of 40,000 temples and monasteries were destroyed, and Buddhism was blamed for the economic decline and moral decay of the dynasty.

In the course of time, 10 Chinese schools of Buddhism emerged, eight of which were essentially philosophical ones that did not influence popular religion. Only two schools have remained influential through today: Chan (school of meditation or Zen Buddhism) and Pure Land (Amitabha-Buddhism). The masters of Chan considered meditation to be the only path to knowledge. In Mahayana Buddhism, worship focused on the Bodhisattva Avalokiteshvara.

Since the seventh century, the ascetic Bodhisattva has been a popular female figure in China. She is called Guanyin, a motherly goddess of mercy who represents a central deity for the ordinary people. Guanyin means "the one who listens to complaints".

In Chinese Buddhism, the centre of religious attention is the Sakyamuni Buddha, the founder of Buddhism who was forced into the background in the sixth century by the Maitreya Buddha (who was called Mile-fo in China, or redeemer of the world). In Chinese monasteries, Sakyamuni greets the faithful as a laughing Buddha in the entrance hall. Since the fourteenth century, the Amitabha school had dominated the life and culture of the Chinese people.

The most influential Buddhist school was the so-called School of Meditation (Chan in China, Zen in Japan), which developed under the Tang dynasty. It preached redemption through buddhahood, which anyone is able to reach. It despised knowledge gained from books or dogmas, as well as rites. Liberating shocks or guided meditation are used in order to lead disciples towards the experience of enlightenment. Other techniques used to achieve final insights were long hikes and physical work. The most important method was a dialogue with the master, who asked subtle and paradoxical questions, to which he expected equally paradoxical answers.

In 1949, the year the People's Republic of China was founded, there were approximately 500,000 Buddhist monks and nuns, and 50,000 temples and monasteries. A number of well-known Buddhist temples were classified as historical monuments.

By the beginning of the Cultural Revolution in 1966, it seemed as if the Red Guards were intent on completely eradicating Buddhism. The autonomous Tibet was hard-hit by these excesses. Only a few important monasteries and cultural objects could be protected, and completely or only partly preserved. Today, there are Buddhists among the Han Chinese, the Mongols, Tibetans, Manchus, Tu, Qiang and Dai (Hinayana Buddhists) peoples.

In the seventh century AD, another type of Buddhism, called Tantric Buddhism or Lamaism, was introduced into Tibet from India. With the influence of the monk Padmasambhava, it replaced the indigenous Bon religion, while at the same time taking over some of the elements of this naturalist religion. The monasteries in Tibet developed into centers of intellectual and worldly power, yet there were recurring arguments. Only the reformer Tsongkhapa (1357–1419) succeeded in rectifying conditions that had become chaotic.

He founded the sect of virtue (Gelugpa), which declared absolute celibacy to be a condition and reintroduced strict rules of order. Because the followers of this sect wear yellow caps, this order came to be known as Yellow Hat Buddhism.

Tsongkhapa had predicted to two of his disciples that they would be reborn as heads of the church. He had therewith anticipated

the continuous transfer of powerful positions within the church – for instance, the position of the Dalai Lama and the Panchen Lama. The Dalai Lama represents the incarnation of the Bodhisattva of mercy (Avalokiteshvara), who is also worshipped as the patron god of Tibet. The Panchen Lama is higher in the hierarchy of the gods and is the embodiment of Buddha Amitabha. The present 14th Dalai Lama, who was enthroned in 1940, fled to India after an uprising in 1959 and has been living in exile since then. The Panchen Lama died in Beijing in January 1989, at the age of 50, after he came to an understanding with the Chinese authorities following the uprising.

In Lamaism, a complex pantheon exists; apart from the Buddhist deities, there are figures from the Brahman and Hindu world of gods and the old Bon religion. Magic, repetitive prayers, movements, formulae, symbols and sacrificial rituals are all means for achieving redemption.

Islam: Islam probably became established in China in the seventh century, and its influence has been very long-lasting. Ten of the 56 recognized nationalities in China profess themselves to Islam. They are the Hui, Uzbek, Uighur, Karach, Kirgiz, Tatar, Shi'ite Tadshik, Donxiang, Sala and Bao'an – a total of 14 million people. The Hui are, as a rule,

<u>Left</u>, Buddha Sakyamuni. <u>Right</u>, mosques are common in northwestern China.

Han Chinese. They are the only group who enjoy the special status of a recognized minority solely on the basis of their religion.

Mohammed was born in Mecca around the year 570 (the exact date is unknown). From the age of 40 onwards, he preached the Koran. Islam soon came to China on two different routes: one was the famous Silk Road, the other from across the sea to the southeastern coast of China. During the Yuan dynasty (1279–1368), Islam finally became permanently established in China. The imperial observatory was built in Beijing and the Arab astronomer Jamal-al-Din was in charge of it.

The policies of the Qing dynasty were –

though it may be oversimplified to say so – hostile to Muslims. In the eighteenth century, slaughtering according to Islamic rites was forbidden, and the building of new mosques and pilgrimages to Mecca were not allowed. Marriages between Chinese and Muslims were illegal, and relations between the two groups were made difficult.

Some of the Muslim sects were declared illegal during the Qing dynasty. Later, the Cultural Revolution led to many restrictions for religious people. Over the last few years, the People's Republic of China has been attempting to bring socialism and religion closer together and achieve a harmony between them. Believers (irrespective of their religion) are expected to be patriotic and law-abiding, but not to give up their faith. Today, there are around 21,000 mosques in China. The Muslims celebrate their festivals, and Chinese-Muslim societies organise pilgrimages to Mecca.

Christianity: Christianity was first brought to China by the Nestorians, in 635. The followers of Nestorian Christianity disseminated their teachings with the help of a Persian called Alopen, who was their first missionary. The symbol of Nestorianism was a cross with two spheres at the end of all four beams. A stele dating from the Tang dynasty is decorated with such a cross and is on display in the museum of Xi'an Province.

For a period, in spite of religious persecutions, this religion had spread to all the regions of the empire, and in some parts of the country was practiced until the end of the Mongol Yuan dynasty. At the same time, initial contacts were made between China and the Roman Catholic Church. The first Catholic church in China was probably built when John of Montecorvino, a Franciscan monk from Italy, arrived in Beijing in 1295.

During the Ming period, Catholic missionaries began to be very active in China. A leading figure among the Jesuit missionaries who played an important role was an Italian, Matteo Ricci. When he died, there were about 2,000 to 3,000 Christians in China.

The Jesuits had used their excellent knowledge of Western sciences in order to forge links with Chinese scholars. Other Catholic orders were more dogmatic and introduced tensions. The Chinese emperors, fed up with the squabbling, persecuted them all.

At the onset of the nineteenth century, the Protestants began their missionary activities. The methods used to convert people were not always scrupulous. Nevertheless, the number of people converted remained an almost negligible minority.

The Vatican had taken an extremely anti-communist stance after World War II; the Chinese ordered that Catholics in China should no longer be accountable to the Vatican. Moreover, the Vatican to this day recognises only the Taiwan government. However, relations are slowing improving.

Left, Virgin Mary shrine in Beijing. **Right**, temple of Man Mo, Hong Kong.

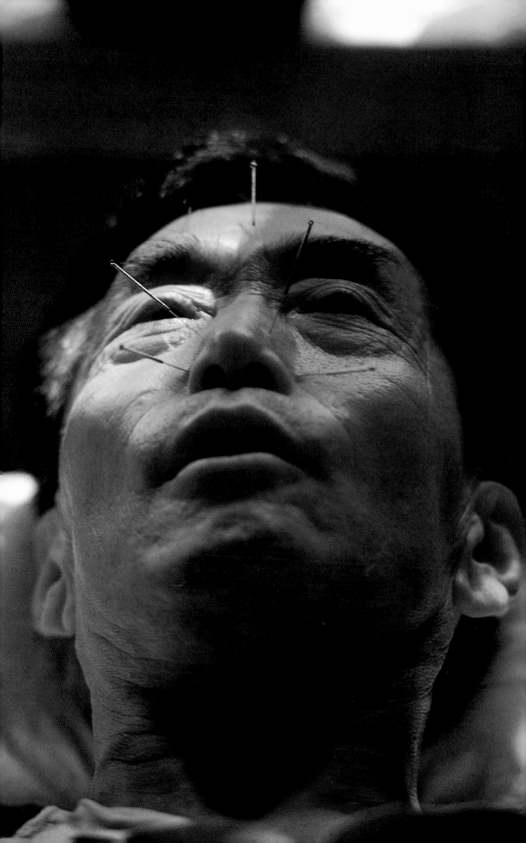

Whenever traditional Chinese medicine is mentioned nowadays, most Westerners immediately think of acupuncture – that small needle that has become increasingly popular all over the world in the last three decades. In some countries, orthodox Western medicine is still somewhat reluctant to accept acupuncture as part of an alternative approach to medicine. However, it is increasingly accepted by many Western physicians, and there is hardly a "pain center" anywhere in the Western world that does not offer acupuncture as a therapy.

Yet medicine in China is not just so-called traditional medicine. In fact, Western-style medicine is the primary form of medical treatment in China. The large public hospitals – *renmin yiyuan* – in all cities use the Western approach (*xiyi*) to treatment almost exclusively. The hospitals for Chinese medicine (*zhonggi*) are smaller, less well-equipped and harder to find.

Nowadays, the Chinese will usually visit a doctor trained in Western medicine if they feel that they are seriously ill and wish to be diagnosed. If no organic failure is found, the patient will go and see a traditional doctor who is far more likely to be able to restore the lost harmony.

Traditional Chinese medicine entails more than just acupuncture. The knowledge of remedies (*zhongyao*) is a very important factor. Patients are treated with different kinds of massage and chiropractics (*tuina*), as well as breathing and movement therapies, such as *taijiquan* (shadow boxing) and *qigong* (breathing therapy).

It is interesting to note that traditional medicine does not only take place within the walls of a hospital. When traveling through China, travelers have many opportunities to observe – even in public places – the efforts of the Chinese to keep healthy.

Wandering through the streets of a Chinese town, again and again one will see farmers in the street selling a certain natural

Left, needles for relieving pain and healing. **Right**, with the help of special charts, this young doctor explains the position of the acupuncture points.

produce. Often it is not obvious that this is a remedy; one would naturally think of it as food. For example, *giou qize* – a small and oval-shaped fruit, carmine red and tasting rather bitter – is used to relieve "congestion" of the liver and for getting rid of "anger". If the look on one's face remains blank, the farmer might add that it is also beneficial against high blood pressure.

Initially, the terminology used in Chinese medicine is odd to us, as Westerners typically differentiate very strictly between the

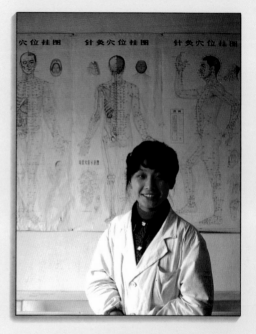

body and the mind. Eating a fruit to get rid of anger doesn't come naturally to us as a treatment.

The pharmacy: In a traditional Chinese pharmacy are the well-known ginseng roots, dried or immersed in alcohol, often looking much like a human figure. In fact, the Chinese character for ginseng contains the sign *ren,* which means person. You will also recognize the acupuncture needles and the cupping glasses made of glass or bamboo.

In the pharmacy there is a unique smell, or rather a mixture of 1,001 scents. And let us assume that you are in the famous Tongrentang pharmacy, which was founded in 1850 and lies in the old part of Beijing, south of Tiananmen. The enormous size of this pharmacy is nearly overwhelming, as is the selection of remedies: small and large eggs, snakes wound up in spiral shapes, dried monkeys, toads, tortoises, centipedes, grasshoppers, small fish, octopi, stag antlers, horns of rhinoceroses, and testicles and penises of various unfortunate – and often endangered – animals. And then there are the thousand kinds of herbs, blossoms, roots, berries, mushrooms and fruits – dried and preserved.

Are these supposed to be medicines? In fact, there is hardly a plant, mineral or animal substance in the world that is not used as a remedy. The *Encyclopaedia of the Tradi-*

ferred to as the "hundred schools". It was the time when ideas were born that were to influence all aspects of life in China for the next 2,000 years – including medicine.

The two most important schools of thought at the time were those of Confucianism and Daoism. Both shared the wish for peace and harmony, but their views on how this was to be achieved differed.

Harmony was interpreted as the interaction of opposite forces, for example, the adjustment of human behavior to ecological and social conditions. If this harmony was interfered with, then the disturbance would result in social or physical illness. The theory of the opposite forces of *yin* and *yang*, the theory of

tional Chinese Pharmacopoeia, published in 1977, has 2,700 pages listing 5,767 substances with medical properties.

Historical roots: The foundations of traditional Chinese medicine were laid over two thousand years ago, in the era of the Warring Empires, a time in which China was split up into many quarreling fiefdoms.

This stage in Chinese history, marked by fighting and misery, lasted a few centuries. So it is hardly surprising that people began to search for a solution to the endless strife. Innumerable thinkers, philosophers and social reformers with as many diverse ideas emerged, a collection of thought often re-

the "five phases of change" and the concept of *qi* were the most influential within the far-reaching theoretical background of traditional medicine. They formed the framework of medical thinking.

At a time when there existed very little knowledge of human anatomy and physiology, these theories provided points of reference. They enabled people to observe not only the relationship of the human microcosm to the macrocosm of the environment, but also the effect that physical and emotional changes have on each other. Thus, the feeling of fury was related to the wind that can come up very suddenly and with elemental force; fury was also brought into connection with a sour type of taste, with muscles and sinews that become cramped due to aggression. The *Inner Classic of the Yellow Emperor*, which is around 2,000 years old, also mentions that people with gall-bladder problems must have fallen ill due to unsatisfied ambition and pent-up anger. Thus, over the centuries, a special form of medicine evolved in China that concentrated particularly on the functional body.

Chinese medicine had some weaknesses. It never developed any surgery that can be taken seriously, and there are many incorrect ideas on anatomy, as anatomical research was in fact never carried out.

lems, however, require a longer healing process despite acupuncture.

A new form of painless acupuncture is that of ear acupuncture, done without needles. Small, round seed kernels are stuck onto certain points of the ear and massaged by the patient every so often. This method is not only very successful in the treatment of pain, but also relieves some allergic complaints such as hay fever.

When you enter an acupuncture clinic, you will notice the similar 1,001 scents of the Chinese pharmacy. This is the typical smell of the *moxa* herb, which is the same as Artemisia, or mugwort. It is considered especially helpful in the treatment of illnesses

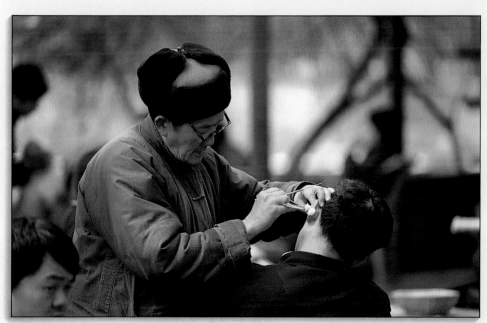

Acupuncture: Certainly not a cure for everything, acupuncture seldom performs the miracles that were often attributed to it in the past. In one aspect, however, its effect is undisputed and valued by a billion Chinese: the relief of pain. While Westerners rely on drugs to moderate physical pain, the Chinese go to the acupuncturist. Many cases of acute back pain, for example, can be cured by sticking just one needle in the *renzhong* point between the top lip and nose. Chronic prob-

Left, Chinese pharmacies often look more like herb shops. **Above**, self-employed helpers care for personal hygiene.

that, in Chinese medical terminology, are classified as "cold", for example, stomach and digestive complaints without fever, certain rheumatic illnesses, chronic pains in the back, and cramped shoulders and necks. The mugwort is formed into small cones and placed on slices of fresh ginger; then it is made to grow slowly. The plant is then placed onto the acupuncture point. Alternatively, it is placed on the end of an acupuncture needle (the so-called "hot needle"), or it is made into the shape of a cigar and rolled back and forth over the skin.

Exercise: At some stage during your travels in China, visit a park at six o'clock in the morning. There, groups of people do certain exercises together.

The most common type of exercise is taijiquan, the so-called shadow boxing. You will probably not be familiar with the qigong exercise, which is often translated in the West as breathing therapy. With certain exercises, which may or may not involve conscious breathing, the patient learns to control qi and thus to influence the course of a particular illness. The qi is a person's vital energy. Guiding one's qi means becoming aware of any part of the body, understanding it and being able to influence it. So there is also a psychological aspect to the qi.

During the Cultural Revolution, qigong

was actually forbidden because it resembled "superstitious" practices too closely.

Yet, in 1980, new qigong groups sprang up throughout the country. It was a lay movement that soon gained a large following. Some forms of qigong involve hardly any movement: breathing and "sinking into oneself" are of prime importance. Other forms, like the "wild goose qigong", entail a lot of movement and are very aesthetic.

The changes of the mental and emotional state follow a certain pattern of movement. The most extreme of these forms is the "crane qigong", which causes violent, sometimes even cathartic emotional outbursts with many people. They scream, cry or laugh, and dance or jump around. They experience what the Chinese call *fagong:* to abandon oneself to spontaneous movements. At the sight of the crane qigong, one's preconceived ideas about the quiet and introverted Chinese become somewhat shaken up, requiring dismissing the stereotype. The popularity of qigong is a clear indication that traditional medicine in China is very much alive and open to further developments.

It's in the diet: For much of China's history, herbalists have given medicinal value to various foods. At times, the distinction between food and treatment can blur.

While the Chinese have little doubt of the efficacy of different foods for treating ailments and improving specific parts of the body, Western science, always empirical, has been somewhat skeptical. Research in Europe and North America, however, has substantiated many claims of the Chinese herbalist. But the research is still tentative.

Consider three traditional delicacies: shark's fin, abalone and bird's nest. These are exquisite parts of an extensive cuisine, eaten in part for their sensory delights. Yet each is claimed to have medicinal value. Shark's fin, for example, is said to benefit internal organs, including the heart and kidneys. Abalone calms those internal organs. Moreover, it regulates the liver and reduces dizziness and high blood pressure. Bird's nest, usually taken in as a soup, cleanses the blood and assures a clear complexion.

Verifying such claims is difficult. The scientific method, which involves controlled experiments using known values and quantities, doesn't lend itself well to the analysis of claims that a food "calms the internal organs." Moreover, to be valid, a result must be independently verifiable. Consideration must also be given to the placebo effect, where a valid result occurs because one believes in something's efficacy. Mind over matter.

Yet extensive research on soy beans and green tea, for example, suggests that components in these two items have substantive medicinal value, perhaps against some forms of cancer. Herbal remedies have gained respect in the West. Why not culinary ones?

Left, the price of shark's fin varies with the quality. **Right**, ancient Chinese inventions included paper and gunpowder, used in fireworks.

DISCOVERIES OF CHINA

The concept that the emperor was the Son of Heaven – and that extraordinary celestial and earthly events were the expression of approval or criticism from above – was the cause for the very early development of astronomical observation in China. The imperial court had its own office of astronomy, and in the 13th century, there were 17 different astronomical instruments at the astronomer's disposal in the Beijing Observatory. Hence, Halley's Comet was first recorded by the Chinese as early as 467 BC. A calendar of 360 days was in use by the 3rd century BC, which successive dynasties tried to improve. In the 13th century, they fixed the

nally consisted of a metal plate with a metal spoon on it, the handle of the spoon pointing to the south. In the 2nd century AD, a seismograph was developed that could show where an earthquake had taken place.

Around 1100, iron foundries in China were already producing quantities of iron and steel that were unmatched in Europe until the 18th century. The use of block and tackle shows that the Chinese understood the laws of mechanics in the 5th century. The so-called Archimedean Screw was used to pump water in the 1st century, and the water wheel in the 4th and 5th centuries.

Irrigation, essential for Chinese agriculture, was important in development of technology.

The written word was always accorded more importance in China than the spoken. This may

length of the year as 365.2424 days, less than a thousandth off from modern calculations.

The Clock Tower of Su Song, built in 1088, is an early example of the highly-developed art of the clockmaker. Chain-driven and powered by a water wheel, it was fitted with a kind of escapement to regulate the wheels to show astronomical movements very precisely.

The *Book of Mathematics* dates from the 3rd century and gives the answers to many astronomical problems. It also deals with the multiplication and division of fractions and the formation of square roots.

Imperial geographers were busy with the deviation of magnetic north from true north even before Europeans were aware that the earth had a magnetic field. The Chinese compass origi-

have been the reason for the early development of paper. Made of mulberry tree bark around AD 200, and of bamboo some 200 years later, paper is still made today all over the world according to the Chinese method.

Printing, however, was not developed until some eight centuries later. Stone rubbing and printing with stamps seem to have been the more economic methods of reproduction of the written word, not least because Chinese script consists of thousands of characters.

In the 9th century, Daoist monks, looking for the elixir of eternal life, mixed charcoal, saltpeter and sulphur, thus discovering black powder. This was used not only for fireworks, but imperial troops in fact used bombs and grenades filled with black powder. ∎

In the early 1980s, *wushu* mania began sweeping through China. In parks and streets everywhere, youngsters maneuvered pretend swords and sticks in a sequence of strange movements. Even today, night after night, Chinese television broadcasts many wushu films, with titles like *The Shaolin Monastery*, *The Sons of Shaolin* or *The Wudang Mountains*. Whole series, which usually combine classical martial arts with patriotic themes, attract viewers of all ages. Early in the morning, there will be older people

practicing *taijiquan* in the parks; others may be doing *qigong* exercises. Even before going to work or school, young people do their training with swords, trying to emulate the acrobatic movements of their screen heroes.

The Shaolin monastery, in the Song Shan range near Luoyang, is the home of most Asian martial arts. Today, followers of qong-fu from abroad make their pilgrimages to the monastery. The bald-headed Shaolin monks, well-known for their inimitable shaolin boxing, recognized the signs of the times a few years back and opened a center for foreigners near the monastery. For a hefty fee, they will teach *shaolin* fighting techniques.

In the traditional wushu centers – for instance, in the district of Gong'an in Hunan province, in the Cangzhou district in the Heibei province, and the Jinan region in Shandong province – around 40 percent of the population, and 70 percent of young people, practice one of the numerous Chinese martial arts. These practices have been adopted by some Westerners in shadow boxing classes and in qong-fu courses.

Be it qong-fu or karate, taekwando or judo, whether popular in Korea, Japan or Scotland, they all originated in ancient China. They were originally used as fighting techniques of one individual against another. Yet, nowadays, they are used primarily for physical training and strengthening of willpower. Many a Chinese youngster dreams of becoming as perfect as a well-known monk and abbot, from the Baoguang Si monastery near Chengdu, who is still able to do a handstand on two fingers even at an advanced age.

Self-defence techniques: Wushu – the art of fighting – is the general term for all these self-defense sports, some of which may be carried out with the fists or the legs, or with the help of swords or lances. The mastery of the various techniques once entailed very esoteric knowledge, which would only be passed on within a family or a monastery, or from master to pupil. Nowadays, wushu is a national sport in the People's Republic of China, with competitions taking place every year. In the first half of this century, all types of wushu – just like traditional Chinese medicine – were less widely known; during the time of the Cultural Revolution, they were considered relics of feudalism and therefore despised. But for the most past, martial arts have enjoyed increasing popularity.

For an outsider, the variety of wushu styles is rather confusing. They are best grouped into four categories: fighting with hands or fists, fighting with swords and other weapons, training in pairs, and training in a group. The various fighting patterns use clever combinations of attack and defense, advance and retreat, movement and silence, acceleration and slowing down, hardness and elegance, pretense and reality.

One wushu technique is "long boxing" or *changquan*, which depends very much on dexterity and speed, and is particularly popular with children and youngsters. Another technique is imitation boxing *xingyiquan*, which favors forceful and balanced movements, and is therefore popular with middle-aged people. *Nanquan*, the southern style of boxing, combines all schools south of the Chang Jiang (Yangzi) and is characterized by small jumps and strong arm movements, often accompanied by loud screaming.

ments of animals, Bodhidarma is said to have developed an exercise that he described as a method of physical training, and this in turn became the origin of shaolin boxing. This type of boxing must surely be one of the most sophisticated Asian martial arts. Shaolin karate, as opposed to many other approaches, applies very hard blows geared primarily to attacking the opponent. Exercises like the "drunk boxing", in which the shaolin fighter feigns drunkenness, or "crane boxing" are amongst the most meaningful exercises.

Nanquan boxing is based on the movements of tigers, leopards, snakes and cranes. This is to some extent also true of shaolin boxing, more common in the north and originating in the Zen Buddhist Shaolin monastery.

Drunks and cranes: The monk Bodhidarma, who founded the Shaolin monastery, came to the heights of Song Shan in 527. He realized that many Buddhist monks were unable to keep up demanding meditation exercises in complete quiet and concentration. Based upon observations of the move-

Left, qigong expert. **Above**, shadow boxing at dawn, Hangzhou.

The monks of Shaolin have served history several times. They worked as bodyguards to the Tang emperor Li Shimin (626–649), helping him defeat his rivals. During the Ming dynasty, shaolin boxing was introduced in Japan; there, it merged with existing martial arts – *jiujitsu*, for instance – and became the famous martial art judo (the soft path). Other martial arts that were also influenced by or developed from wushu are karate and *aikido* in Japan, taekwando in Korea, *siamqu* in Thailand and stick-fighting in the Philippines. Even today, there is a sport called *tangshoudo* in Korea, which means the "Tang way of boxing".

Wushu can also be grouped into an "inner direction" and an "external direction". The latter includes the martial arts mentioned above and shaolin boxing, which is also known as qong-fu abroad. Kung fu simply means a fighting competition. If someone is a good fighter, one says that he has real qong-fu technique. The films from Hong Kong with Bruce Lee made shaolin qong-fu popular in the West, if not trendy.

Taijiquan: In stark contrast to this is taijiquan, or shadow boxing, which takes an "inner" approach. Taijiquan is a gentle method that aims to dispel the opponent without the use of force, and with minimal effort. It is based on the Daoist idea that the principle of softness will ultimately overcome hardness. According to legend, it is also – just like shaolin boxing – derived from the movements of animals. A monk who lived in the remote mountains some 600 years ago is said to have observed the fight between a snake and a crane. While the crane put all his energy into fast, hard blows, the snake adroitly avoided the crane until the crane was so exhausted that the snake won the fight. The monk interpreted this as a confirmation of his Daoist beliefs that soft, round and flexible is superior to the hard and angular. Based upon these conclusions, he developed a method with slowly circling movements, which are geared to breaking the momentum of the opponent's attack and letting it disappear into thin air. It was originally a method of self-defense, but in China, it is mostly older people who use it for meditating and strengthening the body.

It has been proven that shadow boxing dates back at least 300 years. It developed from the self-defense techniques that were inspired by Daoism. In the seventeenth century, when China was ravaged by battles and civil wars, wushu was widely used as a method of self-defense. New techniques were emerging, and by the end of the eighteenth century, the taijiquan style was practiced.

Initially, taijiquan was only known in the villages of the Henan province; the village of Chenjiagou, in the Wen district of the province, is said to be the place where taijiquan originated. It was here that Chen Wanting developed the earliest forms of taijiquan, which were then passed on from generation to generation within the Chen family. Chen's contribution towards further development of

wushu into shadow boxing was by adding new techniques of fighting to the existing ones. He introduced the *daoyin* technique, which concentrated on training the inner forces, and the *tuna*, or breathing exercise. These methods for perpetuating life stem from Daoism and can be traced back to the sixth century. By merging external techniques with inner concentration, the basis was created for shadow boxing: the unity of body and mind in motion, meditation in the movement, and the simultaneous development of inner and outer forces.

Lastly, shadow boxing depends on the application and mastery of the life energy qi, which can be directed to all parts of the body with the help of mental training. Qi must flow and circulate freely in the body. The round movements of taijiquan are derived from this – they can be firm or loose, hard or soft, be directed forwards or backwards, but the movement must always be smooth and flowing. The circulation of the qi around the body is achieved by standing in a particular position, the center of which is below the navel. The trunk remains upright, and all the movements stem from the central point. The movements are carried out very slowly and breathing must be controlled and allowed to circulate freely. Through consistent practice of taijiquan, one eventually comes very close to the ideal of Daoism, namely the wuwei (doing without a purpose).

Peaceful fighting: Taijiquan may be relaxing, but it requires heavy concentration. The word *taiji* is a concept in classical Chinese philosophy used to describe the highest point in the sky (the pole) or the upper side of a cube. Taiji is therefore the principle around which everything revolves, like the center of a circle that always remains in the same position, even if the circle itself turns. The most important aspect of taijiquan is the central point below the navel.

The four most important schools of taijiquan are the *yang* style with its quiet relaxed movements; the *wu* style with compact, gentle movements; the quick and nimble *sun* style; and the traditional *chen* style. From the yang style, the most popular of these, a form with 24 different movements was developed, now commonly seen all over the People's Republic. Like with many other wushu techniques, the individual movements have been given names that point to their origin:

"the white crane spreads his feathers", "parting the mane of a wild horse", "catching the bird by the tail".

Taijiquan can also be practiced with swords and other weapons, or with a partner. For fighting with weapons, one of the four categories of wushu, there are several subcategories: long cutting or stabbing weapons like spears, sticks and wide swords; short weapons like daggers, short swords and hooks; and flexible weapons like the whip with nine sections, the stick in three parts, and the hammer-chain, a chain at either end of which a piece of iron in the shape of a hammer is attached.

In a wider sense, qigong (breathing technique) is also part of wushu. Records show that it dates back 3,000 years. In qigong, certain techniques for regulating the breathing in prescribed positions can bring about concentrated thinking and a state of inner calm; if applied to specific cases, it can improve health and prolong life. There is also a more difficult version of qigong, called *liangong*, with which artists can perform amazing feats: lorries roll over the rib cage, stones are broken on their heads, iron bars broken off with a foot or the head. All wushu methods, especially the gentle ones, rely on

regulating the breathing and letting energy circulate freely.

For psychosomatic illnesses in particular – but not exclusively – wushu techniques are being used therapeutically. There are, for example, experiments being carried out in China using various qigong breathing exercises to treat cancer patients. Studies carried out by Chinese doctors show that taijiquan is successful in treating many illnesses. Taijiquan has a positive effect on the metabolism; amongst other things, it apparently lowers the cholesterol level. High blood pressure is far less common amongst people practicing taijiquan. Depending on age, any one of these methods can be practiced, pro-

vided training is done on a regular basis. For the methods using the "external" approach, the body needs to be moderately supple, while exercises from the "internal" method can be learned even at an advanced age. One can take it up for health or therapeutic reasons, and to gain a new attitude towards life.

Those who learn taijiquan as a martial art must never forget one thing: The highest honor is not to beat one's opponent, but to avoid a fight altogether. Students are accepted based on their attitudes and way of thinking. It is said that taijiquan can make one supple like a child, healthy like a woodcutter, and calm like a wise man.

Above, group synchronization.

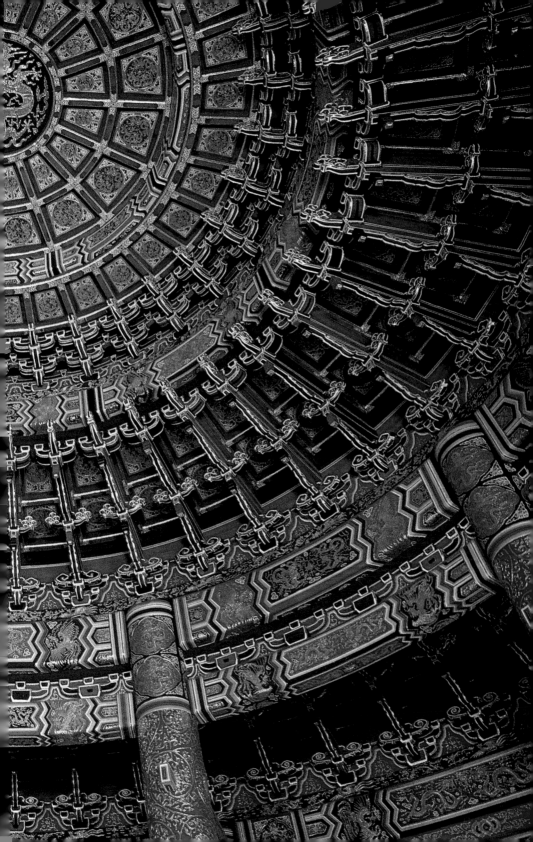

Painting, like most other cultural pursuits in China, has a long history. Cult murals in tombs, temples and palaces, as well as scroll paintings, are known to have existed in the third to first centuries BC. Interest in painting is explained by the extraordinary value the Chinese place – and have always placed – on the art of brush painting.

Brush painting: The importance given to brush painting is due to the intimate association between writing and painting, resulting from the original pictographic character of the Chinese script. As Chinese writing is not phonetic, anybody who is literate in whatever region and speaks whatever local dialect will be able to understand a written text. This nationwide unifying and historically continuous script was therefore always more important than the spoken language; the art of rhetoric – as practiced, for instance, in ancient Greece – never developed in China.

The close connection between writing and Chinese painting is evident from the customary incorporation of written words in most Chinese pictures, such as a poem, the name of the painting, the painter's name and date of completion, as well as the painter's and collector's name stamp. There are also examples of calligraphy where the ideograms stray so far from the characters as to virtually become paintings themselves.

In China, painting comprises monochromatic and colored work in ink on fabric or paper, mural reproductions such as woodblock prints, and calligraphy, as well as some related techniques such as embroideries, woven pictures, and decorative paintings.

Writing and painting utensils are referred to in China as the Four Treasures of the Study. They consist of the brush, ink, rubbing stone and paper – tools held in high esteem by poets, scholars and painters. There are reliable records of brush and ink already being used in the first century BC. Today, a paintbrush consists of a bundle of rabbit fur set in a slim bamboo tube; finer brushes are

made of pine marten fur. These brushes differ from the European watercolor brushes by their softness and, above all, by coming to a very fine point at the end, which allows a brush stroke to be gradually broadened by a movement of the wrist – from a hairline to the full breadth of the brush.

As its French name *encre de Chine* suggests, Chinese ink was only taken up in Europe as a distinct kind of paint in the seventeenth century. There is no doubt, however, that this ink was already widely used in China during the Han period. It is made from the soot of coniferous resin with the addition of glue; ink of good quality even has perfume added – musk in former days, but cloves are now commonly used. The substance is pressed into various wooden molds, giving it the shape of slabs, bars or prisms. Solid ink gained cult significance early on because it was esteemed as the most important calligraphic material.

Ink in solid form is used both for writing and painting, although liquid ink is now also available. However, this deprives the painting process and calligraphy of some of their contemplative attraction, because the rub-

Preceding pages: scene from Dream of the Red Chamber, Beijing; Tiantan. **Left**, porcelain, Song dynasty, Xi'an. **Right**, painting of contemporary painter Li Keran.

bing of ink is not just a practical procedure, but it also attunes one to the artistic activity and aids concentration. The process involves dripping water onto a stone pestle, rubbing solid ink on it and then diluting the solution with water if necessary.

Paper is the usual medium on which to paint. In former days, silk and fine linen were often used, but are now rarely used because they do not allow as much technical refinement as paper does. Paper – itself another ancient Chinese invention, developed by Cai Lun and used from AD 106 onwards – is now produced in different qualities, each offering the painter alternative possibilities depending on absorption and texture.

In China, painting is learned in much the same way as writing – by copying old masters or textbooks, of which *Flowers from a Mustard Seed Garden* is one of the most famous. A painter is considered a master of his art only when the necessary brush strokes for a bird, a chrysanthemum or a waterfall flow effortlessly from his hand. The strong emphasis placed on perfection quickly leads to specialization by painters on specific subjects. In this way, for instance, Xu Beihong (1895–1953) became known as the painter of horses, just as Qi Bai-Shi (1862–1957) was famous for his shrimps.

One of the most favored painting forms in China is landscape painting. Notable characteristics of this form of painting are perspectives that draw the viewer into the picture, plain surfaces (unpainted empty spaces) that give the picture a feeling of depth, and the harmonious relationship between man and nature, with man depicted as a small, almost disappearing, figure in nature.

A peculiar feature is the presentation of the picture as a hanging scroll. It is first painted on silk or on extremely thin paper, backed with stronger paper and mounted in a complicated way on a long roll of silk or brocade. Then a wooden stick is attached at the lower end (or left end, if the scroll is to be displayed horizontally). Typically, the picture was stored away rolled up and brought out only on special occasions to be slowly unfurled, revealing only parts of a scene that were pieced together in the mind of the observer, subtly drawing him into the picture, making him a participant and not just a mere observer. After it had been displayed, the scroll was carefully put away again.

Thus, the picture was handled in order to be looked at – touched by hand while being scrutinized. With horizontal scrolls, always unrolled little by little, the hands were in constant movement.

A similarity applies to the other two forms of presenting classical painting – the fan that needed unfolding and the album leaf that needed pages turned. The underlying thought was to create a bond between picture and observer – an intimate merger – whereas Western painting on panel or canvas impose a rational distance.

In keeping with this, a landscape painting often has a path or bridge in the foreground to bring the viewer into the picture.

Silk and the less-noble arts: Calligraphy, painting, poetry and music are regarded in China as the noble arts, whereas the applied arts are considered merely as honorable crafts. All the same, in the West, these skilled crafts have always held a special fascination. When thinking of China, one thinks of silk, jade and porcelain.

The cultivation of the silkworm is said to go back to the third century BC. Legend has it that planting of mulberry trees and keeping silkworms was started by the wife of the mythical Yellow Emperor Huangdi. For centuries, silk held the place of currency: civil servants and officers as well as foreign envoys were frequently paid or presented with bales of silk. The precious material was transported to the Middle East and the Roman empire via the Silk Road. The Chinese maintained a monopoly on silk until about 200 BC, when the secret of its manufacture became known in Korea and Japan. In the West – in this case the Byzantine empire – such knowledge was acquired only in the sixth century AD. The Chinese had prohibited the export of silkworm eggs and the dissemination of knowledge of their cultivation, but a monk is said to have succeeded in smuggling some silkworm eggs to the West. Today's centers of silk production are areas in the south of China around Hangzhou,

vessels, red and even black clayware with comb and rope patterns, have been found. The Yangshao and Longshan cultures of the fifth to second millennium BC developed new types of vessels and a diversity of patterns in red, black or brown. Quasi-human masks, stylized fish, and hard, thin-walled stoneware, with kaolin and lime feldspar glazes, were created. Later, light-grey stoneware with green glazes, known as *yue* ware – named after the kilns of the town of Yuezhou – were typical designs of the Han period. Even during the Tang dynasty, China was known in Europe and the Middle East as the home of porcelain.

The most widespread form of ancient Chi-

Suzhou and Wuxi; in this region, silk can be bought at a lower price. Hangzhou has the largest silk industry in the People's Republic, while in Suzhou, silk embroidery has been brought to the highest artistic level.

Porcelain: The Chinese invented porcelain sometime in the seventh century – a thousand years before the Europeans did. The history of Chinese ceramic artifacts, however, goes back to neolithic times. Along the Huang He (Yellow River) and Chang Jiang (Yangzi), 7,000- to 8,000-year-old ceramic

Left, calligrapher at work. **Above**, hand painting on porcelain in a factory.

nese porcelain was celadon – a product of a blending of iron oxide with the glaze that resulted, during firing, in the characteristic green tone of the porcelain. *Sancai* ceramics – ceramics with three-color glazes from the Tang dynasty – became world-famous. The colors were mostly strong green, yellow and brown. Sancai ceramics were also found among the tomb figurines of the Tang period in the shape of horses, camels, guardians in animal or human form, ladies of the court, and officials. The Song-period celadons – ranging in color from pale or moss green, pale blue or pale grey to brown tones – were also technically excellent. As early as the

Yuan period, a technique from Persia was used for underglaze painting in cobalt blue (commonly known as Ming porcelain). Some common themes seen throughout the subsequent Ming period were figures, landscapes and theatrical scenes. At the beginning of the Qing dynasty, blue-and-white porcelain attained its highest level of quality. Since the fourteenth century, Jingdezhen has been the center of porcelain manufacture, although today, relatively inexpensive porcelain can be bought throughout China. However, antique pieces are still hard to come by because the sale of articles predating the Opium Wars is prohibited by the Chinese government.

Jade: With its soft sheen and rich nuances of color, jade is China's most precious stone. Jade is not a precise mineralogical entity but rather comprises two minerals: jadeite and nephrite. The former is more valuable because of its translucence and hardness, as well as its rarity. The Chinese have known jade since antiquity, but it became widely popular only in the eighteenth century. Colors vary from white to green, but there are also red, yellow and lavender jades. In China, a clear emerald-green stone is valued most highly. According to ancient legend, Yu, as the jewel is known, came from the holy mountains and was thought to be crystallized moonlight. In fact, jade came from Khotan, along the southern Silk Road.

Nephrite is quite similar to jadeite, but not quite as hard and is more common. During the eighteenth century, nephrite was quarried in enormous quantities in the Kunlun mountains. It comes in various shades of green (not the luminous green of jadeite), white, yellow and black. The oldest jades so far discovered come from the neolithic Hemadu culture (about 5000 BC). The finds were presumably ritual objects. Circular disks called *bi,* given to the dead to take with them, were frequently found. Centuries later, the corpses of high-ranking officials were clothed in suits made of more than 2,000 thin slivers of jade sewn together with gold wire. Since the eleventh century, the Jade Emperor has been revered as the superior godhead in Daoist popular religion. Today, the ring disk – a symbol of heaven – is still worn as a talisman; jade bracelets are believed to protect against rheumatism.

In the jade-carving workshops in present-day China, there are thought to be as many as 30 kinds of jade in use. Famous among the jade workshops are those in Qingtian (Zhejiang province), Shoushan (Fujian province), and Luoyang (Hunan province). Masters of jade work include Zhou Shouhai, from the jade-carving establishment in Shanghai, and Wang Shusen in Beijing, the latter specializing in Buddhist figurines. In government shops, jade can be trusted to be genuine. On the open market and in private shops, however, caution is advised. Genuine jade always feels cool and cannot be scratched with a knife. Quality depends on the feel of the stone, its color, transparency, pattern and other factors. If in doubt, a reputable expert should be consulted.

Lacquerware: The glossy sheen of lacquerware is not only attractive to the eye but is also appealing to the touch. The bark of the lacquer tree (*rhus verniciflua*), which grows in central and southern China, exudes a milky sap when cut, which solidifies in moist air, dries and turns brown. This dry layer of lacquer is impervious to moisture, acid, and scratches, and is therefore ideal protection for materials such as wood or bamboo.

The oldest finds of lacquered objects date back to the fifth millennium BC. Bowls, tins, boxes, vases, and furniture made of various materials (wood, bamboo, wicker, leather, metal, clay, textiles, paper) are coated with a skin of lacquer. A base coat is applied to the core material, followed by extremely thin layers of the finest lacquer that, after drying in dust-free moist air, are smoothed and polished. In the dry lacquer method, the lacquer itself dictates the form: fabric or paper is saturated with lacquer and pressed into a wood or clay mold. After drying, the mold is removed and the piece coated with further layers of lacquer. Vessels, boxes and plates were already being made in this way in the Han period.

During the Tang dynasty, large Buddhist sculptures were produced by the lacquerware process. If soot or vinegar-soaked iron filings are added to the lacquer, it will dry into a black color; cinnabar turns it red. The color combination of red and black, first thought to have been applied in the second century BC, is still considered a classic. In the Song and Yuan periods, simply-shaped monochromatic lacquerware was valued.

During the Ming period, the manufacture of lacquered objects was further refined. The cities of Beijing, Fuzhou, Guangzhou, Chengdu, Yangzhou and Suzhou were renowned for exquisite lacquerware, which was enriched and decorated with carving, fillings, gold paint and inlay.

The carved lacquer technique, which began at the time of the Tang dynasty, reached its highest peak during the Ming and Qing periods. The core, often of wood or tin, is coated with mostly red layers of lacquer. When the outermost coat has dried, decorative carving is applied, with the knife penetrating generally to the lowest layer so that the design stands out from the background in relief. Today, lacquerware is mainly produced in Beijing, Fuzhou and Yangzhou.

body of the metal object. These form the outlines of the ornamentation. The spaces between the rods are filled with enamel paste and fired in the kiln. Finally, metal surfaces not covered with enamel are gilded. During the Yuan dynasty, Yunnan was the center of cloisonné production. However, the golden age of this technique was the Ming period, when the techniques of melting enamel on porcelain were developed.

Ivory: As a craft material, ivory is as old as jade, and early pieces can be traced to as far back as 5000 BC. During the Bronze Age, wild elephants were not a rarity in northern China; some were tamed during the Shang dynasty. The old artist carvers regarded ele-

The most well-known lacquerware is the Beijing work, which goes back to the imperial courts of the Ming and Qing dynasties. Emperor Qianlong (1734–1795) had a special liking for carved lacquerware; he was even buried in a coffin magnificently carved using this technique.

Cloisonné: The cloisonné technique – used to create metal objects with enamel decor – reached China from Persia in the eighth century AD, was lost and then rediscovered in the thirteenth century. In the cloisonné technique, metal rods are soldered to the

Above, precious ivory carving.

phant tusks as a most desirable material from which to make jewelery, implements and containers. The once-large herds of elephants in the south of China thus shrank to a small remnant, and eventually ivory had to be imported. Ming dynasty carvings exemplified the excellent craft skills and superior taste; then, during Qing times, ivory carving was even further refined.

Today's centers for ivory carving are Beijing, Guangzhou and Shanghai. All the ivory is imported from Thailand and several African countries. When buying ivory in China, keep in mind that the import of ivory is prohibited in many countries.

Beijing opera has really only existed for about 200 years, although the origins of theater in China go back much further. Descriptions of dances dating from the Tang dynasty (618–907) show striking similarities to present-day Beijing opera. During the Ming era (1368–1644), Kunqu opera, a form of musical drama, developed, to which many elements of the song, dance and music of the Beijing opera can be traced.

A living tradition: In the old days, as permanent theaters were a rarity, even in Beijing and the major ports, Beijing opera was performed on the streets and in the market places – a sign of its popularity with ordinary people. The Beijing opera was the only way for them to learn anything about life outside the narrow circle of their own day-to-day existence, and was probably their main source of Chinese history. There was hardly a single temple festival during which a theater performance was not given, although the opera performances themselves generally had nothing to do with the religious occasion.

The four main branches of Beijing opera are song, dialogue, mime and acrobatics, united categories that are separated in European theater. There are various forms of Beijing opera. Sometimes music and song are predominant, sometimes mime. In other pieces, fight scenes dominate and the acrobatics are in the foreground, while in others still, the spoken word gets center stage.

The main division is between *wenxi* (civilian plays), and *wuxi* (military dramas), but there are also comedies and skits. Wenxi pieces are more like our conception of drama. They describe domestic, civilian life. The wuxi, on the other hand, consist mainly of fights, and tell of historical wars and battles by making great use of acrobatics.

Many Beijing operas go back to popular legends, folk or fairy tales, or to classical literature such as *The Three Kingdoms, The Dream of the Red Chamber*, or *Journey to the West*. These works are much better known

in China than one might find most literary classics are in the West.

There are four different types of roles in Beijing opera: *sheng*, male lead roles; *dan*, female roles; *jing*, painted-face roles; and finally *chou*, male or female clowns. Each major group is divided into sub-groups. Then there are also extras, such as guards, soldiers, ladies-in-waiting, et cetera. Foreigners often have difficulty with the individual roles. For instance, the *xiao sheng*, or young male lead role of the Beijing opera *The White Snake*,

had to be turned into a *lao sheng* (old man) role for tours abroad. There was often inappropriate laughter during the performances, as the speaking part of the xiao sheng role – a very high, artificial voice – with the falsetto singing, the pink-rouged cheeks and the soft movements seemed effeminate to most non-Chinese.

The dan or female role is the most important part. There are two historical reasons for this. On the one hand, in most of the dramas, stories and novels that form the bases for the operas, a woman is the focus of interest. On the other, the central figure in Chinese dramas has been a woman since the days of the

Yuan dynasty (1271–1368). In general, the dan, who were traditionally played by men, have their faces made up with a white base and various shades of carmine, and a little pale pink around the eyes. They move gracefully with soft, flowing steps. Other characteristics are their half-sung, half-spoken dialogue and a kind of mewing singing.

However, for nearly forty years now, the training of men to sing female roles has been prohibited. The reason given is that this practice has led to "sexual perversion".

Jing, or painted-face roles, portray warriors, heroes, statesmen, adventurers and supernatural beings. Their stage make-up is like a skilfully-made, conspicuous mask.

Masks and costumes: The costumes are based on court costumes of the Han, Tang, Song, and especially the Ming dynasties (1368–1644), as well as from the era of the Manchu emperors (1644–1911). Old wall paintings and drawings of the period in question were studied when the costumes were designed. The costumes of the Beijing opera, however, are by no means realistic. Their symbolic characteristics are particularly obvious in the beggar costumes: they wear silk with colorful patches. While the symbolic colours and patterns of their stage make-up reveal details of character, colour may also be used purely for aesthetic reasons, creating harmony between costume, face and headdress.

Finally, the chou, or the clowns, are easily recognized by their white-painted eye and nose areas. The eyes are also sometimes enclosed in a black square frame. Only real comedies have chou in leading roles, and in other pieces they take secondary parts. They often appear as peasants, servants or other menials, and the coarse colloquial speech used in their dialogues makes the audience laugh. What the other roles achieve through expressive, elevated speech, the chou gains by making use of everyday slang. The jokes of the chou are easy even for a Beijing opera novice to understand, as they are similar to comic characters in theaters worldwide.

The make-up artists can create more than 300 different types of faces.

The history of the mask-like make-up, according to the story, is as follows: Zhuge Liang, a hero from the time of the Three Kingdoms (220–280 AD), had particularly fine, feminine features. For this reason, the great strategist had the idea of painting his face with terrifying colours to frighten his enemies, thus inventing the mask. Red shows a loyal, brave character; black represents a good, strong, slightly rough-diamond and coarse nature; blue symbolises wildness and courage, but also arrogance; yellow indicates a weakened version of the same failing;

green is the sign of an unstable character; orange and grey are signs of age, and a golden mask is worn by gods and goddesses.

Good characters are made up with relatively simple colours, but enemy generals and hostile characters use complicated patterns in their masks. Mysterious characters in the jing roles wear all kinds of colour and pattern combinations. Make-up with the colours green, red and black shows that a character has a limited quantity of the qualities listed above. The addition of green and blue may be a sign that this character rebels before submitting to higher authority.

Cao Cao, one of the main figures from the time of *The Three Kingdoms* and who often

ever said he was going to *see* a Beijing opera, he would have simply sounded ridiculous, for connoisseurs went to listen to an opera. During a lengthy sung portion, they would not watch the stage, but sit with their eyes closed and listening, clapping to the rhythm and thinking about every word in the song."

In Beijing opera, the unnecessary is left out and the emphasis is on the essential.

Props are used sparingly. An oar in the hand of a boatman is enough to make it clear that the scene takes place in a boat. A chair can be just a chair, but it can also be high ground in a landscape. An unlit candle can be the sign that evening is coming on. Every soldier carrying a banner represents a whole

appears on the Chinese stage, is made up in white, with thin eyebrows and sometimes with many zigzagging lines. This shows not only his great age but also his disgraceful character, as white symbolises treachery, poor self-discipline, cunning and guile.

The art of seeing: In China, you never say you're going to see a Beijing opera; rather, you say that you are going to listen to one. Music and song, after all, are the main elements of opera. A famous performer wrote in his memoirs: "If, in earlier years, anyone had

regiment. Riders almost always play two parts, for they also have to portray the movement of the horse – rearing, galloping, and trotting – through mime and gesture, thus turning themselves into centaurs.

But there is also an art to understanding and enjoying this kind of theater. There is great use of convention, so if you want to enjoy Beijing opera, knowing some of the rules is an advantage.

The style of acting is typical of the "non-reality" of Beijing opera. The aim of the actor is not, as in Western drama, to become the character portrayed. The actor distances him or herself from the role and tries to quote

<u>Left</u>, female general in splendid costume. <u>Above</u>, a traitor is accused.

it, to portray events that are connected to the role. No Beijing opera performers ever end up "beside themselves." The closest parallels in the West to the ritual style of operatic performance with its fixed gestures are to be found in classic mime, in ballet and among circus clowns.

You will enjoy seeing Beijing opera when the technique of the performers is perfect and when you can follow the stylized methods of expression. Not that this is easy, since there are more than twenty different ways of laughing and smiling alone. The smallest movement of the eyes, the mouth, a single finger, is full of significance. All has been carefully and painstakingly rehearsed: every move-

be both stylish and correct, so every symbol must have its exact counterpoint in real life. The actor has to follow the rules and conventions. How far he or she is able to deviate from them, with delicacy and certainty, without in any way breaking them, is a measure of talent. Using the medium of Beijing opera, actors can swim on the stage, or a battle can be portrayed taking place in water or in darkness. On stage, embroideries can be created or tea prepared using the art of mime. Everyday things can be translated into the language of the stage. Enacting them, the performer of the Beijing opera shows three things: how the process is being enacted according to the rules, what the character portrayed feels about it, and finally, his or her own interpretation of the action.

Beijing opera is a complete work of art, rather than a realistic drama, although in recent years the use of scenery, lighting effects, and more props has led to some change. The form and performance of Beijing opera make it unique. Today, one question in particular is asked: How is this art form to develop, allowing the new to arise without destroying the old?

Modern competition: Under the influence of foreign culture, modern forms of theater have only begun to develop in China over the last few decades.

Among the influential dramatists are Cao Yu, Tianhan, Guo Moruo and Lao She. The latter wrote *The Teahouse*, performed in Western Europe and Japan.

In the meantime, Western dramatists have also found a sizeable audience in China. Successful performances include – to name but a few examples – Brecht's *Galileo Galilei* and *The Caucasian Chalk Circle*, Arthur Miller's *All My Sons*, as well as various Shakespearean plays. Young dramatists and directors have recently been trying to break with old conventions. London University's Su Liqun's *Zhuang Zi Tests his Wife* was the first play to be staged in English by local actors in over eighty years, while the truly innovative Experimental Theatre of Modern Drama's *Lay Down Your Whip – Woyzeck* combined Chinese street theater with a German anti-fairy tale to deal with, among other things, violence against women.

ment of hand, foot and body are precisely laid down. And they vary from role to role. When a sheng walks, he lifts his feet up and places them slightly to one side. A dan, on the other hand, walks in a slow glide, with little steps, one foot hardly separated from the other. The painted faces take big steps and adopt an upright, proud posture.

In contrast to the other three roles, which demand an upright position, the chou uses his whole body in an expressive, lively fashion. Given the symbolic nature of Beijing opera, this theatrical skill demands excellent coordination from the actors. Just as in a good piece of calligraphy, movement must

Left, elegance and grace on roller skates. **Right**, a novel and acrobatic use of chairs.

LITERATURE

It is not surprising that the written word is more important to the Chinese than the spoken one. Indeed, given the numerous dialects to be found in modern China, the written word – or character, to be precise – is the common means of communication.

Chinese characters developed from a pictographic writing system and not only represent sounds, but also meaning.

The earliest evidence of the Chinese script was found on the so-called oracle bones – tortoise shells or shoulder blades of animals onto which questions regarding the weather, the yield of crops or the outcome of battles were carved. They were then thrown into a fire, and the oracle was interpreted according to the cracks that were formed by the heat. These forms of writing are more than 4,000 years old, and can, of course, not be described as literature, although they provide information on the development of the Chinese script.

Vernacular literature in China took shape as an art form during the Yuan dynasty. Most of the oldest works of literature, however, are from the late Zhou dynasty. The oldest Chinese books were written on strips of bamboo that were fixed together almost like a roller blind. This explains why the traditional way of writing in Chinese runs from top to bottom and from right to left.

Perhaps most famous of early writings for Westerners would be the thoughts of Confucius (551–479 BC). Among the compiled works – probably by his students – are the *Spring and Autumn Annals*; the *Book of Changes*, a system of divination; the *Book of Rites*; and a history of Lu, his native state.

Apart from the classic philosophical works of Confucianism and Daoism, there also exists to this day the "monument to the bound language" called *Shijing* (book of odes, or songs). Legend has it that these songs were collected amongst the peoples of the different states by a civil servant, Cai Shiguan. The government wished to gain insight into the lives of the people with the help of these songs, in order to administer the country more effectively.

It is said that more than 3,000 songs were collected. Confucius selected 300 of them and compiled them in the *Shijing*. The contents of the odes are wide-ranging. There are love songs, songs about the land, and songs glorifying outstanding personalities or personal qualities. Most of the songs in the *Shijing* originate in the area of the Huang He, or the Yellow River.

Poems in the lyrical or epic style play an extremely important part in Chinese literature. To be able to read and write poetry was part of the elementary education of the higher social classes. Students and civil servants of any rank or age were expected to be able to write a poem for any possible occasion. Girls and women who knew how to recite poems graciously were ensured the admiration of the opposite sex. The *Chuzi*, another collection of songs, comes from the south of China. Its creation is attributed to the poet Qu Yuan (c. 322–295 BC).

The Tang dynasty (618–907) was the beginning of the golden age for Chinese poetry. No other period in history has enjoyed such a great number of poets, and works of poetry on such a scale and of such quality. *Quan Tangshi,* the large and complete collection of Tang poetry, contains nearly 50,000 poems by 2,200 poets.

One of the most famous poets of the time was Li Bai, or Li Po, (699–762), who is said to have written his best-known poems in a state of total inebriation. The story goes that he was quite drunk when he was appointed as an official at the palace. Nevertheless, he immediately wrote a poem at the emperor's request that earned him much praise from the public – and, of course, from the emperor.

Du Fu (712–770) must be mentioned together with Li Bai, though his style of poetry is very different. He held office at the court for just a short time, but was forced to flee due to political upheavals. He then led an unsettled, wandering life for a long time, eventually settling in Chengdu, where one can still visit the straw hut – Du Fu Caotang – that served as his home.

From a contemporary point of view, it is hard to say which of the two poets is more significant. Li Bai was a natural talent, free, open and humorous, devoted to nature and close to the Daoists. Du Fu, on the other hand, became a poet through diligence and practice; he was bold and serious, greatly concerned about the political and social situation. His lamentations were closely linked to Confucian ideas.

Prose and fiction, which almost always had an educational aspect, were usually considered trivial and not serious form in ancient China. A status-conscious intellectual would regard it as undignified to concern himself with either of them. (This attitude was to change, fortunately, in the twentieth cen-

from China to the West – India – in order to collect holy scriptures from there. The novel mixes Indian folk stories and legends with Chinese, Buddhist and Daoist elements. Although the story no doubt existed much earlier, the version that is known today is attributed to Wu Cheng'en, who lived in the sixteenth century.

The *Shuihuzhuan*, or *The Water Margin* in English, is a novel dating from the Ming period about robbers; its origins are not clear. The story is partly based upon historical facts

tury.) Nevertheless, there are a number of novels from different epochs that have survived, and which are still read and appreciated by many Chinese today.

Classical fiction: Every child in China knows the novel *Journey to the West* and its famous heroes: the king of the apes Sun Wukong, the pig Zhu Bajie, the monk Sha, and the Buddhist pilgrim and monk, Xuanzang.

The novel describes the adventure of the king of the apes, who, together with the other figures, accompanies the monk Xuanzang

Above left, writer Qu Yuan. **Right**, an old illustration from the novel *Journey to the West*.

about the robber Song Jiang and his companions, who wandered through what is now the province of Shandong, around the end of the Northern Song dynasty (960–1127). Just like Robin Hood and his merry men, Song Jiang and his men fought injustices according to their own code of honor.

They finally submitted to the imperial doctrine and fought against rebels who were threatening the state system. This novel, too, became extremely popular. It is said to have been Mao Zedong's favorite book, although during the time of the Cultural Revolution, it was considered a negative illustration of unnecessary capitulation.

Genre novels: The epitome of the genre novel is *Jinpingmei,* or *The Plum Blossom In A Golden Vase,* dating from the Ming dynasty. In contrast to the novels that are heavily influenced by religion and sometimes have almost fanatical tendencies, *Jinpingmei* portrays people as individual characters and describes the many amorous adventures of its hero, Ximen, in a rather realistic way. Furthermore, this novel conveys a very precise portrayal of social conditions in the sixteenth century. It describes how upstarts and scroungers who gave themselves up to a totally unrestrained life became rampant. It tells of greedy civil servants and of old women who acted as matchmakers; it de-

Hongloumeng, or *Dream of the Red Chamber*, written by Cao Xueqin in the eighteenth century, is rated as the best novel of the Qing dynasty. Many critics consider it China's best novel ever. Its main character is Jia Baoyu, the amorous and sentimental son of a high-ranking official. There are also Lin Daiyu, Xue Baochai and others – twelve girls in all – who are living at the house of the Jia family. The novel describes the prime and decline of the house of Jia. In an imaginative and humorous style, the author has given the male and female members of staff – more than 400 people – individual and distinctive traits, portraying the domestic life of a distinguished Manchu family in all

scribes how idlers and layabouts were curious to find out about the private lives of others, and of Buddhist and Daoist priests who took to womanizing. All in all, it provides a unique portrayal of life as it was lived by the so-called higher echelons of society.

It is not clear who the author of *Jinpingmei* was, but in 1617, a second edition was published, of which a few copies have survived. In 1687, Emperor Kangxi banned the book; yet it continued to be read, and in 1708 it was even translated into Manchurian. Emperor Qianlong again banned the book in 1789. Even today, this book has been on the banned list of the People's Republic.

its detail. Because the novel is so popular, it has given rise to specific research into *Hongloumeng*.

Since the May Fourth Movement of 1919, which amongst other things was aimed at reforming language, prose literature has increasingly been regarded as a means for social change. One of the most outstanding figures in new literature was Lu Xun, a poet, essayist and novelist who believed China needed to modernize through revolution; in his novel *Ah Q,* he uses biting irony to describe the self-destructive and insolent attitude of the underlings who are steeped in tradition and superstition. It was also Lu Xun who, in a brilliant way, introduced the essay form into Chinese literature.

In *The Diary of Sophia*, the author Ding Ling describes the lifestyle of her like-minded contemporaries with sceptical distance. Ba Jin wrote critical novels like *The Family* that, following in the tradition of *Honglou-meng*, describes the decline of a civil servant's family at the beginning of this century.

Also well-known for his critical attitude to society was the author Mao Dun; his novel *Midnight*, for example, exposes the contradictions between foreign businesses and nationalistically-minded entrepreneurs in the Shanghai of the 1930s. Lao She's best-known play, *The Teahouse*, was performed in the

West after the author was "rehabilitated" in the 1980s. In contrast, the author who wrote *Rickshaw Coolie* committed suicide at the time of the Cultural Revolution.

Many writers of this time were sympathetic to the Communist movement, and as this grew stronger, the direction and content of the literature were defined more clearly. After Mao Zedong's speech on art and literature, in Yan'an in 1942, Social Realism was es-

Far left, the Tang poet Du Fu. Left, his contemporary Li Bai, who was very fond of drinking. Above, photo of the most important writer of modern times, Lu Xun.

tablished as the only legitimate form. But other writers were busy singing the praises of workers, peasants and soldiers, and glorifying their struggles against wicked people such as feudal landlords. In 1956, the "period of the Hundred Flowers", some writers expressed dissatisfaction with certain policies. At the end of this period, they were branded as rightists, and their works labeled as "poisonous weeds".

The Cultural Revolution, from 1966 to 1976, virtually halted literary endeavors. Once it was over, however, there was a resurgence of literature. With his story *Scar*, Lu Xinghua gave the name to "wound literature", analyzing the traumas caused by the Cultural Revolution. This wound literature was itself part of the so-called New Realism, which typically looked at society's imperfections. But in 1980, the overriding political goals of China's literature were reasserted. Deng Xiaoping wrote that "it is impossible for literature to be independent of politics. Any progressive and revolutionary worker cannot but think of his works' social influence and must consider, therefore, the interests (of) the nation and the party… The party wishes, without compulsion, that literary workers first consider the public interests."

For most of the decades since 1949, literature in China was impeded by the dictates of Communism's Social Realism. Nevertheless, the 1980s saw a burst of literary creativity in which new literary techniques were tried; most of the 2,000 novels produced from 1979 to the mid 1990s appeared during this decade.

By comparison, only 320 novels were published between 1949 to 1966, and few or none during the Cultural Revolution. Since the late 1980s, some writers have published little, as they have not wanted to risk criticism for expressing views that might be regarded as supporting bourgeoise liberalism. Some writers, meanwhile, have found commercial success by writing pop literature, such as sentimental love stories and martial arts sagas.

At a 1993 meeting of eminent Chinese writers, party general secretary Jiang Zemin, in a speech urging the creation of works that would both satisfy the people and rally the country around the Communist Party, said, "To make socialist literature prosper is the glorious task of literature and art workers."

What would England be without its count-less church spires? Just as inconceivable would be China without its countless pago-das. In keeping with their original religious significance, they are mostly found in places of worship and monastic institutions, or at least near them, and are used for the safe-keeping of relics. These tall and slender towers are also found on hilltops rising high over the landscape. Pagodas assume an aes-thetic vividness as a result of their location and unique form, and this becomes one of the

the enrichment of Chinese architectural forms derived from Buddhism. The word *pagoda* is not Chinese, but was probably adapted from the Sanskrit word *bhagavan*, which has a similar meaning to the English word lord, commonly used to address divinity. In Chi-nese, a pagoda is called *ta*, which earlier was *tappna*, a Chinese rendering of the Indian word *stupa*. (Thus, Bai Ta is Bai Pagoda.)

China's capital city, Beijing, is known above all for its Imperial Palace complex, but the visitor's eye is irresistibly drawn to

enduring impressions of every traveler to China. Nevertheless, the variety of architec-tural styles, materials and forms are at first confusing for the uninitiated.

The first Buddhist missionaries spread the teaching of Buddha across northern India to China. Many Chinese monks later traveled the same route back to India to study ancient writings and to visit the places directly influ-enced by Buddha. In this way, reports of burial rites, religious art and the impressive monastic and temple architecture filtered into remote China.

By way of etymology, too, it can be con-cluded that the pagoda is representative of

another structure, in Beihai Park: Bai Ta, the White Dagoba, rising majestically to the west of the Imperial Palace and above the entire imperial city. The white, massive bell-shaped structure is set on a square base in the style of a Tibetan chörten; it was built in 1651 for the reception of the fifth Dalai Lama at the court of the emperor of China. Who would have guessed that there was a connec-tion, a common origin, between this building and Liuhe Ta (Pagoda of the Six Harmonies) on the Qiantang River, near Hangzhou? These two pagodas cover the entire span of Chinese pagoda design.

There are, of course, pagodas of boundless

diversity throughout Asia wherever the Buddhist religion is present. In the beginning, these buildings were nothing other than burial places. Indian rulers at the time of the Gautama Siddharta, the authentic Buddha, were buried in tombs that consisted of a semi-spherical solid core structure rising from a cylindrical plinth.

The style of Buddhist tombs resembling the Indian stupa can be found in Tibet. The Tibetan chörten were used for the burial of Lama high priests, including the Dalai and

with a surrounding gallery at each level – giving access to one small chapel after another – surmounted by a cylindrical core with a conical shape and a large "umbrella" sitting at its top. Above those are symbols from Buddhist teaching, such as the sun, recumbent half-moon and flames. The White Dagoba in Beijing belongs firmly to this Tibetan chörten tradition.

Chinese style: The diversity in the artistic development and stylistic form of pagodas throughout Asia evolved within China to the

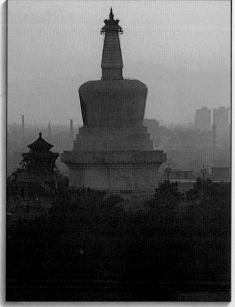

Panchen Lamas; however, in the imaginative world of Tantrist Buddhism, which is dominant in Tibet, the building of a chörten is more meaningful than simply as a mere tomb. It is a symbolic ceremonial act, a result of which is the presence of Buddha manifesting itself in the finished building. The largest building of this kind is the chörten of Jiangzi, a monumental structure that also fulfills the function of a temple. A square four-story base structure rises from a polygonal plinth

Left, beams and roof tiles of Beijing's Tiantan, or Temple of Heaven. **Above**, Temple of Heaven dome; White Dagoba, Beijing.

characteristic elongation of the structure, while dispensing with the plinth. The Chinese pagoda is, to some extent, an overscaled representation of the umbrella-like superstructure built along the central shaft, which in the case of Tantric Buddhist buildings carried as many as thirteen "umbrellas", symbolizing the number of ways of attaining salvation. With Chinese pagodas, the shaft becomes a tower and the "umbrellas" become accessible storys.

The first pagoda structures found in China go back to the third and fifth century AD and were presumably constructed in timber; none of these survive. Later, in the north of China, solid construction using bricks and tiles was adopted, whereas in the south – in the absence of alternative building materials – timber construction continued. The oldest surviving pagoda is found in the district of Dengfeng, near the old imperial city of Luoyang and close to the famous Shaolin monastery. This 40-meter-high (130-ft), twelve-sided Songyue Pagoda was built in AD 523; for over 1,400 years, it has withstood the ravages of weather, natural disasters and revolutions – from the Mongol invasion to the Cultural Revolution.

At the nearby Shaolin monastery, there is another rare sight: Talin, the Forest of Pagodas, a cemetery with more than 200 stone funerary pagodas – the last resting place of monks and abbots. These pagodas are only a few meters high and have, at chest height, a square core to which are attached memorial tablets or small recesses for offerings. Their function and symbolism correspond to the original Indian stupas, but not their architectural style.

Other ancient structures include what are possibly the best-known pagodas in China – the two Wild Goose pagodas in Xi'an. Dayan Ta, the Great Wild Goose Pagoda, was built at the instigation of and to the design of the monk Xuanzang who, in the seventh century AD, undertook an adventurous years-long journey to northern India. It is known to today's Chinese as a legend from the fictional trilogy, *Journey to the West*. The Great Wild Goose Pagoda is used to store his writings and was the religious focal point of a large monastery.

The curious name of this pagoda goes back to a legend supposedly brought back from northern India by Xuanzang. According to his account, it was here that Buddha – whose religious sect forbades the partaking of meat – successfully resisted the temptation of a wild goose. As a warning and reminder of this, a pagoda was erected on the very same spot where he had been tempted.

The smaller 13-story, 43-meter-high (141-ft) Xiaoyan Ta, or Little Wild Goose Pagoda, originally had another name but was simply re-christened, in the course of time, because of its striking similarity to its larger companion, the Great Wild Goose Pagoda. It is of approximately similar age but appears – because of its greater number of storys, its slender form, and its gently-curved topmost point – much more graceful than the monumental and somewhat clumsy Great Wild Goose Pagoda. As solid-brick stepped pagodas, both are typical examples of the Tang-period style.

Tradition of architecture: Just as they adapted Buddhism by rapidly mixing the original teachings of Buddha with traditional superstitions and ancestor worship, so did the Chinese invest the genuine style of the Buddhist pagoda with their own forms and building traditions.

China has been known for its massive tower structures since the Han dynasty. This form of construction was used for city walls, as well as court and palace gates. Chinese

craftsmen developed timber-frame construction to its ultimate form, which can still be admired in the old palaces and temples. Posts and beams satisfy structural requirements and are often built without the aid of glue or nails. Corbels and brackets, artfully combined into incredibly complex structures, support the roofs. Walls resolve into openings or, at least, skillfully pierced surfaces that blend with the natural setting outside. Intricately designed curved roof shapes with finely carved figures encapsulate this style of building that, without a doubt, strongly reflects Daoist philosophy in its aim at complete harmony between people and nature.

The German poet Goethe, who was not unaffected by Chinese philosophy and culture, describes in a poem the unfamiliar turn of creative style. He tells of a Chinese on a visit to Rome; all the buildings, both ancient and new, seem heavy and clumsy to him. He wishes that the poor Romans could understand how fine columns of wood can carry an entire roof, and that carved and gilded beams are a joy to the eye of a sensitive and educated beholder.

Palace architecture: Early antecedents of Chinese palace architecture were found by archaeologists at Erlitou, near Luoyang. Excavations at the Shang dynasty site revealed a terrace that must have been the floor

of Chinese palace architecture are, of course, best observed at Gugong, the Imperial Palace, or some of the other palaces and temples in Beijing – most of which date from the Ming dynasty.

The Imperial Palace best exemplifies the contours of palace architecture. Large buildings like the three great Halls of Harmony, in the front part of the palace, rise from a terrace, which acts as a base but also serves a practical purpose – to protect the halls from any ingress of water. Old texts, however, point clearly to a symbolic and cosmological meaning: "The Heavens cover and the Earth carries." The terrace, in these terms, represents the Earth, and the roof, Heaven.

of some large hall. Architecture later made great strides in the Qin and Han dynasties. The basic plan configuration of later palaces was already fully developed. Timber-frame construction had been considerably refined. The infill panels between the posts and columns that carried the roof became subtle decorative screens. As during the Han dynasty, clay models of these were placed in graves as a parting gift.

Today, the main features and peculiarities

Left, the Great Wild Goose Pagoda at Xi'an, dating back to the Tang dynasty. **Above**, detail of a brick-built stepped pagoda.

The size of a terrace is determined by the ranking of the building in the total context; buildings along the central axis generally count for more than subsidiary ones. This architectural principle can be studied readily at the Imperial Palace. Taihedian, the Hall of Supreme Harmony, has the largest and most splendid terrace in the whole of the palace grounds; in three raised levels, the entire terrace is framed by a finely-decorated marble balustrade.

From the earliest days, the Chinese favored timber as a building material; it was not only easily transported, but it was also very practical. Heavy posts were capable of carrying the roof, while the wood could be carved for decoration and embellishment. For the columns of the Imperial Palace, the hard and precious *nanmu* wood (brought from the southwestern provinces) was used.

In summer, the infill panels between the load-bearing columns of simple houses were easily removed; in winter, the open timber grilles were covered with rice paper to keep the cold at bay. Corbel construction, between the tops of columns and the roof of palacial halls, reached the peak of fine craftsmanship. A visually-confusing impression of longitudinal and cross beams, which involved timber components originally intended just to carry the gutters, becomes

decorative embellishment in palace architecture – but without diminishing their function as load-dispersing elements of the structure. Corbel systems also give a clue as to the social status of the house owner – ordinary people were not permitted to have them.

The roofs of Chinese palaces lend these generally large and massive buildings an air of weightlessness; the slightly upturned eaves and gutters seem to let the entire roof float above the building. Another way of achieving this illusion of floating is the double roof: the roof is constructed in two stages, and the low wall separating the two suggests a small additional story.

The roofs of palaces are covered with glazed tiles. With the Imperial Palace, the emperor's color was yellow, while Tiantan, the Temple of Heaven, is appropriately covered in blue tiles. The tiles at the end are round or half-round decorated finials, and in the Imperial Palace, carry the dragon symbol.

Architecture and superstition: Very conspicuous on palace roofs is the ridge decoration: two dragon-like animals facing each other, while their gaping mouths seem to carry the ridge with their fish-like tails pointing heavenwards. Chinese mythology ascribes to the dragon the ability of being able to make rain. He thus protects the vulnerable timber building against fire.

The mythological beasts at the ends of the ridge of palace roofs have a similar significance: to protect the building from evil spirits. At the same time, the importance of the building can be derived from their number. Ten animals and one immortal decorate the ridge ends of the two-tier roof of Taihedian, in the Imperial Palace. The animals include a lion, dragon, phoenix, flying horse, and a unicorn, amongst others.

Lower down on most of these roofs, one will find a man riding a hen – another common figure intended to protect the building and occupants against disaster. Legend has it that this represents a tyrannical prince from the state of Qi (third century BC). After his defeat and death, the inhabitants of Qi are said to have fixed replicas of him riding on a hen to their roofs in order to keep away disaster and stigmatize the tyrant. Superstition has it that the evil tyrant on the hen cannot leave the roof because the hen cannot carry him in flight.

Such superstitious imaginings are often reflected in Chinese architecture. The so-called ghost wall, for example, was usually put up behind the entrance of all apartments and palaces to bar the entry of evil spirits, as they were believed to be able to move in a straight path only and not around corners. In the large palaces, Jiulongbi, the splendid Nine Dragon Wall, fulfilled this function. Even at the entrance to the government and party offices in Beijing (Zhongnanhai), there is a ghost wall directly behind the gate, complete with quotations from Mao Zedong.

<u>Left</u>, Tibetan Kumbun Chörten, Jiangzi. <u>Right</u>, Longhua Pagoda, Shanghai.

Chiguolema? Have you eaten yet?

This common Chinese greeting reveals the importance of food in China. Although China has experienced countless floods and famines over the centuries, and although the Chinese (over a fifth of the world's population) live on just seven percent of the world's arable land, they have created one of the world's most sophisticated, regionally-diverse and inventive cuisines.

The Chinese passion for food is, perhaps, equaled only by that of the French. Whether it is the annual celebration of the Lunar New Year, the clinching of a business deal, or a family get-together for an anniversary, no expense will be spared on a banquet.

Chinese food is one of the world's most universally-available cuisines, thanks to widespread Chinese emigration to countries throughout Southeast Asia, and to the United States, Australia and many parts of Europe.

As the majority of Chinese emigrated from the southern Chinese province of Guandong, the food of that region – Cantonese – is equated with "Chinese" food in many Western countries. However, with the increasing sophistication of tastes in the West, many Chinese restaurants abroad now offer other regional cuisines, particularly Sichuan and northern food.

But what about food in China itself? Some visitors to China claim that they have enjoyed better Chinese meals back home, and in many cases, this may well be true. China is still in the throes of development, and the quality of produce in some parts of the country is not necessarily of the standard found in other parts of Asia or the West.

Dining out in a Chinese restaurant in a hotel or one of the proliferating private restaurants can either be a superb experience or somewhat of a disappointment. Generally speaking, the large international hotels have fine restaurants (usually with Hong Kong chefs reigning over the Cantonese kitchens). Moreover, those willing to brave the challenges of language will find that the street

stalls in many big cities offer excellent snack food or light meals, such as dumplings and noodles, for an incredibly low price.

Techniques: The different regional cuisines of China share a great many common elements. Owing to the historical scarcity of land and fuel, the inventive Chinese learned to finely cut ingredients so as to reduce cooking time. Meat, fish and vegetables are all shredded, sliced, cubed or diced. Although slow cooking in liquid is sometimes used, the most common method is stir-frying

cut food in a wok over very high heat. Not only does this save on fuel, but it results in a crisp texture and, incidentally, maximum retention of vitamins.

Deep-frying, steaming and braising are also common methods employed by the Chinese cook, but because private homes do not possess an oven, roasted or baked meats are produced only in restaurant kitchens. Cooks throughout China share more or less the same ingredients and seasonings, but it is the way in which these are prepared and combined that provides the differences.

The most popular seasonings are soy sauce, ginger, garlic, vinegar, sesame oil, soybean

Preceding pages: simplicity of dim sum. **Left,** even daily meals are of several dishes. **Right,** sidewalk stir-fry, Hong Kong.

paste and spring onions (scallions). Yet dishes prepared with several of the same ingredients by, for example, a cook in Sichuan and a chef in Guangzhou will be very different.

All Chinese cuisines seek a balance of textures, flavors and colors within a meal. For centuries, Chinese have regarded food as curative or preventative medicine. Certain foods are believed to be either *yin* (cooling) or *yang* (warming); the ideal is to seek a balance between the two. Snake meat, for example, is considered to be fortifying and is therefore a popular winter dish in some parts of the country.

It has been said that the Chinese will eat almost anything with four legs except a table

and anything that flies except a plane. It is, indeed, true that many foods never considered for the table in the West do pass through a Chinese kitchen. Apart from snake meat, bear's paw, dog and other exotic edibles, some everyday ingredients take on a definitely different flavor in China.

Take, for example, the thousand-year egg (also known as a century egg). These eggs are nowhere near that age, of course, and are merely duck eggs pickled for about a month in a mixture of mud, chalk and ammonia until the yolks turn greenish and the albumen a transparent black. Once any prejudices are overcome and the quartered eggs eaten with

a few slices of pickled ginger, many non-Chinese are pleasantly surprised at the discovery of yet another gourmet treat.

Ingredients: Rice is the staple food of the majority of Chinese, although those living in the north traditionally eat food created from wheat flour, such as noodles, dumplings and various steamed, deep-fried or griddle-fried breads. Soybean curd, both fresh and dried in either sheets or twists, provides important protein in a country where the majority of arable land is given over to agriculture, rather than grazing.

Large animals requiring pasture lands – such as the cow and sheep – are replaced in China by chickens, ducks, quails and other poultry, and by the ubiquitous pig. Without doubt, pig is the most widespread meat, while both fresh- and saltwater fish is highly prized and usually excellently prepared.

Vegetables are of supreme importance, but are never eaten raw. (This stems partly from hygienic considerations, as the traditional fertilizer was human waste.) The range of vegetables cultivated in China is vast, particularly in the warmer south, and includes not only those known in the West, but other delights such as a huge range of leafy greens, fresh bamboo shoots, water chestnuts, taro and lotus root. Some common vegetables such as cabbage and white radish are also salted or dried and used as seasoning, especially during the frigid winter months in the cold north.

Regional differences: Being such a vast land, China encompasses a wide range of terrain and produce. Here one can find snowcapped mountains and harsh deserts, mountain gorges slashed by mighty rivers, fertile rice paddies, rich coastal plains and seas teeming with fish. With such climatic and geographic differences, it is not surprising that regional cuisines have developed.

Experts argue endlessly over just how many regional cuisines exist, but it is generally agreed that there are four major styles. These include Cantonese, the food found in the southern province of Guandong (and in neighboring Hong Kong); Sichuan, the pungent food of the western region of China, particularly of the cities of Chengdu and Chongqing; Huaiyang, which includes the eastern Chinese cuisines of Shanghai, Jiangsu and Zhejiang; and Northern cuisine, centered in Beijing but largely inspired by the neighboring province of Shandong, whose chefs monopolized Beijing's restaurant business in the nineteenth century.

Cantonese cuisine: Thanks to the large-scale emigration of Chinese from the southern province of Guandong to elsewhere in the world, this is China's best-known cuisine. Many claim that it is also the finest, and there's no doubt that the fertile south benefits from a benign climate and the widest selection of fresh produce anywhere in China.

Cantonese chefs are renowned for their creativity, their light touch with seasonings and their willingness to incorporate foreign ingredients and flavors. The visitor should not miss the opportunity of sampling the

pers or other vegetables; deep-fried yam balls; tiny spring rolls; and a host of other foods, each more tempting than the previous. Cantonese chefs are also justifiably renowned for their roasted poultry and pork, often served chopped and seasoned with sauces and a touch of sesame oil on a bed of rice.

Although the Chinese do not normally eat dessert, two common offerings at a dim sum spread are melt-in-the-mouth: custard tarts and cubes of coconut milk jelly. Do leave space for these.

Sichuan cuisine: The food of the far western province of Sichuan is the most emphatically flavored in all of China. Much of this emphasis comes from chilies, which appear in many

famous Cantonese array of tidbits known as *dim sum* (or, in Mandarin, *dian xin*). Generally served for breakfast in Guandong, dim sum consist of a selection of steamed or fried foods that are traditionally placed inside tiny woven baskets and wheeled through the restaurant or teahouse on a trolley. There'll be various dumplings filled with mixtures of pork or seafood, wrapped in transparent rice-dough wrappers or the more common wheat-flour *won ton* wrappers; substantial filled buns (*pao*); stuffed mushrooms, chili pep-

guises: dried and fried in chunks, together with other ingredients; ground into a paste with a touch of added oil; as chili oil, and crushed to a powder. Another distinctive Sichuan ingredient is Sichuan "pepper", the dried berry of the prickly ash or fagara.

Some writers claim that the Sichuan love of spicy, pungent food can be attributed to the climate, which is characterized by humidity throughout much of the year, and to freezing winters. Whatever the reason, most visitors to China will find that Sichuan food is full of flavor, and despite the use of chili, is never as hot as a Thai curry or a Korean *kim chee*. There are many excellent Sichuan

Left, filled dumplings, jiaozi. <u>Above</u>, dishes of yin and yang snacks and desserts.

dishes, including duck smoked over a mixture of camphor and tea leaves, then deep-fried, and beancurd scrambled with minced pork and spicy seasonings. This latter dish, *ma po tau fu*, has the bizarre translation of Beancurd of the Pock-Marked Old Woman.

A typical Sichuan eating experience is the fire-pot, or *huoguo*, particularly popular in certain streets in Chongqing. Diners sit around a table that has in the center a type of fondue heated by a gas fire (it used to be charcoal). Seasoned broth bubbles away in the fire-pot, and each diner adds bits and pieces of pre-pared vegetable, meat, fish and beancurd. The food cooks very quickly, and is fished out of the broth using chopsticks or else a special strainer, to be eaten after dipping in sesame oil or a beaten egg. This is a very convivial and warming way to enjoy a meal.

Huaiyang cuisine: The cuisine of the lower reaches of Chang Jiang (Yangze River), especially around Huaian and Yangzhou, gave rise to the term *huaiyang* to describe the food of China's eastern seaboard. A fertile area of "fish and rice", this region has a wide range of agricultural products, as well as abundant fish, prawns, crab and eel. The cooking of Shanghai, Jiangsu and Zhejiang is usually regarded as being part of Huaiyang cuisine, which is not surprising when one learns it was developed by the families of wealthy merchants living in Yangzhou.

The distinguishing feature of Hauiyang food is freshness, particularly when it comes to fish. Natural flavors are regarded as para-mount – no emphatic Sizhuan spicing here. Huaiyang cooks often steam or gently simmer their food, in preference to the faster deep frying. Signature dishes include pork steamed in lotus leaves, Duck with Eight Ingredients, and Lion's Head Meatballs, all of which should be found in any good restaurant around Shanghai.

Northern cuisine: The cuisine of the north tends to be a rustic, home-style cooking making abundant use of onions and garlic, but lacking the variety of vegetables characterizing the cuisines of China's more fertile regions. Northerners generally prefer wheat-based dishes to rice, and one finds a wide variety of noodles; dumplings (*jiaozi*) that are steamed, pan-fried or boiled; breads (once again, fried or steamed); and deep-fried lengths of dough or crullers, excellent with a bowl of sweet or savory beancurd.

Although the indigenous food is relatively simple, Beijing benefitted from the years when it was the imperial capital, attracting people from all over China. The emperor sought out the best chefs in the land, and the first among them could count on being given the rank of minister. It was during these days that the most refined and complex dishes were created, dishes such as Peking Duck, Mandarin Fish, Phoenix in the Nest and Thousand-Layer Cake. Today, the ordinary citizen of Beijing (and, of course, visiting foreigners) can sample these palace dishes in special (but expensive) restaurants.

No visitor should leave without a meal of Peking Duck, which begins when the chef

selects a specially-bred, force-fed duck slaughtered at six months of age. Air is pumped between the skin and the flesh of the duck, the skin painted with a mixture of honey, water and vinegar, and then the duck is dried. It is finally roasted in a special oven and served in three steps. The succulent, crisp skin is tucked into fine wheat-flour pancakes, painted with sweet black-sauce and enlivened with spring onions. After this course, the meat of the duck is enjoyed, with a finale of a soup made from the carcass and salted cabbage.

The Chinese way: Many meals in China are simple affairs: a bowl of rice gruel with pickles, pan-fried dumplings, a noodle soup or a plate of rice with a few shreds of chicken or meat, and a little cucumber. However, a proper family meal will normally consist of the staple (rice, noodles or dumplings), a soup, and three or four freshly-prepared hot dishes. The soup is generally served at the end of a meal, except in Guandong, where the Cantonese sip it throughout the meal to "help down the rice". There is seldom a dessert in the Western sense, although a combination of lychees and almond jelly, or Sichuan pancakes stuffed with a sweet-bean paste, can be found in some restaurants.

If fortunate enough to be invited to a meal in a Chinese home or to an official function,

follow, including seafood, meat, poultry, vegetables, soup, and rice or noodles.

One by one, the prepared dishes of food are placed in the center of the table. Diners help themselves with either a serving spoon, if provided, or with their own chopsticks. It is considered polite to place choice morsels on your neighbor's plate, but be sure to help yourself only to what is nearest you, rather than reaching right across the table. During the course of a meal, the Chinese usually chat, often smoke and drink. Green or black tea, without milk or sugar, is normally served throughout the meal.

Noisiness is a sign that everyone is having a good time, and as the fiery 40–60 percent

be well advised to bring a small gift for the hosts, such as alcohol or cigarettes, or even a gift from your home country. The dining table will be set with bowls and chopsticks, and usually with smaller dishes containing soy sauce, mustard or other seasonings. The number of dishes served will depend on the formality of the occasion. A banquet will commence with a cold dish or hors d'oeuvre. No matter how tempting this is, restrain yourself with the knowledge that there are probably another six or seven courses to

proof Chinese spirits take effect, the volume increases. Beer is also a popular accompaniment to meals, and wines produced by Franco-Chinese ventures are inexpensive and generally acceptable to foreign visitors. The host will constantly urge guests to eat and drink more, but be aware that to finish all the food served implies you are still hungry. Do not be surprised if the dining table takes on the appearance of a battlefield, with bits of bone, pumpkin seed husks, splashes of soup and other detritus being dumped at random.

Another aspect of dining in China is that it is not considered impolite to slurp one's soup or eat with gusto.

Left, outdoor market. **Above**, even the most casual meals are social occasions.

基以造於極莫不整飾之厥費大至於
何則實有故蓋盧溝橋建於金明昌年
拆而重築既費人力又毀成功何如仍舊貫乎則知

PLACES

The first reports in Europe of a people who lived even further east than the Scythians were by the ancient Greeks. They told of a people who produced silk, a process kept secret for centuries by the Chinese under penalty of death. Silk may have been the first commodity of trade between East and West. Exchanges of culture and religion soon followed, with Islam and Buddhism arriving in the Middle Kingdom via the Silk Road. For more than a millennium, in fact, this land route was the only link between Europe and China.

In the early sixteenth century, new opportunities opened up to mercantile Europeans, as Portuguese ships sailed as far as the southern Chinese coast, trading with the Chinese from a base in Macau. The missionaries who followed and ventured into China drew the first European maps of China (and failed miserably in gaining converts). Only the scale of the coastline is correct on any of these early maps – the further the maps extend into the interior, the more distorted becomes the cartography, or it remained blank. One might have said the same about European understanding of China as a whole.

There are no blank spaces left in China today. What were once exotic and remote places are now only exotic. Traveling in China is increasingly easier than one might expect, to the chagrin of old-school adventurers. Contemporary travelers will readily see that China is no monolithic culture. The influence of the Han Chinese may seem ubiquitous, but the rich Turkic culture of Xinjiang, the lively culture of Yunnan, or the lofty mantras of Tibet are just as much a part of China. Travelers may also come to recognize northern and southern differences amongst the Han themselves.

The northern part of China extends from Dongbei in the northeast – known to Westerners as Manchuria – across the Gobi Desert and along the Silk Road to Xinjiang, in the far west. The terrain is often less than gracious. Yet in the north's eastern extent, the Huang He, or Yellow River, has nurtured this territory for thousands of years, giving rise to civilization. Anchoring the Huang He's drainage are, of course, the numerous imperial capitals of Chinese civilization: Xi'an, Luoyang and, finally, Beijing.

The central belt of China follows that most intoxicating of rivers, Chang Jiang, or the Yangzi to Westerners. This river divides China north and south, along the way slicing into the earth to create Sanxia, the Three Gorges, before emptying into the sea near densely-populated Shanghai.

Southern China is of a distinctly different cast. Along the south-east coast are the feisty, entrepreneurial regions centered around Guangzhou and Hong Kong. Further to the west, the faces and languages change, until by the time one has reached Tibet, one feels in a different country. But, as the Chinese will remind travelers, it is still China.

Preceding pages: southern rice fields; Wanli Changcheng; rape-seed field, southeast coast; Hong Kong stock exchange. **Left,** stone tablet on Marco Polo Bridge, outside of Beijing.

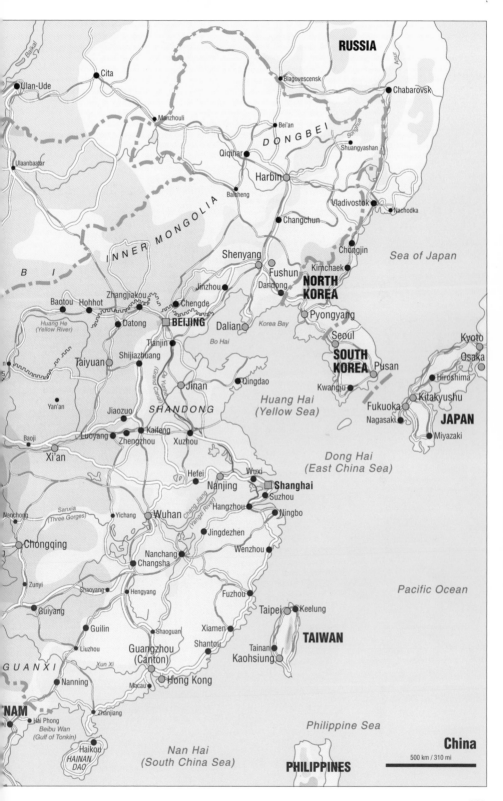

Summer Palace
Haidian Lu

HAIDIAN DISTRICT
Beisinhuanxi Lu
Beisinhuanxi Lu
Beisanhuanzhong Lu

Friendship
Hotel

Dazhong Si
(Great Bell Temple)

Weigong Lu
Xueyuannan Lu
Xueyuannan Lu

Suojafen Lu

Xitucheng Lu

National
Library

Baishiqiao Lu
Gaoliangqiao Lu
Wuta Si
(Five Pagoda Temple)

Jishuitan

XIYU

Deshen

Xiangshan
(Fragrant Hills)
Zizhuyuan Lu

Zizhuyuan Gongyuan
(Purple Bamboo Park)

Xisanhuanbei Lu

Xizhimen

Deshengmenxi Dajie

Xinjiekouwai Dajie

DISTRICT

Jishui
Lake

Deshengmenwai Dajie

Shouduliyuguan
(Sports Hall
of the Capital)
Beijing
Zoo

Exhibition
Centre

Xizhimennei Dajie

Renmin
People's
Theatre

Deshengmennei

Baiyunqu
Xiyuan
Hotel

Xizhimenwai Dajie

Xizhimen

Di'a

Chegongzhuangxi Lu
Sanlihe Lu

Chegongzhuang Dajie

Ping'anlixi Dajie
Chengongzhuang

Battasidong Dajie

Xindanbei Dajie

Xishiku Dajie

Baiwanzhuang Dajie

Lu Xun House
and Museum

Baita Si
(White Dagoba
Temple)

Fucheng Lu

Fucheng Lu

Fuchengmenwai Lu

Fuchengmennei Dajie

Guangji Si
(Temple of Rescue)

XIYU
Beitang
(North Church)
We

Diaogutai
Guesthouse

Fuchengmennan Dajie

Yuetanbeijie

Fuchengmen

Nanlishi Lu

Xisanhuanzhong Lu

Baiyun Lu

Sanlihedong Lu

Yuetannan Dajie

Yuetan
Gongyuan

Xidan Bei Dajie

DISTRICT
Xidan

Yuyuan Lake

Yuyuantan Gongyuan

February 7
Theatre

Taipingqiao Dajie

Xidan
Market

Xidanbei Dajie

Zhongguo Renmin Geming
(Military Museum)

Pikuhutong
Minzu
Wenhuagong
(Cultural Palace of
the Nationalities)

Telegraph
Office

Fuxing Lu
Fuxing Lu
Nanlishilu

Fuxingmen

Fuxingmennei Dajie

Gongzhufen
Jungshibowuguar
Muxidi

Culwei Lu

Yangfangdianxi

Yangfangdian Lu

Broadcast
Building

Changchunjie

Xuanwumenxi Dajie

Nantang
(South Church)

He

Baiyunguan
(Temple of the
White Cloud)

Xuanwumen

Xuanwumenwai

Lianhuachidong Lu

Guang'anmenbeibinhe Dajie

Xinbanmennei Dajie

Xuanwumen
Dajie

Xuanwumen

Luomashi

Lianhua River

Lianhua-
Litus
Pond

Huaibaishu Dajie

Xisanhuanzhong Lu
Lianhuachixi Lu

Guang'an Lu

Guang'anmenwai Lu

Guang'anmennei Dajie

Niujie
Mosque

Niu Dajie

Bo
Wo

Guang'an Lu

Mailandao Lu

Zaolinqian Dajie

Fayuan Si

Guang'ammen

Nanxiange Dajie
Guang'anmennanbinhe Dajie

Nancaiyuan Dajie

Wanshou
Gongyuan

XUANWU
DISTRICT

Xisanhuannan Lu

Sanluju Lu

Baizhifangxi Dajie

Baizhifangdong
Dajie

You'anmen Dajie

Tao
Go

Fengtaipei Lu

Fengtaipei Lu

Daguanyuan
(Grand View Gardens)

You'anmendongbinhe Lu

Yongd

Liangshui River

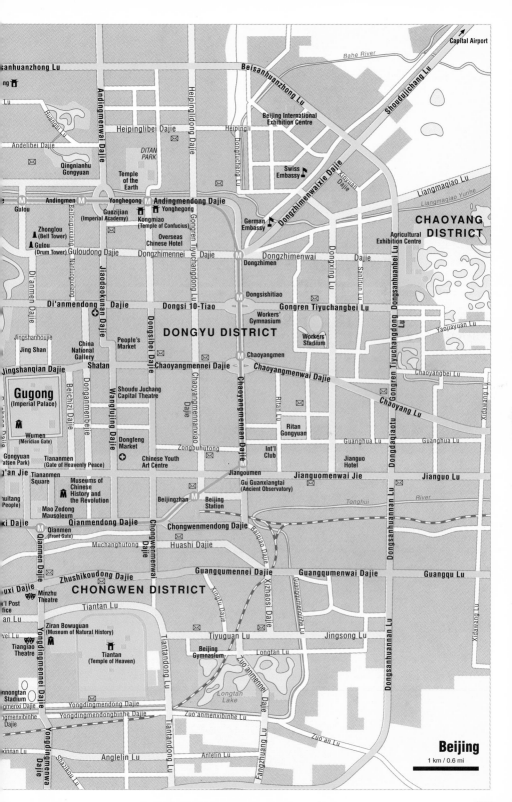

Capital Airport

Bahe River

Beisanhuanzhong Lu

anhuanzhong Lu

Shoudujichang Lu

ng
Lu

Huangsi Lu

Andingmenwai Dajie

Heipinglidong Dajie

Heipingli

Beijing International
Exhibition Centre

CHAOYANG
DISTRICT

Liangmaqiao Lu

Liangmaqiao Yunhe

Andelibei Dajie

Heipinglibei Dajie

Swiss
Embassy

Dongzhimenwaixie Dajie

Xinyuan
Dajie

DITAN
PARK

Dongguchang Lu

Qingnianhu
Gongyuan

Temple
of the
Earth

Agricultural
Exhibition Centre

Andingmen   Yonghegong   Andingmendong Dajie

Gulou

Guozijian
(Imperial Academy)

Yonghegong

German
Embassy

Dongxing Lu

Zhonglou
(Bell Tower)

Kongmiao
(Temple of Confucius)

Gongren Tiyuchangdong Lu

Dongzhimenwai   Dajie

Santilun Lu

Dongsanhuanbei Lu

Gulou
(Drum Tower)

Guloudong Dajie

Overseas
Chinese Hotel

Dongzhimennei   Dajie

Dongzhimen

Yaojiayuan Lu

Dongzhimen

Di'anmen Dajie

Jiaodaokuan Dajie

Dongsishitiao

Dongsi 10-Tiao

Di'anmendong Dajie

DONGYU DISTRICT

Gongren Tiyuchangbei Lu

Jingshanhoujie

Nanluoguxiang

Dongsibei Dajie

Workers'
Gymnasium

Jing Shan

China
National
Gallery

Workers'
Stadium

Chaoyangber Lu

Jingshanqian Dajie

Shatan

People's
Market

Chaoyangmennei Dajie

Chaoyangmen

Chaoyangmenwai Dajie

Chaoyang Lu

Xidawang Lu

Gugong
(Imperial Palace)

Beichizi Dajie

Donganmenbeije

Wangfujing Dajie

Chaoyangmennanxiao Dajie

Chaoyangmennan Dajie

Ritan Lu

Dongdaqiaolu

Guanghua Lu

Wumen
(Meridian Gate)

Shoudu Juchang
Capital Theatre

Dongfeng
Market

Zongbuhutong

Ritan
Gongyuan

Guanghua Lu

Gongyuan
atsen Park)

Tiananmen
(Gate of Heavenly Peace)

Chinese Youth
Art Centre

Int'l
Club

Jianguo
Hotel

'an Jie

Jianguomen

Jianguomenwai Jie

Jianguo Lu

Tiananmen
Square

Museums of
Chinese
History and
the Revolution

Gu Guanxiangtai
(Ancient Observatory)

Dongsanhuannan Lu

uitang
People)

Mao Zedong
Mausoleum

Beijingzhan

Beijing
Station

Tonghui   River

Qianmen Dajie

Qianmendong Dajie

Chongwenmenwai Dajie

Chongwenmendong Dajie

Qianmen
(Front Gate)

Muchanghutong

Huashi Dajie

Baitiao Dajie

xi Dajie

Zhushikoudong Dajie

Guangqumennei Dajie

Guangqumenwai Dajie

Guangqu Lu

uxi Dajie

CHONGWEN DISTRICT

Xingfu Dajie

Xizhaosi Dajie

Guangqumenneile Lu

Xidawang Lu

Minzhu
Theatre

Tiantan Lu

's Post
fice

Yongdingmennei Dajie

Ziran Bowuguan
(Museum of Natural History)

Tiyuguan Lu

Jingsong Lu

an Lu

Tiantandong Lu

vei Lu

Tiangiao
Theatre

Tiantan
(Temple of Heaven)

Beijing
Gymnasium

Longtan Lu

Longtan
Lake

Dongsanhuannan Lu

nnongtan
Stadium
gmenxi Dajie

Yongdingmendong Dajie

Zuo'anmennei Dajie

Zuo'an Lu

gmenxibinhe
Dajie

Yongdingmendongbinhe Dajie

Zuo'anmenxibinhe Lu

Yongdingmenwai Dajie

Shazikou Lu

Fazhayuan Lu

Zuo'an Lu

kinnan Lu

Anglelin Lu

Antelin Lu

Beijing

1 km / 0.6 mi

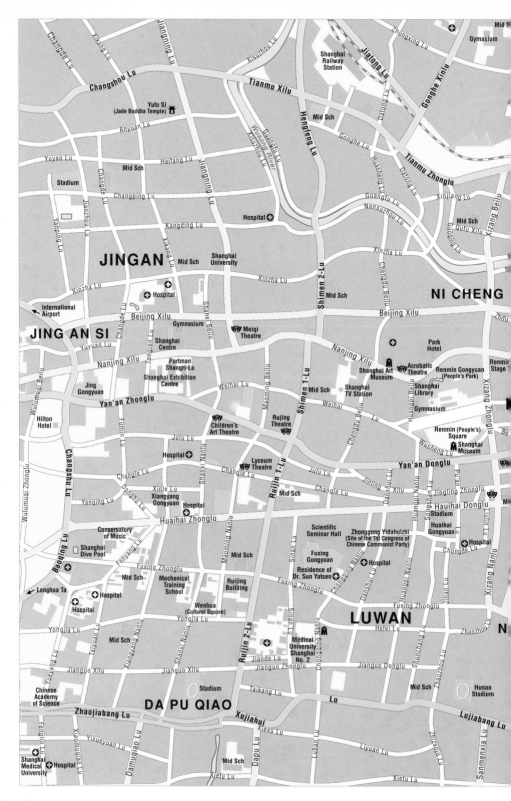

Changde Lu
Xikang Lu
Jiangning Lu
Zhongxing Lu
Gymasium
Mid S

Changshou Lu
Xisuzhou Lu
Tianmu Xilu
Shanghai Railway Station
Jialong Lu
Gonghe Xinlu

Yufo Si (Jade Buddha Temple)
Anyuan Lu
Wusong River
Xisuzhou Lu
Guangfu Lu
Hengfeng Lu
Mid Sch
Gonghe Lu
Datong Lu
Tianmu Zhonglu

Yuyao Lu
Changde Lu
Haifang Lu
Jiangning Lu
Huasheng Lu
Datong Lu
Guangfu Lu
Xinjiang Lu

Stadium
Mid Sch
Changping Lu
Nansuzhou Lu
Mid Sch
Qufu Xilu
Xizang Beilu
Guang Lu

Jiaozhou Lu
Kangding Lu
Hospital
Xinzha Lu

Yanping Lu
JINGAN
Mid Sch
Shanghai University
Shimen 2-Lu
NI CHENG
Zhifu

Xinzha Lu
Xinzha Lu
Chengdu Beilu

International Airport
Hospital
Beijing Xilu
Shanxi Beilu
Mid Sch
Beijing Xilu

JING AN SI
Yuyuan Lu
Gymnasium
Meiqi Theatre
Nanjing Xilu
Park Hotel
Renmin Stage

Nanjing Xilu
Shanghai Centre
Portman Shangri-La
Shanghai Exhibition Centre
Changde Lu
Longchang Lu
Maoming Beilu
Shanghai Art Museum
Acrobatic Theatre
Renmin Gongyuan (People's Park)

Jing Gongyuan
Weihai Lu
Shimen 1-Lu
Mid Sch
Shanghai TV Station
Weihai
Shanghai Library
Xizang Zhong

Wumuqi Beilu
Yan'an Zhonglu
Chengdu Beilu
Gymnasium

Hilton Hotel
Fumin Lu
Children's Art Theatre
Rujing Theatre
Renmin (People's) Square
Be

Changshu Lu
Julu Lu
Shanxi Nanlu
Lyceum Theatre
Ruijin 1-Lu
Julu Lu
Jinling
Shanghai Museum
Wusheng Lu
Yan'an Donglu

Wumuqi Nanlu
Hospital
Changle Lu
Changle Lu
Mid Sch
Changle Lu
Xilu
Huangpi Nanlu
Songshan Lu
Jingling Zhonglu

Baoqing Lu
Yanqing Lu
Xinle Lu
Xiangyang Gongyuan
Huaihai Zhonglu
Hospital
Sinan Lu
Hauihai Donglu
Huaihai Gongyuan
Stadium
M

Donghu Lu
Fenyang Lu
Conservatory of Music
Shanghai Dive Pool
Scientific Seminar Hall
Zhonggong Yidahuizhi (Site of the 1st Congress of Chinese Communist Party)
Hospital
Chongde Lu

Fuxing Zhonglu
Mid Sch
Mechanical Training School
Maoming Nanlu
Mid Sch
Ruijing Building
Fuxing Gongyuan
Residence of Dr. Sun Yatsen
Chongqing Nanlu
Hospital
Danshui Lu
Huangpi Nanlu
Fuxing Zhonglu

Longhua Ta
Hospital
Wenhua (Cultural Square)
Yongjia Lu
Ruijin 2-Lu
Sinan Lu
LUWAN
Hefei Lu
Zhaozhou Lu

Yongjia Lu
Taiyuan Lu
Mid Sch
Xiangyang Nanlu
Shanxi Nanlu
Medical University Shanghai No. 2
Jiande Lu
Chongqing Nanlu
Shunchang Lu
Jinan Lu
Xizang Nanlu

Chinese Academy of Science
Jianguo Xilu
Jianguo Xilu
Jianguo Zhonglu
Jianguo Donglu
Mid Sch
Hunan Stadium

Zhaojiabang Lu
DA PU QIAO
Stadium
Xujiahui
Taikang Lu
Lu
Lujiabang Lu

Fenyang Lu
Yixueyuan Lu
Xiaomuqiao Lu
Xiexu Lu
Dapu Lu
Lihan
Liyuan Lu
Sanmenxia Lu

Shanghai Medical University
Hospital
Mid Sch
Xietu Lu
Xietu Lu

156

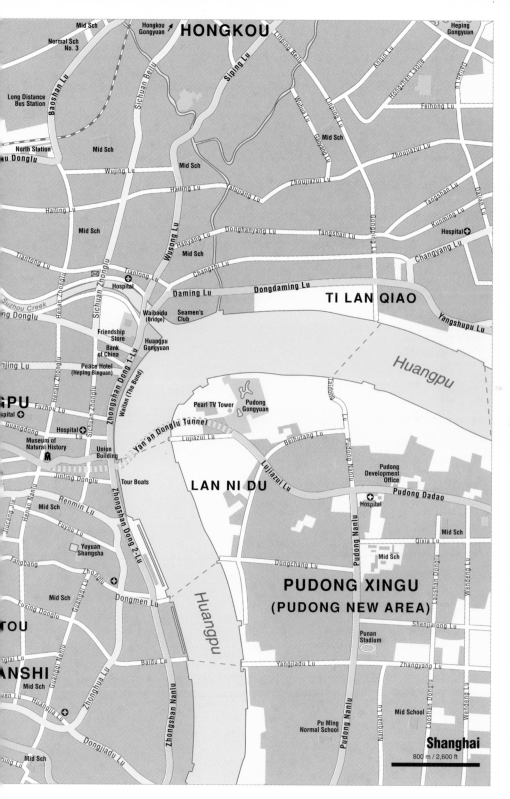

Mid Sch
Normal Sch No. 3
Hongkou Gongyuan
HONGKOU
Heping Gongyuan
Long Distance Bus Station
Baoshan Lu
Sichuan Beilu
Siping Lu
Linping Beilu
Wuhai Lu
Linping Lu
Baoyang Lu
Anqin Lu
Hongzhen Laolu
Feihong Lu
Hi Fengci
North Station
Mid Sch
Mid Sch
Mid Sch
Wujing Lu
Hailing Lu
Yalujiang Lu
Zhoujiazui Lu
Zhoujiazui Lu
Tangshan Lu
Dalian Lu
u Donglu
Hailing Lu
Wusong Lu
Hanyang Lu
Donghanyang Lu
Tangshan Lu
Hospital
Kunming Lu
Changyang Lu
Tiantong Lu
Mid Sch
Mid Sch
Tiantong Lu
Changzhi Lu
Gongping Lu
Henan Zhonglu
Sichuan Zhonglu
Hospital
Tiantong Lu
Daming Lu
Dongdaming Lu
TI LAN QIAO
Suzhou Creek
ng Donglu
Waibaidu (Bridge)
Seamen's Club
Yangshupu Lu
njing Lu
Friendship Store
Bank of China
Peace Hotel (Heping Binguan)
Huangpu Gongyuan
Zhongshan Dong 1-Lu
Waitan (The Bund)
Huangpu
GPU
spital
Fuzhou Lu
Henan Zhonglu
Sichuan Zhonglu
Pearl TV Tower
Pudong Gongyuan
Guangdong
Hospital
Yan'an Donglu Tunnel
Lujiazui Lu
Beihufang Lu
Pudong Nanlu
Museum of Natural History
Union Building
Lujiazui Lu
Pudong Development Office
Jinling Donglu
Tour Boats
LAN NI DU
Hospital
Pudong Dadao
uicang Jie
Henan Nanlu
Mid Sch
Renmin Lu
Zhongshan Dong 2-Lu
Qixia Lu
Mid Sch
Laoshan Donglu
Wandeng Lu
Fuyou Lu
Yuyuan Shangsha
Mid Sch
Fangbang
Zhongh
Dongchang Lu
PUDONG XINGU
(PUDONG NEW AREA)
Fuxing Donglu
Mid Sch
Dongmen Lu
Huangpu
Shenjiatong Lu
OU
Punan Stadium
Baidu Lu
Yangjiadu Lu
Zhangyang Lu
nglai Lu
Guangqi Nanlu
Zhonghua Lu
ANSHI
Mid Sch
en Lu
Huangbu Lu
Zhongshan Nanlu
Pudong Nanlu
Nanquan Lu
Laoshan Donglu
Wandeng Lu
Dongjiadu Lu
Pu Ming Normal School
Mid School
Mid Sch
Shanghai
800 m / 2,600 ft

157

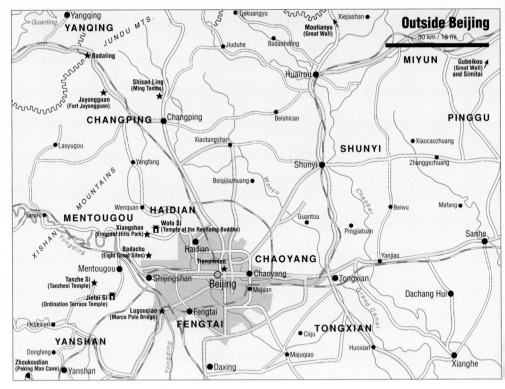

Outside Beijing

30 km / 18 mi

Guanting

YANQING
Yangqing
Tjekuangyu
Xiejiashan
Moutianyu (Great Wall)
Jiuduhe
Badaoheling
Huairou

MIYUN
Gubeikou (Great Wall) and Simitai

JUNDU MTS.

★ Badaling

Shisan Ling (Ming Tombs) ★
Beishicao

PINGGU

Juyongguan (Fort Juyongguan) ★
CHANGPING
Changping
Xiaotangshan

Laoyugou

SHUNYI
Shunyi
Xiaocaozhuang
Zhanggezhuang

Yangfang
Beiqijiazhuang

Wenyu

MOUNTAINS

Yanchi
Wenquan
HAIDIAN
Wofo Si (Temple of the Reclining Buddha)
Guantou
Pingjiatuan
Beiwu
Mafang

Chaobai

Xiangshan (Fragrant Hills Park) ★
MENTOUGOU
Haidian
Yanjiao
Sanhe

Badachu (Eight Great Sites) ★
Tiananmen
CHAOYANG
Chaoyang

XISHAN
Yongding

Mentougou
Shijingshan
Beijing ○
Chaoyang
Majuan
Tongxian
Dachang Hui

Tanzhe Si (Tanzhesi Temple) ★
Grand Canal

Jietai Si (Ordination Terrace Temple)
Lugouqiao (Marco Polo Bridge) ★
Fengtai
Cigu
TONGXIAN

Hebeicun
FENGTAI
Majuqiao
Huoxian
Xianghe

YANSHAN
Dongfeng
Yongding
Daxing

Zhoukoudian (Peking Man Cave)
Yanshan

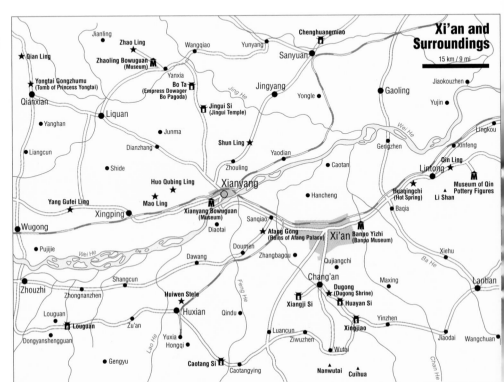

Xi'an and Surroundings

15 km / 9 mi

Jianling
Zhao Ling ★
Wangqiao
Yunyang
Chenghuangmiao
Sanyuan

Qian Ling ★
Zhaoling Bowuguan (Museum)
Yanxia
Jingyang
Gaoling
Jiaokouzhen

Yongtai Gongzhumu (Tomb of Princess Yongtai) ★
Bo Ta (Empress Dowager Bo Pagoda)
Jing He
Yongle
Yujin

Qianxian
Jingui Si (Jingui Temple)
Wei He
Lingkou

Liquan
Junma
Gengzhen
Xinfeng

Yanghan
Dianzhang
Yaodian
Qin Ling ★

Liangcun
Shide
Zhouling
Shun Ling ★
Caotan
Lintong ★
Museum of Qin Pottery Figures

Huo Qubing Ling ★
Xianyang ○
Hancheng
Huaqingchi (Hot Spring) ★
Li Shan
Li Shan ▲

Yang Gufei Ling ★
Mao Ling ★
Xianyang Bowuguan (Museum)
Baqia

Xingping
Sanqiao
Wei He
Diaotai
Afang Gong (Ruins of Afang Palace)
Xi'an
Banpo Yizhi (Banpo Museum)

Wugong
Doumen
Zhangbagou
Qujiangchi
Xiehu
Lantian

Pujijie
Dawang
Chang'an
Maxing

Shangcun
Dugong (Dugong Shrine) ★

Zhouzhi
Zhongnanzhen
Huiwen Stele
Xiangji Si
Huayan Si
Yinzhen

Louguan
Huxian
Qindu
Xingjiao
Jiaodai
Wangchuan

Dongyanshengguan
Zu'an
Luancun
Ziwuzhen
Wutai

Gengyu
Caotang Si
Caotangying
Nanwutai ▲
Cuihua ▲

Feng He

Ba He

Chan He

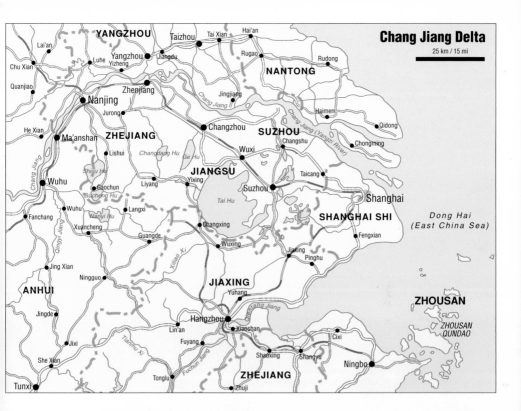

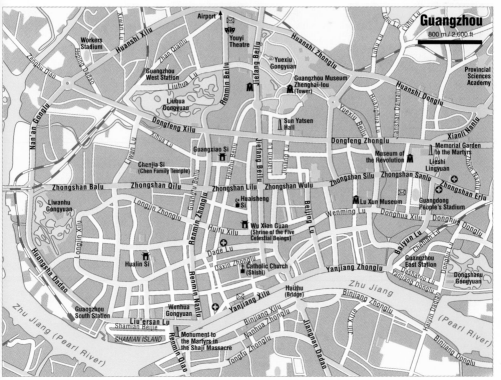

THE NORTH

Taking the top half of China and collectively – and perhaps naively – calling it "north" lends itself, if not careful, to the suggestion of a homogenous quality. Indeed not. Emphatically not. The differences between northwestern China and northeastern China are as fundamental as between left and right.

Yet there are unifying threads of history, if not culture, slicing across northern China. The so-called Silk Road – a German geographer's moniker – extended from east to west, or west to east, if one prefers, linking the mysterious lands of West Asia and Europe, including the waning Roman Empire, with the emperors of the Han dynasty. Its importance faltered after several centuries, however, when the southeastern coast took on commercial importance.

The capitals of China's ancient rulers were mostly in the northeast – Xi'an, Luoyang, Beijing. Due west of the Korean peninsula and not all that far from the steppes of Mongolia, a fact not absent from Beijing's history, Beijing was the center of the universe until imperial rule collapsed in 1912. Although not China's largest city, Beijing – Northern Capital – is best known today for the Imperial Palace, one of the world's wonders, and as seat of China's Communist government.

Northeast of Beijing hovers Dongbei – literally, East-North – but better known to outsiders as Manchuria. Geographically and politically, this area has often been of uncertain mind. In this century alone, Dongbei has been under Japanese, Russian and Chinese control, and the influences from Korea, especially near the border with North Korea, are considerable and deeply embedded.

Beyond Beijing, whipping westward over the rocky hills and mountains like a restless serpent, is Wanli Changcheng – the Great Wall. An ancient line of defence against nomads from the dark edges of the earth that lost its usefulness centuries ago, it has retained its timelessness, particularly where the tourists don't flock.

The northeast is also home of Confucius and of the Eight Immortals of Daoism. More fundamentally than even these philosophical undercurrents, it is home to the source of Chinese civilization: Huang He, or the Yellow River. Along its course is Xi'an, from where the first emperor of a unified China, Qin Shi Huangdi, made ancient history. Huang He then loops northwards, towards the Mongolian steppes and the beginnings of the Silk Road.

Along this Silk Road, China exported, yes, silk to the world's shadowy peripheries, and imported Buddhism and Islam. To the west, beyond the Gobi Desert and ancient Buddhist caves, is a land of superior simplicity and grace, and of Islam. There are also glacier-peppered mountains and waterless basins, and an emptiness that is nevertheless embracing, if not intoxicating.

Preceding pages: late autumn street traffic, Luoyang. **Left,** Foxiangge, the Summer Palace outside of Beijing.

DONGBEI:
MANCHURIAN NORTH

North of Beijing lies a cold and mostly industrial region of three provinces: Liaoning, Jilin and Heilongjiang. With a blending of Chinese, Korean and Russian influences and peoples, the area sometimes takes on a muddled cultural identity. It has also been an area of conflict and power struggles, including border fights between the former Soviet Union and China. Before that, the area was abused by the Japanese in World War II, and then was the staging area for fierce battles in the Korean War.

The Chinese call this area **Dongbei**, which literally means East-North. To the west, the northeastern provinces border the Mongolian steppes, and to the east, the Korean peninsula. The old name of Manchuria, still in use outside China, goes back to the fact that this was once the territory of the Manchu, rulers of the Qing dynasty.

The Manchu had prohibited the settlement of Han Chinese in this region. Not until the middle of the last century was a major settlement of Han Chinese permitted, under the pressure of an expanding population and the confusions of the Taiping Rebellion (1850–1864). Up until the end of the 1970s, the Manchu were considered to have been completely assimilated with the Han Chinese; but in recent years, the special customs and traditions of the Manchu are once more being emphasized. During World War II, the Japanese attempted to separate this region from China by setting up the puppet state of Manchuguo under the rule of the last Chinese emperor, Puyi. Today, about 100 million people live in this northeastern region.

From Beijing, it's possible to cross northeastern China by the Trans-Siberian Railway; the train travels via Shenyang, Changchun, Jilin, and Harbin, and via Qiqihar, Hailar and the border town of Manzhouli to Russia. Shenyang, the capital of Liaoning Province, is 840 kilometers (520 mi) from Beijing. It takes 12 hours to get there by express train; by plane the distance is covered in an hour and a half.

A rail journey from Beijing takes about 12 hours, traveling for long stretches along the coast of Bo Hai. Apart from the seaside resort of Beidaihe, it also passes the town of Xingcheng, which dates from Ming period and has many interesting sights and is also a popular resort. A good time to travel to Shenyang – and northeast China in general – is in summer, as the long winters are bitterly cold.

Shenyang: An important meeting point of several transport routes in the northeast, Shenyang is also one of the most important industrial cities in China. With a population of nearly six million people, Shenyang is sometimes known by its Manchurian name of Mukden.

Although Shenyang's history – and that of the entire province of Liaoning – can be traced a long way back into history, the city did not gain any importance until the Song dynasty, when it became a center of trade for nomadic livestock breeders. Its rise to prominence came during the Qing dynasty – Liaoning was, and still is, the home of the Manchu, the Qing emperors. Today, more than half of the Manchu ethnic minority live in this province.

In Liaoning Province itself, there are several autonomous regions inhabited mainly by Manchu; displays of traditional Manchu culture are put on specially for foreigners nowadays. In the autonomous Xiuyuan district is a museum of Manchu art and culture.

In Liaoning, the greatest building from the time of the Manchu Qing dynasty is the **Imperial Palace**, or Gugong, in Shenyang, the most complete and best-preserved palace complex after the Imperial Palace in Beijing. It was built in 1625, after the Manchu had declared Shenyang to be their capital, and contains more than 300 buildings in an area covering more than 60,000 square meters (650,000 sq ft). This palace, which was maintained after the Qing emperors later moved to the capital of Beijing, was the residence of Nurhachi, the founder of the Qing dynasty, and his successor Abahai (Hong Taiji in Chi-

Left, cooling off in northeastern waters.

nese). The main buildings – an amalgamation of Chinese, Manchu and Mongol architecture – are the Chongzheng, the Qingning Palace, the Dazheng, and the Wensu Pavilion.

Of the three **imperial Qing tombs** in Liaoning Province, two are in Shenyang: the Northern Imperial Tomb, Beiling – built in 1643 for Nurhachi's son Abahai and now in the middle of a park in the north of Shenyang – and the Eastern Imperial Tomb, Dongling, the final resting place of Nurhachi, eight kilometers (five mi) outside of the city. The third tomb, Yongling, built by Nurhachi for his ancestors, is in the Xinbin district.

Also worth seeing in Shenyang is **Shishen Si**, a Lamaist temple dating from the seventeenth century and located in the western part of the city. The **Liaoning provincial museum** is also worth a visit.

From Shenyang, the train leaves the main line and goes southwards towards **Anshan**, some 80 kilometers (50 mi) from Shenyang. Anshan is a city of millions, and perhaps the largest iron-and-steel works in China is to be found here, producing 20 percent of the nation's steel. Anshan is a jumping-off point for a pleasant visit to the scenic **Qian Shan**, a mountain blanketed with ancient pines, pavilions, temples and monasteries dating from the Ming and Qing periods. Temple markets are still held here every April.

From Anshan, the journey continues south through broad fields of millet and soybean to the tip of the peninsula, where the port of **Dalian (Lüda)** lies. The ice-free harbor is one of the most important in China in the north, a fact reflected in its conquest by Japan during World War II and the Soviet Union's takeover of it afterwards; it was returned to China only in the 1950s.

The city, surrounded by greenery in the summer, is also a popular place for holidays and excursions, not least because of the extensive beaches and the mild maritime climate. The main impression of the city, which lies in a bay, is of a busy port with broad streets and big squares planted with greenery. Don't miss the opportunity to visit one of the numerous fish restaurants here. Well worth a visit is the nature park of Laohutan, right by the sea.

From Dalian, the town of **Ganjizi**, to the north of the bay, is accessible by bus or taxi. In Ganjizi is a brick tomb dating from the Han dynasty with interesting wall paintings. Some 60 kilometers (40 mi) from Dalien and east along the coast is **Lüshun**, once known as Port Arthur; the harbor has, however, lost much of its former importance.

Towards Korea: Southeast from Shenyang via Benxi, or northeast from Dalian, are **Dandong**, near the North Korean border, and the mountainous vistas of Dagu Shan. From Dandong, the railway carries on into North Korea as far as its capital, Pyongyang. For those who want to say they've nearly set foot in North Korea, boats carry visitors to within a few meters of the North Korean side of the Yalu River.

The main route from Shenyang runs east at first, to the nearby industrial town of **Fushun**, where there is a prison

Women in traditional clothing at a festival in Shenyang.

for war criminals, and where the last emperor, Puyi, was imprisoned until 1950. Outside of Fushun is one of the world's biggest open-pit coal mines, producing over 20 million tons yearly.

To the east of Fushun and an overnight journey by train is **Tonghua**, a wine-producing town in the southeast of Jilin Province. Apart from sights such as a monastery and the mausoleum of Yangjingchu, there is a wine cellar.

From Tonghua, **Ji'an**, on the Chinese-Korean border, is accessible by train or bus. Ji'an lies on the upper course of the Yalu River and was once the capital of the Korean kingdom of Koguryo. There are numerous tombs in the vicinity, but only some of them can be visited. Ji'an lies in the middle of an autonomous region of China's Korean minority. There are about two million Koreans living in China, and more than 60 percent live in Jilin.

The capital of this autonomous region – there are two such regions in Jilin – is **Yanji**, where the Koreans also have their own university. At Ji'an, the border river Yalu is only some 30 meters (100 ft) wide, and the life here is quite idyllic. In the summer, women chat across the border while doing their laundry, and children from both sides swim in the river together, although it is not officially permitted to swim to the opposite bank.

The Korean ambiance, by the way, is not noticeable here alone. Some parts of Shenyang, Changchun, Jilin and Mudanjiang, too, feel rather Korean – people wear Korean clothing, signs are written in Korean, and Korean is the primary language of commerce. (In Shenyang, there is a cemetery dedicated to the memory of the Chinese who died in the Korean War.)

North of Yanji, surrounded by beautiful scenery, lies the town of **Mudanjiang**. The most famous peak along the Chinese-Korean border is **Baitou Shan** (White Head Mountain), with its crater lake, the beautiful Lake of Heaven. In its clear waters, creatures like the one believed to dwell in Loch Ness have reportedly been seen several times; the

Dongbei's weather is harsh on its people.

last sighting was in 1981. (Nearby is a waterfall, one of the sources of the Sungari river.) This mountain is considered sacred by Koreans and the Manchu, and it lies in the center of the **Changbaishan nature reserve**, which covers 2,000 square kilometers (770 sq mi) and is China's largest reserve.

In **Changbai Shan** (Ever White Mountains), which lie along the Chinese-Korean border, many animals survive that have become extinct elsewhere – sables, snow leopards, tigers, and bears. Excellent ginseng grows here, too.

Like many other mountain ranges in China, Changbai Shan has its own Tianchi (Lake of Heaven), a volcanic crater lake that is just under 15 kilometers in circumference.

Into Manchuria: From Fushun onwards, the railway turns north until it reaches the provincial capital of Jilin, **Changchun**. On its way, the train runs through huge fields of grain; here in the northeast, there are still enormous farms owned by the state. From the train, however, old villages with their mud huts

can be seen. The town of Changchun (Eternal Spring), on the Yitong River, did not become important until the end of the last century, when it was the terminus of the Manchurian railway, built by skilled Russian labor.

In 1932, the town, then known as Xinjing, became the seat of the government of the Japanese puppet state of Manchuguo. Today, the town still shows signs of Japanese urban planning in its ruler-straight boulevards. The **palace of Emperor Puyi** has once more been restored to its old form.

Changchun, an industrial and university town, is also well-known for its car-manufacturing works. Because of its large parks, Changchun is often also known as the "town of woodland". A great many films are produced here in one of the biggest film studios of the People's Republic of China. Most films that are internationally-known, however, are produced elsewhere, for example, in Xi'an or in the large coastal cities.

From Changchun, the journey continues via the Trans-Siberian Railway to **Harbin**, the capital of Heilongjiang Province, with its population of over three million. The distance from Beijing to this point is almost 1,400 kilometers (900 mi), and the train covers it in 18 hours. Harbin (Place for Drying Fishnets) can also be reached by plane from Changchun and Beijing.

The city lies along the river Songhua, which joins Heilong Jiang to the north. The impression of this industrial city is one of industrial sites and newly-built apartment houses that all look alike and are a familiar sight all over China. A marked contrast is in the older, sometimes almost European-looking residential areas.

Many anti-communist Russians fled here after the October Revolution of 1917, and formed the majority of the inhabitants together with those Russians already living here. After World War II, most of them went back to what was then the Soviet Union.

Here, too, were the gruesome and inhumane experiments of the Japanese army's Unit 731, for decades after World War II denied by the Japanese govern-

Warm day, Dalian beach.

ment. The unit's existence was only recently acknowledged by Japan, after a Japanese scholar uncovered documented proof. Over 4,000 prisoners of war – both Asians and Allies – died as a result of experiments involving cold, heat, chemicals, injections of viruses and plague, and live dissection.

Some districts of Harbin are still reminiscent of Russian cities today. Russian influences can be detected in the architectural style of many of the buildings, not least in the old churches with their unmistakable onion domes. There are over a dozen Christian churches in Harbin, many of them built in neo-Gothic style. Another of the city's few interesting sights is Jile Si, a temple built in 1924 in the Nangang district.

The winters are very cold, and temperatures can fall as low as minus 38°C (–36°F). For this reason, ice-sailing is one of the most popular sports in Harbin. Every year during the winter, there are also large exhibitions of ice sculpture in the city. Human figures, pavilions and entire palaces are hacked out of ice.

Near **Yichun**, to the north of Harbin, there is an ancient forest along the Tangwang River composed mainly of Korean pines; this has now been declared a nature reserve and is a perfect place for long hikes.

The train from Harbin runs on to the northwest towards the Russian border. After three hours of traveling is **Daqing**, China's biggest oilfield.

About 260 kilometers (160 mi) from Harbin to the northwest, in the swamps around the lake Zhalong, is a nature reserve where rare red-crowned and white-naped cranes live.

Not far to the west of Qiqihar, the train route towards the Russian border crosses into **Inner Mongolia**, passing through the Greater Xingan range. The first town in Inner Mongolia is Hailar, in the middle of the Mongolian steppe, which has a Siberian atmosphere. On the Chinese side, the journey ends in Manzhouli, where you can begin the journey, which lasts several days, to Moscow and eventually onwards to Europe and Berlin.

Ice Lantern Festival, Harbin.

BEIJING: NORTHERN CAPITAL

The country around Beijing was already settled in prehistoric times, proven by the discovery in the small town of Zhoukoudian, southwest of Beijing, of the skull of *Sinanthropus pekinensis* (Peking Man). More recently, since about a thousand years ago, the city has served as primary and subsidiary residence for a series of dynasties. Under the rule of the Mongol emperor Kublai Khan in the thirteenth century, it was known as Khanbaliq (City of the Khan), an especially splendid and magnificent winter residence of the emperors.

The city did not receive its layout, which still survives today, until the rule of the Ming dynasty. In traditional Chinese thought, the world was not imagined as the flat, round disk of the Ptolomaean vision in the West, but was conceived of as a square. A city, too – and especially a capital city – was supposed to be square, a reflection of the cosmic order and adhering to its geometrical definition, with a north-south and east-west orientation of roads and buildings. In no other city in China has this basic idea been fulfilled as completely as in ancient Beijing.

Geomantic design: The third Ming emperor Yongle is considered the capital's actual planner and architect. In 1421, he moved his government from Nanjing to the city of Beiping (Northern Peace) and renamed it as Beijing (Northern Capital). In a bad attempt at transliteration by Europeans, the city became known as Peking in the West – a name that persists in some instances, such as with the cuisine specialty, Peking Duck. (Nobody calls it Beijing Duck.)

The plans of Yongle followed the principles of geomancy, the traditional doctrine of "winds and water," which strives to attain a harmonious relationship between human life and nature. Screened from the north by a semicircle of hills, Beijing lies on a plain that opens to the south, an auspicious direction, as it was toward the south that the generos-

ity and warmth of *yang* was thought to reside. Likewise, all important buildings in the old city face south, thus protected from harmful influences from the north – whether winter Siberian winds or enemies from the steppes. Thus, it was not by chance that south-facing Qianmen – the Outer Gate to the city – was the largest, most beautiful, and most sacred of its kind. The hill of Jing Shan, to the north of Gugong, the Imperial Palace, was probably created according to geomantic considerations as well.

A theoretical line from north to south divides the city east and west, with the axis centered on the Imperial Palace; important buildings and city features were laid out as mirror images on either side. Ritan (Altar of the Sun), for example, has its equivalent in Yuetan (Altar of the Moon). Planned in an equally complementary way were Xidan and Dongdan, the eastern and western business quarters, which today still serve as shopping streets.

Some of the most notable buildings of both old and new Beijing are to be found

on the north–south axis itself. From the north: Zhonglou and Gulou (Bell and Drum Towers), Jing Shan (Coal Hill), and the Imperial Palace. From the south northwards: Qianmen (Outer Gate), Tiananmen, and the Imperial Palace, lined up one after the other like pearls on a string. In the middle of this north–south chain of historically-significant buildings lies the heart of ancient Beijing, the Dragon Throne, from which the emperor, ritual mediator between heaven and earth, governed. This was considered the center of the physical world, thought of as a gigantic grid. The city, and the world, and everything within, are clearly given a defined place in a hierarchy, depending on how far they are from the center. This imperial throne is embedded in a majestic palace, which is also square and surrounded by high purple walls on all sides – the so-called Forbidden City. Around it lies the imperial city, which in earlier times also formed a square surrounded by walls.

Part of the old imperial city was defined by a chain of lakes. Today, the northern part forms the center of Beihai Gongyuan (Beihai Park). On the shores of the central and southern waters lies **Zhongnanhai**, since 1949 the Communist Party's forbidden city. Only highly-placed officials and important state guests are permitted inside.

Crowded around the old imperial city was a sea of mainly single-story houses. Curved like the crests of waves, the roofs of this inner city were not allowed to rise above the height of the Imperial Palace. Here, the tasteful homes of the wealthy and of influential officials were to be found. Even nowadays, this part of Beijing is still considered to be the actual inner city, or old city. However, only a few monumental gates of the mighty defensive walls that once surrounded Beijing have survived – Qianmen in the south and in the north, Deshengmen.

Adjoining the inner city to the south was an outer city. In Qing times, the former was residence for the Mongols, the latter for the Chinese. In the Chinese area, the doors of the houses were lower,

Entrance to Zhongnanhai

the *hutong* (as the alleys of Beijing were known) were narrower, and the rice bowls were less well-filled. Instead of tea, people drank hot water. Instead of satin boots, they wore sandals. However, bored Manchu officials and wealthy merchants sometimes fled their respectable surroundings for the Chinese district's tea and bath houses, brothels, specialty restaurants and bazaars – all competing for the favors and money of literati, monks, mandarins, and, from time to time, the occasional prince in clever disguise.

Even today, things are livelier to the south of Qianmen than in other parts of the city. The gourmet restaurants remain crowded. **Dazhalan**, a small street running at right angles to the boulevard of Qianmen Dajie, has old established shops and businesses of excellent reputation, and is still an attraction for people from the Beijing suburbs as well as the provinces. Not far away is **Liulichang**, a shopping street restored to its original style for tourists, which has almost everything that China can offer by way of art and kitsch. The number-one shopping district today is still **Wanfujing**, a street that runs in a northerly direction from the Beijing Hotel and is now lined with fashionable boutiques and fast-food restaurants, lending it the appearance of a street in Hong Kong or Singapore.

Outside these historic city districts, however, huge concrete tower blocks have sprouted. In the northwest lies the scientific and intellectual quarter, including China's most famous universities, Beijing and Qinghua. The Chaoyang district, to the east, is the largest industrial area of the city. Bicycles still crowd the streets, but the cyclists are segregated from the motorized vehicle traffic, and today there is a flood of cars and buses that jams city streets and the multiple-lane ring highways that encircle Beijing. The local public transport system is insufficiently developed and hopelessly overcrowded, although the subway system is more tolerable for visitors, and faster.

The rhythm of the seasons is similar

Bird fanciers.

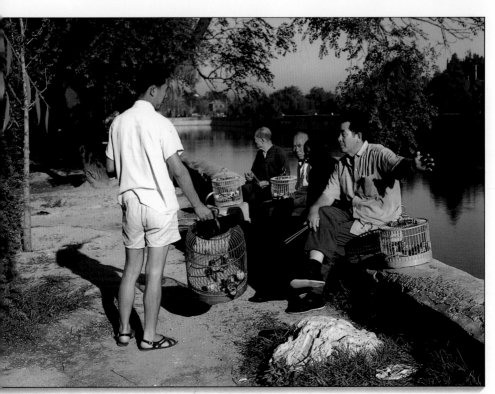

to that in central Europe. The summers are hot and long, winters cold and dry. When sandstorms whirl through the city in spring, Beijing hardly dares to breathe. The fine dust forces its way through cracks and crevices in homes, which are badly insulated. Moreover, vehicular exhaust, massive construction projects and industrial output have turned Beijing into a polluted city – the air is thick and dusty and leaves people red-eyed and scratchy-throated.

Yet an early morning walk through a park – any park – reveals undreamed-of impressions: the sound of a moon fiddle accompanied by an aria from a Beijing opera; the chirping of birds, their cages hung in the trees; the sight of graceful sword dancers and noiseless *taiji* practitioners; and more recently, gymnastics accompanied by disco music for the elderly. (Indeed, Beijing seems at times a city of dancing: ballroom, folk, disco.)

People in this crowded city grab every meter of available space and make use of it. Grassy spots by freeway entrance ramps are used for evening exercises.

The broad plazas outside the Forbidden City are turned into dance halls that would make Lawrence Welk proud. The steps and empty concrete expanses in front of office buildings are shared by grandparents and grandchildren.

Imperial Palace: In the ancient past, in the early morning when the fourth guard watch of the night was proclaimed by powerful strokes from Gulou, the Drum Tower, the mandarins in the imperial city would push aside their silken bed curtains, dress and tidy up, then step into their porter-carried litters, which bore them to the imperial morning audience in **Gugong**, the Imperial Palace. A eunuch would show them their place, arranged according to rank, and there, kneeling in silence, they would receive instructions from the emperor on the Dragon Throne.

Behind the walls, more than 10 meters (30 ft) high, and within the 50-meter-broad (160-ft) moat, life in the palace was dictated by a multitude of rules and taboos. (Entrance was denied to ordinary mortals, of course.) Today, **Wumen, or Meridian Gate.**

the gateway serves as a gigantic entrance for visitors; it leads to one of the most fascinating displays of Chinese cultural history, and to what is probably the best-preserved site of classical Chinese architecture.

In 1421, after 17 years of construction, the Ming emperor Yongle moved into the palace, and up until the founding of the republic in 1911, the palace was residence and center of the world during the reign of 24 emperors – from the Ming dynasty up until the last emperor, Puyi. It has 9,000 rooms in which an estimated 8,000 to 10,000 people lived (including 3,000 eunuchs, as well as maids and concubines), all within an area of 70 hectares (180 acres).

The entire site can be divided into two large areas: **Waichao**, the Outer Court, in the south, and in the rear, **Neiting**, the Inner Residence.

Approaching from **Wumen** (Meridian Gate) are the three great halls and courtyards of the outer area. **Taihedian** (Hall of Supreme Harmony) is the first and most impressive of these, and at the

same time it is the largest building in the palace. In its center is the skillfully-carved, gold-colored **Dragon Throne**, from which the emperor ruled over the Middle Kingdom. This was also where the most solemn ceremonies – the New Year's festivities or enthronement of a new emperor – were held. The courtyard held up to 90,000 spectators.

On the other side of the imposing architecture of the Outer Court, to the north and separated from it by **Qianqingmen** (Gate of Heavenly Purity), lies a labyrinth of gates, doors, pavilions, gardens and palaces. This was the residence of the imperial family, mostly female, as the emperor and castrated eunuchs were the only males permitted to enter here.

The center of this private section is formed by three rear halls, **Sanhougong**. However, the emperors did not live there after the Qinq period, but carried on state business primarily in front of **Qianqinggong** (Palace of Heavenly Purity). Actual political intrigues and maneuvering took place in the inter-

Dragon
Throne.

linked rooms to the left and right of this palace. Here, the more influential eunuchs and concubines were rivals for power and influence within the court; this was the scene of plots and intrigues, and of deaths – natural and unnatural.

The well in the northeast, just behind **Ningshougong** (Palace of Peace and Longevity), was the place of one such episode. A concubine of Emperor Guanxu had dared, in 1900, to oppose the ambitious Empress Dowager Cixi. As punishment, the concubine was rolled up in a carpet and thrown down into the narrow shaft of the well by eunuchs.

Government guides can be hired – for a princely sum – outside the Forbidden City, and there is also a helpful and informative audio tape that can be rented. Note that Westerners may be asked by Chinese tourists to pose repeatedly in family and group photos; although most people in Beijing have long since grown accustomed to seeing foreigners, most Chinese tourists are from outside Beijing, and foreigners are still something of a curiosity.

Nestling closely against the southern walls of the palace, near Tiananmen, **Zhongshan Gongyuan** (Sun Yatsen Park) continues to display the impressive imperial architecture and landscaping. In the park, there used to be a temple honoring the gods of the earth and of fertility. The triumphal arch near the southern entrance was originally set up in a different place in honor of the German ambassador, Baron von Ketteler, who was murdered at the beginning of the Boxer Rebellion.

The former shrine of the imperial ancestors, now known as the People's Cultural Park and functioning as something of a college for continuing education, dates from the Ming dynasty. Here, the ancestral tablets of the imperial forebears, which the emperor was required to honor, were kept.

On 1 October 1949, Mao Zedong, Chairman of the Communist Party, proclaimed the founding of the People's Republic of China from **Tiananmen** (Gate of Heavenly Peace). Today, his portrait gazes south from this spot onto **Tiananmen Square**, which was quad-rupled in size during the 1950s so that up to a million people could gather in the square. Rallies of the Red Guards took place here during the Cultural Revolution, as did the 1989 democracy demonstrations, ending only when the government – after pulling the plug on the world's media – used the army and tanks to oust the demonstrators, resulting in many deaths.

In the center of the square is an obelisk, unveiled in 1958 as a monument to the heroes of the nation and a perfect example of the Socialist Realism style. In 1959, **Renmindahiutang** (Great Hall of the People), on the west side of the square, was officially opened. This is an impressive building in the Soviet Neo-Classical monumental style, and where the People's Congress meets. The massive facades of the **Museum of Chinese History** and the **Museum of the Revolution** border the square to the east.

After the death of Mao, a mausoleum for him was built. Even today, when the teachings of the little red book of quotations have long gone out of fashion,

Old Summer Palace.

except for tourists, people from all over China visit **Mao's mausoleum**, filing respectfully past Mao's embalmed body, lying in a rose-hued, glass enclosure.

Just steps away from the mausoleum, visitors get a graphic picture of how socialism is being consigned to the dustbin of history by a feverish consumerism, as visitors are ushered through a small bazaar where everything from Mao busts to laundry detergent are for sale.

To the northwest of the Imperial Palace, in the grounds of today's **Beihai Gongyuan** (Northern Lake Park), was the winter residence of the Mongol emperor Kublai Khan. Now, only legends remain of his former palace on **Qinghuadao** (Jade Island), the site of **Bai Ta** (White Dagoba), 35 meters (115 ft) tall and a Buddhist shrine dating from 1651, built in the Tibetan style. At the foot of the shrine, on the shores of the wide lake that dominates the park, imperial cuisine in appropriate style is available in Fangshan, a gourmet restaurant. Tuancheng (Round Town), in the southern part of the grounds, was

once the administrative center of the Mongol Yuan dynasty. From here is a good view of Zhongnanhai (Southern and Central Lake), site of the Politburo and State Council grounds.

Summer palaces: The great aesthete and Qing emperor Qianlong, who ruled from 1736 to 1795, had a huge masterpiece of landscaping and architecture created in the northwest of Beijing: **Yuanmingyuan** (Garden of Perfect Purity), or more commonly in English, the Old Summer Palace. Structures here were in the Western style, built according to plans by an Italian Jesuit and based upon European models such as the palace of Versailles. Only ruins remain today; during the Second Opium War (1856–1860), British and French troops ravished the palace and reduced it to rubble.

The dynasty built a replacement nearby, in the grounds laid out by Qianlong as a place of retirement for his mother. The new summer residence took on special interest for the famous (or infamous) Empress Dowager Cixi, who

Summer Palace.

fulfilled a wonderful, if rather expensive, dream in 1888. Using absconded money that had been intended for the building of a naval fleet, she constructed **Yiheyuan** (Garden of Cultivated Harmony), or the Summer Palace. Originally a concubine of the third rank, Cixi had placed herself on the Dragon Throne after the death of the emperor and ruled in an unscrupulous and self-centered way for 50 years, in the name of her young child.

As in every classical Chinese garden, water and mountains (usually represented by rocks) determine the landscape of Yiheyuan: the lake **Kunming** covers three quarters of the total area of more than 30 square kilometers (10 sq mi); on its shore is **Wanshou Shan** (Hill of Longevity). Over bridges and up stairs, through gates and halls is the massive **Foxiangge** (Pagoda of the Incense of Buddha), which crowns the top of Wanshou Shan.

In the eastern corner is a special jewel of the classical Chinese art of garden design, **Xiequyuan** (Garden of Joy and Harmony), a complete and picturesque copy of a lotus pool garden from Wuxi.

In order to make it more difficult for strangers to spy into the grounds, **Renshoudian** (Hall of Benevolence and Longevity) was built right next to the eastern gate, **Dongmen**, now the main gate. Behind it lay the private apartments of Cixi; today, these rooms are also a theatrical museum. Here, Cixi used to enjoy operatic performances by her 384-strong ensemble of eunuchs.

Of light wooden construction and decorated with countless painted scenes from Chinese mythology, **Changlang** (Long Corridor) runs parallel to the northern shore of the lake, linking the palace's scattered buildings into one harmonious whole. It ends in the vicinity of **Qiuyangfang** (Marble Boat), a ridiculous mockery in which Cixi, looking out over the lake, had tea.

Tiantan: Twice a year, a splendid and magnificent procession of some 1,000 eunuchs, courtiers and ministers would leave Gugong, the Imperial Palace, for **Tiantan** (Temple of Heaven) to the **Tiantan.**

south. Only twice a year, then, would the western gate be opened for the emperor, and each time he would spend a night of fasting and celibacy in **Zhaigong** (Palace of Abstinence) prior to the ritual ceremonies of sacrifice the next morning. At the winter solstice he expressed thanks for the previous harvest, and on the 15th day of the first month he begged the gods of sun and moon, clouds and rain, thunder and lightning to bless the coming harvest.

Set in the middle of a park of 270 hectares (670 acres), Tiantan, an outstanding example of religious architecture, dates from the Ming period. Destroyed several times, including by lightning, it was last rebuilt in 1890, and has been open to the public since 1949. The temple grounds are square, although the northern edge follows a semicircle, a symbolic expression of the fact that the emperor, in offering his sacrifices, had to leave the square-shaped earth for the round-roofed heaven.

An exquisite example of Chinese wooden buildings, constructed without the use of a single nail, is the round, 40-meter-high (130-ft) **Qiniandian** (Hall of Prayer for Good Harvests). With its three levels and covered with deep blue tiles that symbolize the color of heaven, the roof is supported by 28 pillars. The four largest ones, in the center, represent the four seasons; the double ring of twelve pillars represents the 12 months, as well as the traditional divisions of the Chinese day, each comprising two hours.

In the south of the park lies a white, circular marble terrace, **Hianqiutan** (Altar of Heaven), and the so-called **Echo Wall**, famous for its acoustics.

Temples and shrines: As an imperial city, the Beijing of Ming and Qing times was not just a favored place for magnificent palaces and broad parks. Here, also, the great religions of China had impressive sacred buildings. Unfortunately, many of the Buddhist, Daoist, and Tibetan shrines and temples, along with mosques and churches, were damaged or destroyed during the Cultural Revolution, or were earlier turned into factories, barracks or schools after 1949.

Yonghegong.

However, the most important religious sites have been restored and reopened.

Fayuan Si (Temple of the Source of Buddhist Doctrine), a Buddhist shrine dating from the seventh century, is probably the oldest surviving temple in the city, located in the southwestern Xuanwu district. Today, it is a training center for Buddhist novices.

Just around the corner, on Niu Dajie, is the oldest mosque in Beijing, **Niujie Mosque**. The style of the building, which is almost a thousand years old, is an interesting combination of traditional Chinese architecture and elements of Arabic and Middle Eastern influence.

The most magnificent and most elaborately-restored sacred building in Beijing is **Yonghegong**, a Lamaist temple in the northeast of the old city. Originally the private residence of a prince, it was turned into a monastery when its owner was promoted to emperor in 1723; according to ancient Chinese custom, the former residence of a Son of Heaven had to be dedicated to religious purposes once he left. From the mid 1700s,

this was a center of Tibetan art and religion, which at the same time offered the central imperial power welcome opportunities for influencing – and controlling – ethnic minorities in Tibet and Mongolia. In the three-storied central section of **Wanfuge** (Pavilion of Ten Thousand Happiness) is a statue, 23 meters (75-ft) tall, of the Maitreya Buddha, which is supposed to have been carved from a single piece of sandalwood. Only a few steps away is the **Kongmiao** (Temple of Confucius), inviting a quiet look. Dating from the Yuan dynasty, it now houses part of the metropolitan museum.

On the other side of the Imperial Palace, due west along Fuxingmennei Dajie, **Baiyunguan** (Temple of the White Cloud) was once the greatest Daoist center of northern China. Today, a small group of monks lives here – only old and young. Due to the political climate between 1960 and 1976, a middle-aged generation of monks doesn't exist.

For a look at Beijing as a working city, not just a collection of temples and imperial buildings, walk through its narrow neighborhood streets. A bustling area, west from the top of Qianmen, is Dazhalan, a narrow and crowded *hutong* filled with vendors selling pirated CDs, T-shirts and electronics. An area of antiques is nearby on Liulichang. Visitors can also take a pedicab tour of a hutong here, which is a bit sanitized but nonetheless allows visitors to peer into a traditional, and fast-disappearing, way of life in Beijing.

The temples that lie at a distance from the dusty asphalt of the inner city and the suburbs have their own special charm. **Biyun Si** (Temple of the Azure Clouds), with its impressive Pavilion of 500 Luohan and its 35-meter-high (115-ft) stupa, lies at the feet of the Western Mountains and next to **Xiang Shan** (Fragrant Hill).

Not far away is the extensive complex of **Wofo Si** (Temple of the Reclining Buddha). Its main attraction is a reclining bronze figure depicting Buddha shortly before his entry into nirvana. A miniature train takes visitors from the bottom of the hill to the temple.

Western Mountains, near Xiang Shan.

LIFE IN THE HUTONG

In a region formerly protected by the Great Wall, Beijing was once hidden behind its own city walls. And within the city walls were its citizens, each with a wall built around their own homes and courtyards, or *siheyuan*.

Today, ring roads and walls of high-rise buildings have taken over the function of the city wall, itself a victim of town planning. In the city center, faceless buildings of the 1950s protect an inner core, a labyrinth of crumbling old grey alleyways, some dating back several centuries. These are the *hutong*. Once the center of life for Beijingers living outside the Imperial Palace, hutong are now threatened with eradication by urban redevelopment.

Hutong history: Beijing is a Mongol city. The nomadic conquerors who made Beijing their capital brought their way of life and language with them.

Horses were part of their lifestyle. Wells were dug and horse-troughs, *hut* or *hot* in Mongolian (as in *Hohhot*, the capital of the province of Inner Mongolia), were set up. The people of Beijing, attempting to assimilate, turned these Mongol wells into the Chinese hutong.

Mongols or no Mongols, Beijingers could hardly leave their houses and homes lying unprotected amid the horse-troughs. All they had to do was close up the small spaces between the houses with a wall and privacy was restored. It was even simpler to build on to the wall of their neighbors, although no one was allowed to build so as to block another householder's route to water. In this way, the tangle of hutong grew, just wide enough to let a rider through.

The houses and courtyards, hidden away and boxed in, are themselves closed off with wooden gates, on which one can often see carved characters intended to bring good fortune to the house owner and to his trade. Just inside the gates are the ghost walls. Apparently, a Chinese ghost can only move straight ahead; the ghost wall bars any further progress beyond the gate.

Courtyard culture: Traditionally, the introverted architecture of these Chinese courtyard tells much about the Chinese family. In a traditional hutong courtyard, there will be a few trees and many flowers and cacti, in front of which are the family bicycles. Three or four single-story buildings overlook the courtyard.

In the siheyuan of families who are higher in the social order, a second and third courtyard may adjoin the first. There may be two small "ear courtyards" to the sides, which contain the kitchens or serve as storage spaces. But this type of housing has become a rarity, as space is needed for the ever-growing population. What were once single-family dwellings have now been adapted for four or five families.

Increasingly, many of these hutong courtyards are filled with plywood shanties housing migrants from the countryside. Most of these hutong buildings today are, in fact, hopelessly overcrowded. But even in such courtyards, there is always space for a chessboard to be spread out.

The names of each hutong tell its story by describing the life it contains. Some indicate professions or crafts: Bowstring Makers' Lane, Cloth Lane, Hat Lane. Some lanes, if mostly populated by a single family, are named after that family.

Many names are due to the shape of the lane. The Buffalo Horn Curve is, of course, curved, as is the Dog Tail Lane, of which there are at least eight in Beijing. Sometimes the names echo the military organization of the Manchu: Mongol Camp, Muslim Camp, or Camp by the Incense Burner all go back to former troop positions. ∎

Hutong in western Beijing.

OUTSIDE BEIJING

Great Wall: It's been said that the only construction by human hands visible to the naked eye from space is **Wanli Changcheng**, the Great Wall. (It's difficult to find documentation of exactly who saw it from space, and when.)

It winds its way like an endless slender dragon from the Yellow Sea through five provinces and two autonomous regions and up into the Gobi Desert. The very earliest stages of the building of the wall date from the fifth century BC, but the present course was basically determined around 220 BC by Qin Shi Huangdi, the first Chinese emperor and the founder of the empire. He had smaller, previously-constructed sections linked and extended northwards to ward off the horse-riding nomads. Soldiers and peasants from all parts of the country were conscripted, spending several years of their lives building this "wall of ten thousand *li*" – Wanli Changcheng.

(One li is about 500 meters.) Blocks of rock weighing several hundred kilograms had to be heaved up the steep slopes, and many people paid with their lives for this project.

From ten in the morning until three in the afternoon, the pass of **Badaling**, the section of the wall that is most accessible from Beijing, turns into a tourist carnival. The avalanche of visitors streams past countless stalls selling souvenirs promoting this great symbol of Chinese civilization. Then it moves in two different directions, attempting to conquer the steep climb. From the high points are views of the breathtaking scenery, where the mighty wall climbs up and down in the midst of a fascinating mountain landscape.

The scenery at **Mutianyu** is almost as imposing. This part of the wall, some 120 kilometers (75 mi) to the north of Beijing, was restored a few years ago and is less busy than Badaling. Parts of the wall here remain as they were – it has not been rebuilt – so visitors have a better sense of its antiquity. The walk is **Great Wall.**

difficult but not treacherous. Cable cars take visitors from the bottom of the hills nearly to the wall itself.

Ming tombs: A visit to Badaling is normally combined with a trip to the **Shisan Ling**, the Ming tombs. Protected by a range of hills to the north, east and west, the tombs of 13 of the 16 Ming emperors lie in this geomantically-favorable spot. Entry from the south on the valley floor passes through numerous gates of honor along Shendao (Soul Path), flanked by the stone guardians of the tombs. The guard of honor of twelve human figures represents civil and military dignitaries and officials; there are also lions, horses, camels, elephants and mythical creatures – 24 stone figures form the animal guard of honor.

Two of the 13 tombs are open to the public. **Chang Ling** is the final resting place of Emperor Yongle. The mound of the tomb has not been excavated, and one can only admire the magnificent hall of sacrifice. In Yongle's day, in the fifteenth century, human sacrifice was by no means unusual; 16 imperial concubines accompanied him on his journey to the underworld. In Wanli's reign (1573–1620), this terrible custom was no longer practiced. The entrance to **Ding Ling**, the 27-meter-deep (89-ft), dank vault of Wanli, was long sought for in vain, located only in 1957. His primary wife and one concubine are buried with the emperor.

Day trips: Tianjin, Chengde and Beidaihe attract many visitors from Beijing out for the day – usually on a day-trip by train. **Tianjin** has a population of seven million and is one of China's major cities. Some 140 kilometers (90 mi) to the southeast of Beijing, it is noted for its port and its carpets. Because of its architecture, Tianjin has more of a city atmosphere than Beijing.

Chengde, formerly Jehol, was the summer residence of the Qing emperors and, at the same time, a politically-important meeting place for the leaders of ethnic minorities. The "palace for escaping from the heat" – a translation of Chengde – is surrounded by a magnificent park.

LOWER HUANG HE: SHANDONG & QUFU

The bridge over **Huang He** (Yellow River) at Jinan, Shandong's provincial capital, is most decidedly not an architectural sensation. But it is still pointed out with pride by Chinese to visitors, a symbol of the apparent taming of the Huang He, one of the two fateful rivers of China. The river has changed its course countless times over the centuries, resulting in disastrous floods in the western part of Shandong. Not until 1933 did its lower course find its present outflow into Bo Hai (Bo Sea). Half the province of Shandong (Mountainous East) lives off the fruitful flood plain of the river, despite the devastation.

Culturally and historically, **Shandong Province** – with 75 million inhabitants one of the most populous provinces – is a region with a wealth of traditions. This was the home of the important ancient states of Qi and Luo, and perhaps more importantly, the thinker Confucius came from Shandong.

The province was the home of the famous, noble-spirited "bandits of Liangshan Moor". In the same spirit as England's Robin Hood, they distributed among the peasantry the spoils they had taken from the more wealthy.

Here, too, the secret Society for Peace and Justice had its beginnings, which was to enter history with the English name of Boxers – and the Boxer Rebellion – around the turn of the century.

Malicious tongues claim, not without justification, that there's nothing worth seeing in the provincial capital of **Jinan**, with a population of about two million people. All the same, there are many fountains in its parks, and pleasure-boat rides on Daming, the Lake of Great Purity. Weifang, in the middle of the peninsula, is famous for its New Year pictures and kites. In the north is **Yantai**, with its inviting beaches and scenery. Not far away, on a high rock projecting into the sea, is Penglai, home of the Eight Immortals of Daoism.

Dao mountain: A mere 80 kilometers (50 mi) away, in a sort of religious counterpoint, is the mountain of **Tai Shan**, a Daoist national shrine.

In popular Chinese religion, mountains are considered to be living beings. Their stabilizing power perpetuates the cosmic order; they create clouds and rain. Tai Shan, the Exalted Mountain, is the most easterly of the five sacred mountains of Daoism, and, as life comes from the east, it is the holiest of all five. It is supposed to have risen from the head of Pangu, the creator of the world according to Chinese mythology.

Tai'an is the name of the town at the foot of the mountain. In its center lies **Daimiao**, a magnificent temple honoring the god of Tai Shan. Daimiao is a complex of more than 600 buildings, including Tiangongdian (Hall of Heavenly Gifts), one of the most massive classic temple halls in China. It contains a monumental fresco that is more than 60 meters (200 ft) long. Less than half a mile to the north of the temple, at Daizong Fang (Gate of the God of Tai Shan), lies

the starting point of the seemingly-endless ascent to the 1,545-meter-high (5,070-ft) summit. In earlier years, emperors and mandarins were carried up the 6,293 steps in litters.

Pilgrims and travelers need a whole day for the journey, or they can cheat a bit and ride to a halfway point by minibus, then ascend by cable car almost as far as the summit. But those who take the quick way miss the splendid variety of this open-air museum: temples, pavilions, shrines, stone steles, inscriptions and waterfalls. A little way off the main path, the text of the *Diamond Sutra* has been engraved in a huge block of stone. The 1,050 characters, each some 50 centimeters (20 in) high, are considered a masterpiece of the calligrapher's art. Once past Zhongtianmen (Middle Gate of Heaven), the ascent becomes steeper. Passing Wudaifu Song (Pines of the Fifth Order of Officials), which, according to legend, were given this title by emperor Qin Shi Huangdi after sheltering him from a thunderstorm, the path leads to Nantianmen (Southern Gate

Sunrise on Tai Shan.

of Heaven), which is the entrance to the realm of the immortals on the summit.

Up here where it is pleasantly cool in summer and uncomfortably cold in winter, the path leads to the main shrine of the mountain, **Bixia Si** (Temple of the Princess of the Azure Clouds). As the daughter of the god of Tai Shan, the princess of the azure clouds is an attraction for rural people, particularly women, who come to pray for the well-being of their children and those yet to come. The Jade Emperor is the supreme Daoist god, and a small temple dedicated to him is accordingly placed on the actual summit of the mountain. If the air is clear, the view is overwhelming. However, all too often, there are clouds just below the ridge of the mountain, and even the main attraction of Tai Shan, the much-praised natural spectacle of the sunrise, can only be seen in all its splendor on less than 100 days annually.

Confucian heritage: In 1919, during a visit to Beijing, Kong Linyu died at the age of 76, but not before he fathered two girls. He was a descendant of the philosopher and moral teacher Kong Fuzi (Master Kong in English). The name was later latinized to Confucius.

According to tradition, the two daughters could not continue Kong Linyu's line. But his concubine was in the fifth month of her pregnancy. Rival factions of the Kong clan posted guards outside the chamber of the pregnant woman. Still, all the doors of the house were opened, so as to make it easy for the "wise ancestor", Confucius, to find his way back for rebirth. On 23 February 1920, Kong Decheng was born, representing the 77th generation after Confucius. Succession was assured, and the "first family under Heaven" heaved a sigh of relief.

However, 17 days later, Kong Linyu's main – and childless – wife poisoned her rival and the mother of the heir. The murder almost went unpunished. A distant relative who provided the poison took opium, at the time a favored method of committing suicide.

The scene of this family drama was the **Kong residence** in Qufu. Originally

Tomb of a descendant of Confucius, in Qufu.

built in the sixteenth century during the Ming dynasty, this mansion was home to the Kong clan until 1948, when, with the imminent threat of a Communist takeover of China, the last of the line left for exile in Taiwan.

The outside of the residence looks rather plain, but with its 450 to 600 rooms (published accounts vary), it is in fact something of an extensive mansion. Several hundred servants were once employed here in the front part of the building, the Yamen, which consists of administrative buildings and audience halls. In the rear part, which could only be entered by a few selected servants and ladies' maids, were the living quarters of the ducal Kong family. The contents of the residence consist of valuable works of art, calligraphy, articles of clothing and extensive archive material. Nowadays, there is a hotel in the western wing.

Now geared for bus loads of tourists, a quieter **Qufu** was the home of Confucius. He was born in this neighborhood and taught for many years, trying to influence everyday practical politics with his moral doctrine.

This is also where Confucius died; he is buried in **Konglin**, the forest belonging to the Kong family a few kilometers north of town, under a simple grass-covered mound. The way to the mound is lined with human and animal figures in stone, a custom otherwise reserved for emperors.

In imperial times, Qufu was *the* sacred town of China, almost on the same level as Jerusalem or Mecca. Still bearing witness to this former status is the size and splendor of **Kongmiao,** the Confucius temple in the center of the small town. A temple is supposed to have been built on this site as early as 478 BC, one year after the death of Confucius.

Coming from the south, a three-story, 23-meter-high (75-ft) pavilion, whose origins date back to the eleventh century, pops into view. Passing the 13 pavilions in which steles with imperial inscriptions are kept, the road leads to the eighteenth-century Dachengdian, at

Kongmiao, ceremony in front of the main hall.

30 meters high the main hall of the temple, in which the sacrificial rites in honor of Confucius used to be carried out. Unique from an artistic and historical point of view are the 28 stone pillars, which are reported to have 1,296 dragons carved on them. The yellow color of the roof, a color otherwise reserved exclusively for the Imperial Palace, once again emphasizes the position of the great philosopher Kong Fuzi in Chinese tradition.

Ever since the Han dynasty, the increasing reverence accorded to Confucius has gone hand in hand with the continuous and unstoppable growth of the prestige and power of his successors. The importance of Confucian thought in upholding the state was acknowledged by the imperial house, insofar as they increasingly awarded the Kong family more titles, privileges and land. Towards the end of the last century, the successor of the "Wise One" was one of the wealthiest property owners in the country, presiding over his own judicial system and a private army.

German desires: Ferdinand von Richthofen – baron, geographer and adventurer – had been keeping a lookout for a place in which Germany could realize its colonial ambitions on Chinese soil. In 1897, two priests of the Catholic Steyler Mission were killed by Boxers, providing an excuse for the German emperor, Wilhelm II, to establish a colony in the Far East.

Before the first German frigates and gunboats moored in the harbor, **Qingdao**, the Green Island, was still a little fishing village. The military superiority of Germany forced the Chinese into an agreement to lease the Bay of Kiaochow (now known as **Jiaozhou**) to them. German officers, sailors and businessmen were soon promenading up and down the Kaiser Wilhelm Ufer and dining in the seafront Prinz Heinrich Hotel. They drank beer from the Germania brewery, which is still exported all over the world today under the name of Tsingtao (the old Wade-Giles spelling of Qingdao). This beer, however, owes its excellent flavor not only to the brewing expertise of the former colonial rulers, but to the excellent water of **Lao Shan**, a nearby range of mountains with wild and beautiful scenery, and many Daoist temples.

There is still evidence of a colonial past in Qingdao, where the nineteenth-century neo-Gothic style of the buildings is reminiscent of small German towns. There are bright, red-tiled roofs, half-timbered façades, sloping gables, triangular windows in the attics, the tall towers of the Catholic cathedral, and, a special little jewel, the former governor's palace, which has the flair of a Prussian hunting lodge. It is left to the Chinese pagoda on top of what was once known as Bismarck Hill, around which the houses of the town are grouped, to restore the actual cultural surroundings.

The German presence in China did not last long. In 1914, at the beginning of the World War I, Japan conquered the German colony.

Even though the suburbs of Qingdao are now rather unattractive, the town has preserved its character as a holiday and seaside resort.

Left, Catholic cathedral, Qingdao.

CONFUCIUS

Next to Daoism and Buddhism, Confucianism is the great doctrine that has left a lasting impression on life in China for more than 2,000 years. It has determined behavior for all areas of social life, right down to the smallest detail. Even today, certain ways of behaviour and certain views in China can be explained with reference to Confucian tradition.

Confucius is known in Chinese as Kong Qiu. (It was the Jesuits who latinized the Chinese title Kong Fuzi, "Master Kong", to Confucius.) He was born in 551 BC, a member of an impoverished aristocratic clan in the state of Lu, in the southwest of modern Shandong Province. China did not yet exist as a single unified nation, and states within its territory were constantly struggling for supremacy.

In this age of great social upheaval, Confucius appeared, a traveling teacher who tried to influence the fate of the country through his group of pupils and through direct contact – as adviser or minister – with the ruler. His ideal was the virtuous ruler whose example would lead all his subjects to keep moral standards. The kingdom whose ruler did not measure up to this moral standard must inevitably fall. Natural catastrophes and bad harvests were a sign that a ruler's mandate had been withdrawn.

Apart from this belief, the recognition of hierarchy, whether expressed in family relationships or in loyalty to the ruling house, is the cornerstone of Confucian thought. Relationships between human beings, and not speculation about the existence of any God, are the focal point. Confucius tried to restore the *li* customs and rites, which were believed to date back to the wise rule of the Zhou dynasty, but which had fallen into disuse. In these matters, he could be considered a traditionalist.

Yet he was ahead of his time in his rationalism and enlightenment, which caused him to dismiss the mysticism connected with rites. A human being should try to be truly good. Nobility is not determined by birth, but by an attitude of mind and the actions resulting from it. Nobility of mind and a hierarchical order of ruler and subject, ancestor and descendant, father and son, man and woman, old and young, teacher and student, form the basis for right action that keeps in mind the well-being of all humanity.

Confucius died in 479 BC and was buried in Qufu, in Shandong Province, where the temple built in his honor can still be visited. Even today, generations of Kongs are able to trace their descent in a direct line from Confucius.

During Confucius's lifetime, his teachings met with little response from the rulers. Under Emperor Qin Shi Huangdi (221–206 BC), followers of Confucius were even buried alive and their writings burned. However, the Han dynasty raised Confucianism to a state doctrine, for it offered them a problem-free system of administration and a strengthening of the power structure. Apart from a short predominance of Buddhism, Confucianism has been inextricably bound up with the imperial system ever since, and has formed the ethical basis of Chinese society.

The Communists, however, saw an ideological opponent in Confucianism. During the Cultural Revolution, their struggle came to a head with an anti-Confucius campaign, which was, however, less of a debate about the contents of his teaching than a defamation of his character.

Over the last few years, attempts have been made to hold an examination of, and debate about, Confucianism. ∎

Portrait of Confucius in the robes of court official.

XI'AN: CRADLE OF CIVILIZATION

The cradle of Chinese civilization anchors itself at the bend of **Huang He** (Yellow River), in the central provinces of Shaanxi and Henan. Here, in the fertile valleys of the loess-covered landscape, the ancestors of the Han Chinese settled in the third century BC. The fertile soil encouraged establishment of settlements, with the river irrigating the land. Too, the erratic personality of the river – flooding and changing course with regularity – forced people to work in close cooperation. Eventually, the first and strongest states of ancient China developed in this region.

Xi'an, capital of Shaanxi Province, lies in the protected valley of the river Wei, a few dozen miles west of the Wei's confluence with Huang He. From this valley, the emperor Qin Shi Huangdi unified China for the first time.

During the Tang dynasty (618–907), Xi'an was the largest city in the world. Chang'an (Heavenly Peace), as it was called back then, was linked to many central Asian regions and Europe via the Silk Road. Thousands of foreign traders lived in the city.

For more than 1,000 years, Xi'an served as the capital for nearly a dozen imperial dynasties. Following the demise of the Tang dynasty, however, Xi'an's importance began to evaporate. Its historical importance blossomed once again in 1936, when two generals of the Kuomintang kidnapped their leader, Chiang Kaishek, and forced him to cease his civil war with the Communists and cooperate with them against the Japanese – an incident considered to be pivotal in modern Chinese history.

Today, Xi'an is a modern industrial town known for its aviation and textile industries, and for its several universities and research institutes. About five million people call Xi'an home, and it is an important center for travel into China's interior. This old imperial capital is easily reached from all the important cities in China. A direct flight from Beijing takes about two hours, while the train journey of around 1,165 kilometers (725 mi) takes almost 24 hours.

Xi'an's climate has moderate seasonal variation. The winters are not too cold, while in summer, the temperature can rise to 30°C (85°F). At the beginning of spring and autumn, the days are pleasantly cool; the rainy season lasts from July to October.

Wheat and cotton is grown in the region around Xi'an. In some villages, one might find the traditional loess cave dwellings, which are increasingly being replaced with modern brick buildings.

Old imperial center: While the center of Xi'an retains its historical layout from the Tang dynasty, it is largely overwhelmed by modern buildings, heavy traffic and a persistent haze choked by exhaust of cars and buses that leaves residents with reddened eyes and sore throats. The air hangs heavy.

In its earlier days, the metropolis was surrounded by a large wall. The city itself stretched over nine kilometers (6 mi) from east to west, and nearly eight

kilometers (5 mi) north to south. All roads in the town itself were built in a classic Chinese grid pattern, running straight north-south and east-west, meeting at right angles.

While the grid layout persists today, the layout of the ancient city is not quite identical with the modern one. Back then, Dayan Ta (Great Wild Goose Pagoda) was in the center of town. Although the walls built during the Tang dynasty are no longer there, 14 kilometers (8 mi) of the wall from the Ming dynasty still surround the center. The city has been rebuilding the 12-meter-thick (40-ft) walls, and the moat outside the wall has also been reconstructed and integrated within a park.

Modern Xi'an has wide, tree-lined avenues that give shade in the hot summers, and, too, help distinguish Xi'an from most other provincial capitals, which are bleak and monochromatic.

In the city center, where the city's two main roads intersect, is **Zhonglou** (Bell Tower). This renovated 23-meter-high (75-ft) tower, which dates from 1384, is encircled by downtown's shopping and commercial center. From Zhonglou east runs **Dong Dajie**, with many shops and restaurants. From Dong Dajie to the north is **Jiefang Lu**, leading to the railway station.

One of the biggest free markets in Xi'an is not far from Zhonglou, towards the south of the town. Its many snack bars are run by Hui Muslims selling delicious food, such mutton-filled sesame rolls.

A few minutes' walk from Zhonglou to the northwest is **Gulou**, the Drum Tower. Resembling the Bell Tower and dating from the eighteenth century, it was rebuilt after the 1949 Communist revolution. The Drum Tower highlights the Muslim quarter to the west. (Some 60,000 Hui Muslims live in Xi'an.) Lined with souvenir and other shops, alleys winding through the Hui neighborhoods lead to **Da Qingzhen Si** (Great Mosque). The mosque, which dates back to the Ming period and has been renovated several times, bears more resemblance to a Chinese temple with

Hu fu, a tiger figure from the Qin dynasty.

its inner courtyards. The main prayer hall is accessible only to Muslims.

Farther along the road, in the direction of Xi Dajie, is **Ximen** (Western Gate), one of the remaining 13 gates encircling the ancient city. In the hall above the gate are interesting historic exhibitions and displays.

Near the south gate of the city wall, **Nanmen**, and in a former Confucian temple is **Shaanxi Sheng Bowuguan**, the provincial museum, with more than 4,000 exhibits in three buildings, much of it relating to the Silk Road.

The first building has a chronologically-arranged exhibition about Chinese history from earliest times to the end of the Tang dynasty, with well-preserved artifacts (including unusual bronze objects). The museum's centerpiece is the collection of stele, with around 1,100 stone tablets on which ancient Chinese texts, including those of the Confucian classics, are engraved. The third section of the museum houses animal sculptures in stone, Tang dynasty stone friezes, bronzes and jewels, as well as Buddhist sculptures and ceramic tiles from the Han dynasty.

The museum, one of the best and most important in the nation, regularly holds special exhibitions.

Outside the city walls and about one kilometer from Nanmen, the 43-meter-high (141-ft) **Xiaoyan Ta** (Little Wild Goose Pagoda) was built in the eighth century. It was severely damaged during an earthquake eight centuries later, but was repaired in the late 1970s.

More significant than this pagoda, however, is the 73-meter-high (240-ft), seven-story **Dayan Ta** (Great Wild Goose Pagoda), anchoring the southwest end of Yanta Lu. It was built at the beginning of the Tang dynasty, in the seventh century. A noted monk, Xuanzang, went on a pilgrimage to India in 629, returning much later with many Buddhist scriptures, which were stored in the pagoda and translated into Chinese. Although only a few buildings remain of the original temple complex of 13 courtyards and over 300 rooms, a few monks have returned.

Below, Dayan Ta, Xi'an; right, countryside embroideries.

Near that pagoda, in the south of the city, is a true gem: **Shaanxi History Museum**. Opened in 1992, the modern museum is housed in a handsome building with clear and attractive displays, arranged in chronological order and labeled in English. There are displays of terracotta horses and soldiers, Ming and Qing pottery, and bronze cooking vessels that sit on tripods from the Shang and Zhou dynasties.

Terracotta warriors: The museums in the city proper give but a glimpse of Xi'an's greatest and most important attraction: **Bingmayong**, the underground Army of Terracotta Warriors.

This vast treasure lies 35 kilometers (20 mi) south of Xi'an, at the foot of Li Shan. In 1974, peasants digging a well uncovered these life-size figures of horses and warriors figures. (Visitors are sometimes invited to meet one of those farmers, if said visitors are willing to buy a book that he will autograph.)

The terracotta army is but part of a grand tomb, **Qin Shihuang Ling**, built by the first Chinese emperor, Qin Shi Huangdi. The main tomb of the emperor is about one kilometer to the west of the terracotta warriors. According to historic surveys, a splendid necropolis apparently depicting the whole of China in miniature is centered under the 47-meter-high (154-ft) mound. The necropolis itself is said to be immense in size; in order to open up the entire necropolis, 12 villages and half a dozen factories in the area would have to be relocated.

According to old records, the ceiling is said to be studded with jewels depicting the sky, and mercury was pumped in mechanically to create images of flowing rivers. (Trial digs have revealed high contents of mercury in the soil.) The official entrance to the tomb has yet to be found.

Several hundred thousand workers spent 36 years building the tomb, which the emperor, at the age of 13, ordered to be built shortly after he ascended the throne. It is also said that all of the workers and supervisors involved in its design and construction were buried alive within the tomb. Rumor has it that

At an unearthly attention for centuries.

the emperor was so superstitious and fearful that he only had the necropolis built to deceive people and is, in fact, buried somewhere else.

Some of the approximately 7,000 terracotta figures from the excavations have been restored by archaeologists and are exhibited in a hall built above the excavation site. Scientists continue to dig for more figures, and visitors can watch the work in progress while walking the site's perimeter.

The figures are arranged in typical battle formation in 11 corridors, comprised of officers, soldiers holding spears and swords (many of them authentic weapons), and others steering horse-drawn chariots. Each figure is about 1.8 meters (5 ft 9 in) tall, and each head has been individually modeled with unique facial expressions.

In the main hall of the exhibit building is a model of the entire necropolis (main tomb and other tombs); videos are shown of the excavation work. There are now three buildings in which to view the terracotta figures and weapons; other areas might one day be excavated. Another building, set up as a small museum, contains a sensational exhibit: the miniature model of a bronze chariot, with horses and coachman, from the Qin dynasty. The carriage was discovered in 1980 and is similar to carriages used by Qin Shi Huangdi on his inspection tours, alive and above ground.

Outside Xi'an: On the way back to the city is **Huaqingchi** (Hot Springs of Huaqing), in use for over 3,000 years. There are baths and pavilions in the park area, which would be pleasant enough if not for the throngs of tourists. This is where, during the Tang dynasty, the most famous concubine in China, Yang Guifei, bathed. A reproduction of the bath she is said to have used can be seen. Farther up in the mountain is the place where Chiang Kaishek was recaptured by two of his own generals during an escape attempt, after he had been taken prisoner in 1936.

A visit to the neolithic settlement of **Banpo** is interesting, 10 kilometers (6 mi) to the east of Xi'an. Some relics,

including ceramics from the Yangshao culture, are exhibited. The excavated village shows the outlines of houses and cooking areas, and is part of the museum. There is still debate about whether the people living here 6,000 years ago were a matriarchal community.

Further afield, about 60 kilometers (40 mi) from Xi'an, is **Xianyang**, the capital during the reign of Qin Shi Huangdi. Few traces are left of the legendary palaces said to exist here then. There is a museum in a former Confucian temple that contains more than 3,000 artifacts from the time of the Warring Kingdoms, and also the Han and Qin dynasties. The collection of miniature terracotta horses and soldiers, from the Han dynasty and each about 50 centimeters (20 in) in height, is particularly impressive.

Seventy kilometers (40 mi) to the northwest of Xi'an is **Zhao Ling**, the tomb of Taizong, an emperor of the Tang dynasty. The tomb also contains, in addition to that of Taizong, 167 burial sites for the other members of the imperial family. The site, near the town of **Lingquan**, covers over 20,000 hectares (50,000 acres).

About 85 kilometers (50 mi) to the northwest of Xi'an is **Qian Ling**, the joint burial place of the Tang emperor Gaozong and his wife, the empress Wu Zetian. The tomb itself has not been opened – the approach to the tomb is guarded by a "ghost avenue" of large stone sculptures of animals and dignitaries. There is a group of 61 stone sculptures, with their heads missing, apparently representing foreign dignitaries. The peasants of the region and time are said to have knocked the stone heads off when there was a famine, which they believed was caused by the presence of these foreigners.

Six of the 17 smaller tombs nearby have been excavated. A few minutes from the main tomb are the tombs of Princess Yongtai and Prince Zhanghuai. The tombs contain exquisite frescoes from the Tang dynasty.

Yan'an: Mao Zedong's Long March from Jiangxi ended in the town of Wuqi

Excavations at Banpo.

in 1936. The leaders then established their base of operations in Yan'an, staying for a decade. This small market town of just under 50,000 people is 270 kilometers (170 mi) to the north of Xi'an, where the Yan river cuts a path through the dry mountains.

Yan'an can be reached from Xi'an by overland bus (24 hours) or by plane (one hour). It can also be reached by plane from Beijing, Shenyang and Taiyuan. If taking the overland bus from Xi'an to Yan'an, stop at **Huang Ling** to visit the tomb of Huangdi, the Yellow Emperor. The tomb has long been a place of pilgrimage for Chinese.

Bao Ta, the pagoda that dominates Yan'an, originates from the Song dynasty and was restored in 1950.

Until the 1970s, when Yan'an was the national center of pilgrimage of the Cultural Revolution, it was as well known as Gugong, the Imperial Palace in Beijing. The headquarters of the military commission of the Chinese Communist Party, along with the houses of the communist leaders Mao Zedong and Zhu De, are still preserved in the Fenghuang mountains north of Yan'an. The Museum of the Revolution contains over 2,000 documents and objects from the Yan'an period, which is still praised by many older functionaries of the Chinese Communist Party as the "golden revolutionary era".

There are also some interesting Buddhist and Daoist temples in the area surrounding Yan'an.

Around Yan'an it is still possible to see the caves that are typical of this central loess landscape, and which were used during World War II by the leaders of the Communist Party and Red Army.

Hua Shan: In an easterly direction from Xi'an, 120 kilometers (75 mi) by train, is Hua Shan, one of the sacred mountains of China. Its name means "flowering mountain," and its cultural significance, extending far back into history, is Daoist. There are numerous temples on the mountain up to its top.

The ascent via the lower north summit to the 2,100-meter-high (6,900-ft) south peak starts at **Yuquan Yuan** (Garden of the Jade Spring), seven kilometers (4 mi) east of Huayin. The ascent takes at least half a day. Behind Yun Men (Cloud Gate), where there is a fine view, the path climbs steeply upwards; it's helpful not to suffer from vertigo. Many visitors and Daoist pilgrims ascend to enjoy the sunrise.

Luoyang: The train from Xi'an to Luoyang, east of Xi'an, takes about seven hours. The train passes through the town of **Sanmenxia** (Three Gate Gorge), where one of the largest hydroelectric power plants in China was built.

While Xi'an was the capital of the Western Han dynasty (206 BC–AD 9), the residence of the emperors of the subsequent Eastern Han dynasty (AD 25–220) was in 3,000-year-old Luoyang, sometimes called the Eastern Imperial City. In fact, Luoyang, like Xi'an, served as the capital for several dynasties – ten, to be exact, flourishing during the Tang and Song dynasties, then gradually losing its importance to the increasingly prosperous coastal towns.

Just prior to the Communist victory in 1949, the town had few residents (esti-

Good-luck charm.

mates range from 20,000 to 100,000) and appeared desolate. This changed after 1949. Luoyang became an industrial city with the construction of many factories, including the first tractor factory in China. Numerous monotonous-looking working-class districts were added, so typical of many of China's industrialized cities; today, Luoyang has all the unpleasant features accompanying such a development. An attempt has been made to make it more pleasant by creating green spaces.

The **provincial museum** is fairly central, offering an overview of the historic development of the town and its environs, from the neolithic period to the Tang era. Not far from the museum, in Wangcheng Yuan, are two underground tombs from the Han dynasty, which were excavated at a different location in the 1950s.

In the old town, to the east, one can still see a few houses in the style of the Song, Ming and Qing dynasties. To the south, about eight kilometers (5 mi) from downtown, is the tomb of General Guanyu, who is worshipped in China as the god of war and is quite popular. A stele erected at the mound of Guanyu's tomb has been engraved with the biography of the general, who came from Shu in the third century.

To the east, 13 kilometers (8 mi) outside of Luoyang, is **Baima Si** (White Horse Temple). This monastery, founded in AD 68, is said to be the oldest Buddhist monastery in China. The name of the temple reflects an old legend about two monks on a white horse who delivered Buddhist scriptures to Luoyang. Statues of the two monks and their burial places can be seen here. Unfortunately, only a few ruins remain of the old monastery complex. The restored monastery itself houses more than 60 monks of the Zen Buddhist order, and is again a center for followers of Zen Buddhism. To the east of the temple is a pagoda from the Song dynasty, **Qiyun Ta** (Skyscraper Pagoda).

The most spectacular cultural and historically-important site outside of Luoyang is **Longmen Shiku** (Longmen

Longmen Shiku.

Caves), 13 kilometers (8 mi) south of town and along both sides of the Yi river. These Buddhist caves were created between the fifth and seventh centuries, with most of the figures and grottoes sponsored by noblemen of the time – there are over 1,300 grottoes and 700 niches containing 40 pagodas, 2,780 inscriptions and more than 100,000 statues and images.

Many of the most beautiful sculptures were stolen at the turn of the century and now reside in museums in the West, or else in private collections. Nevertheless, together with the grottoes at Datong and Dunhuang, the Longmen caves are still a unique record of Buddhist creative art, reflecting different styles, from the northern Wei dynasty to the Tang dynasty. The biggest statue is more than 17 meters (56 ft) tall, and the smallest one, less than two centimeters.

The structures on the western bank of the river are well preserved, including the sculptured stone figures and grottoes. The most striking part of the site is **Fengxian**, a temple that contains that 17-meter-tall (56-ft) central Buddha statue, surrounded by bodhisattvas and heavenly guards. The ears of the Buddha are two meters long. The statue was completed in 676 during the reign of the Tang emperor Gaozong, said to have been inspired by the empress Wu Zetian.

Shaolin on Song Shan: Some 80 kilometers (50 mi) southeast of Luoyang is **Shaolin Si**, a monastery. This Temple of the Small Forest at the western edge of **Song Shan** can be reached in about three hours by car on a reasonable country road, traveling through the countryside and villages.

The Shaolin monastery is known beyond China's frontiers for the special form of unarmed combat developed by its monks over the centuries, and is considered as the cradle of Chinese forms of martial arts, including qong-fu.

If expecting a remote and romantic retreat where the wisdom of the ages is passed along in a realm of meditation and solitude, toss aside that foolish thought right now. Shaolin has become a major tourist stop, if not a tourist trap, in addition to being a place of pilgrimage. In recent years, a training hall – mainly for wealthy foreigners – has been built next to the monastery, obscuring the peaceful landscape. Expect to encounter tour buses and hawkers.

The founder of the monastery, Bodhidharma, reportedly sat in front of a rock face and meditated for a decade. As a result, his silhouette is said to have been imprinted on the rock. Bodhidharma is now considered the founder of Chinese Zen Buddhism, derived from a Buddhism that arrived from India in 527.

The Shaolin monastery has been ravished several times over the centuries, most recently by Red Guards during the Cultural Revolution. (One might also say by increasing tourism.) It has, of course, been restored in recent years and once again houses monks. In **Qianfodian** (Thousand Buddha Hall), one can still see depressions in the stone floor of this main hall of the temple, reminders of the tough combat exercises performed by the monks.

Southwest of the monastery is **Talin**

Taiji practice with sword.

(Pagoda Forest) and its 220 tombs, the oldest of which probably dates to the Tang dynasty.

Several other sights can be reached from **Dengfeng**, a small town in Song Shan: the Daoist temples **Chuzu'an** (Temple of the First Patriarch) and **Zhongyuemiao** (Zhongyue Temple), in which sacrifices to Song Shan were once made. Four big iron figures in combat position guard the pavilion in which the emperors used to make their sacrifices. Also worth a visit is **Guanxingtai**, an observatory built in 1279 and located 15 kilometers (9 mi) southeast of Dengfeng, in the small town of Gaocheng.

Zhengzhou: Located around 80 kilometers (50 mi) northeast of Dengfeng is the town of Zhengzhou, on the south bank of Huang He (Yellow River). The capital of Henan Province, Zhengzhou can be reached by plane from several airports in China; the town is also an important railway junction for the Shanghai–Xi'an and Beijing–Guangzhou lines.

Although it was already populated during the Shang period, the town did not attain great significance until the construction of the railway lines at the end of the 1800s.

During World War II, it was attacked several times by the Japanese due to its importance as a railway junction. The Kuomintang troops blew up the dikes of Huang He as a defense against the Japanese. Hundreds of thousands of Chinese tragically lost their lives in the subsequent flooding. The breaches in the dikes were repaired only in 1947, with American assistance. In the 1950s, Zhengzhou, badly damaged during the fighting of 1948–1949, was turned into an industrial and manufacturing area.

Zhengzhou's so-called Old Town, with its maze of narrow alleys and remnants of the city wall, is worth a look. A monument for the victims of a general strike of railway workers in 1923, which was brutally suppressed, stands in the commercial center, commemorating one of the most important milestones in the history of Chinese workers. There is a

Talin, near Shaolin.

permanent exhibition about Huang He in Zhengzhou, along with the requisite provincial museum.

Kaifeng: East from Zhengzhou along the railway line to Shanghai and south of Huang He is Kaifeng.

From the time of the Warring Kingdoms (476–221 BC), the town served as the capital for seven dynasties, flourishing especially under the Song dynasty. The 12-meter-long (39-ft) scroll painting, *Upriver to the Qingming Festival*, dating from the Song period and now stored in the Imperial Palace in Beijing, describes life in this flourishing commercial town. The town later went into a decline. In 1644, the dikes of Huang He were opened to stop advancing Manchu soldiers, and over 300,000 people lost their lives in the flooding.

Fortunately for traditionalists, Kaifeng did not become a contemporary industrial center, and so it still has the look of an old Chinese town, although specific tourist sites are few.

In the northwestern part of Kaifeng is **Tie Ta** (Iron Pagoda), which originates from the Song dynasty. With 13 stories and over 50 meters (160 ft) high, its name comes from the rust color of the bricks, which from a distance look like cast iron. The most ancient, best-preserved building in the town is **Po Ta** (Fan Pagoda), which is three stories high and contains numerous Buddha figures in various niches.

Other sights in Kaifeng are Yuwangtai (Old Music Terrace), Longting (Dragon Pavilion) and the **Xiangguo monastery**, in the town center. Built in AD 555, for many centuries the monastery was the center of Buddhism in China. It was destroyed in a catastrophic flood in 1644, but was later rebuilt. An octagonal pavilion with a remarkable ceiling made of wood is worth noting, as is a gold-plated statue of Guanyin made from *gingko* wood.

Kaifeng is also known for once having a sizeable settlement of Jews, a fact recorded by Marco Polo. Their synagogue ceased to exist in 1850, although a stele at a supermarket commemorates the former site of the building.

Loess cave dwellings.

UPPER HUANG HE: THE YELLOW RIVER

The second-longest river in China, Huang He, or the Yellow River, nurtured the development of ancient Chinese civilization. Shallow and erratic in its course (it has shifted numerous times, as much as 200 kilometers in its lower stretch), the river is not especially important as a waterway of commerce. Nevertheless, over the centuries, Huang He provided nourishment for the crops that would feed China's expanding population. And, too, it would sometimes decimate both population and land.

Approximately 5,500 kilometers (3,400 mi) in length, the river got its name because of the yellowish sediment – desert soil carried down by the winds – in the water.

An eight-hour train journey from Beijing towards the west leads to the large town of Datong, in Shanxi Province. From there, the train continues through Hohhot, the provincial capital of Inner Mongolia, towards Mongolia and then into Russia and finally to Europe. Alternatively, from Hohhot, travelers can head west via Baotou, Yinchuan and Lanzhou, and then further to Ürümqi; the Ürümqi express train takes about four days from Beijing.

While the northern railway line leads directly into the steppe and desert areas of the vast Gobi, the other line follows Huang He, the Yellow River, whose scenic valley lazily stretches through Baotou in a southwesterly direction towards Lanzhou.

On the journey from Beijing to Datong, visible are parts of the 2,400-kilometer-long (1,500-mi) **Wanli Changcheng (Great Wall)**, which in the past marked the frontier of Chinese civilization and extended from Gansu Province to Huang Hai, the Yellow Sea. The journey continues through the hilly loess landscape of the north, passing numerous villages surrounded by clay walls, with mud houses and ancient cave dwellings. Life here is not pleasant. The cold north winds leave dust constantly in the air. The average annual temperature is only 6°C (43°F); during the height of summer, the thermometer rises to 38°C (100°F), while in winter it can fall to –30°C (–22°F).

Datong: Lying 1,200 meters (4,000 ft) above sea level in the north of the coal-producing province of Shanxi, the industrial and coal-producing town of Datong gained its historic importance from the central Asian peoples who, in AD 386, founded the Northern Wei dynasty (386–534). The Wei rulers, sympathetic to Buddhism, undertook the construction of the **caves at Yungang**, the construction of which was completed in the Tang dynasty.

The caves are the greatest sight in Datong, about 15 kilometers (10 mi) to the west of town and at the base of the hills of Wuzhou. In the 53 caves, there are more than 51,000 statues; the biggest is 17 meters (56 ft) tall; the smallest is less than two centimeters high. There are also numerous reliefs in the caves.

Spread along a hillside with a height of more than 1,000 meters (3,000 ft), the

Preceding pages: Xuankong Si, a hanging monastery near Heng Shan. Left, Buddha statue at the caves of Yungang. Right, Buddhist monk.

Yungang caves suffered both natural erosion and plunder. Around 1,500 figures were broken during the first decades of this century, or else were taken abroad and are found today in North American or European museums.

On the way to the caves is the restored Guanyin Hall, dating from the Liao period; it was completely destroyed during the Cultural Revolution.

In Datong itself, there are the **Huayan monasteries**, as well as the **Shanhua Monastery**, founded as early as the Tang dynasty.

Some buildings and figures can still be seen in the two Huayan monasteries, which are 1,000 years old. Several of the clay figures in the main hall of the Lower Huayan Monastery date back to the Liao period. The frescoes with themes from Buddhist legends are also interesting. What is unique is that all entrances to the temple buildings face the east – the Liao were sun worshippers who prayed to the east. The main hall, with five gold-plated Buddha statues, dates to the Jin dynasty.

After the demise of the Liao and Jin dynasties (1115–1234), Datong gradually declined in importance and served only as a fortification for the Ming emperors. **Jiulongbi** (Nine Dragon Wall) in the old city dates from the Ming period. With colored, glazed bricks, it was once the entrance to a palace in which the thirteenth son of the first Ming emperor lived.

From Datong, there a lovely excursion through the loess landscape to **Heng Shan**, 60 kilometers (40 mi) to the southeast and one of the five sacred mountains in China. Here, five kilometers (3 mi) outside the town of Hunyuan, the 1,400-year-old **Xuankong Si** (Hanging Monastery) nestles against an enormous rock, supported by extra support poles. From there, one can travel by bus to the mountain range **Wutai Shan**, which includes one of the four sacred mountains of Buddhism. The Buddhist god of wisdom, Manjusri, is still worshipped in the numerous monasteries along Wutai Shan. During the Ming period, there were more than 300 monasteries

The Manchu storm the Great Wall.

here, of which only a few remain. **Foguang Si** (Temple of the Light of Buddha) and the temple of Nanchan are worth mentioning.

Taiyuan: A bus journey of 175 kilometers (110 mi), which takes a day, goes from Wutai Shan to Taiyuan, with more than two million inhabitants and the capital of Shanxi Province. The climate is moderate; in January, temperatures fall to minus 12°C (10°F); in July, the average temperature is 25°C (77°F).

Shanxi cuisine is a notable experience in Taiyuan, as this industrial city offers little else. Worthy samplings include *tounao* (a thick soup of mutton), lotus roots, yam, herbs and rice wine, and *shaomai*, consisting of steamed dumplings made of wheatmeal.

Taiyuan's history goes back to the Spring and Autumn Period (770–476 BC). The town was opened to outside trade at the beginning of this century with the construction of a railway line, expanding into an industrial town after the Communist revolution in 1949. The area surrounding Taiyuan is rich in important historic relics of great beauty. Just 25 kilometers (16 mi) outside of town, on the slopes of Xuanweng, is the temple of **Jin Si**, with its Shengmudian (Mother Goddess Hall) where numerous painted clay figures are stored, considered amongst the most important artifacts of the Song period. In the southeastern suburbs of Taiyuan is the Ming-period **Shuangta Si** (Two Pagoda Temple), which has become the symbol of the town, and the temple of **Chongshan**, whose construction goes back to the Tang dynasty.

Not far from Taiyuan are the Daoist Longshan caves and the Dayun temple, in the town of **Lingfen**. The provincial museum in the town center contains a collection of Buddhist stone statues from the fifth to tenth centuries, and a collection of ancient sutras from the third and fourth centuries.

Inner Mongolia: Returning to Datong, the next stop along Huang He is **Hohhot**, capital of the province of Inner Mongolia. Be prepared for the journey, as it takes about 13 hours by train from Beijing to the east.

A large city, Hohhot lies at the southern outskirts of the **Gobi Desert**, on a high plateau on the edge of the Mongolian grassland. Mongols form a minority in Inner Mongolia, making up around 15 percent of the total population. It is thus not surprising that, today, Hohhot looks more like a Han Chinese town than a Mongolian one. (In the sixteenth century, Hohhot was founded by the Mongol sovereign Altan Khan as a Mongolian settlement.)

There are some buildings of religious interest in Hohhot. The 400-year-old monastery of Dazhao, renovated in 1985, houses a well-stocked library with splendid scriptures. Also of note are the Lamaist temple Xilitu Zhao, dating from the seventeenth century, and Wuta Si (Five Pagoda Temple), from the eighteenth century.

To see authentic Mongolian life, travel to the grass steppes, to Baiyunhesha (170 km/100 mi), Wulantuge (80 km/50 mi), or Huitengxile (130 km/80 mi). Although tourism has already intruded, it's possible to gain an insight into the

Wuta Si in Hohhot.

life of Mongolian nomads living in the distinctive tent known as a *yurt*. A visit to the grasslands in summer is particularly interesting because of the traditional *naidam* festival, when horseriding games, wrestling and archery are on offer. Mongolian specialities such as mutton and lamb are served, either roasted or grilled over an open fire.

Three hours' train journey from Hohhot is **Baotou**, the steel city of the grasslands. Baotou was once an important trading center; from the seventeenth century onwards, the Qing emperors systematically populated the town with Han Chinese.

The Mongols once called this area Land of Red Deer; in socialist China, it became an important center for the iron-and-steel industry. Baotou stretches along the banks of Huang He, which crosses Inner Mongolia as far as 800 kilometers (500 mi). There are few interesting sights in Baotou to lure the traveler; nevertheless, a sturdy vehicle is useful for reaching **Wudangzhao**, a Lamaist monastery in the Daqing mountains, 75 kilometers (50 mi) away.

One can also take an excursion to the **tomb of Genghis Khan**, 120 kilometers (75 mi) south in Yijinhoroqi. There is a small, village-style museum at the mausoleum displaying Mongolian customs and traditions.

Yinchuan: From Baotou, the train heads onward southwest to Yinchuan, the capital of the autonomous region of **Ningxia**. Yinchuan has nearly a million inhabitants, and is the city of the Hui, or Chinese Muslims. Over four million people live in the autonomous region itself; some 30 percent are Hui Muslim, who, because of their Islamic dress, are visibly different from the Han Chinese.

The landscape along Huang He alternates between fertile plains and arid regions. Closer to Yinchuan, the landscape becomes greener and more fertile. To the north and west of the river, the desert-like landscape stretches to the river bank; steppes alternate with fertile areas that have been artificially irrigated with water from Huang He. The Chinese used the river over 2,000 years ago to irrigate the land in this area

by building canals. The irrigation systems were extended over the centuries and the canals continue to form the basis of Yinchuan's wealth.

Huang He has, however, frequently played a devastating role in Chinese history – when it floods, it covers thousands of square kilometers of farm land. The river is 5,450 kilometers (3,400 mi) long; its middle part crosses the provinces of Gansu, Ninxia and Inner Mongolia and, further on, forms the border between Shanxi and Shaanxi provinces before reaching the northern plain.

Deposits and sediments have turned it yellow, hence its name. This was not always the case, however; it used to just be called the River. Only during the Han dynasty did it begin to be called the Yellow River, or Huang He. This may be the result of the vast deforestation that took place in central China from the sixth century onwards.

Vessels can use only part of Huang He; its estuary on the Shandong peninsula is so shallow that no boat connection to the sea is possible. Over the last

Mongol nomads in front of their *yurt*.

2,000 years, the river has changed course twelve times, with the resulting floods causing great devastation. Nevertheless, over the centuries the river has benefited people where they were able to tame and farm the floodlands.

The area around Yinchuan is still the most fertile, wealthiest part of Ningxia. The bare, mountainous southern part of the autonomous region is the poorest area of China.

A rapidly-growing industrial town, Yinchuan has a history going back more than 1,500 years. The division between the old and new town is clearly recognizable. The old town can easily be explored, on foot or bicycle.

To the north of the old town, the 54-meter-high (177-ft) **Bei Ta**, or Haibao Ta (North Pagoda), dates from the seventeenth century and is worth a visit, with a good view of the town, its surroundings and Huang He.

In the southwest of the old town is the 64-meter-tall (210-ft) **Xi Ta** (West Pagoda), whose roof is made of green ceramic tiles. The most interesting con-temporary sight in Yinchuan is its old town, with the many small shops and snack bars around the city gate, which resembles Tiananmen, in Beijing. The Muslims predominate here: the white caps of the Hui are everywhere, and many of the Muslim restaurants are recognizable by their blue signs.

Located just 30 kilometers (20 mi) outside of Yinchuan is **Xixia Ling Mu**, the ancient burial site of the Western Xia dynasty and containing the tombs of eight kings and 70 other graves.

A lovely bus-ride from Yinchuan southwards via Wuzhong leads to the hydroelectric power plant in the gorge **Qingtong**. From here, take a boat on the very muddy Huang He to the 108 pagodas on the other bank. In the south of Ningxia, in the caves near Guyuan in Xiumi Shan, is a 19-meter (62-ft) statue of Buddha. From Qingtong Gorge, continue in the direction of **Zhongwei**. Near Zhongwei, the Tengger desert skirts the river's banks.

Lanzhou: Spend the night in Zhongwei and take the train the next day for

Camel herd on the Mongolian steppes.

Lanzhou, capital of Gansu Province and one of the poorest regions in China. Ethnic minorities, including Tibetans, are settled here.

With over two million inhabitants and stretching along the upper reaches of Huang He, Lanzhou is a modern industrial town and the center of Chinese nuclear research. Unfortunately, the town does not live up to its name – Orchid City – and only in the old town can one still sense the town's 2,000-year history.

The best view of the town and river is from **Baita Shan** (White Pagoda Hill), on the northern bank of the river. Near the bridge is a small Muslim market, where one can find spicy noodles, lamb kebab and oriental bread on offer in the small snack bars.

A 600-year-old temple site is located on a slope in **Wuquan Gongyuan** (Park of Five Springs), in the north of the town. **Chongqing Si** (Chongqing Temple) contains a five-meter-tall (16-ft) bronze statue of the Buddha, dating from 1370, and a five-ton iron bell from

1202. The zoo is in Wuquan Gongyuan. The neolithic pottery and bronze artifacts from the Zhou period in the **provincial museum** are worth seeing. Do not miss the most splendid exhibit in the museum – the *Flying Horse of Gansu*, from the Eastern Han dynasty.

In summer, there are boat trips on Huang He (if the water isn't too shallow) to the caves at **Bingling Si**, 100 kilometers (60 mi) from the city and jutting out of the water. The trip takes about three hours, and one highlight is the large number of Buddha figures carved into the sandstone by several artists in the fifth century. The largest is nearly 30 meters (90 ft).

The journey of 260 kilometers (160 mi) to the monastery at **Labrang** takes about eight hours and is fairly strenuous. The monastery was founded in 1710 and is one of the most important monasteries of the Yellow Hat sect. If there is sufficient time, it is worth making the trip, but allow around three days for the journey.

Along the way, an excursion to the gorges of **Liujia** near the river is an equally worthwhile trip.

The journey along Huang He ends in Lanzhou. From here, **Xining**, the capital of Qinghai Province to the west, can be reached in three to four hours by train. Not far from Xining is **Ta'er Si**, the Kumbum monastery, which is important to Tibetan culture – the present Dalai Lama was born near here. From Xining, the railway carries on to **Golmud**; from here, Lhasa is within reach by bus or other ground vehicle.

The hearty traveler could also continue towards the northwest, passing **Jiayuguan**, the end of the Great Wall, and then venturing due west, crossing **Dunhuang** along the old northern Silk Road route, with its famous cave grottoes, the oasis Turpan, and then finally reaching **Ürümqi**.

In a southwesterly direction, the railway goes from Lanzhou through the hilly, furrowed landscape to **Gansu Province** in the Wei River valley. The Wei is one of the numerous tributaries of Huang He that accompanies a journey to Xi'an.

Left, temple protector. Right, guardian deities, Huayan Si, Datong.

THE SILK ROAD: ACROSS THE NORTH

China's vast west is accessible to travelers along the classic Silk Road. Historically, the trade route was never known as the "Silk Road". A German geographer, Ferdinand Freiherr von Richthofen, gave it that romantic name in the late 1800s.

To the north looms the **Gobi**, one of the world's great deserts. Covering around 1.3 million square kilometers (500,000 sq mi), the Gobi ranges in elevation from 1,000 to 1,500 meters (3,000–5,000 ft) above sea level. Noted for its vicious sand storms and extreme summers and winters, the Gobi holds important reserves of coal and oil.

This ancient trade route starts in the old capitals of Luoyang and Chang'an (now called Xi'an), reaches Huang He (Yellow River) at Lanzhou, then skirts westward along deserts and mountains.

Heading west: The Silk Road divides into two routes at the oasis of Dunhuang. The northern route goes to Hami, another oasis, then winds along Bogda Shan to the oasis of Turpan. It then comes close to Ürümqi, ascends across several mountain passes through the Tian Shan range to Karashahr and Korla and – via Kuqa, Kysyl, Kumtura, Aksu, Tumtchuk and Lailik – finally finishes at Kashi (Kashgar).

The southern route leads from Dunhuang between the river oases on the northern slopes of Kunlun Shan (Altyndagh) and the sand desert of Taklimaken Shamo, in Tarim Pendi (Tarim Basin). Hidden in this expanse of nothingness is Lop Nur, a dried salt lake where China tests its nuclear weapons. The best-known oases along this route are Charklik, Cherchen, Endere, Niya, Kerija, Chotan and Yarkand. In Kashi, the two routes rejoin together.

Ancient trade: In AD 200, this transcontinental route linked the Roman Empire in the west with the Han dynasty of China. Trade was carried on by foreign traders who belonged to neither of the two old empires, however.

Before the discovery of the sea route to India, the Silk Road was the most important connection between the East and West. It experienced its last great era during the time of the Mongols, when the entire route from China to the Mediterranean was part of one empire. At that time, Nicolo and Marco Polo (1254–1323) traveled from Kashi to eastern China along the southern route.

The overland link quickly lost its importance as seagoing trade developed. In recent times, it has been replaced in China with the Lanzhou-Hami-Ürümqi railway line, the last part of which was completed in the early 1990s.

Lanzhou to Jiuquan: The varied loess landscape and the many contrasts offered by the desert make the overland journey between Lanzhou and Jiuquan, an ancient crossroads and garrison town, truly extraordinary. In the south, the distant snow-covered peaks of **Qilian Shan** flank the railway line. The train reaches the flat, 800-kilometer-long (500-mi) Gansu corridor when it arrives at the old administrative and garrison town of **Wuwei**, which became a district capital in 115 BC. (The Flying Horse, a bronze statue from the Eastern Han period and excavated in 1968, comes from near Wuwei. The original is now in a museum in Beijing; a beautiful replica is in the provincial museum.)

Zhangye, the capital of the district of the same name, is 60 kilometers (40 mi) to the west. Zhangye, founded in 121 BC as a garrison town, has a bell tower (originally a drum tower) in the town center. It dates from 1509, with a bell from the Tang period. The wooden pagoda found here also dates from the Tang period; its first six floors, out of a total of eight, are actually made of brick.

Jiuquan, a thriving industrial town, was founded in 111 BC as a garrison outpost. Between 127 and 102 BC, the Han emperors relocated nearly a million peasant families here, including at least 700,000 victims of a devastating flood in Shandong. Nowadays, the old town quarter around the drum and bell towers is changing, like much of China; small alleys are being torn down and modern buildings erected.

Preceding pages: dissicated mountains line the Silk Road. **Left, Huo Shan, the Fiery Mountains.**

Renmin Gongyuan (People's Park) at the edge of the town was built as a memorial to General Huo Qubing. The general is said to have once been given a barrel of wine by the Han emperor Wudi (140–87 BC) as a reward for defeating the Xiongnu, thought to be related to the Huns who, in the fifth century AD, overran eastern Europe. To let his soldiers enjoy the wine, too, he watered it down with water from a spring. The spring is in front of a landscaped garden in a modest, rectangular basin.

Out in the nearby desert, China's Long March rockets are tested and launched into the heavens.

About 15 kilometers southwest is the Buddhist temple site of **Wenshu Shan**. At the time of the Qing emperor Qianlong (1736–1795), 300 monk's cells are said to have existed here, but they were demolished by rebellious Chinese Muslims after 1865. The small Qianfo Dong, or Mogaoku (Thousand Buddha Caves), with their poorly-preserved paintings, date from the Northern Wei period (386–535).

A good 30 kilometers (20 mi) further to the west is **Jiayuguan**, since 1372 a part of the western end of Wanli Changcheng, or the Great Wall. The fortification, 1,800 meters (5,800 ft) above sea level, was completed four years after the victory of the Ming dynasty. A square inner courtyard is enclosed by walls and two gates. On top of the 10-meter-high (33-ft), 640-meter-long (2,100-ft) wall are 17-meter-high (56-ft) watch towers from the late Ming and the early Qing periods. The wall was first restored around 1507, and again during the Qing period, and then once more in recent years.

At the southern entrance, towards the town of Jiayuguan, rises an elevated, pavilion-like stage. Dignitaries used to watch plays from the pavilion opposite on the right-hand side. The wall, from the Ming period and still intact, stretches southwest to the foothills of Qilian Shan and approximately northwards to Bei Shan. The structure, which dominates the landscape, is particularly impressive when approached from the west. A

Desert of western China.

monument with the inscription "Strongest Fort of the World" has stood outside the West Gate since 1809.

Weijin Bihua Mu, eight tombs from the Wei dynasty (220–265) and the Jin dynasty (265–420), are situated around 20 kilometers (12 mi) to the northeast. They contain wall murals depicting scenes from everyday life.

The old town of **Yumen**, which can only be reached by funicular railway, lies around 60 kilometers (40 mi) to the west. The town has little charm, but **Changma Dong** (Changma Caves), 60 kilometers (40 mi) farther to the southeast, have been built in similar style to certain grottoes of Mogao, near Dunhuang, south of the main road and railway line.

At both **Hongliuyuan** and **Anxi**, the road to Dunhuang turns off to the southwest away from the railway line, crossing the river Shule.

About 40 kilometers (25 mi) before Dunhuang is a well-preserved watchtower dating from 1730, an example of the type of communications used at that time. By daylight, flag signals were given from the top platform; at night, fire signals lit the night.

To reach Dunhuang by rail, travel to Hongliuyuan. From there, continue southwest for several hours by bus. After crossing the drained plain of Shule He, near the village of Zhangjiaquan in the flat desert to the west, remnants of the Great Wall from the eastern Han period are visible. The structure of clay-and-fascine construction is surprisingly easy to see.

Dunhuang: The oasis town of Dunhuang lies in an irrigated cotton-producing oasis.

The **museum** near the hotel has some local finds, visual displays, and models of the oasis, reflecting the historic significance of this settlement. Between cotton fields and threshing areas at the edge of the town, **Baima Ta** (White Horse Dagoba) is reminiscent of Beijing's White Dagoba. This is where the white horse of the famous traveling Indian monk Kumarajiva (344–431) is said to have died.

There are 492 grottoes at the **caves of Mogao**, some 25 kilometers (15 mi) southeast of the town. Of these, around 70 can be visited. The first caves are said to have been built by the monk Lezun in 366, the last ones carved out at the time of the Mongolian conquest in 1277. After that, Mogao sunk into oblivion, until the monk Wang Yuanlu settled here at the turn of this century. The first cave he opened is the one now numbered 16. In the next cave, he found more than 40,000 manuscripts. The Hungarian-British explorer Sir Aurel Stein bought 6,500 manuscripts from Wang between 1907 and 1914; a Frenchman bought a further 6,000 scripts.

The grottoes show an uninterrupted history of Chinese painting, particularly of landscapes, over a period of nearly a thousand years. Visiting them is the high point of any journey along the Silk Road. But because of the inadequate information, travelers need to be well prepared for contingencies. The following suggestions give the numbers of the individual caves in square brackets.

The paintings, from the Northern Wei (386–535) period, are mainly concerned with Buddhist legends and saints such as Kumarajiva [272]. The Jataka of King Sivi [275] depicts the self-sacrifice of a monarch for a dove. The four excursions of Buddha Sakyamuni [27] confront him with the real world. The Jataka of the Deer King [257] shows the rescue of a deer and the punishment of a hunter. The victory of Buddha over the Temptor Mara [254] and the Jataka of the Sacrifice of Prince Sudana for a hungry tiger [254] are other examples. Many paintings [263 and 249] depict the figure of the preaching Buddha.

The form and contents of painting developed further under the Western Wei and the Northern Zhou (535–589) dynasties; scenes from daily life, such as hunting scenes, now begin to appear [240]. One Jataka describes how 500 reformed bandits recovered their eyesight [285].

The representation [285] then turns towards bodhisattvas and guardians of the world. Flying elves, male Gandharva

Left, caves at Mogao. **Right**, express train from Beijing to Ürümqi.

[290] and particularly female Apsara [404] became important subjects.

In the Sui period (589–618), further Jatakas [419] and legends from the Lotus Sutra [419] or from Buddha's entry into nirvana [295] appear. The blackening by time of the often-used white lead gives the outlines of the figures a particular charm. The depiction of people becomes more realistic [303], and there is a first depiction of Paradise [420]. The paintings from the Tang period (618–909) exude beauty and perfection. There are representations of the Western Paradise [329, 217, 172], which is of significance for the Jingtu (Pure Country Sect), but also of worldly sponsors [329] and scenes of meditation [172], a picture of the historic monk Xuanzang [217], pictures of orchestras [220] and weddings [445], pictures of ploughs in the rain [23], of dancers and musicians [320], and again paintings of Buddha's entry into nirvana [158], monks studying [201], battle scenes [12], servants [17], and finally landscapes such as Wutai Shan [61].

One of the most beautiful caves [323] shows an Indian Buddha statue made from sandalwood being presented to the reigning emperor.

In the subsequent Five Dynasties Period (to 960), the formal mastery of the painters is preserved; sponsors such as the King of Khotan [98] are painted more realistically. Under the Northern Song (960–1126), interesting pictures of temples [61] and Arhats (Luohan, disciples of the Buddha) [97] are painted. After that, the artistic creativity declines. However, there is one masterpiece from the first Yuan period showing the bodhisattva Avalokiteshvara [3], with a thousand arms and a thousand eyes.

Purely touristic attractions in Dunhuang are **Yueyaquan** (Lunar Lake) and **Mingsho Shan** (Singing Sand Mountain). A day-trip to **Yumen Guan** (Jade Pass), 70 kilometers (40 mi) away, gives a good view of the landscape from these ruins of a Han-period border town.

Xinjiang: The population of the Xinjiang, actually an autonomous region and China's largest province, is

Even in the desert, there are traffic rules.

predominantly Islamic. The Uighur people of this autonomous republic speak Turkish and are Muslims; they constitute approximately 45 percent of the total population. The Han Chinese population has increased from eight percent in 1940 to over 40 percent. Han Chinese live mostly in the larger cities and in new settlements, where the youth from the huge towns of the east, who were "sent to the countryside" after 1958, have settled. The smaller oases and nomad areas – and also the agricultural areas in the north of Xinjiang – are still predominantly populated by people of the Uighur and Kazakh minority groups.

The capital of this autonomous region, **Ürümqi**, which lies 900 meters (2,900 ft) above sea level, is a huge town. About 75 percent of its one million population are Han Chinese and only 10 percent each are Uighur and Hui; it is the departure or destination point for all journeys around Xinjiang. The development of industry here has resulted in substantial environmental pollution in recent years.

The museum is worth a visit. Apart from significant archaeological finds, it also exhibits life-size models of the houses and tools of the most important nationalities in the region.

In the old town, there are (again) numerous small mosques and bazaars full of activity. A pavilion in the style of a Chinese garden lodge and a small pagoda, both symbols of the town, are located on **Hong Shan** (Red Mountain), which also offers a good view of the town. The town itself has modern highrises. Older buildings date from the time of the Soviet presence, including the main post office and the state guesthouse. The walls and gates described in 1936 by Sven Hedin were demolished some time ago.

It is worth taking an excursion to **Tianchi** (Lake of Heaven), due east some 100 kilometers (60 mi) from Ürümqi and lying 1,900 meters (5,800 ft) high on the slopes of **Tian Shan**, at the foot of the 5,445-meter-high (17,864-ft) Bogda Shan, a secondary mountain range of Tian Shan; the journey passes

Tianchi, Lake of Heaven, in Tian Shan.

some scenic landscape. The lake is complete with tourist facilities.

Just 150 kilometers (90 mi) west of Ürümqi is the Chinese settlement of **Shihezi**, whose structure and layout go back to its colonization under the Qing emperor Qianlong (1736–1795). The town, with over 100,000 inhabitants, is typical of the Han Chinese pioneering towns in areas with artificial irrigation.

Turpan: To the east of Ürümqi, **Turpan** can be reached from Ürümqi in a half-day bus journey or by rail; the station is 60 kilometers (40 mi) from the town. The road leads eastwards through the desolate industrial belt of Ürümqi, then through pastures along the northern slope of Tian Shan to **Dabancheng**, a market town near a pass leading to the richly-forested valley of the Baiyang He (White Poplar River). At the end of the Baiyang He, the road reaches a stony desert stretching to the edge of **Turpan Pendi** (Turpan Basin). This oasis, 150 kilometers (90 mi) long from east to west, is a depression 150 meters below sea level, second in the world below sea

level only to the Dead Sea. To be precise, the exact low point is **Aydingkol** (Moonlight Lake), a salt lake in the basin that is drying up and is 154 meters (505 ft) below sea level.

In summer, the temperature in the oasis, bordered in the north by Tian Shan and in the south by Kuruktag, rises to 47°C (117°F).

Only a few old buildings have been preserved in Turpan. **Sugong Ta** (Emin Minaret), built with clay bricks in 1776, and the sparsely furnished mosque next to it are the symbols of the town.

In an ancient and fantastic underground irrigation system, the **Karez wells**, melting water from the mountains is channeled to the oasis over long distances via gravity and underground to prevent the water from evaporating. The subterranean canal system is over 3,000 kilometers (1,800 mi) in length.

The local museum shows relics from the Silk Road, mummies from the Astana graves, silks from the early period of transcontinental trade along the route, and funerary objects.

Sugong Ta, the Emin Minaret in Turpan.

Towards the east, **Huo Shan** (Fiery Mountains) – a range of bare sandstone mountains rising up to 1,800 meters (6,000 ft) – stretch for 90 kilometers (60 mi). In direct sunlight, the temperature rises up to 45°C (110°F). As a barrier to the search of legendary sutras, the mountain range achieved fame in the novel *The Journey to the West*, which describes the travels of Xuanzang. Born in Luoyang around 602, Xuanzang entered a Buddhist monastery at the age of 13, quickly becoming an expert in the religious scriptures. He departed for India in 629 with the support of the Tang emperor Taizong (627–649), studied and debated at the Buddhist academy Nalanda, near present-day Patna. He returned after 17 years to China with 657 scrolls, taught in Chang'an (present-day Xi'an), and died there in 664.

Just 50 kilometers (30 mi) from Turpan is the ruined city of **Gaochang**, the ancient Karachotcha or Khocho. The town was founded as a garrison under the Han emperor Wudi (140–86 BC) and became a prefecture around 400 BC. In AD 460, it declared its independence from the partly Turkish rulers. In 640, the Tang emperor Taizong (627–649) took it back from Qu Wentai, the last independent ruler. During its heyday, it had 30,000 inhabitants and more than 30 Buddhist monasteries; remnants of some of these, where Xuanzang preached in AD 639, can still be seen. Around 1300, the town capitulated after 40 years of fighting, during which the irrigation system was destroyed. Today, one can see the division of the town into a center with sacred buildings, and into suburbs with bazaars and housing estates.

Next door, to the northwest, is **Astana** (or Sanbao, Three Citadels), a burial ground with well over a thousand tombs. Several tombs, mostly dating from the fifth and sixth centuries, are open to visitors; their wall murals depict the earthly world: earth, gold, jade and stone, six types of geese that are also assigned characteristics, and three mummified bodies. Tombs from the Han period contain wall murals with everyday scenes. Similar murals are in the tomb

Uighur children at a spice stand.

of Zhang Huaiji, from the Tang period.

To the north of Gaochang, on Huo Shan, is the ancient cave monastery of **Bezeklik** (or Qianfodong, Thousand-Buddha-Caves). The trip through the Murtuq canyon begins at a watchtower dating from the Qing period (around 1770), located opposite the cave monastery site Samgin (Murtuq). It was used from around 450 to the thirteenth century. The caves of Bezeklik – around 70, of which only some can be visited – have been carved into the cliff face some 80 meters (300 ft) above the western bank of the river.

The plunder of valuable paintings by German and British archaeologists (Albert von Le Coq, Albert Grünwedel, and Aurel Stein) damaged the pictorial representation of the Buddha and bodhisattvas in caves number 29 and 39. After 1860, Islamic fanatics destroyed most of the facial depictions. Nevertheless, the remains are somewhat interesting still. Work on the caves began around 430; the monastery was later abandoned in the 1200s.

Ten kilometers (6 mi) to the west of Turpan is the ruined city of **Jiaohe Gucheng** (Old City by Two Rivers), which in the past was called Yariko or Yarkhoto, founded in the Han period and the center of a kingdom until the fifth century. Jiaohe lies on a plateau between two rivers, a natural fortification. Civil wars and lack of water at the time of Mongol rule (ca. 1230) brought the town to ruins. The central sacred site and the remnants of Buddhist monasteries and stupas in the northwest, which are most prominent among the ruins, are still well preserved. It's easy to distinguish between the bazaar and artisan quarters near the eastern gate and the ancient settlements. The remains of underground dwellings, which offered protection from the summer heat and the freezing winter, are of special interest.

Kashi: Much further to the west, on the other side of the great vastness of Tarim Pendi, the city of **Kashi** (Kashgar) lies 1,300 meters (4,270 ft) high on the bank of the Tumen river, in the middle of an

Bezeklik.

irrigation oasis with cotton and other agricultural cultivation. The population of a quarter of a million is predominantly Uighur. Kashi only first became Chinese around 200 BC, again during the Tang period, and finally during the period of the Qing emperors Kangxi (1662–1722) and Qianlong (1736–1795).

Kashi is the furthest away from the ocean of all the big towns; it is closer to Moscow, Islamabad, Delhi, Kabul and Teheran than to Beijing. The borders of Kyrgyzstan (120 km/75 mi), Tajikistan (160 km/100 mi), Afghanistan (300 km/ 190 mi) and Pakistan (400 km/250 mi) are close.

The climate is extreme: in winter the temperature can fall to –24°C (–11°F), and in the summer months it regularly reaches above 40°C (104°F). The frost-free period lasts 220 days annually.

Aitika (Id Kah Mosque), in the town center, was renovated in 1981 and is China's largest mosque, able to hold 6,000 worshippers. With a central dome and two flanking minarets, the building, dating from 1445, dominates the town.

Behind the gate are open, tree-lined squares for prayer; 100 meters behind is the Great Prayer Hall, open only for Friday prayer. A stylized picture of the Ka'aba of Mecca adorns the entrance to the Great Prayer Hall.

Side halls are covered in precious carpets. The steps in front of the side walls are a popular meeting place, particularly for the elderly. On religious feast days, up to 50,000 worshippers come for Friday prayer.

To the north runs an extremely lively bazaar street with barber shops, book and fur traders, blacksmiths, bakers and, directly by the mosque, dentists. The covered bazaar, where mostly cloth, haberdashery and food are sold, is extensive and rambling.

A stroll through the bazaar ends up at a modern shopping avenue, with the striking Minzudian (Department Store of the Minorities), along with craft shops and workshops. Opposite the entrance to the covered bazaar along the Great Square are snack bars, tea houses and numerous small shops. No donkey or

The faithful gather for prayer in front of Aitika, Id Kah Mosque, in Kashi.

horse-drawn carriages, the traditional means of transport, are allowed here. Instead, they stop at the northern edge near the street leading to the mosque.

Directly where the horse carriages stop is **Qini Bagh** (Chinese Garden), which was the British Consulate from 1895 to 1947 and is now a hotel, where mostly Pakistani traders and individual travelers and backpackers stop.

In a building in front, the state travel agency has a local office and offers cars for rent. The main buildings are in danger of crumbling, though the site retains its historic charm for the moment. The once-famous wine gardens have had to make way for a bus parking area. One can still sense the atmosphere from the time of Sir George MacCartney, who resided here for 28 years. Explorers such as Sven Hedin, Sir Aurel Stein and many others frequented the house.

The former Russian and then Soviet consulate at the other end of the town, used as such between 1865 and 1961, is now a hotel. At the time of Consul Nikolaj Petrowski, the rival of MacCartney, the European explorers also called here. The newer buildings are from the time of the Soviet advisers.

Xiangfei Mu, the Abakh Hoja mausoleum, dates back to the sixteenth century, and was renovated in 1980. Abakh Hoja (Aba Hezhuo), who died in 1583, was an outstanding political and Muslim religious leader in Kashi.

His sarcophagus, one of 57 here that house 72 of his descendants, lies on an elevated pedestal in the center of the central building's main hall, which is reminiscent of a mosque (but not facing Mecca), and is flanked by slightly leaning minarets. In the near left corner is the sarcophagus of Xiangfei (Fragrant Concubine), the daughter of the last Hoja and source of the mausoleum's popular name.

According to legend, Xiangfei is said to have refused to sleep with the emperor Qianlong, who had abducted and taken her to Beijing after the repression of a rebellion in 1758. Since she would not consummate the relationship, she was forced to commit suicide by the empress dowager – the emperor's mother.

Her body was taken back to Kashi in a carriage, the remnants of which are exhibited in the small mosque.

Jakub Beg, the leader of the rebellion of 1877 that was repressed by the Qing rulers, is buried in the nearby cemetery. The exact location of his grave is no longer known. The memorial built in 1887 by the Imperial Russian Geographic Society for the German traveler Adolf Schlagintweit, who was murdered here in 1857, can also no longer be found.

The most important weekly event is the Sunday market (*basha*, a Chinese version of bazaar), still held by the banks of the Tumen, which has several bridges over it and steps leading to town. Tens of thousands of visitors, buyers and sellers come to this market, reputedly the biggest in Asia.

The market area, which is divided into sections selling similar goods, offers grain and flour, camels, sheep, cows, yaks and horses, fur and leather products, wood, doors and furniture, spices and salt, bread, vegetables, and cloth. The numerous market alleys are lined

with tea shops, snack bars, hairdressers, workshops and bakers. The cattle market is particularly lively in the mornings, carrying on through lunch.

Nearly all the central Asian minorities visit the market – Pakistani traders are there in great numbers – giving it an international atmosphere.

The **mausoleum of Mahmud al Kashgarli** (1008–1105) was built outside of Kashi. The building, which is about 40 kilometers (25 mi) away along the road to Pakistan, towers over a mosque once destroyed in an earthquake.

A portrait of Mahmud hangs in the entrance hall, and on his sarcophagus lies a copy of his main work, *Divan Lugat Atturk*, written between 1072 and 1074 while he was in exile in Baghdad. It is one of the oldest Arabic-Turkish dictionaries, with 7,500 entries.

Mahmud came from the house of the ruling Karachanid family and was one of the most important scholars of his time. Exiled from Xinjiang after the clan's overthrow in 1058, he return to Kashi shortly before his death. The mausoleum is visited by Turkish travelers. Farther to the southwest, 190 kilometers (120 mi) from Kashi at the beginning of the high peaks of the Pamir range, is the lake of Karakul. The ice-covered peaks of Muztagata (7,546 m/24,700 ft) and Kongur (7,719 m/25,300 ft) rise up here. The second and third highest peaks in the Pamirs, it's said that they can be seen from Kashi on an exceptionally clear day.

The Buddhist **Sanxian Dong** (Caves of the Three Immortals), on a sheer rock face by the Qiakmak river, are somewhat less interesting than those of Bezeklik or Dunhuang.

The residence of ancient rulers, Hanoi (Halvoi), which flourished during the Tang and Song dynasties and was abandoned in the eleventh century, is today a ruin with few remnants, amongst them the Mor pagoda and the Karez irrigation systems. It lies 30 kilometers (20 mi) to the east of Kashi.

Taxkorgan: About 250 kilometers (150 mi) south of Kashi is Taxkorgan (or Sariköl, Stone Tower), 3,600 meters (11,800 ft) above sea level. It is the last outpost in China before entering Pakistan, and is the capital of an autonomous district of the same name; a majority of Tadzhik people live here. According to accounts by Ptolemy (around AD 140), traders from East and West used to trade their goods here.

From Taxkorgan, continuing south leads to Pakistan's **Karakorum range** (Black Wall).

In Kashi, Pakistanis offer hotel accommodation in the Hunza Valley of Pakistan. The 750-kilometer-long (470-mi) track across the **Khunjerab Pass**, at 4,700 meters (15,400 ft), is sometimes difficult, either because of weather or else due to more secular unrest. The pass was reopened in 1986 after prolonged disturbances in the area, but is often not very safe or comfortable because of uncertain weather.

About 270 kilometers (170 mi) south of the pass is the nearest airport in Pakistan, at Gilgit. Along the mountain road are many wall murals, engravings, and sculptures from the era of the Silk Road. Too, there is exquisite scenery.

Left, dunes of Taklimaken Shamo. **Right**, northern eyes.

THE CENTER

While much of ancient China's roots are found in the northeast, much of China's contemporary history – the last two centuries – is along the central stretch of its eastern seaboard, and along the corridor etched into the terrain by Chang Jiang, more commonly known to Westerners as the Yangzi.

The great city of Shanghai is not known for imperial buildings or court intrigues, nor for its depth of ancient history. Its important history is rather recent, starting in the last century with the foreign concessions that divided up the city amongst the colonial powers.

Shanghai came into being as a city of commerce, and as with all great centers of commerce, monuments were of little importance. This may be changing, however. China has decided that Shanghai, its largest city with over 14 million people, is to be its cornerstone for the twenty-first century. No small feat, considering the depth of China's past 40 centuries. But over US$40 billion worth of new infrastructure is being poured, quite literally, over the nineteenth-century colonial residue, reshaping not only the contours, but the personality of the city. Marking the achievement will be a 459-meter-high (1,506-ft) financial center, the world's tallest building when completed in 2001.

Upriver along the Chang Jiang, the vast delta region is pock-marked with industrialization, which has masked the traditional textures of cities such as Suzhou, Wuxi, and Hangzhou. As the southern terminus for the Grand Canal, or Da Yunhe, which connected northern and southern China, Hangzhou was once a thoroughly important and critical city.

Further upriver, but not by much, Nanjing has taken on less of the industrial veneer that now personifies most Chinese cities. Nanjing is a little bit greener, and a little bit more gracious. Perhaps its memorialized reminder of the Japanese rampage in World War II has left it a little more appreciative.

Further west is Sanxia, the Three Gorges. A century ago, travel through the gorges was probably the world's most difficult commercial river journey. Now, the gorges are a routine tourist excursion, although with still the same exquisite scenery. In a few more years, however, the scenery will be different: a new dam is under construction, the world's largest. Its reservoir will extend westward 500 kilometers, and the gorges will be 185 meters shallower.

Beyond the gorges is Chongqing (or Chungking to the old colonial brigade), a bit of an odd city for China, as it sits on a rocky promontory, not a flat expanse.

In the center of China, not exactly on the Chang Jiang, is Sichuan, China's most populous province with more than 10 percent of the country's population. Long protected by mountain ranges on three sides, Sichuan is home to a rather spicy cuisine, and also to the few remaining giant panda bears in the world.

<u>Preceding pages</u>: sailors relaxing on leave along the Bund, Shanghai.
<u>Left</u>, autumn foliage over a temple roof.

SHANGHAI

Back in what some might consider its glamorous colonial days, Shanghai was called the Paris of the East. Today, a more accurate description might be Heir to Hong Kong.

Shanghai is undergoing an impressive transformation just as rapidly as possible. Where there were once neighborhoods of small houses, there are now high-rises. Where there were once handsome brick, colonial-era buildings, there are now glitzy hotels. To visit Shanghai is to visit a giant public-works project: new highways, new ports, new bridges, new office towers – all of it unfolding at a dizzying pace.

The intent of all this urban revamping is nothing less than to make Shanghai a world-class regional center of banking and finance, on par with Singapore and Hong Kong. Marking this ambition will be the **Shanghai Financial Center**, what will be the world's tallest building – 459 meters (1,506 ft) – when it's completed around 2001.

On a less lofty level, Shanghai sits on the river **Huangpu**, an 80-kilometer-long tributary of Chang Jiang, the Yangzi, that provides Shanghai ("upriver to the sea") with ocean access. Administratively, Shanghai is a metropolis without a province, made up of both surrounding rural districts and a dozen city districts.

People and more: Locals and outsiders agree on one thing: *Ren tai duo* – There are too many people in China's largest city. The greater metropolitan area has over 14 million inhabitants; the city proper itself covers 375 square kilometers (145 sq mi) and has eight million inhabitants – if not more, as keeping tabs on the population is tricky. Whatever the exact number, the density is amongst the highest in the world, with almost 19,000 people crowded into every square kilometer.

People of Shanghai are very individualistic, speaking a dialect that nobody else can understand, eating a different cuisine, and generally considering themselves to be light-years ahead of their nearest competitor, Beijing. Indeed, a thriving art scene, pulsating night life and a cosmopolitan air makes Beijing seem a bit dowdy in comparison.

Walking down Shanghai's fashionable commercial district is like stepping into a somewhat grimy Tokyo, Hong Kong or Miami – but still flashy, trendy and youthful. Unfortunately, other than the shopping boulevards of Nanjing Lu and the Bund, Shanghai is not especially a walker's paradise. (But street signs are in pinyin, of considerable help to foreigners.) Too, for getting away from the central district, the bus routes are somewhat Byzantine, and the buses themselves an exercise in chaos.

However, the ever-expanding subway system – now in the northern and western neighborhoods, and soon to cross the river eastwards – is superb.

Distinctly a city of commerce, the region was already a trading center in AD 960, flourishing for centuries and becoming an important trading port of wine houses, temples, shops, schools

and storehouses. Japanese pirates were attracted by this wealth, and after numerous attacks upon Shanghai's honor, a protective wall was built in the sixteenth century. (It surrounded the old city center – just south of the Bund in a circular area defined by the roads of Renmin and Zhonghua – until 1912.)

While the wall eventually humbled the Japanese pirates, it failed to impede colonial Western greed. As a result of the Opium Wars in the 1840s, the British imposed upon China the Treaty of Nanjing, which, among many things, opened up Shanghai. Without too much delay, a number of European powers established communities in Shanghai.

These foreign concession areas took up most of what is now central Shanghai, save for the old walled Chinese part of the city.

Radicalism is a Shanghai tradition. The Communist Party was founded in Shanghai in 1921, and the Cultural Revolution not only began here, it kept its headquarters in Shanghai. But despite the enthusiasm of the Red Guards to demolish everything not defined as Socialist Realism – and that included anything foreign, Buddhist, or simply old – many buildings from colonial times have survived. But many may not survive China's push to modernize.

On the waterfront: One gets a first impression of this modernization along Zhongshan Dong Lu, which parallels the western bank of the Huangpu. Most foreigners know this road as the **Bund** (Waitan). At night, the Bund is a lengthy outdoor people-watching corridor of both locals and foreigners, packed with hustlers selling everything from Mao's red books of quotations – only tourists buy them now – to sex.

Here, too, along the Bund, directly opposite the Peace Hotel, the Shanghai day starts before dawn, with people doing *taijiquan* and other exercises.

If joining them, then afterwards consider heading to the so-called Breakfast Alley, which runs parallel to Nanjing Dong Lu, the best-known shopping street running from the Bund westwards, and near Sichuan Lu, which runs north and

The river of Huangpu.

242

south. There are all sorts of local dishes available, including *baozi* (steamed buns), *youtiao* (dough pockets fried in lard) and, of course, strongly-sweetened Shanghai coffee.

It is often said that Shanghai is nothing but a consumer's paradise, bereft of culture. Street activity along the Bund and Nanjing Lu would certainly enforce Shanghai's reputation as a shopper's paradise – not limited to just clothes, silk or electronics, but also traditional theater props and musical instruments, art and even stamps.

Book shops selling mostly antiquarian books are concentrated in Fuzhou Lu, south of Nanjing Lu, and can be reached via Henan Lu.

The **Peace Hotel** (Heping Binguan), known as the Cathay Hotel in the old days, offers a 1930s atmosphere. Views of the Bund and Shanghai skyline are excellent from its eighth floor. Have breakfast on old silver plates and meditate on the transforming waterfront.

Shanghai harbor is the third-largest in the world and an important factor in the city's industrial prowess. Across the river from the Bund, on the eastern side, is **Pudong Xingu** (Pudong New Area), swampy farmland before 1990 and now under development as a special economic zone.

But this is not just another urban development project. Pudong is a massive US$40 billion undertaking that will significantly redefine Shanghai. It will have a new container port, a new international airport, acres of new high-rises and skyscrapers. Numerous tunnels and bridges are under construction to connect Pudong with central Shanghai. (One hopes that the civil engineers for Pudong have studied Shanghai's subterranean history. Since 1920, when the problem was first noticed, Shanghai has sunk several meters.)

If for some reason you are unable to locate Pudong from your perch on the Bund, look once more across the river for the impossible-to-miss **Pearl TV Tower**, an observation and broadcast spire on the other side of the river, with globes lit up in bright colors at night.

he Bund.

Colonial concessions: At the northern extent of the Bund, near the Friendship Store and **Huangpu Yuan** (Huangpu Park), the boulevard crosses the **Suzhou**, a canal from the northwest that joins the Huangpu where it makes a tight ninety-degree bend. Huangpu Yuan is said to have had signs prohibiting "dogs and Chinese" from entering the foreign enclaves. The bridge, Waibaidu, is usually crowded with pushing pedestrians and cyclists. Formerly called Garden Bridge, Waibaidu connected the American and British districts until, in 1863, both merged into the International Settlement (Shanghai Zujie), which stretched west and east. From 1937 onwards, the bridge defined the border with the Japanese-occupied territory north of the Suzhou. The Seamans Club, which used to house the Russian consulate, is still a meeting place for seamen and students from around the world.

North to Hongkou: North of the Suzhou, Huangpu Yuan and Waibaidu, Sichuan Lu leads northwards into Hongkou, which has retained some of its old southern Chinese charm. Laundry is draped from balconies on bamboo canes, and in the side streets, elderly people sit outside on stools to chat, chop vegetables, play cards or guard the bedding airing out in the street.

An evening walk through the streets of Hongkou can be enlightening, although the canals emit a terrible odor in summer. There are several cafes where young workers congregate, but the night now comes alive with loud nightclubs, discos, karaoke bars and restaurants.

At the edge of the northern part of Sichuan Lu is **Hongkou Gongyuan**, one of the loveliest parks in Shanghai. Within the park is the grave of Lu Xun and a museum commemorating Lu Xun, no doubt the most famous Chinese writer of this century. He lived in Shanghai from 1933 until his death in 1936, and his former home on Dalu Xincun, a side alley of Shangyin Lu, is just a few minutes east of the park.

Hongkou was already in Japanese hands before the occupation of 1937, and had the nickname of Little Tokyo.

Morning taijiquan on the Bund.

In fact, a large percentage of Shanghai's resident 30,000 Japanese lived in Hongkou. Ironically, given Japan's alliance with Nazi Germany, Little Tokyo became a haven for Jewish refugees from Europe. Until 1941, China was one of the last countries open to immigrants, requiring neither entry visa nor proof of financial means. Although these conditions were tightened after 1939, the Jewish community – considered a valuable asset in Shanghai – gave others assistance with money and job opportunities. By 1939, 14,000 refugees had reached Shanghai. In 1943, some 15,000 Jewish refugees lived in the Hongkou ghetto, built by the Japanese after demands from their Nazi allies.

Due west of Hongkou a few kilometers is the **Shanghai Railway Station**, which opened in 1988. Here, the day begins even earlier than in the parks, and on every corner, stalls offer breakfast dishes. Nearby is the northern terminus for the subway system.

West of the train station, on the other side of the canal Suzhou, is **Yufo Si** (Jade Buddha Temple), on Anyuan Lu. The temple is famous for its two Buddha statues made of white jade, brought back from Burma (Myanmar) as a gift by the monk Huigen, in 1882. The statues were brought to Shanghai in 1918, when the temple was completed. One of the statues, of the Sleeping Buddha representing his entry into nirvana, is a special rarity. However, the other white-jade statue of the Seated Buddha – two meters (6 ft) tall, decorated with jewels and weighing 1,000 kilograms – is the more famous. About 70 monks are in residence, overseeing religious and tourist activities, and operating a restaurant.

Central Shanghai: West of the Bund and Huangpu, wedged between Yan'an Lu to the south and Nanjing Lu to the north, is **Renmin Gongyuan** (People's Park). Once a race course of the powerful *taipan* in the 1860s, most of the area is now a parade ground for rallies and the occasional demonstrations, such as in 1987, when students demanded an improvement in their material conditions and freedom of expression. Lo-

cated inside the former racecourse club, on Nanjing Lu, is the well-stocked and renovated **Shanghai Library**.

On the other side of Nanjing Lu is the **Acrobatic Theater**, exhibiting bronzes from 1700 to 1400 BC, along with the entire range of Chinese ceramic art, paintings and calligraphy.

A little east along Nanjing Lu and due north of the park is yet more colonial history, the **Park Hotel**, where glamorous festivals were once held under its glass dome.

South of and adjacent to People's Park is **Remnin Square**, home to the new and impressive **Shanghai Bowuguan** (Shanghai Museum). The modern facility – some of its newest galleries opened in 1996 – boasts a spectacular collection in a superb setting. Visitors can rent audio guides that can be programmed to provide information, in several languages, about specific exhibits. There are impressive bronze wine vessels, with carved animal masks, from the Shang period; ancient food steamers fitted with vessels

for hot water to keep food warm; Ming pottery with brilliant blue designs of flowers; celadon vases; and stone statuary from the Han and Tang periods. Opened in 1996 were new galleries devoted to painting, jade, stamps, ethnic minority art, furniture and calligraphy.

The Old City: From the north, paralleling Sichuan Lu, Henan Lu intercepts Renmin Lu, which together with Zhonghua Lu defines a circle outlining the edge of the old city. The city walls paralleled this ring road until 1912, when they were knocked down, the moats were filled in, and the two streets were laid down.

Chenghuangmiao (Temple of the Town God) was at the heart of the old city. Its restoration is rather touristy. Better to spend time next door in **Yuyuan Shangsha**, a bazaar and park, Yuyuan (Garden of Joy). Here, as befits a bazaar, one can find tens of thousands of trinkets and lots of merchants hustling for your coin. Don't be put off by the exterior of the various restaurants. Give them a try. The best one is certainly the

Residue European atmosphere, hotel restaurant.

Huxinting tea house, which, as the name confirms, lies in the middle of the small lake and whose famous zigzag bridge leads directly to Yuyuan. A bit of traditional China is preserved here, but increasingly, young people come to chat or read the newspaper. Various musicians meet here weekly to play traditional Chinese music.

Legend has it that the gardens of Yuyuan were built in the sixteenth century by the eccentric and gifted landscape architect Zhang Nanyang. Yuyuan covers an area of almost four hectares (12 acres), with artificial hills, lakes, and pavilions connected by zigzagging bridges. One can well imagine how this park served as the home base for the rebels of the Society of Small Swords during the Taiping rebellion. Today, an exhibition about this secret society is located in their former headquarters, the Spring Hall.

The alleys around Yuyuan show a different side of colonial Shanghai. If one doesn't succumb to a tendency to romanticize that which is, in fact, poverty, the alleys offer a realistic impression of the normal living and housing conditions of the people in Shanghai.

To the south: In the south of the city, on the road with the same name, is the **Longhua Ta**, a temple built in 242 and since destroyed and rebuilt several times. The temple site consists of seven halls that, since the end of the Cultural Revolution, are being used once more for religious purposes.

Considerably closer to central Shanghai, the former French Concession – founded in 1862 and in the southwest part of downtown, in the district of **Luwan** – has kept its own character with French-inspired architecture and the many avenues. Huaihai Lu, formerly Avenue Joffre and the counterpart of Nanjing Lu with its shady trees, is perhaps the more pleasant choice for shopping or just strolling. It has many shops and cafes, still reflecting French and Russian influence. (Many Russian emigres once lived here.)

Famous people resided here, given its proximity to the culture of the Old City. **Sun Yatsen's residence**, Sun Zhong-shan Guju, was on Xiangshan Lu, south of Huaihai Lu, near Fuxing Yuan. Mao Zedong and Zhou Enlai also lived and worked in this area. At Xingye Lu 76 and east of Fuxing Yuan is the founding place of the Chinese Communist Party, **Zhonggong Yidahuizhi**.

And last, though not least, perhaps the most important man of Shanghai prior to 1949 lived here: Du Yuesheng, the boss of the Green Gang, who after the victory over the rival Red Gang was one of the most powerful personalities in Shanghai. He lived on Ninghai Lu, between Yan'an Lu and Jingling Lu. The Green Gang, a mafia-type organization, controlled the opium trade, prostitution, gambling halls and anything else that was part of Shanghai's underworld. Without the backing of Du Yuesheng, it is unlikely that Chiang Kaishek could have carried out his bloody struggle against the Communists. The Who's Who of 1937 lists all his positions and services, and he is described as a "well-known benefactor." He died in 1951 in Hong Kong.

BEYOND SHANGHAI: HANGZHOU & SUZHOU

"In heaven above there is paradise, on earth there are Suzhou and Hangzhou." Repeated like a mantra, this well-known line of poetry is about what are considered to be the garden spots of the country. Small in scale, full of charm and home to quiet spots tucked away amid fussy cities, even today these towns along **Da Yunhe (Grand Canal)** – which runs north and south – live up to the reputation of the poem by Yang Chaoying, who lived and wrote during the Yuan dynasty.

The origins of Da Yunhe go back to the period of the Eastern Zhou dynasty (770–256 BC). Since the end of the thirteenth century, this waterway has stretched north to south over a distance of more than 1,800 kilometers (1,100 mi); it crosses the provinces of Zhejiang and Jiansu towards Beijing and connects the rivers Qiantang, Chang, Huai and Huang.

Like the Great Wall, Da Yunhe was assembled from smaller pieces. Preparing for war, the king of the state of Wu had a canal built from Suzhou to Chang Jiang (Yangzi River). It was completed in 495 BC, and was 85 kilometers (50 mi) long. A few years later, the canal was extended to Yangzhou, and the two rivers Chang Jiang and Huai He, in the north, were linked. Numerous myths and legends exist around the building of the canal system. One tells of how the Sui emperor, Yangdi, who reigned between 605–618, had ordered a link to Yangzhou be built to enable him to admire the heavenly *qiong* flower.

The flower, however, had the last revenge by wilting after the canal was built. Nevertheless, the emperor's fascination created a link from what was then the capital, Luoyang, to Beijing in the north and to Huai He in the southwest and, subsequently, from Zhenjiang to Hangzhou. As a result, the capital Luoyang was eventually connected with the north and with the economically-important southern region by a canal

system of 2,700 kilometers (1,70[...] Using the canal, the customs tr[...] that were collected in the area were transported to the capital. Also transported were commodities – the Zhenjiang/Jiangsu region could produce three rice harvests per year, as well as silk, porcelain and other items for the court. Rare wood and bricks, used for the Imperial Palace in Beijing, were transported on the canal system as well.

The Yuan dynasty (1271–1368), which made Beijing the capital, extended the canal system, thus connecting the capital directly with Hangzhou and shortening the distance by about 1,000 kilometers (620 mi), to 1,800 kilometers (1,100 mi). The canal may not yet be finished. Currently, officials are studying ways to improve the canal to alleviate water shortages in the north.

For travelers, Da Yunhe is an interesting route for a boat journey. However, as it is a working canal, the sights are not always pleasant. The banks along the canal are heavily industrialized, and the water is often filthy with trash and debris; the stench from the waters can be overwhelming. That said, it is a slice of life away from the metropolitan hubs.

Hangzhou: At the beginning of the twelfth century, the Chinese court was defeated in its battle against the "northern barbarians" and fled south from Nuzhen. In 1138, the newly-formed empire of the Southern Song dynasty took Hangzhou as its Xingzai, or Temporary Residence. As the seat of the dynasty, the town flourished, as officials, writers and scholars moved to there as the dynasty blossomed. It had already been a fortified town since the Tang period, when in the seventh century the building of the Da Yunhe had strengthened its presence, as Hangzhou was the southern terminus for the canal.

The city of Hangzhou was the subject of many poems in the Tang period, such as in the work of the poet Bai Juyi (772–846), who became governor of the town and had a dam built at Xi Hu (West Lake) that still bears his name, Baidi. The poetess Li Qingzhao, who lived from 1084 to around 1150, and who had escaped to the south, was inspired by the colorful background of Hangzhou to write many poems. Hangzhou became well-known during the Southern Song period; its population increased from less than half a million to over one million, thus making Hangzhou one of the largest cities in the world at the time. It was nearly destroyed in the second half of the nineteenth century, during the Taiping rebellion, and not much of antiquity remains now of this town. The city walls and gates have disappeared, and the numerous old canals have been filled in.

Today, Hangzhou is the capital of Zhejiang Province, one of the most prosperous regions in China. Its products include silk and Longjingcha (Dragon Well Tea), and its pharmaceutical industry and academy of arts are well-known throughout China. Over a million people live in the city, which covers 429 square kilometers (165 sq mi).

While it is a good walking town, Hangzhou, and particularly Xi Hu, the main attraction, is a tourist trap, with many visitors, especially weekend travelers and honeymooners from nearby Shanghai.

It is said that every Chinese city has a **Xi Hu**, a West Lake. In fact, there are around 30 West Lakes in China; Hangzhou's is perhaps the most famous. Legend has it that Xi Hu was created from a pearl dropped by a phoenix and a dragon. Originally, Xi Hu was only a bay on the river Qiantang, but since the Tang period, it has been extended into a lake that now covers 5.6 square kilometers (two sq mi). Its eastern shore is close to the town, while the other shores are surrounded by forested mountains often shrouded in mist, which gives the landscape a romantic allure.

Sudi, the Su Causeway – named after the poet Su Dongpo (1037–1101), who was governor from 1071 to 1089 – leads from the northern shore, near Hangzhou Hotel, to **Huagang Guanyu** (Flower Bay Park) in the southwest. The large site goes back to the Southern Song period. Today, the park – containing rare flowers, peonies, rocky landscaped areas, pavilions and numerous small

Da Yunhe, the Grand Canal, connects Hangzhou with Beijing.

fish ponds – is twice its original size. Across Baidi (Bai Causeway), named after Bai Juyi, is the largest island in the lake, **Gu Shan** (Solitary Hill). On its southern side is **Zhongshan Gongyuan** (Sun Yatsen Park), which was originally part of the palace gardens of the emperor Qianlong (r. 1735–1796). The palace from the Song period was destroyed during the Taiping Rebellion.

To the west of the park is the **Zhejiang Museum**, founded in 1929 and exhibiting the oldest rice finds in China – more than 7,000 years old and discovered in 1973, in Yuyao. To the northwest is **Wenlange** (Pavilion of Literary Waves). Adjacent to the east are pavilions and a small pagoda of Xilingyinshe (Xiling-Die Culting Company), founded in 1903.

At the end of Gushan Lu is a bridge, Xiling, which connects the island to the mainland. In the southern part of the lake is **Xiaoyingzhou** (Island of the Small Seas), which was created in 1607 as an artificial coral reef. It was designed as a generously-arranged garden, with pavilions and bridges in such a way that it encloses four lakes, which contain lotus flowers and carp. The island can be reached only by boat, which depart from four places: Hubin Gongyuan (Seashore Park) on Hubin Lu near the city; the observation point Liulangwenying (Listening to the Orioles) on the east side of the lake near the Children's Palace; at Huagang Guanyu (Flower Bay Park); and on Gu Shan (Solitary Hill), at Sun Yatsen Park. Much of the shore is lined with observatories, pavilions and tea houses.

The pagoda at **Baochu** to the northeast stands out against the sky, a symbol of the city. It was built in 968, and destroyed and rebuilt several times. The present pagoda dates from 1933 and is 45 meters (150 ft) high.

Slightly to the west is **Geling**, a hill that has a tea house where retired men often meet to talk and play checkers amidst bird cages, a nice setting for an early morning stroll or run.

On the northwestern shore of the lake is **Yuefei Mu**, the mausoleum and ancestors temple of General Yue Fei. This

Hangzhou's Xi Hu, or West Lake.

symbolic figure of Chinese patriotism, who is still mentioned in modern Chinese literature, was executed in 1142 as a result of intrigues. His name was rehabilitated shortly afterwards, and he is now honored at this burial site with the temple built in the thirteenth century. In the hall of honor are paintings that depict the life and fate of the general; there is also a statue of him. This temple, too, was badly destroyed during the Cultural Revolution, but some original artifacts from the Song period have been preserved, including figures that protect the path to the funeral mound. In front of the vault, the general's opponents are depicted in a kneeling position; these statues, made from iron, are from the early nineteenth century. Chinese visitors still spit on them in fury, which shows how strongly the general remains in the Chinese consciousness.

In the west of the town, at the end of Lingyin Lu, which is easily reached by bus, is the beautifully-situated **Lingyin Si** (Monastery of the Hidden Souls), a popular attraction from where one can see **Feilai Feng** (Peak that Flew from Afar). The monastery was founded in 326 by the Buddhist Indian Hui Li. He thought he saw in the Peak that Flew from Afar a part of the Gradhrakuta Mountain in India, thus the inspiration for its name. Since the second half of the tenth century, the rock walls of the mountain have been carved with about 300 sculptures and inscriptions; the earliest figure is thought to date from 951. A group of three Buddhist deities are at the right hand entrance to the **Qinlin cave**.

Past these figures is the monastery, one of the ten most famous Buddhist monasteries in China. The most popular figure is at the foot of the mountain: the fat-bellied Buddha from the Song period, one of the most touched and photographed figures anywhere and believed to bring good luck. Up to 3,000 monks used to live in the 18 pavilions and 75 temple halls on the mountain peak. Behind the entrance gate to the temple and two stone columns inscribed with Buddhist texts is Tianwangdian (Hall of Heavenly Kings), where an-

Hangzhou's Xi Hu, or West Lake.

other statue of the Maitreya Buddha can be seen, guarded by the two Heavenly Kings standing at its side. In Daxiongbaodian (Precious Hall of the Great Heroes), which lies behind two nine-story pagodas from the tenth century, is the gilded statue of the Buddha Sakyamuni, which is more than nine meters (30 feet) high and made of precious camphor wood. It is the tallest figure made from this material in China.

About nine kilometers (5 mi) southwest of Xi Hu and near the zoo (Dongwuyuan) is **Hupaoquan** (Spring of the Running Tiger), whose origin or discovery is surrounded by various legends. The water of this spring has extremely high surface tension, and floating coins on it has become a national sport. The water tastes good and can be sampled in a nearby tea house in Dinghui Si, a Tang-period temple.

Towards the northwest is the village of **Longjing** (Dragon Well), which is often acclaimed as a sight worth seeing. Visitors will be hectored constantly in Hangzhou to buy some of the tea from

Laughing Buddha at Lingyin Si.

this village, which is somewhat touristy, with obligatory introductory speeches and a guided tour through shops. For the most part, workers abandoned the tea industry here and returned to private farming some years ago, and the vessels used communally in the past for drying the tea leaves are now set in motion only when the tourist buses arrive. An excursion to one of the surrounding villages, such as **Meijiawu**, about 20 minutes by car to the south of Hangzhou, is probably more worthwhile. If fit enough, the trip through the lovely landscape with its famous bamboo grove can be made by bicycle, hired in town. This village also grows tea, and the villagers, who have not yet been overrun by tourists, are very hospitable and willing to explain tea production.

Southwest of the lake on **Yuelun Shan** (Moon Mountain) near the Qiantang river, is **Liuhe Ta**, the Six Harmonies Pagoda, first built in 970 to protect the town from flooding. It later served as a lighthouse and was meant to pacify the dragons brought in by the floods. The

pagoda, 60 meters (200 ft) tall, has seven inner and thirteen outer stories, whose original bricks are from the twelfth century, while the outer wooden parts were renovated around the turn of the nineteenth century. In the town itself, where the tea houses and cafes have reopened and daily life carries on in the little alleys, **Fenghuang Si** (Mosque Temple of the Phoenix) on Zhongshan Zhong Lu is of historical and cultural significance. It was originally built in the Tang period; after being destroyed several times, it was restored in 1984. Fenghuang Si is one of only a few preserved mosques in China and contains numerous Arabic inscriptions.

As in all towns, a visit to the open market is well worth while, as are the silk factories, which give a sense of the complexity of silk production as well as of the working conditions in a traditional Chinese factory.

One way to avoid the summer heat and the crowds is to head for **Mogan Shan**, 60 kilometers (40 mi) to the north. Buses go from Hangzhou to this very beautiful mountain of waterfalls and bamboo groves, almost 800 meters (2,600 ft) above sea level.

Shaoxing, located 60 kilometers (40 mi) to the east of Hangzhou, is accessible directly by train. The town is known throughout the world for its rice wine. Every year the Shaoxing brewery produces about 40,000 tons of wine and has been receiving praises for its excellent quality since the seventh century. Shaoxing was once the Temporary Residence of the emperor, for twenty months during the Southern Song period, and is linked to Da Yunhe.

Shaoxing has never enjoyed the same importance as Hangzhou. The town has yet to be discovered by tourism, which in no way detracts from the charm and atmosphere of this small, but very lively and beautiful, provincial town. Lu Xun, the most famous modern Chinese writer, was born in Shaoxing, in 1881, and both his birth place and the **Lu Xun museum** can be visited on Duchangfang Street. They display an example of the traditional Chinese style of living, as well as

Qingming festival pilgrimage, Lingyin Si.

photographs and documents from the life of Lu Xun. Another noted writer and revolutionary grew up in Shaoxing: Qui Jin (1875–1907), one of the first feminists in China. She was executed in 1907 after an abortive uprising against the imperial system. The house where she lived, on Hechangtang near the crossroads of Jiefang Nanlu and Yan'an Lu, gives an impressive picture of the life of a civil servant's family during the late Qing dynasty, exhibiting photographs and documents from her life.

Just east of the town is **Dong Hu** (East Lake), an artificial lake created towards the end of the Qing period. The boats, which are typical of this area with their black canopies, are steered through the bizarre seascape by the boatsmen using their feet. Caves with calligraphy can be seen. A few kilometers southeast of the town, at the foot of **Kuaiji**, is the tomb of the legendary emperor Yu, who is said to have tamed the water by building dams and changing the course of rivers. A temple was first built on the mountain in 545; the present site is, however,

from the Qing dynasty, and comprises several large and small halls and pavilions, which hold numerous mythical figures and a tombstone of Yu.

Tai Hu: Between the two provinces of Zhejiang and Jiangsu is Tai Hu, the third-largest lake in China and covering 2,420 square kilometers (930 sq mi) and peppered with 48 islands. Here, one has a romantic view of a landscape in green and blue, veiled with fine mist and the subject of many poems. The residents have a more pragmatic view of the lake: they use it to catch fish, and to breed ducks and geese as well as to grow lotus and water chestnuts. However, the most important economic factor in the area is the cultivation of mulberry trees and silkworms.

The largest island, **Dongting Xishan**, covers 90 square kilometers (35 sq mi). The point of highest elevation, Piaomiao Feng (Blurred Peak), reaches 336 meters (1,102 ft). Also of interest is the peninsula Dongting Dongshan, to the south of Piaomiaofeng. The island Dongting Xishan can be reached from

A moon gate, typical in southern Chinese gardens.

Xiaomenkou on the southern bank of Tai Hu, from Wuxi in the north and from Suzhou by boat; there is also a boat connection to the peninsula.

On this island is a cave that is an old Daoist sacred center lying in the Linwu range. It wasn't until 1985 that it was uncovered from the mud of Tai Hu. A large number of religious artifacts and utensils were discovered, some of which are now exhibited in the provincial museum in Suzhou.

In the west of the mountainous peninsula Dongting Dongshan, whose highest elevation is the 293-meter-high (961-ft) Muli Feng, is **Zijin'an** (Purple-Gold Monastery), which dates back to the Tang period.

After being destroyed, it was rebuilt in the second half of the fourteenth century. The 16 Luohan statues and the statue of Guanyin, goddess of mercy, are special attractions in this particular monastery; the sculptures are said to have been made by the Hangzhou sculptor Lei Chao and his wife in the Southern Song period.

Suzhou: Even if Hangzhou has overtaken its sister town as the most popular destination for the Chinese, Suzhou – known as the town of gardens and canals – is at least as charming as its rival town on the West Lake. While Hangzhou has its large and grand lake, Suzhou is home to small intimate garden spots tucked away behind houses and hidden between narrow streets. Even when it rains, as it often does, the narrow streets and cobblestone walks are given a softened, misty aura that make Suzhou a relaxing, romantic diversion from the chaos of the cities. Be warned, however, that development is overtaking quaintness and tradition.

Suzhou was mentioned in 484 BC, since it was, for a few years, the capital of the state of Wu during the Period of the Warring Kingdoms (475–221 BC). It flourished as a trading and silk center in the early sixth century, linked with the capital through Da Yunhe, the Grand Canal. Its most prosperous period was during the Ming and Qing dynasties, when many officials, scholars and art-

Chinese garden in Suzhou.

ists settled here and local traders grew rich. This wealth was largely invested in the 150 gardens that make Suzhou so famous today. The principle of Chinese garden construction – creating an illusion of the universe in a small space – is clearly evident here. Water trickles between unusually-shaped, rocky crags; small islands are connected by canals and zigzag bridges; winding paths lead to tiny garden spaces with fountains, carefully manicured plants and fish ponds. A walk through the small alleys in the town, along the canals, and through the gardens has a special charm in the misty mornings, when the bus loads of tourists haven't yet marched through.

In the northeast of the town, on Qimen Street, is **Zhouzheng Yuan** (Garden of the Foolish Politician), which covers four hectares (9 acres) and is the largest garden in Suzhou. Wang Xiancheng, a retired court official, had it built in 1513 on the spot where the poet Lu Guimeng lived during the Tang period. It is said that Wang's son, a gambler, lost the property through gambling. During the Taiping Rebellion, when Suzhou was substantially destroyed, the Taiping clan made this garden its headquarters from 1860 to 1864. The largest part of the area is covered in ponds, close to pavilions connected by zigzagging bridges. The ponds are full of lotus flowers; one pavilion is consequently called Hehua Simian Ting (You See Lotus Everywhere). Paths wind along willow-tree-lined shores to various viewing points.

Directly next to this garden is **Lishi Bowuguan** (History Museum), where the history of Jiangsu Province is depicted. Farther west on Xibei Lu is **Beisi Ta** (North Temple Pagoda), its current manifestation from the seventeenth century. The present pagoda dates from the Southern Song period, although two thorough restorations occurred in the second half of the seventeenth century. A splendid view of Suzhou can be had from the top of the 76-meter-high (250-ft), nine-story tower, which is built in an octagonal shape. There is a tea house with refreshments behind the pagoda.

On the western edge of the town, in the street of the same name, is **Liu Yuan** (Garden for Lingering In). Aptly named, it is a garden with many nooks and crannies, in which getting lost is a pleasure. A garden was first created here in the sixteenth century, but the current one was created in 1800 by its proprietors. The Garden for Lingering In is considered a prime example of a southern Chinese garden of the Qing era, and thus belongs to the gardens protected as national cultural monuments. Here, too, a pond forms the center of the garden; it is lined with many paths, halls and pavilions. There are some interesting pieces of furniture and some especially beautiful artifacts in the halls. Another specialty is a six-meter-high (21-ft) stone from Tai Hu that has been erected in the northeastern courtyard.

Opposite Liu Yuan is **Xi Yuan** (West Garden), which together with Liu Yuan once formed a single large area owned by an imperial official, Xu Shitai. His son had a temple built here that, after being destroyed by the Taiping, was reconstructed. At the back of Daxiongbaodian (Precious Hall of the Great

Pagoda near Suzhou.

Hero), the goddess of mercy, Guanyin, is portrayed.

Further west is Luohantang (Hall of the Luohan), where 500 gilded Luohan representations are exhibited; each face is different. Particularly fascinating is the depiction of the monk Jigong, whose facial expression changes depending upon where the observer stands. One of the nicest gardens is the Garden of the Fisherman's Net.

Beyond a series of tacky souvenir shops – ubiquitous outside all of these gardens – is a secluded, quiet spot for meditation, reading or simply watching elderly patrons while away the morning over tea. (The tea houses in these gardens, it should be said, are somewhat disappointing, failing to capture the romanticism of the gardens themselves, in part because the workers talk at a decibel level out of sync with the peaceful nature of the place.)

This garden might be more accurately described as a home whose open, airy rooms are connected by a series of walks, streams and gardens. Rock sculptures, moss, small trees, flowers and miniature pines are all artfully arranged.

About one kilometer further to the west, in the village of Fengqiao, is **Hanshan Si** (Monastery of the Cold Mountain), named after the seventh-century monk Han Shan, a Zen Buddhist fond of drink who became famous as an eccentric poet. Thought to have lived in the seventh century, Han Shan's poems have been translated into Western languages and are worth reading.

The monastery was built in the sixth century, though the current buildings were rebuilt after being destroyed during the Taiping revolt. In the monastery are statues of Han Shan and his companion Shi De. Visitors can buy stone rubbings and poems written by the two monks. Hanshan Si is a popular place for the festival of the Chinese New Year, and if you like noise and festivities, don't miss it.

In the southwest of Suzhou are remnants of the **old city wall** and **Panmen**, a gate from 1351, whose origins are thought to date back to the fifth century

Back-alley canals, Suzhou.

260

BC. Towards the city in a northerly direction, directly behind the wall, is **Ruiguang Ta** (Happy View Pagoda) and **Kongmiao** (Confucius Temple). Opposite on Renmin Lu is **Canglangting** (Garden of the Blue Wave Pavilion). This relatively small garden was built in 1041 by the poet Su Shenqing. In the center on an artificially-created hill is a pavilion. The harmonic structure of the winged roofs is impressive; they are partly covered in leaves, merging into the groves of bamboo and Cyprus trees.

Further north in the direction of the town, on Renmin Lu, is **Yi Yuan** (Garden of Harmony), which was created in 1876 when an imperial official acquired the former property of the fifteenth-century minister Wu Kuan and transformed it into this garden. In the eastern part are pavilions and buildings, in which paintings and calligraphy are exhibited. The western part is designed to enhance the natural landscape.

Opposite the Garden of Harmony begin the alleys of the old city. At the northern edge of Guanqianjie is the Daoist **Xuanmiaoguang** (Temple of Mysteries), now partly occupied by a bazaar. The temple is thought to have been founded around 270; only San-qingdian (Hall of the Three Pure Ones), dating from 1180, remains of the original 31 halls. The gilded statues of the Three Pure Ones are in the hall. Around the temples are numerous small shops, food stalls, restaurants and many of the sweet shops for which Suzhou is noted throughout China.

Northeast of this busy scene, between Lindun Lu and Yuanlin Lu, is a garden called **Shizilin** (Lion Grove), which was landscaped by a Buddhist monk in the fourteenth century around a temple. The rock shapes are worth a look. The biggest one is **Shizi Feng** (Lion Peak), which has a labyrinth of narrow paths and many caves.

Wuxi: The history of Wuxi, reached from Suzhou either by railway in under an hour or by boat on Da Yunhe in about six hours, goes back to the early centuries BC, when the town was called Youxi

Clay figures from Wuxi.

– literally, "there is tin." The tin reserves must already have been exhausted by the Han dynasty, as since that time it has been called Wuxi, or "there is no tin." Tin or not, Wuxi's importance grew with the completion of Da Yunhe, and its modest wealth was achieved, as in the whole region, through agriculture and extensive silk production.

Today, there are nearly a million people living in Wuxi, and tourism plays an increasingly important role for the town, but as a crossroads and departure point more than for any intrinsic interest.

The mild climate, soil and sufficient water make the region around Wuxi one of the most fertile in China – the Chinese call it "land of fish and rice." The town itself offers few sights, but its charming landscape and its close proximity to Tai Hu mean it is a popular destination for excursions and day trips. One special attraction is Da Yunhe, which flows through the town, and its arched bridges. Qingming Bridge over the canal, in the southeast of the town, is architecturally interesting.

In the western part of the town is **Xihui**, a park of 44 hectares (111 acres) whose name comes from Xi Shan (Tin Mountain), 75 meters (246 ft) high, and the 300-meter-high (990-ft) Hui. The park was created between the two mountains in 1958.

On top is the octagonal **Longguang Ta** (Dragon Light Pagoda) from the Ming period, with a wonderful view over the town and Tai Hu. Hui is famous for its water, which comes from Tianxia Di'erquan (Second Spring under Heaven). There are pavilions and temple halls under ancient trees, with inscriptions from Tang and Song times.

Hui is known for the small figures that have been made from the hill's clay. The material has been popular since the Ming period because of its malleability and hardness after firing. Adjacent to Xihui is **Jicheng Yuan** (Garden of Delight), barely covering a hectare and constructed around five centuries ago.

In the southwest of the town is **Mei Yuan** (Plum Garden), constructed at the end of the last century. In its center is a rock garden surrounded by thousands of plum trees. In spring, the garden is one expansive sea of blossoms – and of visitors.

Another site, **Li Yuan** (Shell Garden), is in the southwest of the town near Wuli Hu (Five Li Lake), an offshoot of Tai Hu. West of Li Yuan, Baojie Bridge leads to **Yuantouzhu** (Tortoise Head Island), whose artificially-created shape with many small hills is supposed to represent the head of a tortoise. In the past, court officials and rich families lived in this area, and there are the pavilions, pagodas and tea houses typical for this lovely landscape.

Nearby is an example of a strange tourist site that is popping up around in China, **Space City**. For some reason, Wuxi has taken on this moniker, and this combination museum and amusement park offers a ride on a simulated rocket launch and a walk through a planetary landscape that combines science with Star Wars fiction.

Outside of Wuxi: Excursions from Wuxi into the surrounding area are worthwhile, either on a day-trip by bicycle, which can be hired anywhere, or a trip lasting several days.

Some villages now offer tourist programs, which in some cases include accommodation in usually good hotels with equally good food; there is also, at times, the possibility of staying with a family. In any case, this is not only a chance to see the lovely countryside, but also to get an impression of rural life in this wealthy region.

For almost 1,500 years, the area around Wuxi has produced silk. Most people here cultivate silkworms as a popular and profitable sideline. The young worms, spread out on rice-straw mats, are fed with juicy mulberry leaves and then put on bundles of rice straw, where they spin a cocoon in less than a week, usually in five days.

Between April and November, one can observe this activity on many farms. The cocoon is washed in silk-spinning mills and then the silk thread is pulled, which can measure more than 1,000 meters (3,000 ft). Several threads are then spun together into a durable yarn that can be woven.

Right, Buddha Sakyamuni, Lingyin Si monastery.

NANJING

Here, in one of the most beautiful cities of China, the struggle between China's rapid development and the preservation of its past can be distilled down to the question of trees. Nanjing's wide avenues are lined with stately sycamore trees, three and four rows deep in some places, that provide a welcome sea of green. But the pressure to accommodate new high-rises, hotels, automobile traffic and a growing population has meant the trees are starting to be felled. As one elderly resident laments, the trees used to provide a canopy of shade from the harsh summer sun. Now, she says, it is more difficult to find a cool, shady spot.

Trees are especially important. Together with Wuhan and Chongqing, Nanjing is considered one of the "three furnaces" of China. In the summer, temperatures rise above 40°C (104°F).

Yet even with a population of five million, Nanjing, the former capital of the rich province of Jiangsu, still offers a respite from the frantic, congested pace of nearby Shanghai and Beijing to the north. From the park-like setting of its famous university to the forested Zigin Shan (Purple Mountains) in the east, Nanjing offers an atmosphere that few other Chinese cities can match.

Nanjing can easily be reached by train, boat or plane. There is an express train, which began running in 1996, that zips from Shanghai in just over two hours, and without any stops in between. Arrival by train from the north crosses China's longest river, Chang Jiang (Yangzi), via the great **Nanjing Changjiang Daqiao** (Yangzi Bridge), which was opened in 1968. The bridge, to the northwest of the city, is a symbol of Chinese independence and national pride. When relations between the former Soviet Union and China were severed in 1960, the Chinese built the bridge – which had been mostly a Soviet project up to then – with their own design and resources. It took 9,000 workers more than eight years to construct the bridge, struggling against the strong

currents of Chang Jiang. The bridge is an important symbol of progress for Nanjing, as its construction helped spur further development. Today, Nanjing is a center for shipbuilding and engineering industries, as well as the chemical and petrochemical industry in China.

More interesting for travelers, however, is Nanjing's reputation as a center for higher learning. This status makes it one of the easiest places to find English-speaking guides – or just someone to have a conversation with over a beer.

Historical depth: The region has been populated for more than 5,000 years, and the history of Nanjing itself dates back to the fifth century BC. Between the third and sixth centuries AD, Nanjing was the capital of southern dynasties at a time when foreigners were ruling in the north of China. Little has been preserved from that era, however, with the exception of some animal sculptures and stele outside of Nanjing, and in the Buddhist cave grottoes in nearby Qixia.

Nanjing reached national importance during the Ming dynasty, whose first

emperors had their seat of government here in the Southern Capital – a literal translation of the name Nanjing – at least until they transferred it to Beijing, at the beginning of the fifteenth century. The well-preserved **city wall** in Nanjing dates from this period, and is best viewed from the **Zhonghuamen** (Zhonghua Gate), in the south of the city. Although not terribly symmetrical, the wall had a circumference of over 30 kilometers (18 mi), with an average height of 12 meters (40 ft). Taking two decades to construct, the wall had 13 gates as defensive ramparts and barracks. Several of the gates remain standing today, including Zhonghuamen, a good reference point for navigating Nanjing.

In the city itself, the **Shitoucheng**, a partially-preserved wall to the north of Mochou, is a reminder of Nanjing's turbulent history. There is a secluded wooded walk that follows the path of the wall, and sections of the stone are still visible. A small park nearby hosts a military museum and park with models of aircraft and rockets.

Rape of Nanjing: In the same section of town, near **Jiangdongmen** (Gate on the Eastern Bank of the River), is the somber **Datusha Jinianguan**, a memorial to the Nanjing massacre and an appropriately simple stone building with a plain facade. Inside is a quiet, darkened exhibition of photographs, maps and witness accounts that document the arrival of Japanese troops in December of 1937, and the brutal rapes, burning and looting of houses and historical relics, and the slaughter of some 300,000 Chinese that occurred over the next six weeks. Over 20,000 cases of rape were reported, including gang rapes followed by execution. Those who survived sometimes ended up as Japanese Imperial Army "comfort women," as the Japanese now call those Asian and European women held prisoner for sex.

Most silencing is a viewing hall overlooking a mass grave, one of many of the *wan ren keng* (pit of ten thousand corpses) that the Japanese left behind. Any question about China's lingering resentment over Japanese occupa-

Nanjing Changjiang Daqiao.

tion is answered by this sign in the museum: "We must be on guard against any attempt to distort the history of Japanese aggression or to mollify aggressive war by the forces in Japan."

The concern of the Chinese to memorialize the massacre is not one of vanity or self-pity. The Japanese, including government officials, have persistently denied the magnitude of the massacre, if not denying it completely. More people, mostly civilians, died at Nanjing from the Japanese massacre than from the atomic bomb at Hiroshima, yet Japanese textbooks refer to the massacre as a "minor incident". Among those in government denying the massacre have been cabinet ministers – including the foreign, justice and education ministers – university professors, and the politically-feared right-wing establishment.

City center: The **Xinjiekou** traffic circle marks the center of the city. Here, the largest hotel, the Jingling, towers above the traffic, but there are other hotels under construction that will tower above it. To the southwest is **Mochou**, a lake named after the Mochou (Lady Without Sorrows), who is said to have lived here in the fifth century. Various Qin pavilions pepper the area.

Nearby, the **Chaotiangong** (Chaotian Palace) dates back to the Ming dynasty and is considered one of the area's best-preserved Confucian temples. (It has been used for this purpose since the middle of the last century.)

Also in the southern part of the city, near Zhonghuamen, is a lively market area known as **Fuzimiao**, a maze of shops, street stalls selling food, and carnival attractions, all centered around the site of a Confucian temple. Nearby is a museum built in the memory of peasant revolutionaries.

To the north, on the other side of the Xinjiekou traffic circle, are **Gulou**, the Drum Tower, and **Zhonglou**, the Bell Tower, near the leafy campus of **Nanjing University**. The streets in this part of the city are filled with lively student cafes and eateries. There is a beautiful view of Nanjing from Gulou, used as an exhibition hall. Nearby is a permanent

Bicycle guard.

open market; it is also worth walking from here to Shanxi Square, a busy local market. Nearby is a small museum honoring a contemporary leader, former premier Zhou Enlai, who died in 1976 and remains popular today.

In the eastern part of the city is **Nanjing Bowuguan** (Nanjing Museum). Its display of ceramics, bronzes and porcelain from Nanjing and the province of Jiangsu covers 5,000 years of history. The most important exhibit is a 2,000-year-old shroud from the Eastern Han dynasty, made from 2,600 green jade rectangles sewn together with silver wire.

Like much of China, there is considerable mixing of historical periods in Nanjing's monuments and historical residue. For example, the first Ming emperor, Zhu Yuanzhang, had a wall erected on the foundations of an existing wall that had been built of reddish sandstone in the third century, which is still preserved today. Nearby, to the south of Zhonghuamen, is **Yuhutai** (Rain of Flowers Terrace), where in the fourth century, according to legend, the Buddha made flowers rain from the sky. Today, there is a memorial in the park to Communists and their supporters who died in 1927 at the hands of Chiang Kaishek and his nationalists.

Outside of Nanjing: Ruins to the northeast of Nanjing, near **Zijin Shan** (Purple Mountains), offer a glimpse of the era from the Ming dynasty. Here, in the foothills, was **Mingxiao Ling**, mausoleum of the first Ming emperor Hongwu (Zhu Yuanzhang). Unfortunately, it was plundered during the Taiping uprising in 1864. A "sacred path" that has been preserved, however, is lined with stone animals and soldiers and leads directly to the tomb.

A bit farther to the east of the mausoleum is another of a modern-day leader. **Zhongshan Ling**, the mausoleum of Sun Yatsen, was built here after the death of the founder of the republic in 1925; the body of Sun was moved here in 1929. The complex covers an area of eight hectares (20 acres). A Cantonese, Sun Yatsen wanted to find his last rest-

Zhongshan Ling.

ing place here amidst the lovely Zijin mountains. An avenue lined with beautiful trees has 392 granite steps that lead to the white memorial hall, its roof covered with blue ceramic tiles. The vault is slightly below the memorial hall; various inscriptions on the walls reflect the political heritage of Sun Yatsen.

To the east of the mausoleum in Linggu (Valley of the Souls) is the **Linggu Si**, a temple built at the end of the fourteenth century. Only the temple site of Wuliangdian, which has been restored several times and has been built entirely from stone and without any wooden rafters, remains of the former large structure. The area is popular with Nanjing residents with its pines.

Behind Wuliangdian is the 61-meter-high (200-ft) **Linggu Ta**, a pagoda built in the 1920s in memory of the victims of the Northern Campaign of 1926–27. There is a magnificent view of the surrounding landscape from the top floor. Visible atop the mountain stands an **observatory**, built in 1934 and extended in 1949. It has a museum with old and new astronomical instruments. A cable car to the observatory provides a splendid view of Nanjing.

The park on **Xuanwu**, a lake in the north of Nanjing, offers pavilions and small islands linked to the shore by dams and curved bridges. With its attractive lotus-covered ponds and willow trees, Xuanwu provides an ideal atmosphere for a quiet time. A 15-kilometer-long (9 mi) promenade follows the shores of the lake. There is also a small zoo in the park, and an open-air theater and aquarium. A small tram ferries visitors around the lake, as well. At night, retirees flock to the park for evening walks and sessions of *taiji*.

Some 12 kilometers (7 mi) north of the city rises **Yanziji** (Swallow's Rock), which gets its name from its appearance when viewed from Chang Jiang. Northeast there are tombs of rulers and noblemen from the time of the Three Kingdoms and the Southern dynasties. The stone sculptures of animals and mythical figures, some more than three meters (10 ft) high, line the paths between the tombs.

There are several ways of traveling from Nanjing to other towns and areas. One is through picturesque fields planted with rice, wheat and vegetables, although these rural oases are quickly making way for industrial factories. The railway stops first in **Zhenjiang**, made famous from Marco Polo's travels. Zhenjiang is situated on the southern bank of Chang Jiang, in a colorful countryside of green hills and bamboo groves.

Seventy kilometers (40 mi) northwest of Nanjing lies **Yangzhou**, which flourished between the tenth and fourteenth centuries. Marco Polo spent several years here.

At that time, Yangzhou attracted many poets and artists. The Academy of Art of the "Eight Eccentrics," whose paintings can be seen in the Yangzhou museum, is famous. Yangzhou played an important role for Japanese Buddhists; this is where the monk Jian Zhen began several expeditions to the Japanese islands in the eighth century. In recent years, Japanese Buddhists have given donations to erect a memorial hall for the monk.

ear Ming mbs.

CHANG JIANG: THE RIVER YANGZI

The longest river in China is called, appropriately enough, Chang Jiang – Long River. Meandering eastwards for approximately 6,000 kilometers (3,500 mi), Chang Jiang begins in the southwest part of the Qinghai Plateau on Geladandong, the main peak of Tanggula Shan. Its course ends just north of Shanghai, where its eight-mile wide mouth empties into Huang Hai, the Yellow Sea, near Shanghai.

Along the way, the river flows across nine provinces, with its 700 tributaries draining an area of nearly two million square kilometers (700,000 sq mi) – nearly 20 percent of the total geographic area of China, and one-quarter of the country's arable land.

From the delta just north of Shanghai, an area with what is probably China's highest population density, the river is navigable by ocean-going vessels to Wuhan, nearly 1,000 kilometers (600 mi) upstream. Along this lower stretch (which is, in fact, known Yangzi in this area, its local name changing upriver two more times), the river flows through most of China's important industrialized area, not to mention centers of such trades as silk weaving, embroidery, lacquer work and carving. It is impossible to underestimate the importance of the Chang Jiang.

The government feels that the river can be even more important to China by accelerating growth in the interior provinces, increasing the river's navigability, and controlling disastrous floods. Along the section of the river famed for its gorges, Sanxia, China has begun building a hydroelectric dam at Sandouping that will eventually form the world's largest storage reservoir.

The dam itself will be two kilometers wide and 185 meters (607 ft) tall. When filled, the new reservoir waters will extend west over 500 kilometers, as far as Chongqing. The reservoir will be up to 175 meters (575 ft) deep.

Scheduled for completion in the first decade of the next century, the intent of the dam is in many ways understandable, given that the interior provinces have economically lagged way behind the booming coastal regions.

But the dam and reservoir will permanently alter the picturesque landscape, by submerging sections of the gorges and forcing entire riverside communities to move, perhaps as many as one million people. The water level through the Three Gorges will be raised 185 meters – higher than some of the rocky spires now bordering the river.

Wuhan: The film *Gunboat Up the Yangtse* introduced the river to modern Westerners. Everyone who saw the movie knew that large boats could travel as far as what is now the industrial, somewhat bland city of Wuhan – more or less halfway between Shanghai and Chongqing, the river's navigable stretch. The river's course from here to the ocean is not terribly interesting or picturesque, and thus is therefore avoided by most foreign tourists.

After the 1860 Treaty of Tianjin made

Preceding pages: junks on the Chang Jiang. **Left,** boats are lifted up in the Gezhouba lock. **Right,** the jade Buddha in Guiyuan Si, Wuhan.

Hankou – one of three municipalities that merged to create Wuhan – a free port, the colonial powers of Great Britain, France, Germany, Russia and Japan established themselves here and divided the former village into concessions. From here, they sought to colonize the inland provinces of China. Wuhan district, which is the city's largest, is still characterized by colonial architecture.

Wuhan, which has four million inhabitants, is today better known to foreigners and Chinese alike as a starting or finishing point for excursions through Chang Jiang's three famous gorges, Sanxia. This jumping-off point gives Wuhan an attractive position with which to capitalize on tourists, but surprisingly, the city has done little to enhance its tourist trade. Getting around the city – after the construction of a new bridge and new roads, and development of modern hotels – is easy enough. But Wuhan itself isn't particularly attractive. But if passing through, consider spending a day on an urban ramble here. **Huanghelou** (Yellow Crane Tower)

on She Shan (Snake Mountain) in Wuchang district has been carefully restored, and the surrounding buildings have been rebuilt in traditional Chinese style. The original Huanghelou is said to have been built in the third century, only to be destroyed and rebuilt numerous times, most recently in 1884. The pagoda-like building holds exhibitions of calligraphy and paintings, and windows on every floor offer different vantage points from which to view **Changjiang Daqiao**, the bridge across the Chang Jiang. Exactly 1,156 meters long (3,793 ft) with eight piers, it was the first bridge across the Chang Jiang. Built between 1955 and 1957 for rail and road traffic, the bridge was critical for the development of the economy and created an urgently needed transportation link between the north and south of China.

On the edge of the town is a large lake area, **Dong Hu** (East Lake), situated in a huge park that has a number of other sights. There is a nice view across the entire lake and park area from

Changjiang Daqiao (Yangze Bridge), Wuhan.

276

Huguangge (Sparkling Lake Pavilion). The lakes are a popular spot for members of the many institutes located in this part of the town. But despite the visitors, particularly in the hot summer months when temperatures in Wuhan rise to around 40°C, it is a pleasantly cool place because of its enormous size.

Near Donghu Yuan (East Lake Park) is the restored Hubei provincial museum, worth a visit, particularly because of its unique set of well-preserved chimes from 430 BC.

Guiyuan Si, a Buddhist temple from the sixteenth century, is in the center of Hanyang. It has not yet been restored, although it was not destroyed during the Cultural Revolution. A walk through the halls and courtyards adds a certain nostalgic charm to it. The painting of the bodhisattva Guanyin shows the goddess of mercy standing on a tortoise, giving the temple its name.

Cruising upriver: Boats travel in both directions, but traveling down-river, from Chongqing to Wuhan through the gorges, is naturally faster and takes two nights and three days. Upriver takes five days. Negotiating a boat trip can be confusing. There are upscale cruises with hotel-like accommodations and dining rooms, casinos and entertainment. At the other end of the scale are local boats in which travelers bunk four or six to a cabin and fend for themselves in regards to meals. The boats that leave daily at various times from Wuhan to Chongqing were once called Dongfanghong (East is Red) during the days of the Cultural Revolution. Today, they have been renamed after their home ports Chongqing, Hankou or Shanghai. Boats have different classification systems, so for each cruise, it is important to ask what exactly is meant by first-, second- or third-class.

Wuhan to Sanxia: The first stop upriver from Wuhan to Chongqing is the town of **Yueyang**, a river port located in Hunan Province on the southern edge of Hubei Province, and on the eastern shore of Dongting.

The best-known sight in this town of 200,000 greets the traveler south of the

Small day-tour boats.

river: **Yueyanglou** (Yueyang Tower), one of the most famous pavilion towers in the region, if not China. Numerous songs have been composed about it since the Tang period (618–907), but the restored building currently dates from the last century.

The tower is flanked on both sides by two pavilions, Xianmeiting (Plum Blossom of the Immortal Pavilion) and Sanzuiting (Three Drunks Pavilion). Dongting Hu, one of the largest inland lakes in China, is linked to the Chang Jiang by several rivers, canals and lakes, and serves as a water reservoir for the river. During the rainy season, it takes up to 40 percent of the waters from the Chang Jiang; in droughts, it returns its water to the river, and its area is reduced by almost a third.

The lake contains a wealth of fish, is a breeding place for rare waterbirds, and in the summer months, its shores are covered in the red and green hues of blooming lotus plants.

About 200 kilometers (120 mi) west of Wuhan is **Shashi** (Sand Town), still in Hubei Province. This town, which by Chinese standards is small with only about 200,000 inhabitants, has few sights to offer. Zhanghua Si was founded in 535, but its present structure dates from the Ming period and contains two beautifully-worked jade Buddhas. There is also the seven-story-high Wanshoubao Ta (Pagoda of Eternal Life).

Yichang, the last stop before reaching the gorges, is an industrial town. If you want to break your journey here, enjoy a short excursion by bus to see how the Chang Jiang emerges from the gorges at the Nanjing Pass, six kilometers (4 mi) away.

The famous battle between the state armies of Shu and Wu (AD 221) took place here. The king of Shu and leader of the army, Liu Bei, lost the battle. It is vividly remembered in Chinese history as a victory of a weak army over a numerically much stronger army by the use of tactical skills.

After his defeat, Liu Bei was forced to flee through the gorges of the Chang Jiang to Baidichen.

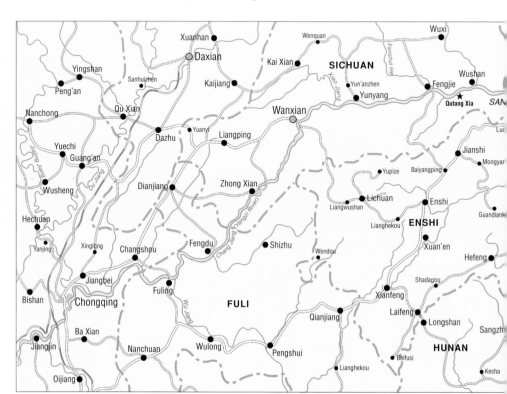

Sanxia (Three Gorges): Just behind Yichang, boats enter an enormous lock. In front is **Gezhouba**, the biggest dam in China thus far: 2,500 meters (8,200 ft) wide and 47 meters (154 ft) deep. It was completed in 1986 and supplies electricity to the surrounding provinces. A new town has grown up in recent years along its banks. However, the dam's construction was controversial, since the dam has raised the water level of the upper course and has possibly increased the actual danger of flooding.

Gezhouba will one day have a mate. West of Yichang, work has begun on what will, when completed, be the world's largest dam. The **Three Gorges Dam** has already proved controversial, because it will be enormously costly, over a million people will have to be moved, and it could cause environmental problems. The water level through the gorges will be raised 185 meters.

But the scheme has boosted tourism to Sanxia, the Three Gorges, with visitors arriving to see them before the transformation. There are vivid depictions all along the river of just how much the terrain will be changed. Markings on the rocky walls of the river mark the depth; a quick calculation shows visually just how much of the gorges will be flooded. Already there are signs that construction work will severely pollute this stretch of the river, as debris and garbage now rush down the river past the passing cruise boats.

The lock of Gezhouba lets several boats through at a time, negotiating a height change of up to 30 meters (100 ft). Upstream of the dam, four rock faces, resembling silhouettes, emerge on the southern bank of the river. With a bit of imagination, one can recognize the four famous heroes from the novel *Journey to the West*, which is known throughout China. They are the ape king Sun Wukong, the Buddhist master Xuanzang, the pig Zhu Bajie and the monk Sha.

The entire length of the three gorges is about 120 kilometers (75 mi). From the dam and upriver towards Chongqing, the three gorges are Xiling Xia, Wu Xia,

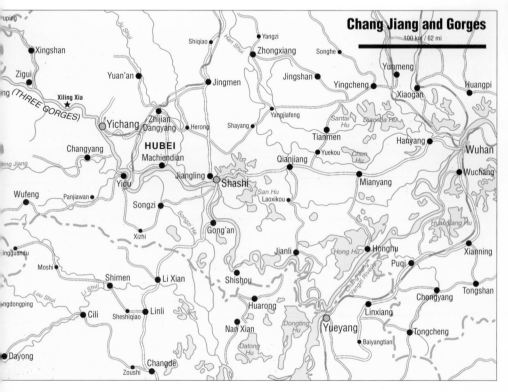

and Qutang Xia. The first and longest gorge is **Xiling Xia**. This 78-kilometer-long (48-mi) gorge is really made up of several smaller, well-named gorges.

From the north, the river is overlooked by Huanglingmiao (Yellow Hill Temple). The main hall of the temple, which is said to date from the Han period, is dedicated to the ruler Yu. About half way into Xiling Gorge, the river is divided by a sand bank.

The peculiar shape of the next small gorge earned it the name Niugan Mafei Xia (Horse-Lung and Ox-Liver Gorge); hidden behind it is the 120-meter-long (390-ft) abyss of Qingtan (Blue Cliff). Bingshu Baojian Xia (Precious Sword Gorge) also got its name from its appearance: a rock that juts up like a sword and from legend.

Zhuge Liang, a famous military leader from the period of the Three Kingdoms (220–280) and brother-in-arms of Liu Bei, is said to have written a military manual; not finding anyone worthy of becoming his successor, he hid the manual beneath the rock. Since then, the Chinese have waited for a military commander who has the capabilities of moving the rock and freeing the valuable book.

The mouth of **Xiangxi** (Fragrant River) on the northern bank signals the end of Xiling Gorge. The boat passes Zigui, the home of the famous poet Qu Yuan (330–295 BC) who, according to legend, drowned himself in despair over the occupation of his home state Chu by the armies of the Qin empire. (The whole of China still celebrates the Dragon Boat Festival in his honor.)

Despite its name, the 40-kilometer-long **Wu Xia** (Witches Gorge) is relatively calm. As with so many places in China, the gorge, surrounded by twelve mountain peaks, is steeped in legend, and loudspeakers on the boats hardly stop bellowing out all the lore.

One of these stories includes that of the youngest daughter of Xiwangmu (Western Heavenly Mother), who helped the legendary Emperor Yu conquer the water and who now keeps watch over the river from the highest peak, Shennu

The water acquires a yellow color during the rainy season.

Feng (Fairy Peak), with her eleven sisters – a Chinese Lorelei who does not bring misfortune to the seafarers but rather protects them. The border between the provinces of Hubei and Sichuan runs through Wu Xia.

Entry into the third gorge, **Qutang Xia** (Bellows Gorge), is breathtakingly-beautiful. Although it is only eight kilometers long and thus the shortest of the three, it is probably the most fascinating of the gorges. Perpendicular walls rise up from the river, narrowing it to a width of 100 meters (30 ft) and requiring the helmsman to exert great concentration in steering the vessel through the narrow gap. Swirling brown water reveals that underneath the smooth surface are treacherous maelstroms.

Traveler reports from the 1920s and 1930s offer an exciting account of the journey through the gorges with cargo boats and junks. The boats had to be towed upstream, and the coolies carried out heavy work that could, at times, end in death if one of the men lost his footing on the paths hewn into the rock and pulled his mates, who were all chained together, down into the abyss.

The crossing of the Qutang Xia in a normal cargo boat required more than a hundred trackers, hired from among the peasants in the surrounding areas. But even then, the relatively short distance took several days, depending on the water level.

There is a saying that to reach Sichuan is more difficult than to reach heaven, and traveling through these narrow gorges gives that saying real meaning. Until this century, this passage was almost the only way to get from eastern China to Sichuan Province, which is surrounded by nearly impassable mountain ranges.

Sanxia to Chongqing: After passing through Qutang Xia, the boat passes the settlement of **Fengjie**, and to the east, **Baidicheng**, City of the White Emperor. Legend has it that a ruler from the time of the Eastern Han dynasty (AD 25–220) saw a white dragon emerge from a well outside his palace. He considered it a good omen and henceforth

Porters cover the mud.

called himself White Emperor. In the main hall of the palace are figures of two army generals of Shu from the time of the Three Kingdoms (221–263), Liu Bei and Zhuge Liang. (After the military defeat at Yichang, Liu Bei was forced to flee to Baidicheng, and on his death bed named Zhuge Liang as his successor.)

The next large town is **Wanxian**, for a long time a trading center and port for ships traveling through the gorges. An impressive and steep staircase leads upwards to the city near the mooring. Stunning is the realization that all of these steps – and hundreds more leading to a city park – will be submerged after the completion of the dam project.

Now, the steps lead to the market street, where at almost any time during the day or night, traders offer local produce and bamboo goods to buyers coming from the boats.

Wanxian is particularly famous for its oranges and pomelos, and it is the place where Chinese travelers on the river like to get their provisions.

About five hours from Wanxian, on the northern bank of the river, is **Shibaozhai** (Stone Treasure Stronghold). During the reign of emperor Qianlong (1736–1797), a temple was erected on a rock rising up 30 meters (100 ft) from the northern bank of the Chang Jiang. According to legend, there was a small hole in the temple wall, from which enough rice trickled to feed the monks, thus the name, Stone Treasure. However, when the monks became greedy and thought they could get even more rice if they made the hole bigger, the treasure dried up.

As the ascent to the temple was very tiring, a pagoda-shaped pavilion was built against the rock at the time of emperor Jiaqing (1796–1820). Its eleven stories reach as far as the temple, and so one can easily climb up to the temple from inside the pavilion.

Fengdu, which is also on the northern bank of the Chang Jiang, has been named after a dam and the mountain range surrounding the town. It is really called the Ghost or Devil Town, be-

Left, Shibaozhai **Pagoda.** **Right,** old stone pagoda by the river.

cause from the time of the Tang dynasty (618–907), statues of demons and devils have been housed in numerous temples. Visitors can take a cable car to several of the temples, which often have the feel of a cheap carnival fun-house, with statues of ghosts and demons and grotesque scenes of torture.

Chongqing: The journey upriver, which has covered nearly 700 kilometers (435 mi), ends in Chongqing, in Sichuan Province and rare among Chinese cities, as it is built on a rocky promontory hugging the river, not on a flat expanse. Actually, it sits right at the confluence of two rivers, where the Jialing joins the Chang Jiang; it has always been an important trading center due to its location.

During the Tang period (618–907), Chongqing was called Yuzhou, and it is still called Yu, for short, today. The emperor Zhao Dun, of the Southern Song dynasty (1127–1279), had renamed it Chongqing, or Twin Fortune, after two lucky events: he first became prince of the prefecture, and then later became emperor.

"When the sun shines in Sichuan in winter, the dogs bark". This proverb is particularly apt for Chongqing.

Through most of the winter, from around October to March and when temperatures can fall to 4°C (39°F), the town is shrouded in fog that rises from the rivers, depressing the spirit.

During World War II, when the Japanese occupied parts of the country and the Kuomintang government under Chiang Kaishek had fled to Chongqing, the town was bombed for several summers by the Japanese. Then, people were grateful for the winter fog, as no Japanese reconnaissance planes flew over the city, and so no bombers.

This city of 14 million people threatens at time to expand beyond control. In response, rather ugly-looking high-rises have been built in the center.

Chongqing is not constructed on traditional grid lines. The houses in the old city center are typical of the architecture in this region, clinging to the slopes with their black roofs resembling swallows nests; the top floor has a door to the

Dazu Buddha.

street and the lower floors overlook one of the two rivers.

Two cable cars link the river banks, and a bridge over the Chang Jiang, completed in 1982, has relieved the pressure on the ferries. Another bridge, supplementary to the existing one across the Jialing, has been built farther north, creating a link between the districts of Shapingba and Jiangbei.

The old city area around **Jiefangbei** (Liberation Square) is full of small meandering alleys. Steep steps lead from the tip of the peninsula down to the river banks, studded with moorings. At the tip of the peninsula is a small pavilion, **Chaotianmen** (Door Facing Heaven). The flood level is marked here, as a reminder of the last big flood in 1982, which covered a large area and caused great devastation.

Not far from Chaotianmen, hidden in a narrow side street, is a small Buddhist temple, **Luohan Si**. Noted for 500 painted terracotta sculptures called *arhat*, it has been restored in recent years. In the evening, there is a brilliant

view of the whole city from **Pipa Shan**, the city's highest point.

Beyond Chongqing: Heading out of town towards Beiquan (Northern Springs), a bus journey leads past numerous industrial buildings and paper factories, whose waste emissions create pollution problems on Jialing Jiang.

Beiquan, an idyllic park on the river bank, is a refreshing retreat after the hurly-burly of the city. Bathe in the warm spring, whose temperature is 35°C (95°F). Some 25 kilometers (15 mi) further on is **Nanquan** (Southern Springs), in a park with a lake suitable for swimming or rowing.

Dazu, 160 kilometers (100 mi) west of Chongqing, can be reached by bus in around five hours. The bus journey, through pleasant countryside, is in itself an experience.

Thousands of Buddhist sculptures and reliefs are scattered among the nearly 40 hills. Construction began in the ninth century, when many Buddhists fled from persecution to Sichuan. They found patrons in Dazu to build these places of special worship.

On **Bei Shan** (North Mountain), within walking distance of the town, is a site called Amitayus-Dyana-Sutra, with more than 600 figures that depict the teachings relating to Buddha Amitabha, worshipped as Master of the Western Paradise. A white stone pagoda stands on the opposite hill.

More impressive is **Baoding Shan** (Treasure Mountain), 15 kilometers (9 mi) northeast of Dazu. The sculptures cut into the mountain are larger and more colorful here, showing scenes that represent the teachings of Buddhism. One hall contains a Guanyin sculpture with 1,007 arms.

Nearby is a Sleeping Buddha, a 31-meter-long (102-ft) prostrate figure symbolizing the passing of Buddha into nirvana. An aspect in these scenes is that the ethical principles of both Buddhist and Confucian origins are interwoven, representing the efforts made by the Buddhists at that time to present their teachings as compatible with the Confucian teachings of the state, somewhat important at the time for one's health.

Left, steps to a town along the river. **Right**, street trader in Chongqing.

SICHUAN

Sichuan is China's most populous province, with approximately 10 percent of the Chinese population – more than a hundred million people – living in a land area of 567,000 square kilometers (219,000 sq mi). Among this population are national minorities such as the Yi, Tibetans, Miao, Hui and Qiang, who live mostly in the three autonomous regions of the province.

The lowlands of Sichuan, surrounded by high mountain ranges to the north, east and west, has a climate very favorable to agriculture – warm summers and not very cold winters, with high humidity, allowing cultivation throughout the year. Even during the winter months of January and February, the peasants supply the country's markets with fresh fruit and vegetables

The picturesque terraced plots, typical of the basin at the center of the province, can produce up to three harvests in a year. The farmhouses, often built in a timber-frame style, are scattered between the fields and are surrounded by shade-giving bamboo groves.

The main grain of the region is rice; a large amount of rape seed is also grown, which supplies most of the cooking oil used in China. Towards the end of March, Sichuan's plain glows yellow with the blooming rape-seed fields. Along the edges of many of the terraced fields are mulberry trees, the food for the silkworm industry that many peasants have as a lucrative sideline. Other agricultural products in the relatively wealthy province include oranges, mandarins and pomelos, vegetable oil, sugar cane, camphor, raw lacquer, wax, tea and bamboo, which, amongst other things, is used as raw material for the intricate Sichuan wickerworks.

The forests in the western mountain region are rich in fir and deciduous trees, and in rare animals. This is the home of the giant panda, which has increasingly been pushed into ever higher mountain regions by human settlements, and is now threatened with eventual extinction, although the Chinese government is increasing its efforts at preserving the species.

Unfortunately, the ruthless economic exploitation and environmental pollution are visibly affecting these regions. Some areas have been put under special environmental protection to maintain the flora and fauna at its present level, at least, and to carry out research.

Today, the province, which in past centuries was not easily accessible and thus preserved a rich tradition, is linked to the rest of China through numerous routes. Chengdu is the center for air traffic, and can be reached easily and quickly from towns and cities including Beijing, Shanghai, Wuhan, Guangzhou, Xi'an, Kunming, Lhasa and Hong Kong.

There are numerous direct railway links between Sichuan and almost all other Chinese provinces, and the stretch between Chengdu and Kunming counts amongst the most beautiful train journeys in the country. The line between Chongqing and Xi'an slithers across hairpin bends, and through numerous

tunnels and across many bridges, cresting the Qinling range, to the north beyond Sichuan.

The two regions of Shu and Ba were part of present-day Sichuan under the first emperor of a united China, Qin Shi Huangdi. These prefixes still appear as abbreviations for Sichuan. Around the year 1000, during the Northern Song dynasty, four districts were created to facilitate administration. They were called Chuan Xia Si Lu (four districts of Chuanxia), and were later abbreviated to the modern name Sichuan.

Chengdu: The capital of the province, Chengdu, lies in the center of the Sichuan basin. The town, which is more than 2,000 years old, now has around four million inhabitants. In contrast to some other Chinese urban centers, Chengdu has preserved a special atmosphere – it is how we imagine China to have been in the past. Of course, rapid modernization will soon cast a shadow over said special atmosphere.

Chengdu was already the political, economic and cultural center of western

Sichuan by 400 BC. During the Five Dynasties Period (907–960), Meng Chang (935–965), a ruler of the later Shu, had numerous hibiscus trees planted on the city walls, so the town became known as the City of Hibiscus.

Built on flat ground, the town can easily be explored on foot or by bicycle. It has almost a southern aspect, with its colorful old streets lined by scores of small restaurants and remaining crowded till late into the evening with traders, buyers or people out for a stroll.

You could eat your way through the countless specialities by visiting the snack bars or tea houses, which often have free performances of Sichuan operas or other songs, or instrumental pieces to entertain guests having the popular jasmine tea.

Wuhou Si (Temple of the Duke of Wu), in a southern suburb of Chengdu, was built by the king of the Cheng empire in the last years of the Western Jin dynasty (265–316). During the Ming period (1368–1644), the temple was merged with the nearby site of Zhaomieliao, a temple dedicated to the memory of Liu Bei.

The temple site as seen today was rebuilt in the Kangxi era of the Qing dynasty, in the late 1600s. There are more than 40 sculptures of famous personalities from the Shu and Han periods, as well as numerous memorial stones, scrolls and sacral implements.

On the southwestern outskirts of Chengdu, by the Huanhua stream, is the park containing **Du Fu Caotang** (Hut of the Poet Du Fu). Du Fu, a poet from the Tang dynasty (618–907), had sought refuge in Chengdu with his family. He built a straw hut on the property of a helpful friend, then lived there for three years in very modest circumstances. He is said to have written more than 240 of his popular and much-read poems here.

The memorial to Du Fu has been renovated or rebuilt several times during the subsequent dynasties. The present site in the park dates from two different periods: the governing period Hongzhi of the Ming dynasty and the governing period Jiaqing of the Qing dynasty. Included at the site are the

Mao statue, Chengdu.

Gongbu Temple, the Shishi Pavilion and the study inside the hut, next to which is a temple. Handwritten and printed examples of the poet's works, in various editions, are on display.

Wangjianglou (River Viewing Pavilion Park) stands on the southern bank of Jin Jiang, in the southeastern part of town. It was built during the Qing dynasty in memory of Xue Tao, a famous female poet of the Tang dynasty. Today, this area is a public park with several towers and pavilions. Most refreshing are the large stands of bamboo.

The Chongli Pavilion, which is 30 meters (100 ft) tall and has four floors, is particularly noticeable because of its striking ornaments, green-glazed tiles and red-lacquered columns. More than a hundred varieties of bamboo – including such rare varieties as spotted and square bamboo – have been planted here in honor of Xue Tao, who is said to have loved bamboo. The poetess is said to have fetched water from the well on the site to make the paper that she used.

It is worth visiting **Wangjian Mu** (tomb of Wang Jian), in the west end of town. Wang Jian (847–918) was a general in the last days of the Tang emperor Lizhu's rule (between 904–907), and was the first ruler of the newly-founded state of Shu, in present-day Sichuan Province. The building, which is 19 meters (33 ft) high, has three burial chambers. The center chamber contains a sarcophagus between two rows of stone figures; a frieze runs along three walls depicting musicians and dancers.

If so inclined, one might visit the zoo. Although it is not especially pleasant, Chengdu zoo has several pandas.

However, if inclined to see giant pandas, and not a zoo, head north of town for six kilometers to the **Giant Panda Breeding Research Facility**, which is much better than the zoo – the living environment for both the giant and lesser pandas is more natural, and there are plans yet to enlarge the facility. Established in 1990 and open to the public since 1995, there are about a dozen pandas living here, and excellent exhibits and a museum.

Sichuan's mountains are home to the giant panda.

Outside Chengdu: Eighteen kilometers (11 mi) north of Chengdu, in the town of Xindu, is the famous Buddhist **Baoguang Si** (Precious Light Monastery). It is thought to have been founded during the Eastern Han dynasty and to have housed more than 3,000 monks in the tenth and eleventh centuries. The site was burned down during the Ming period and then rebuilt in 1670. The oldest building on the monastery site is the 30-meter-tall (100-ft) **Sheli Ta**, a pagoda in the front courtyard and the only one to have survived the Ming-period fire. A Buddha relic is kept in the abbot's rooms. The 500 relatively well-preserved Luohan statues from the Qing dynasty are worth the visit.

Dujiangyan, on the upper course of Min Jiang and 50 kilometers (30 mi) from Chengdu, is an irrigation project over 2,000 years old. Built from 306 to 251 BC, the irrigation network was capable of irrigating 500,000 acres (200,000 hectares) of land shortly after its completion; today, 600,000 acres (240,000 hectares) of agricultural land are supplied with water from the system. There is a three-meter-tall, 1,900-year-old stone statue of Li Bing, the builder, in Fulongguan (Pavilion of the Dragon's Defeat), erected in the third century to commemorate the success. There is a nice view over the site from here. Erwangmiao (Two Kings Temple) was built in honor of its architects.

Emei Shan: An increasingly popular – and thus busy – area, the Emei mountain range is southwest of the Sichuan basin and 160 kilometers (100 mi) from Chengdu. The town Emeixian, at the foot of the mountain range, can be reached either by bus or train from Chengdu. The journey takes about three hours. Alternatively, it's possible to get off the Kunming-Chengdu train at Emeixian. There are minibuses from Emeixian to **Baoguo Si** (Baoguo Monastery), dating from the sixteenth century. The temple, built on a slope, comprises four halls, each one constructed in a more elevated position than the previous. There are also various exhibition halls with artifacts, calligraphy and

Street cobbler.

paintings. Baoguo Si is only one of many temples and monasteries – over 150 are said to have been built here over the centuries – scattered throughout the mountain range. Many decayed when they were no longer inhabited, or have been destroyed. Today, only twenty can be visited.

Emei Shan was named after its shape: a curved eyebrow. The Daoists started erecting their temples here in the second century, and as Buddhism strengthened from the sixth century onwards, the mountain became a sacred place of Buddhism. In fact, it is one of the four sacred Buddhist mountains. There are rare animal and bird species on Emei Shan, and up to 200 different types of butterfly.

Near Baoguo Si, by a small pond under some trees, is a former rest house for political cadres, now called Hotel Hongzhushan. Day trips to the mountain are convenient from here, as are excursions lasting days. Guest houses have been built next to the hotels.

Steps lead from Baoguo Si up to the peak. A road was built some years ago to the Jieyindian Pavilion, at an altitude of 2,670 meters (8,800 ft), and now buses go to within six kilometers (4 mi) of the 3,100-meter-high (10,170-ft) **Jinding** (Golden Peak). About 20 meters (70 ft) below the summit is **Jinding Si** (Golden Peak Temple), with a 20-meter-long (66-ft) bronze hall.

In favorable weather conditions is a remarkable natural phenomenon on the peak. If the sun is in the right position, an observer's shadow is cast onto the clouds below the peak, and an aura of pastel rainbow colors forms around the silhouette. The Buddhist pilgrims, of whom there are still many, interpret it as a special sign when they experience this natural phenomenon. In the past, some pilgrims would throw themselves from the peak, imagining that this led directly to the longed-for nirvana. (One can also see this phenomenon from an airplane above clouds.)

At the bottom of the stone steps are several monasteries; the larger ones often offer food and shelter during the two-and-a-half-day descent. The further on up the mountain, the more expensive the food, since everything, including the coal for the kitchen stoves, has to be carried up by porters. Arrive before 5pm at a monastery offering shelter, when it's easier to get a bed in a separate room, rather than sleeping on the floor in the temple halls with the many other hikers.

About 10 kilometers (six mi) below Jieyindian is **Xixiangchi** (Elephant Bathing Pool), a relatively large temple built against a rock and offering a lovely view of the surroundings. According to legend, this is where the elephant of Bodhisattva Samantabhadra (Puxian) took his bath. Visitors can participate in the predawn religious ceremonies.

Below the Xixiangchi, the descent divides into a relatively steep but shorter path to **Wannian Si** (Temple of Eternity) or a longer, but more beautiful, path to Qingyinge (Pure Sound Pavilion). Often on the upper part of the path are a battalion of rude, pushy monkeys demanding a toll of peanuts or fruits. If provoked – or if they don't accept one's excuse of having no offerings – they

Porters offer special services, Emei Shan.

may become aggressive; there are cases where the monkeys have grabbed cameras and clothes from people.

Further along the path is a small gorge, **Yixiantian** (A Thread of Sky), through which winds a stream lined by lush vegetation. **Wannian Si** (Temple of Eternity) stands at the lower end of the steeper path, at about 1,200 meters (3,900 ft). It was built in the fourth century and is said to have consisted of seven halls. Today, only one 16-meter-high (50-ft) hall remains. The square structure, with a dome roof and made of bricks without rafters, is typical of the architecture of the Ming dynasty. It contains a bronze figure, from around 920, of Bodhisattva Samantabhadra atop on a white elephant. According to legend, this bodhisattva came to Emei Shan riding on the white elephant.

The northern and southern path join again at **Qingyinge** (Pavilion of Pure Sound), where the two streams Black Dragon and White Dragon also join, the source of the pure sounds. The pavilion serves as a rest house now, with proper meals being served on two floors. A few kilometers further along the Dragon Stream is a picturesque little settlement, Lianghekou, where there is a bus every hour back to Baoguo Si.

Leshan: Reached by bus from Emeixian railway station in less than an hour, Leshan, which is over 1,300 years old, lies at the confluence of the Qingyi, Min and Dadu rivers, south of Chengdu. Once the proverbial sleepy town, its popularity with Chinese tourists is furiously modernizing Leshan.

The most important sights are on the mountains **Lingyun Shan** and **Wulong Shan**. On the cliff face of Lingyun Shan (Mountain Reaching to the Clouds), Buddhist monks in the eighth century spent 90 years carving a huge, seated Buddha figure, **Dafo**. The head of the 71-meter-high (233-ft) Buddha is 15 meters (50 ft) long, and is covered with more than 1,000 snail-shaped hair knots. Over 100 people could stand on his foot, over eight meters wide (30 ft).

According to legend, the Buddha was built by monks from Lingyun monas-

Left, sleeping monk. Right, Dafo, tallest statue in China.

tery to tame the swift currents of the river. The reason that the figure is well preserved is that inside its hollow body, invisible from the outside, gutters were carved to drain the rain water.

Lingyun Monastery lies on the mountain above the Buddha figure. Its buildings originally date from the Tang period (618–907), but have been renovated several times in the course of the centuries. Next to the monastery rises the 38-meter-high (125-ft) **Lingbao Ta** (Soul Pagoda) from the Song period (960–1270), a square brick building with five floors inside, but thirteen storys outside, each decorated with a Buddha.

Wuyou Si, which also dates to the Tang period, stands on the mountain of the same name, and is very well preserved. Inside are the gold-plated, wooden figures of Buddha Sakyamuni, Manjusri and Samantabhadra.

Nature reserve: In the northwest of Sichuan and close to the border with Gansu Province, the **Jiuzhaigou Nature Reserve** has been open to visitors for some years. It is advisable to join an organized tour led by a reputable travel agency, since travel into this area can be extremely difficult, especially during the rainy summer months, when torrential rain and mud slides often make the way impassable to traffic.

Jiuzhaigou is about 500 kilometers (300 mi) due north of Chengdu. It lies about 2,500 meters (8,200 ft) above sea level, and covers an area of 148,260 acres (60,000 hectares), framed by forested mountains and high mountain peaks covered with eternal snow. Lush vegetation alternates with grass steppes, lakes, rivers and waterfalls.

The Tibetan people in the region have a legend about the creation of Jiuzhaigou: An immortal called Dage and a fairy called Wunuosemo are said to have lived deep in the mountains. They fell in love. One day, Dage gave Wunuosemo a mirror as a present, which he had polished to a high shine with the wind and the clouds. Unfortunately, she dropped the mirror and it broke into 108 pieces, which changed into the 108 lakes of the Jiuzhaigou, the Nine Village Valley.

Rice terraces, Sichuan.

THE SOUTH

It was in the south of China, particularly along the southeastern coast, where Deng Xiaoping's economic modernization program took root, and germinated, and prospered. In hindsight, it was both a bold and a necessary experiment, designed to gradually introduce a market economy to China. Not everyone got to participate, especially outside of the select special economic zones, but they could watch the lucky ones prosper. It was learning by example.

The idea of commerce is not an extraordinary notion in southeastern China. Guangzhou was already an international port in the ninth century, and by the 1500s, when the Portuguese arrived in a showy flotilla, the area had replaced the Silk Road as the trade route of choice into China. For over a century, until 1842, Guangzhou held China's international trade monopoly, the only port open to outsiders. (Through lazy transliteration, the provincial name of Guangdong somehow ended up coming out of European mouths as Canton.)

Southeast China's other port of note has not the historical depth of Guangzhou, but it has an uncanny entrepreneurial depth, unmatched anywhere in the world. Hong Kong has eclipsed its coastal neighbors, for the moment at least, by returning to Chinese sovereignty. A British colony – coerced from China in the nineteenth century – until 1997, Hong Kong became the definitive capitalist free-market no-holds-barred port. What happens now as a definitive capitalist free-market port (and maybe still no-holds-barred) in a Communist country is anybody's guess. Return to these pages, in a later edition and in another decade, for an update.

Inland from the coast, to the west, the land turns more tropical, and the languages and people more distinctive. The terrain in Guilin has seduced poets for centuries, of whatever art form. What geologists call limestone karst is, in fact, the romantic blending of misty towers and surreal reality found in old Chinese brush paintings.

To the south, Yunnan borders Burma, Laos and Vietnam, and thus it shares the ethnic groups that give this southern region a distinctive feel and ambience. There are no wondrous architectural delights, and no stupendous archeological revelations to be found by travelers in Yunnan. There is just the grace of land and people.

Tibet, of course, doesn't belong in a section titled "The South" any more than one called "The West" or anything else. But this book's rigid, dogmatic structure has it following the southern chapters, and so it is here, under protest. In any case, Tibet needs no introduction, no clarification, no summarization. Tibet has simply the loftiest and most unique culture anywhere, and it must be encountered one-on-one to be believed.

ON THE COAST
IN THE SOUTHEAST

The southeastern coast, primarily mountainous **Fujian Province**, is a lush, green landscape with a harsh, classically-rugged coastline.

Or so one might think, looking at the map and remembering that the region is noted for the meditating practitioners of Daoism. In fact, much of this area, certainly at least the urban centers, both large and small, are aesthetic disasters, having long ago yielded to the monotonous industrial-and-proletariat concrete of a developing China. If looking for pretty sites and sights, head elsewhere. If looking for modern urban China, for better or for worse, continue onwards.

Lying opposite Taiwan, across **Taiwan Haixia** (Taiwan Straits), Fujian has long been a source of Chinese emigrants to the world, and a large number of overseas Chinese now living in Taiwan, elsewhere in Asia, and in America came from Fujian.

Despite the strained, awkward relations with Taiwan, which China considers one of its provinces, China has encouraged Taiwanese investment in Fujian. (Taiwanese investment in China is over US$20 billion.) Indeed, cities like Xiamen are veritable magnets for Taiwanese investors, entrepreneurs and tourists, many of whose families originally came from Fujian. Here, too, Taiwanese are more likely to be welcomed by mainlanders, as they share the same dialect and cuisine – and may often be distantly related.

Shantou: A port in the eastern part of **Guangdong Province**, Shantou can be reached by flights from Guangzhou (Canton). Shantou spreads over 245 square kilometers (95 sq mi) and has just under one million inhabitants.

Shantou is one of the smallest of China's four original special economic zones (SEZ), and it has attracted overseas Chinese investment and is developing rapidly.

The town offers little of historic interest, though like most Chinese cities, it has a **Zhongshan Gongyuan** (Sun Yatsen Park), by the bank of the Meixi (Plum River) and not far from Zhongshan Lu on its southern flank. The park, which has been constructed on an island and is linked to the town by three bridges, consists of a generous combination of water and green areas. In the southwest of the park is Yuemei Huayuan (Botanical Garden). Western influence dating from the eighteenth century is still noticeable in the city, but in contrast to Shanghai, with its reasonably well-preserved colonial buildings, Shantou looks neglected.

Two islands can be reached from the harbor in the south of the city. To the southeast of the town is the small island of **Mayu Dao**, which has a stony shore in the east, as well as a sandy beach. In the southern part, a pavilion with the poetic name Guanhaiting (Sea View) has been built. In the north of the island is the Tianhaigumiao (Temple of the Sea God) and the temple of Maguang.

Zhangzhou: A two-hour ride by bus from Xiamen and on the Jiulong Jiang

(Nine Dragon River), Zhangzhou has been noted in historical narratives since the seventh century. Long known as a center for foreign trade and as a port, Zhangzhou is home for around 300,000 people living within 265 square kilometers (100 sq mi).

The most important sight in the town is **Nanshan Si** (Southern Mountain Temple). Built during the Tang dynasty, it was destroyed and rebuilt several times. The present site originates from the Qing dynasty. Daxiong Baodian (Precious Hall of the Great Hero), in the middle of the site, houses three gilded and seated Buddha statues. Note the huge copper bell, which weighs 700 kilograms (1,500 lbs), from the Yuan dynasty.

Xiamen: It takes about two hours to get from Zhangzhou to Xiamen, with a population of over half a million. Reachable by air from many cities in China, Xiamen (previously known as Amoy) is probably the best-known urban area of Fujian Province.

An important port for a long time, in the seventeenth century it became a center of historic battles. The last loyal supporters of the Ming dynasty sought refuge here from the new rulers, the Manchu of the Qing dynasty. The notorious Ming general Koxinga (Zheng Chenggong) used Xiamen as his base to attack the Manchu in the north, raising an army of 800,000 soldiers and pirates. Failing in his fight against the Manchu, he fled to Taiwan and kicked the Dutch off the island.

Later, the island of Gulangyu, in front of the town, became a foreign enclave under the 1842 Treaty of Nanjing.

Geographically, Xiamen is ideally located, with a pretty coastline and harbor. However, development in recent years has turned what was a quiet vacation spot into a boisterous, exhaust-choked metropolis yielding to the demands of rapid development. In fact, Xiamen is the number one focus of Taiwanese investment in China.

Xiamen does boast one innovation that other Chinese cities could well emulate – it has outlawed car honking. After experiencing the cacophony of

Factory for rubber products, Xiamen.

traffic noise in other Chinese cities, visitors will be amazed – and pleased – to discover that the honking ban here is obeyed and works, and motorists actually seem to drive more safely.

One of the worthwhile places for an excursion is **Wanshi Gongyuan** (Garden of the Ten Thousand Rocks), to the east at the top of Huyuan Lu. The area covers 80 hectares (200 acres) and includes a lake, large green areas, a pavilion and a botanical garden. In the east are Taiping Shan and Taiping Yan (Taiping Rock), with a small temple from the Tang period. In the south of the park, on Shitou Shan (Mt Lion Head), are Ganlu Si (Temple of the Sweet Dew) and Tianjie Si (Temple of the Heavenly Kingdom), dating from the second half of the seventeenth century. South of the park is **Wulao Shan** (Mountain of the Five Elders).

It is possible to walk across the mountain to the temple of **Nanputuo** in the south, north of Siming Nanlu, on whose opposite side is the campus of **Xiamen University**. The temple was founded during the Tang period, but its present structure belongs to the Qing period. It is dedicated to Guanyin, the goddess of mercy, and there are three statues of the goddess in the third hall, Dabeidian (Hall of Great Mercy).

The pavilion behind the temple houses not only valuable old Buddhist scriptures, but also specimens of calligraphy from the Ming period, bells from the Song period, a Guanyin statue with eight heads and 24 arms from the Ming period and made of white porcelain, and Buddha statues carved from jade.

A memorial hall for writer Lu Xun has been built on the university campus. Lu Xun was one of the sponsors of the **Anthropological Museum**, which opened at the university in 1952 and is located on Siming Nanlu. It contains a reproduction of Peking Man, oracle bones from the Shang period, early bronzes, and extensive works of art.

The most popular excursion spot is the small island of **Gulangyu**, which can easily be reached in five minutes from the mooring point near the Lujiang

Hotel. Visitors can swim or sunbathe on the island, which is 1.6 square kilometers (half a square mile) in size and has two landmarks: Longtou Shan (Dragon Head Hill) and Hutou Shan (Tiger Head Hill). East of the southern beach is Shuzhuang Huayuan, a garden created in 1913 by a Taiwanese who was fleeing from the Japanese. It has been designed in the style of the gardens of Suzhou. Lianhua'an (Lotus Nunnery), which is directly behind the gate to Dragon Head Hill, is also worth visiting. There are a number of memorials to Zheng Chenggong, or Koxinga, on the island; a memorial hall, Zheng Chenggong Jinianguan, was built in 1962.

The island was once a center for artists and musicians, and walking through the narrow streets, one is likely to hear the melodious chords of pianos.

Beyond Xiamen: Three hours by bus north of Xiamen is **Quanzhou**, founded in 700 and once one of the most important ports in China. In the Song dynasty, population was half a million; today, about 400,000 people live here.

In addition to the Islamic traders who came to Quanzhou in the seventh century, two Muslim missionaries also settled here. The **Yisilanjiao Sheng Mu** (Holy Islamic Graves) on Ling Shan (Soul Mountain) bear witness to their presence. In the eastern part of town, the hill is easily reached on foot.

Qingjing Si (Muslim Temple of Calm and Clarity) on Tumen Jie is another example of the strong Islamic influence. It is said to be a copy of a mosque in Damascus and was built in black and white granite in 1009, on commission from Arab traders.

Northwest of this mosque, on Xi Jie and easily recognized by two richly-decorated pagodas from the tenth century, is **Kaiyuan**, a temple erected in 686 and substantially extended in subsequent centuries. At six hectares (17 acres), it is one of the largest temple sites in China today. There are five Buddha statues in Daxiong Baodian (Precious Hall of the Great Hero). The middle one, Buddha Sakyamuni, is said to be a present from the Tang emperor

Kaiyuan, in Quanzhou.

Xuanzong. East of the Kaiyuan temple is **Haiwaijiaotongshi Bowuguan**, the Foreign Trade History Museum. Its main exhibit is an ocean-going junk from the Song period, discovered and lifted from the Bay of Quanzhou in 1974.

A lovely three-kilometer walk to the north leads to **Qingquan Shan** (Mountain of the Clear Spring), once a Daoist center. The only thing remaining is a five-meter-high (16-ft) figure of Laozi from the Song period, which is said to have stood in the center of a Daoist temple. From here, a path leads to **Mituo Yan** (Amitabha Rock) with its five-meter-tall (16-ft) statue of the Buddha Amitabha, from the Yuan period. On the way to the highest point, the 490-meter-high (1,600-ft) Wutaiding, you pass the temple **Cien Yan** (Rock of Granted Grace), which has a special attraction in the form of a statue of Guanyin from the eleventh century. Other sights worth seeing are Shisun (Stony Bamboo Shoots) on Gui Shan (Tortoise Mountain) to the west, and Jiuri Shan (Mountain of the Ninth Day), which is nearly five kilometers northwest of the town on Jin Jiang.

Fuzhou: Three hours by bus from Quanzhou is Fuzhou, something of an industrial quagmire on the banks of Min Jiang. The city is immensely popular with Taiwanese tourists, however.

Fuzhou's history dates back to the second century BC, when it was the residence of the kingdom of Yue. Its importance as a port grew from the tenth century onward, and was opened to foreigners in 1842 as a result of the Opium Wars. The town, which has over a million inhabitants today, was occupied by the Japanese from 1940 to 1945.

There is a good view of town from the 60-meter-high (195-ft) hill of **Yu Shan**. At the northwest edge of the hill is **Bai Ta**, the White Pagoda, built in 904 and restored several times. A library is housed in the temple of the same name, **Baita Si**. East of Baita Si is the temple **Qigong Si**, erected in honor of the Ming general Qi Jiguang (1528–1587), who had successfully fought against Japanese pirates. Opposite Yu Shan rises the

Narrow bamboo rafts are used by Fuzhou-area fishermen.

85-meter-high (280-ft) hill Wushi, with a seven-story pagoda dating from 941. **Xi Hu**, or West Lake, in the northwest of the town, is a popular spot for excursions. It was constructed in the third century, but has been considerably enlarged this century.

Another worthwhile excursion is **Hualin Si** (Splendid Forest Temple), established in 965 at the foot of a 45-meter-high (148-ft) hill, Ping Shan, in the north of town. Only the main hall remains of the original structure; the other buildings are Qing period.

Outside Fuzhou: There are several rambles outside Fuzhou. Drum Mountain, approximately 15 kilometers (9 mi) to the east, is particularly interesting and can be reached by bus. Numerous religious buildings are set in a lovely landscape, including **Yongquan Si** (Temple of the Sparkling Spring), from 908, of which 25 halls are still preserved. Two other temples outside the town are **Linyang**, nine kilometers (12 mi) away on Beifeng Shan, and **Chongfu**, at the foot of Beiling Shan. Built in 977, its preserved buildings date from the second half of the nineteenth century.

In Zhejiang Province, the harbor towns of Wenzhou and Ningbo are the largest in the province after the capital city of Hangzhou. But don't go out of your way to visit them, unless passing through and in the area.

Wenzhou lies on the south bank of Ou Jiang, 30 kilometers (20 mi) from its estuary. Wenzhou's importance as a port has grown since the revolution in 1949. The varied directions of Chinese development are clearly apparent in this ancient 2,000-year-old city. **Jiangxin** (Island at the Heart of the River), easily reached by ferry and in the town's north, is the main attraction. Pagodas stand on the island's two hills, which were originally two islands but were joined during the Song dynasty. The eastern pagoda was built in 869, the western in 969.

Almost a day's trip away is **Ningbo**, on the railway network. Ningbo first became an important port during the Tang period, and flourished during the Southern Song dynasty (1127–1179), when Hangzhou was the capital. Much of the old money of pre-World War II Shanghai came from Ningbo. Today, 600,000 people live in the city, which continues to be an important junction.

The private library **Tianyige**, on Changchun Lu, to the west of Yue Hu (Moon Lake), is of significance. Set up in the sixteenth century by the scholar Fan Qin, it once held about 70,000 valuable manuscripts, of which several thousand are still preserved, most of them in Hangzhou.

In the south of the town rises the 30-meter-high (100-ft) **Tianfeng**, a pagoda first built in the Tang dynasty; its present form dates from 1330. In the central **Zhongshan Gongyuan** (Sun Yatsen Park) is Qita Si, now a monastery.

Baoguo Si (Protection of the Land Temple) is more than 15 kilometers (9 mi) to the northwest, built during the Song dynasty. Daxiong Baodian (Precious Hall of the Great Hero) is the oldest preserved wooden structure in the province. **Tiantong Si** (Temple of the Heavenly Child), 35 kilometers (20 mi) to the east, was built in 757 as an important center of Zen Buddhism.

Putuo Shan: One of the four sacred Buddhist mountains in China, the island of Putuo Shan is accessible by boat from Ningbo. Before 1949, more than 2,000 monks and nuns lived in over 200 monasteries, with origins going back to the eleventh century. Intentionally or not, the island fits most preconceptions of pre-industrial China, as the enthusiasm of increasing numbers of Chinese tourists might indicate.

Puji Si (Monastery of Complete Redemption) was built in this century, while **Fayu Si** (Monastery of the Law) dates from the sixteenth century. **Yangshi'an** (Poplar Branch Convent), to the west with its two-meter-high stone picture of Guanyin, goddess of mercy, dates from 1608.

The third largest is **Huiji Si** (Convent of the Enlightened Redemption). Lying on a hill in the north of the island, it was founded during the Ming period, and was considerably extended in the following centuries. Pilgrims come here on the 19th day of the second lunar month for the birthday of Guanyin.

Right, traditional gentleman.

306

GUANGZHOU

The mythical origins of booming Guangzhou are not the most auspicious. As legend has it, five celestial beings, riding on the backs of five flying goats, landed here and founded Guangzhou. Goats don't do much for engendering civic pride in an economic powerhouse and gateway to the West. Yet the name Yangcheng, or Goat City, was once affixed to this city. Even today, the evening newspaper is called *Yangcheng Wanbao* (Goat City Evening News).

But goats are spunky and independent, and in Guangzhou, one grasps a palpable sense of China's energy, and of its breakneck pace in transforming itself into an international player. Guangzhou is a boisterous urban mass with all the blemishes one equates with modern cities: air thick with pollution, streets crowded with cars and trucks, blocks of cramped housing overflowing with people, and an invigorating chaos.

At the mouth of **Zhu Jiang** (Pearl River), Guangzhou lies 45 kilometers (28 mi) upriver from Humen (Tiger Gate), also called Bocca Tigris on old maps. Around five million people live in the greater metropolitan area, with over two million within the city's boundaries. Like many of China's cities, Guangzhou's population is probably much higher than official figures.

Climatically, Guangzhou is a temperate, subtropical city. The Tropic of Cancer runs a few miles to the north, and for a few days in July, the sun lies directly above the city. The rainy season parallels the hot summer months, when daily afternoon showers are typical.

Flying goats notwithstanding, Guangzhou probably was founded in 214 BC as an encampment by the armies of the Qin emperor, Qin Shi Huangdi (221–210 BC). At first the town was called Panyu; the name Guangzhou first appeared during the period of the Three Kingdoms (222–280). During the Tang period (618–906), the city was already an international port, but remained second to Quanzhou – Marco Polo's Zaytun –

for centuries. In 1514, the Portuguese flotilla commanded by Tome Pires reached Guangzhou. The province's name in the Cantonese dialect is Guangdong, from which the Portuguese derived the name of Cantào. From Cantáo came Canton, which came to be used in all European languages.

From 1757 to 1842, Guangzhou held a trade monopoly in China, as it was the only Chinese port opened to the foreigners. Traders were obliged to cooperate contractually with Chinese merchant guilds; this arrangement planted the seeds for the subsequent *comprador bourgeoisie*.

After the overthrow of the Ming dynasty by the Manchu in 1644, nationalist ideas survived longer in Guangzhou than in other parts of China. Yet, at the same time, close contact with overseas Chinese (*huaqiao*) ensured the continuation of an openness to the world and a desire for reform in the city. (Openness, in turn, would eventually spawn revolutionary zeal.) Trade with the East India Company increased, particularly the

importation of opium. The profits financed colonial expansion, however, and did not benefit the local Chinese population, and China's silver reserves were depleted to pay for the imports. This culture of dependency helped nurture revolutionary ideas and motivate secret societies, which preserved the ideals of the Ming period and fostered a determination to restore this last Chinese dynasty to power.

In 1839, the Chinese commissioner Lin Zexu ordered the confiscation and destruction of 20,000 chests of opium, leading to military intervention by Great Britain in the First Opium War (1840–1842). The resulting Treaty of Nanjing led to the opening to foreign trade in Guangzhou, Shanghai, Xiamen, Fuzhou and Ningbo, and the gift of Hong Kong to England. In 1858, in a reactionary fit by the Chinese, foreign traders were required to limit their base of operations to the island of Shamian, at the mouth of Zhe Jiang. After the Second Opium War (1856–1860), they settled in other parts of Guangzhou and continued trading.

Following the overthrow of the Qing dynasty in October, Guangzhou became the center of the movement led by Sun Yatsen (Sun Zhongshan) and the headquarters of the Kuomintang (KMT), the first modern party in China. In a period of cooperation between the KMT and the Communists, Mao Zedong worked and taught at Guangzhou's Institute of Peasant Movements, and Zhou Enlai and Lin Biao at the Military Academy.

The modernization of Guangzhou began in the early 1920s; most of the main streets defining the city today were built then. A feverish sense of urgency in construction – it took only 18 months to build 40 kilometers (25 mi) of road – is evident even today. Throughout the city, high-rises, hotels, bridges and new highways now seemingly materialize overnight. During that modernization in the 1920s, the remainder of the old city wall was pulled down, and a collection of junks on the river was removed.

Urban personality: The personality of Guangzhou differs significantly from that of the north. The language of

Colonial architecture, Shamian.

Guangzhou, Cantonese, is incomprehensible to northern Chinese, who typically speak Mandarin. Cantonese has nine tones, instead of the four tones in the Mandarin dialect. While it is urban, Guangzhou has been marked more by trade than industry, in contrast to Shanghai, although light industry is now important in Guangzhou.

The area around Guangzhou was overcrowded even 200 years ago, and many peasants from the region emigrated to Southeast Asia, America and Europe. As a result, Cantonese is the most common dialect among overseas Chinese. Likewise, the same is true for Cantonese cuisine, which is the most varied of all Chinese cuisines but is often mocked by other Chinese.

Thus the language, cuisine and boisterous, crowded look of Guangzhou is often familiar to foreigners – it is the look and feel of Chinatowns in North America, Europe and Australia.

Old Guangzhou: In the southwest of the city, the island of **Shamian** is a preserved relic of the colonial past. The small island was divided in 1859 into several foreign concessions, primarily French and British. After 10pm, Chinese were kept off the island by two iron gates and narrow bridges. The former Catholic and Anglican churches have been reopened for worship, and most of the former trade and consular buildings are now used as government offices.

Opposite the canal that separates Shamian from the town itself, and where houseboats are occasionally moored, begins the so-called **Bund**, which continues along the waterfront to **Haizhu**, the oldest steel bridge across the Zhu Jiang and built in 1933. About 100 meters to the east of the bridge, which connects the eastern end of Shamian with the mainland, is a memorial. Here, in 1925, Chinese demonstrators died in a hail of bullets fired by foreign troops guarding the foreign quarters.

About two kilometers further east, to the northeast of Haizhu, the 50-meter-high (160-ft) double towers of the **Catholic cathedral** are visible. Built in the early 1860s, the cathedral was left to

The bridge of Haizhu.

decay after 1949, and left to decay even more during the Cultural Revolution. In the 1980s, it was restored and now holds services under the auspices of the Patriotic Catholic Church, banned from having contact with the Vatican.

To the north of the bridge, half way down Shamian towards the mainland on Qingping Lu, is **Qingping Shichang** (Market), occupying the side alleys around the main roads of Renmin Nan Lu and Nuren Jie. This district has flourished since the reforms of 1978 and is always quite crowded with shoppers and those seeking a snack. One of the first places to develop under China's gradual adoption of market economics, the area was for years a capitalist oddity.

To the east is **Wenhua Gongyuan** (Culture Park), with roller-skating rinks, an open-air theater, theater halls, art exhibitions and performances by the School of Acrobats. Nearby is the well-stocked Department Store of the South (often called Nanfang Department Store), on the corner of Renmin Nan Lu, lined with shops and also known as

Taiping Lu, in honor of the Taiping Rebellion of 1850–1864.

Xiajiu Lu leads to Guangdong, a restaurant. Behind it, in a narrow side alley named Shangxia Jie, is **Hualin Si**. This temple is said to have been founded by an Indian monk in 526, although the existing buildings date from the Qing period. There are 500 statues of Luohan – pupils of the Buddha – in the main hall. A statue of Marco Polo with brimmed hat, however, was lost during the Cultural Revolution.

Near the crossroads of Renmin Zhong Lu and the sixth section of Zhongshan Lu (Sun Yatsen Street), in Guangtalu south of Zhongshan Lu, is **Huaisheng Si**, a mosque dating back to 627 and founded by a trader who was said to be an uncle of Mohammed. At that time, Arab traders visited China, so the legend may well contain some truth, although it does not give sufficient evidence for an exact date of the foundation of the mosque. The 25-meter-high (82-ft) minaret, **Guang Ta** (Naked Pagoda), dominates the area, although new

Construction breather.

high-rises are competing for the skyline. The mosque is a cultural center for Guangzhou's 5,000 Muslims.

To the north of Zhongshan Lu, a fairly narrow street leads to **Liurong Si** (Temple of the Six Banyan Trees); its **Hua Ta** (Flower Pagoda) is a symbol of the city. Liurong Si, said to date back to the fifth century, was named in 1099 in a calligraphic tribute from the poet Su Dongpo (1031–1101).

The main hall contains statues of the Buddha, eight Luohan figures, the god of medicine, and the goddess of mercy, Guanyin. The statues date from the Qing period. Visitors can climb up the nine-story pagoda behind the main hall; unfortunately, the view is marred by numerous skyscrapers. Today, the temple is the local headquarters of the Chinese Buddhist Association.

A few hundred yards northeast is **Guanxiao Si**, a temple preserved during the Cultural Revolution on orders from Zhou Enlai. Local legend has it that the temple is older than the town; it dates from the time between 397 and 401. Some of the present buildings were, however, built after a big fire in 1269, and most probably only after 1832.

Dongtie Ta and **Xitie Ta** (Western and Eastern Iron pagodas) date from early in the city's history. There is a seven-meter-high (23-ft) stone pagoda behind the main hall, with sculptures of the Buddha placed in eight niches. It is thought to date from 967, but was only put in its present location at the beginning of Mongolian rule. The halls reflect several styles from different eras.

To the northwest, in a formal garden near Jiefang Bei Lu, **Sun Zhongshan Jiniantang** (Sun Yatsen Hall) is easy to spot with its eye-catching blue roof tiles. The hall, built shortly after the death of Sun Yatsen in 1925, now houses a large theater and lecture hall that can seat 5,000 people. **Yuexiu Gongyuan**, due north, is a beautiful example of a landscaped park. It is dominated by **Zhenhailou** (Tower Overlooking the Sea), a memorial to the seven great sea journeys undertaken by the eunuch Zheng He; between 1405 and 1433, he traveled

Downtown skyline.

to east Africa, the Persian Gulf and Java. Today, the tower houses a museum on the history of Guangzhou.

Restored after the Cultural Revolution, **Chenjia Si** (Chen Family Temple) dates from 1894 and lies on the western part of Zhongshan Lu. It has six courtyards and a classic layout, and is decorated with friezes manufactured in Shiwan. Gardens surround a small lake with rowboats. There are also tennis courts, a swimming pool, badminton courts and a gym. The family name Chen is one of the most common in Guangdong Province. Families of that name from throughout the province donated money to build this temple.

Nearby, not far from the train station, is a shaded park devoted to the cultivation of orchids. The north of the town is dominated by **Baiyun Shan** (White Cloud Mountain), six kilometers (4 mi) away and accessible by cable-car.

Eastern districts: In the east of the city, on Zhongshan Lu, is the former Kongzimiao (Confucius Temple). It lost its religious function during the "bour-

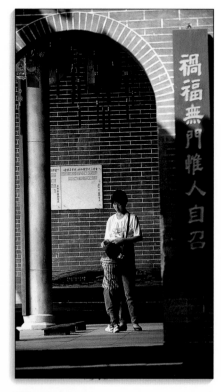

geois revolution" in 1912. In 1924, the **Peasant Movement Institute** (Nongmin Yundong Jiangxisuo) was opened here, in effect the first school of the Chinese Communist Party. The elite of the Communist Party taught here: Mao Zedong (his work and bedroom can be viewed), Zhou Enlai, Qu Qiubai, Deng Zhong, Guo Moruo and others. This is also where Mao developed his theory of peasant revolution.

After the collapse of the workers' uprising in 1927, the Communists were forced to retreat for a time from the cities. A park and memorial, **Lieshi Lingyuan** (Memorial Garden for the Martyrs), was created in 1957 in memory of the uprising and its nearly 6,000 victims. The temple is mostly of Ming-period construction.

Directly east of it is **Guangdong Geming Bowuguan** (Provincial Museum of the Revolution), a reminder of the role of the Kuomintang and its predecessors since the First Opium War.

South of Zhongshan Gan Lu are the old buildings of Guangdong University, where China's first modern author, Lu Xun, lectured in 1927. An exhibition is dedicated to him. Until 1927, the All Chinese Trade Union Federation was located nearby. Liu Shaoqi, the revolutionary and later president of the People's Republic – and a victim of the Cultural Revolution – worked there.

In the northeast, near the zoo on Xialie Lu, is a memorial park built in 1918 for the 72 victims of the uprising in 1911.

Outside Guangzhou: The town of **Foshan** (Buddha Mountain), with more than one million people, is home to **Zumiao** (Ancestor Temple), a famous Daoist temple whose history goes back to the Song dynasty. It was renovated in 1372, and contains a 2,540-kilogram (2-ton) bronze statue of the Northern God, Zhenwu, from around 1450. There is also a small museum on the grounds, which has relics dating back to the Han period. The buildings – most of which were built during the Qing dynasty – have been decorated with ceramics produced in the factory of **Shiwan**, located in a suburb. (Shiwan ceramics were also used in the Chen temple, in Guangzhou.)

Left, amidst the old. **Right**, hotel bellboy.

HONG KONG

Hong Kong Island

However barren it may have been a century ago, nobody standing in the middle of Hong Kong Island could ever imagine it as anything but a great metropolis. Fifty-story buildings seem more common than 10-story buildings.

Central District: Hong Kong's Central District is home to Hong Kong's banks. Most difficult to miss, from nearby or from across the harbor in Kowloon, is the 368-meter-high (1,209-ft) **Bank of China** (sixth tallest building in the world), designed by the American-Chinese architect I.M. Pei. The building's distinctive sharp angles point directly at other financial institutions, presumably to project bad *feng shui* upon them.

There are few truly historic buildings to give real character to Central. The colonial-style **Supreme Court Building** once housed the legislative council. The Victorian-Gothic **St John's Cathedral**, inaugurated in 1849 and Hong Kong's oldest Anglican church, is tucked away on Battery Path Road. But these buildings are aberrations.

The place to begin a Central ramble is at the **Star Ferry Terminal**, where the Star Ferry arrives and departs for Kowloon. Blinking at the right of the piers is the unmistakable polka-dotted **Jardine House**, whose distinctive round windows have inspired the Chinese to nickname the building as the House of a Thousand Orifices.

Just behind is the **General Post Office**. Across the street, to the west from the post office and Jardine House, are the shiny towers of **Exchange Square**, one of the most modern office complexes in the world and the home of the Hong Kong Stock Exchange.

Western District: If one was foolish enough to try and identify the "real" Hong Kong, one would think inevitably of the **Western District**, which begins at Possession Street, and sprawls west to Kennedy Town. More practically, Western's atmosphere emerges around

Central Market, near the fringes of the busy Central district. Western was the first district to be settled by the British, but, today, there is virtually nothing British about this area. It is a traditional Chinese urban society at its purest, known as a last refuge of the Hong Kong Chinese artisan.

At the corner of Hollywood Road and Ladder Street is the temple of **Man Mo**, built around 1840. Tourists regularly throng through Man Mo – but this doesn't inhibit the temple's regular worshippers, who create thick clouds with their burning joss offerings.

Victoria Peak – *The* Peak to those who have made it to society's top – wasn't always regarded with such awe. During the first six years of the colony's history, hardly anybody traveled to its inhospitable heights. It wasn't until 1888, when the **Peak Tramway** (actually a funicular railway) was opened, that the Peak became *the* Peak. Everybody who was (and is) anybody longs to live on the Peak. The best way to see the Peak in all its bucolic glory is by walk-

ing around **Lugard Road**, which begins just opposite the Peak Tram's upper terminus, 395 meters (1,305 ft) above sea level. Accessible at tram stops along the way are the Botanical Gardens and Zoological Gardens.

Wanchai: Nightlife in Wanchai was not meant for the Peak's elite. In the late 1940s, it was a hangout for sailors, and during the 1960s, it offered rest and recreation to thousands of American, Australian and New Zealand soldiers and sailors on leave from Vietnam.

Here are brightly-lit fruit markets, souvenir shops, second-hand bookshops, tailors, gaudy hostess clubs, topless bars, discos, and raucous English-style pubs.

Nobody thinks about Wanchai for culture, but it does harbor the **Hong Kong Arts Centre**: 15 floors of auditoriums, rehearsal rooms, theater workshops, and the offices of numerous cultural organizations. Across the street is the famous and respected **Academy for Performing Arts** (APA).

Fenwick Pier, where warships often berth, is just up Harbour Road, behind the APA. This section of Harbour Road (called Wanchai North) has the HK$3 billion **Hong Kong Convention and Exhibition Centre**, a vast center including the **Grand Hyatt** and **New World Harbour View** hotels.

Two blocks to the south of Hennessy Road is a far more Chinese section of town. Here are famous Chinese furniture-makers working right out on the street, and also two well-known Chinese temples: **Pak Tai**, home to a three-meter (10-ft) copper image dating from 1604, and **Chai Kung Woot Fat**, where believers who have overcome illnesses leave offerings in the form of mirrors with lucky inscriptions. The temple interior is dazzling.

Western District was the first Hong Kong suburb occupied by Europeans. They soon deserted it and moved to a spot they deemed healthier, optimistically naming it **Happy Valley**.

In 1841, shortly after Happy Valley was settled, the colony's residents created the edifice that has made Happy Valley world-famous: the Hong Kong

Academy for Performing Arts.

Jockey Club's Happy Valley Racecourse. During the October-to-May racing season, it attracts thousands of racegoers (about 35,000 a running).

Causeway Bay: Really a bay until the 1950s, when it disappeared in a land reclamation project, Causeway Bay is one of Hong Kong's more modern districts. What remains today is occupied by the **Hong Kong Yacht Club**, on Kellett Island (once a real island), and a typhoon shelter for small boats. At sunset, one may be besieged by a gaggle of women offering a chaste ride in one of their "floating restaurant" sampans, decks filled beam to boom with tables and chairs. Kitchen sampans then pull up, vying for orders and showing off their fresh prawns, crabs and fish. Seafood, noodles, congee, omelettes – just about anything edible can be prepared in the precariously-floating kitchens.

Causeway Bay's modern history began in 1973, when the **Cross-Harbour Tunnel** was opened. This underwater freeway, one of the largest tunnels in Asia, crosses to Kowloon.

Stanley: Take public transportation along the coast to Turtle Cove, then to Stanley Village, once a thriving Chinese capital long before the British set foot here. The town was founded in 1770 by a pirate, Chang Po Chai, who had captured the island. From Stanley, travel to **Repulse Bay**, whose beach has been widened several times its original size and improved, and which has everything except peace and quiet.

Aberdeen: With a character unlike any other town in Hong Kong, Aberdeen's charm is its typhoon-proof anchorage, home to about 20,000 of Hong Kong's 70,000 "boat people" and their 3,000-plus junks and sampans. A colorful 30-minute ride through Aberdeen Harbour reveals its chaotic atmosphere, the incredible sea life and the dynamism of this city upon the water.

Kowloon

The name Kowloon is made up of two Chinese words, *gau*, meaning nine, and *lung*, or dragon. Tradition says that a

Causeway Bay at dusk.

boy emperor who once lived here noticed that there were eight hills, so he called them the Eight Dragons. A servant pointed out that an emperor is considered to be a dragon; therefore, the eight hills plus the boy emperor were the nine dragons – *gaulung*. In fine colonial fashion, this was transliterated to English as *kowloon*. Although Kowloon is a mere 10 square kilometers (3 sq mi), it is the place that most people remember after a visit to Hong Kong.

The traditional focal point of **Tsimshatsui**, at the tip of the peninsula, is the **Star Ferry**. Where the old clock tower stands was the Asian end of the *Orient Express*, from London. Nearby is the **Peninsula Hotel**, where people stayed before boarding the train, and now a classic in its own right. Behind it is a new tower wing.

Across the street is the egg-shaped **Space Museum and Planetarium**. Next to it is the **Museum of Art** and the Cultural Centre.

Nathan Road was named after Sir Matthew Nathan, a major in the Royal Engineers who built the road and later became Hong Kong's governor, in 1904. During Nathan's time, this road was a meandering track lined with banyan trees. Citizens used it to drive out to the countryside in horse-drawn buggies for Sunday picnics. Nathan's futuristic notion that Nathan Road would one day be part of a big commercial center seemed so laughable at the time that his road was called "Nathan's Folly."

Yaumatei: Northwards on Kowloon's Canton or Jordan roads surges into the **Yaumatei**, a district known for its large typhoon shelter, where Hong Kong's boat people anchor their floating homes. It has been said that some citizens of Yaumatei's boat city live a lifetime without setting foot on shore. Inhabitants can get a haircut, medical aid, go to school or attend a church service – all without going ashore.

Just inland from the teeming waterfront is **Shanghai Street**, a matrimonial avenue well-known for its traditional shops selling old-fashioned gold ornaments and other such items for a Chi-

Shopping nightlife, Kowloon.

nese bride's trousseau. Yaumatei's **Temple Street**, originally famous for its temples, is now renowned for its **night market** that lights up after the sun goes down. In the Temple Street area are four temples, grouped together in **Public Square Street**.

The colony's main **Tin Hau Temple** was built on these shores more than 100 years ago. Land reclamation has forced it to move inland, but Yaumatei's boat people hike to it regularly to worship gods, particularly Tin Hau, the protector of fisherfolk.

Mongkok and Sanpokong: Hong Kong is well-known as perhaps the most densely-populated place on earth. Within Kowloon is a district with the highest population density in Hong Kong – **Mongkok**. Here live an estimated 165,000 people per square kilometer. The shops along this stretch of Nathan Road boast many bargains not found on the lower and pricier end.

Sanpokong, one of Kowloon's first manufacturing areas, is located just opposite **Kai Tak Airport** in a crowded and dirty jumble of streets, bordered on one side by Choi Hung Road and on the other side by Prince Edward Road. Businessmen who visit the colony's factories know the place well. For tourists, the only reason to come here would be to browse through factory outlet stores.

New Territories

Many visitors to Hong Kong concentrate on bargain-hunting in Central and Tsimshatsui. But a day should be spent exploring the New Territories, which include the area right down to Boundary Street, in Kowloon. But most people here say you're not really in the New Territories until you've traveled beyond Lion Rock Tunnel and Laichikok.

Head out towards **Castle Peak**, or towards Shatin and Taipo. On the Castle Peak side of the Kowloon peninsula is **Laichikok Amusement Park**, which has been entertaining people for decades and is one of the world's few places to enjoy Chinese opera and ice skating in the same compound. Another attrac-

Temple wishes for the new year.

tion, the **Sung Dynasty Village**, is a recreation of part of a village that existed in China 1,000 years ago. Near Castle Peak itself, adjacent to the LRT station, is a huge temple called **Ching Chuen Koong**, home for aged people who have no relatives or means of support. It is also a repository for many Chinese art treasures and a library of 4,000 books, which document the history of Daoism.

A must on any trip around the New Territories is **Lau Fau Shan**, a huge fishmarket near Yuen Long and where there is a restaurant with an entryway and walls decorated with thousands of oyster shells.

Near Yuen Long are the walled villages of **Kam Tin**. The most popular for visitors is Kat Hing Wai, which is often mistakenly referred to as the Kam Tin Walled Village.

There are 400 people living at Kat Hing Wai, all with the same surname – Tang. Built in the 1600s, it is a fortified village with walls six meters (18 ft) thick, guardhouses on its four corners,

arrow slits for fighting off attackers, and a moat. The "authenticity" may seem spoiled by some of the modern buildings inside, complete with television aerials peeping over the old-time fortifications, but there is still only one entrance, guarded by a heavy wrought-iron gate. Visitors can enter the village for a nominal fee, but in earlier times, that gate kept out undesirables.

The **Hong Kong Railway Museum**, complete with vintage stock, is housed in the former Tu Po Market KCR station. Not far away, but with its own railway station, is **Tai Po Kau**.

Whether entering **Shatin** by road or rail, travelers are often amazed to find a bustling metropolis in the middle of the agricultural New Territories. Massive housing projects occupy fields where, just a few years ago, the greatest activity was water buffaloes pulling plows in rice paddies. The New Town Plaza is a massive shopping and entertainment complex, while Riverside Plaza Hotel, along the banks of the Shing Mun River, is another modern addition.

One of the New Territories' walled villages.

The **Shatin Valley** has several places of worship, of which three are worthy of note. First is the **Temple of 10,000 Buddhas**, which can be reached by climbing 431 steps up the hillside above the Shatin Railway Station. There, you will find a main altar room with 12,800 small Buddha statues on its walls.

An additional 69 steps up the hill is the **Temple of Man Fat**, where you can meet the man who created this temple and pagoda complex – even though he died a long time ago. Called Yuet Kai, he was a monk who spent a lifetime studying Buddhism and living a meditative life. His greatest concern was immortality. When he died, he was buried, but, according to Chinese custom, his body was later dug up to be reburied in its final resting place.

Monastery in the New Territories.

From either of these two places of worship, look down on a third one that is much more in tune with the present-day spirit of Hong Kong: the Hong Kong Jockey Club's **Shatin Racecourse**. Thousands of punters (the grandstands hold 75,000) religiously go there every October-through-May horse-racing season to bet money on the ponies and then pray for good fortune.

Outer Islands

Of all the outlying islands, the greatest in size, and perhaps in atmosphere, is **Lantau**, with a land area twice that of Hong Kong Island. In some ways it is still not too late to experience on Lantau the rural village lifestyles that have endured unchanged. But time is short. Hong Kong's new **international airport** on reclaimed land along the island's north shore, is certain to introduce changes, especially with new roads and bridges connecting the island to both Kowloon and Hong Kong Island.

Lantau is dominated by the ragged and two-part **Lantau Peak**, rising 935 meters (3,086 ft) high at the heart of lizard-shaped Lantau.

A particularly good trail circles the blue **Shek Pik Reservoir**, on the west slopes of Lantau Peak. This 21,000-million-liter (5,500-million-gallon) res-

ervoir gathers most of the freshwater carried from Lantau's heights by rushing streams and rivulets.

For those who land at **Silver Mine Bay**, Lantau's main visitor point, regular buses travel from there along Lantau's southern resort coast to the brightly-painted red-and-gold **Po Lin Monastery**. Here, in a large visitors' dining house, enjoy a good vegetarian lunch served by Po Lin's resident monks.

West of Po Lin, in the direction of Tung Chung on Lantau's north coast, is an excellent walking path that traverses mountain ridges and small canyons, and crosses over rushing streams en route to Lantau's **Yin Hing Monastery**, a haven rich with traditional Buddhist paintings and statues. This monastery sits on a slope and commands a fine view of the surrounding mountains, farming country and the blue South China Sea.

For those who would like to break up their Po Lin area tour with a local-style high-tea hour, there is a proper tea plantation and teahouse, **Lantau Tea Gardens**, just a short walk away from the Po Lin Monastery. The teahouse has rooms for rent, barbecue facilities and a free camping area.

While on the northern side of Lantau, try to visit **Tung Chung**, an old fortress and bay that curves around the pointed southern tip of little Chek Lap Kok Island. On a hill overlooking this little harbor, you'll spot an old fort that was built in 1817.

Expansive Lantau is also understandably famed for its many long, smooth and often empty beaches. The finest sandy sweeps are on the southeast coastline that arcs from **Cheung Sha**, south of Silver Mine Bay, to **Tong Fuk**. The most popular and crowded beach (probably because it is the easiest one to reach) is Silver Mine Bay Beach; a resort of the same name is near the Silver Mine Bay ferry landing.

The third-largest of the outlying islands, and somehow less well-known both to visitors and local people, is **Lamma Island**. It is nicknamed Stone Age Island because of its archaeological association with some of the earliest

Bronze Buddha, Po Lin Monastery.

settlements in Hong Kong, and perhaps also because it is, as yet, reasonably free of high-rise buildings, cars, commercialism, and pollution-spewing factories. Although it is just over eight square kilometers (5 sq mi) in size, Lamma is rich in green hills and beautiful bays, and because it's mountainous, there is little cultivation. Eroded mountain tops dominate the grassy lower slopes.

Lamma is an island totally devoted to fishing, with a small population of less than 6,000 people (which includes a surprising number of expats who want to "get away from it all" and commute to urban Hong Kong daily for work). Although Lamma has a regular ferry, it has remained relatively undiscovered – much to the joy of those who live there.

Cheung Chau, a dumbbell-shaped isle – with hills at either end and a village nestled in a connecting rod of land – is narrow enough to walk from Cheung Chau Harbour on its west side to Tung Wan Harbour on the east in a few minutes. Cheung Chau is a fishing island, with a few farms in its more distant reaches, and its main town is a tangle of alleyways. There is no vehicular traffic, a unique Hong Kong phenomenon that gives the island an automatic serenity. Cheung Chau's sense of community is strong, but it does not exclude the visiting stranger. People here are more friendly than the hurried city dwellers in Hong Kong's Central District.

The island was once the haunt of pirates. One of the greatest pirates of all, Cheung Po Chai, used to hide out on this island when he was in danger.

Once a year, the whole island community comes together for a big Bun Festival, a celebration held to exorcise wandering and malicious ghosts who have been unable to find rest in this world. The festival, *Ching Chiu*, originated many years ago after the discovery of skeletons, perhaps the remains of people killed by pirates. Afterwards, the island was plagued by misfortunes; a Daoist priest recommended that offerings should be made to the restless spirits of the dead, and thus the festival.

Fishing boat in an outer island.

MACAU

A Portuguese colony, Macau does not revert to Chinese sovereignty until 1999, two years after Hong Kong. Yet it is a convenient extension of travels to Hong Kong. With the return of that former crown colony in 1997, the Chinese are preparing for that of Macau.

At one stage in early Eurasian history, Macau was *the* Asian seat of Roman Catholicism. Bishops here controlled all of the church's missions from Goa to the Moluccas and Nagasaki.

The first stop is usually **Penha Hill**, atop which stands the magnificent **Bishop's Palace**, unoccupied for many years but partly open to the public. From there, one can see across to Macau's Inner Harbor, and about a kilometer beyond, China. From another point, the Outer Harbor approaches and the island of Taipa, which is connected to the peninsula by a bridge, are visible.

It has been said that peninsular Macau has more churches per square mile than Vatican City. Perhaps the most striking Macau church is the towering facade of **St. Paul's**, with its impressive grand staircase. Historians call it the finest Christian monument in the Far East.

The first church at this site was destroyed by fire in 1601; construction of a new one began the following year. The present classical facade was added before 1630. In 1835, another fire destroyed St Paul's adjacent college, a library reputed to be the best east of Africa, and, again, the church itself. In 1904, efforts were made to rebuild the church, but, as is clear, little was done. Today, the facade of St Paul's is Macau's most enduring visitor symbol.

If touring by taxi, the driver usually races on to one of the colony's Chinese temples, but ask instead to go to **Monte Fort (St Paul's Fortress)**, which overlooks the facade. This fortification was built in the early 1620s. When Dutch ships attacked and invaded Macau in 1622, the half-completed fortress was defended by 150 clerics and black slaves. A lucky cannon shot by an Italian Jesuit hit a powder keg carried by the invaders; the badly-injured Dutch retreated.

Temples: Tours here always include the Chinese temples of A-Ma, for which Macau is named; Kun Iam, famous for the table on which the first Sino-American treaty was signed in 1844; and Lin Fong (Lotus).

The temple of the goddess **A-Ma** squats beneath Barra Hill, at the entrance to Macau's Inner Harbor. It is the oldest temple in this Portuguese territory, said to date back 600 years to the Ming dynasty. It was here, in 1557, that Macau was ceded to Portugal. The original temple was said to have been erected by Fukinese fishermen and dedicated to Tin Hau, the patron goddess of fishermen and others at sea.

The second temple complex of **Kun Iam** (in Cantonese, Kuan Yin) is dedicated to Buddhism's goddess of mercy, Guanyin. Some secondary temples in this complex are dedicated to A-Ma. The present temple dates back to 1627 and was built on the site of an earlier fourteenth-century temple.

Facade of St Paul's.

The third temple, **Lin Fong**, built in 1592, is quite near Macau's nineteenth-century **Portas do Cerco** (Border Gate). In the old days, it served as a guest house for mandarins traveling between Macau and Guangzhou. Its most recent restoration took place in 1980, but it is still an excellent example of classical Buddhist architecture.

Most tours make a quick visit to the **Dr. Sun Yatsen Memorial House**. Dr Sun, who established the first republic after the fall of emperor Puyi, is revered in both China and Taiwan. Although opened after he died, the memorial is near where he practiced medicine at nearby Kiang Vu Hospital. (He was one of the first Western-trained Chinese doctors in this area.) His birthplace is across the border, in China's Cuiheng.

Two other areas often missed by quickie tours – but very accessible by walking or by taxi – are the **Camões Garden** and the **Dom Pedro V Theatre**. The renovated eighteenth-century building now houses the Orient Foundation, though it was once the residence of the president of the select committee of the East India Company, the all-powerful firm that for centuries "ruled" from India to the South China Sea.

Gambling: Sleepy Macau is also vicariously known as the Las Vegas of the East, or, if European, the Monaco of the East. Indeed, gambling is the main reason that over six million visitors each year – 80 percent of them from Hong Kong – make the 64-kilometer (40 mi) sea cruise across the Pearl River estuary to Macau.

Macau's casinos, each one virtually packed everyday, feature Western and Chinese games of chance. If tired of conventional craps, roulette, baccarat (*chemin de fer*) or blackjack, try Chinese *fantan* or *pai-kao*.

Macau islands: The "other Macau" is not on the peninsula, but consists of the two islands of **Taipa**, connected to the mainland by an arching bridge, and **Coloane**. The islands' cobble-stoned villages have grown a bit, but are still charming – a cross between Iberian villages and Chinese farm communities.

Colonial influence.

GUILIN:
LIMESTONE WONDER

"The river is like a green silk belt, and the hills are like turquoise jade hairpins", wrote the Tang scholar and writer Han Yu (768–834).

Artists have immortalized their impression of this bizarre landscape – with its round mountain tops – in countless poems and paintings. Today, photographers have taken up the aesthetic calling, trying for just one more image. Many of those photographers are travelers from around the world, making it one of the top destinations in China, together with Beijing, Shanghai and Xi'an. Arriving in Guilin at sunset must be one of the most breathtaking approaches Asia.

The area around Guilin owes its exquisite beauty to an ancient geological process in which limestone formations were forced up from the sea bed more than 300 million years ago. Erosion then shaped the hills and peak tops, leaving at the same time numerous subterranean caves and caverns within the eerie rock formations.

What brings nearly every traveler eventually to Guangxi and especially Guilin is the region's unyielding and surreal landscape. The area's tableland has a predominance of limestone that has been deeply weathered and eroded down to a landscape that geographers call karst – sharp pinnacles and cliffs above ground, with trees seeming to defy logic if not gravity as they sprout from vertical surfaces, and labyrinthian caves and grottoes below ground.

Until the end of the 1970s, it was a quiet, sleepy place. But since then, this town on **Li Jiang** (Li River) has undergone incredible development because of tourism, the practice of which is quite easy nowadays with flight connections to Shanghai, Beijing, Guangzhou and Hong Kong. Other parts of Guilin can also be easily reached by train and overland bus, or by car.

Guangxi: The Guangxi region is in the southern subtropical part of China. Summers are long, hot and humid; the best times to visit are spring and autumn. Guilin itself is in the northeastern part of the Zhuang Autonomous Region of Guangxi, home of the Zhuang minority people, the largest national minority in China. More than 40 million people live in Guangxi, which borders on Vietnam in the south. Of Guangxi's population, approximately one-third are Zhuang, with another five percent belonging to various other minorities, including the Yao, Miao, Yi and Dong. These small minorities are settled predominantly in the more remote western and northern parts of Guangxi.

Guilin, which today has around half a million people, acquired its name from the local cassia trees, whose blooms carry their sweet scent through the entire town in autumn. (In fact, Guilin means cassia tree forest.)

According to historical records, Guilin is said to have been founded in 214 BC. At that time, the Lingqu Canal was being built under the regency of the first Chinese emperor, Qin Shi Huangdi. The

Preceding pages: karst limestone defines Guilin's landscape. **Left**, the Li Jiang. **Right**, household chores, Li Jiang.

canal still exists today, connecting the central Asian plain with southern China and Southeast Asia, via the Chang (Yangze), Li and Zhu (Pearl River).

Guilin and Guanxi have a tradition of sheltering refugees. In 1647, the Ming imperial court established a temporary settlement here during their flight from the Qing Manchu. Nearly three centuries later, hundreds of thousands of northern Chinese sought refuge in Guilin from the advancing Japanese during World War II. And in 1949, Guilin was one of the last towns to be taken by the Chinese Communists in their fight against the Nationalists.

Guilin and its surroundings are still mostly agricultural, but this is limited by the numerous mountains in the whole of Guangxi. The landscape is characterized by terraced rice paddies, water buffalos, bamboo groves and farmers working in the fields. *Jujube*, a type of date, is harvested here, and Guilin is famous for its spicy *guilinjiang*, a pepper sauce.

Guilin itself is not particularly attrac-tive. There are still many old, somewhat rundown houses, but a building boom started with the arrival of tourism several years ago. Many modern hotels have sprung up, and the face of Guilin has changed considerably. Indeed, some would say that it's become thick with traffic, bustling and peppered with scam artists preying on tourists.

In the center of town and around Zhongshan Lu are many large and small souvenir shops, clothes boutiques, small hotels, and, in between, an increasing number of snack bars and small restaurants offering snakes and frog legs.

North of the centrally-situated Lijiang Hotel, on Ronghu Bei Lu, is the 150-meter-tall (500-ft) **Duxiu Feng**, the Peak of Unique Beauty. Leading to the top are exactly 300 steps.

Nearby, are the **ruins of Wang Cheng** (Royal Residence), dating from the late fourteenth century. A bit further west, by the bank of Li Jiang and at the corner of Binjiang Lu and Fengbei Lu, rises **Fubo Shan**. The hill is probably named after a general from the Han period who

Ludiyan, or Reed Flute Cave.

had defended the inhabitants against attackers. Along the way to Fubo Shan is a two-ton bell, along with a huge cooking pot from which more than 1,000 people could apparently be served. Both are from a former temple. On the south slope of Fubo Shan is a cave, where a dragon, who had a beautiful pearl to light his cave, is supposed to have lived. A fisherman stole the pearl, but brought it back quickly when he discovered to whom it belonged.

On the eastern slope of the mountain is **Qianfo Yan** (Thousand Buddha Rock), with around 300 Buddhist sculptures from the Tang and Song dynasties. Further north is **Diecai Shan** (Mountain of Colored Layers). Atop the 220-meter-high (730-ft) mountain is a wonderful view of Guilin and Li Jiang. There are also Buddhist sculptures and calligraphy in the caves of Diecai Shan.

On the eastern bank of Li Jiang – easily reached by crossing Jiefang bridge – is **Qixing Gongyuan** (Seven Star Park). Its seven hills are laid out according to the star pattern of the Ursa Major (Big Dipper) constellation. There are several illuminated caves in the mountain; the most famous is the Seven Star Cave with its inscriptions and poems. **Luotuo Shan** (Camel Mountain) has an interesting shape, resembling a seated dromedary. There is also a bonsai exhibition and a small zoo in the park.

Almost six kilometers northwest of the city center is **Ludiyan** (Reed Flute Cave), which goes 250 meters (800 ft) into the mountain's interior. The cave takes its name from the reeds – used to make flutes – that once grew at the entrance of the cave. That same entrance is now clogged with hawkers selling to tourists. There are many bizarre stalactites and stalagmites along the way inside resembling pagodas, people, lions and mushrooms, lit by colored lights. There is no limit to the imagination. The most beautiful spot of the tour is a subterranean water landscape, which resembles the landscape around Guilin and Li Jiang. The most impressive place inside the cave might be the Crystal Palace of the Dragon King, less because

Yangshuo.

of any dragon and more for its capacity to hold 1,000 people.

Li Jiang: A boat trip from Guilin to Yangshuo on peaceful **Li Jiang** (Li River) is perhaps the high point of any visit to Guilin. The boats – and at times there seems to be an armada of them – leave from Jiefang Bridge, near the Lijiang Hotel. Smaller boats usually leave from Xiangbi Shan (Elephant Trunk Hill).

The cruise from Guilin to Yangshuo, about 60 kilometers (40 mi) away on the winding and twisting Li Jiang, is unusually expensive and takes four to five hours, passing the many exotic mountains whose shapes have inspired and fired the Chinese imagination: Elephant Trunk, Old Man, Pagoda and Hole mountains.

Cormorant fishermen in narrow bamboo boats, bathing children, water buffaloes, small settlements, and women doing their washing can be seen along the way. Sometimes the water level is so low that the boats can only depart from the settlement of Yangdi. The second part of the journey, however, is perhaps more interesting.

Yangshuo, south of Guilin and the end of the boat journey, is today a developed village that thrives mainly on tourism, especially budget and backpack travelers. During the day, it is less than serene. Nonetheless, when the boat tourists have departed, the village streets become tranquil again.

From Yangshuo, there is a bus back to Guilin (about two hours' journey). The trip leaves an impression of the varied landscape and of the many traditional tombs, as well as an insight into Guilin agriculture.

Beyond Guilin: Northeast of Guilin is **Sanjiang**, a settlement from the Song dynasty. In the other direction, southwest of Guilin, in the center of Guangxi, is **Liuzhou**, an expanding industrial town of over half a million people, and picturesque and typically southern Chinese. The main attraction is Dule Yan (Dule Rock) with its numerous karst caves. Another area with a beautiful landscape is the settlement of **Guiping**, about 130 kilometers (80 mi) southeast from Liuzhou.

The capital of the Autonomous Region of Guangxi is **Nanning**, southwest of Guilin and only 160 kilometers (100 mi) from the Vietnamese border. Here, travelers can visit a museum of the autonomous region, an institute for national minorities, and a cultural center where the villages of eleven national minorities have been reconstructed in an open-air museum. Its two-million-plus residents are sharing in a rapidly-expanding consumer affluence, obvious from the blossoming of stores.

Southwest of Nanning, near the Vietnamese border and the river **Zuo Jiang**, is a landscape nearly as fantastic as that in Guilin. In Ningmeng district, there are centuries-old rock paintings along a steep rock face.

The route from Guilin via Liuzhou towards Guangzhou (or the other way by boat) passes **Wuzhou**, a small town that is also surrounded by a magnificent landscape. The coastlines of Guangxi, however, have so far hardly been opened up to tourism.

Left, cormorant fishing. **Right,** Guilin portrait.

YUNNAN: THE SOUTHWEST

"South of the clouds" is a loose translation of the name of China's southwestern province, **Yunnan**, bordered by Burma (Myanmar) to the west and Laos and Vietnam in the south.

Southwest China is said to have been ruled by six princes in the eighth century. The story goes that one of these princes made the long journey to the imperial court of the Tang emperor for an audience. When asked from where did he come, he replied that his home was even farther to the south than the rainy area in southern Sichuan. In response, the emperor created the name Yun Nan, which in literal translation means "Cloud-South". The Ming emperors (1368–1644) later used Yunnan mostly as exile for troublesome intellectuals or uncooperative bureaucrats. While the Chinese imperial dynasties didn't consider the region to be outside of their jurisdiction, they did see it as outside of Chinese culture, where only barbarians – and exiled miscontents – lived. At any rate, those banished to Yunnan were usually forgotten.

Yunnan is home to a great variety of peoples. In fact, there are over two dozen different nationalities on the Yunnan-Guizhou high plateau, mostly peasants in the mountain villages. The Yi, Naxi, Bai and Dai are amongst the most populous groups in the province; in the towns, Han Chinese predominate.

There are no grand buildings, archaeological finds or cultural artifacts to be found in Yunnan; it is the unspoilt countryside, rare animals, rich flora and the variety of ethnic groups and their cultural traditions that attract the traveler.

Sichuan to Yunnan: Many towns and regions in southwest China were long closed to foreigners. And while, until a few years ago, the few accessible towns could only be reached via **Kunming**, it is now possible to travel throughout the southern region.

The railway journey from the plain of Sichuan leads gradually up to the Yun-

nan-Guizhou Plateau, which on average lies at an altitude of 2,000 meters (6,560 ft). The landscape is unspoiled; bare mountains rise majestically, the few trees pointing their green foliage defiantly skywards. Calm rivers dominate the valleys, and only where nature permits it – in narrow valleys hemmed in between river and mountain slope – have people settled. The railway itself looks like an alien enterprise from a distant place. Nevertheless, it is a lifeline for what was once an almost-forgotten region.

On the Sichuan border, the town of **Dukou** – of no particular merit for the traveler other than its history – is an artificial creation, constructed out of nothing and as uninviting as many of the Siberian settlements that probably served as an example in the 1950s. The pioneers of Chinese industrialisation were attracted by the lucrative ore deposits rather than by the beauty of the area. All the inhabitants are from other provinces, and the indigenous people, particularly the Yi, living in their moun-

tain villages, have ignored them. But, increasingly, one must travel further into the mountains to find villages where the old traditions still survive. Village houses are sparsely furnished, almost without any furniture. The fireplace is in the middle of the large room on the floor, surrounded by three stones that symbolise the presence of a deity and must not be touched. Hospitality is shown by offering plenty of spirits.

Lijiang: The road westward from Dukou to Lijiang, the area of the Naxi people, crosses several mountain passes and narrow gorges. Huge rocks, tumbling waterfalls and wild streams make one aware of the force of nature.

Worth a visit is Heilongtan (Black Dragon Pond), in Lijiang, which offers a marvelous view of Yulong Shan. In the small park is Wufenglou (Five Phoenix Pavilion), which exhibits Naxi cultural artifacts. A small institute dedicated for research into Naxi culture is also located in this park.

The sky and the earth are still in close proximity in Lijiang. **Yulong Shan** (Jade Dragon Mountain), whose highest peak Shanzidou (5,600 m/18,360 ft) dominates the open Lijiang plain, gives credence to the proverb, "When the sky and the earth were not yet separated, trees could walk and stones could speak", from the Dongba scripts of the Naxi, preserved in an old picture scroll. The mountain was first climbed in the 1960s.

In summer, the slopes below the snow line bloom with azaleas of all colors, and countless medicinal herbs attract collectors. Cattle, goats, yak and Tibetan oxen graze on the pastures at the foot of the mountain. One of the biggest gorges in the world, the 16-kilometer-long (10-mi) **Hutiao Xia** (Tiger Leap Gorge), is located on Yulong Shan. The canyon itself is between 2,500 and 3,000 meters (8,200–9,800 ft) deep and, at its narrowest point, is 30 meters (100 ft) wide. The Jinsha Jiang (upper part of Chang Jiang, the Yangzi) surges at the bottom of the gorge.

Naxi people: The origin of the Naxi is still not clear. It is thought that they settled many thousands of years ago in

Yulong Shan, the Jade Dragon Mountain.

the northwest of China, in the modern provinces of Qinghai, Gansu and Sichuan, before being driven south by central Asian invaders.

The Naxi have for some decades attracted a lot of interest from ethnologists worldwide, who are interested both in the Naxi hieroglyphics and in their customs and social structures. The Naxi are amongst the few groups in the world where remnants of matriarchal organization are still clearly recognizable. Women carry out both the heavy and the important tasks, and are dominant in family life.

The costume of the Naxi women serves as a cushion on the back to ease the pressure of heavy loads. Two large and seven smaller, circular ornaments adorn the back, symbolizing the sun, moon and stars – the firmament. The shoulders of Naxi women, bent by heavy work, are turned skywards day and night.

It is women who choose their partners, in festive rituals. The chosen man spends only evenings with "his" woman over the years; he continues to work and live in his mother's house. Female members of the family have the privilege of their own room where they can receive their lovers, while the male members of the family have to share a room.

Where women are in charge, the men naturally seek escape in entertainment. They are considered to be keen singers, dancers and musicians.

The number of Dongba shaman still alive and practicing in the Naxi culture is estimated at 30 to 40, some working at an official institute that was founded a few years ago. They are helping to decode the Naxi picture script.

Er Hai Hu: Many of the more than twenty different minority peoples in southwest China still show traces of matriarchal social structures. This is also the case with the Bai, who are predominantly settled in the area around the lake Er Hai.

The charm of the landscape, the mild climate, even in winter, and the hospitality of the people made the town of **Dali** a favorite with foreigners soon after its opening. The enterprising peo-

Bai musicians.

ple of Dali have quickly adjusted to the needs and quirks of foreigners. Backyard restaurants offer soft drinks, coffee and hot chocolate, as well as pizzas and hamburgers.

Dali takes its name from a proud and powerful empire that ruled in southwest China from the tenth to thirteenth centuries, before Kublai Khan, the great Mongol emperor, conquered this remote corner of the empire. The Bai had already created a kingdom – Nanzhao (738–902) – three centuries earlier. The last and well-preserved relics of that culture are in the **caves of Shizhong Shan** (Stone Bell Mountain), in **Jianchuan** on the way from Lijiang to Dali.

The caves contain both religious sculptures and several depictions of the kings of Nanzhao. The Nanzhao stele, a 3-meter-high (10-ft) monolith from the eighth century, can still be seen at the site of the former Nanzhao capital, Taihe. Its inscriptions give an indication of the political and economic system of the Nanzhao kingdom.

Well-known throughout China are **Santa Si** (Three Pagodas), in Dali. The central pagoda, which at 70 meters (220 ft) is the highest, dates from the ninth century and once stood in the center of a temple. During restoration work in 1978, more than 600 different artifacts were discovered. Long hidden in the buildings, they date from the seventh to tenth centuries – bronze mirrors, medicines, Buddha sculptures of gold and a phoenix made of silver.

The pagodas of Santa Si are painted white. The Bai call their ancestor White King, and their language, which resembles Mandarin Chinese, is called "white language". And while Bai itself means white, the color's significance is still not known. However, Bai women prefer strong, bright colors – particularly red – in their clothing, amongst the most colorful clothing in southwest China.

The culture and religion of the Bai blends in a unique way its own traditions with neighboring Chinese, Indian and Tibetan influences.

In the area's numerous small temples, the Buddha, Laozi (founder of Daoism),

Fisherman on Er Hai, near Dali.

Guandi (a war god), and Lama deities are worshipped equally. On the day before the full moon, a food-and-drink celebration often takes place in temples, and the monks tell fortunes and produce horoscopes – for a donation.

Kunming: The capital of Yunnan province, Kunming, and its nearly three million inhabitants are situated on a 2,000-meter-high (6,500-ft) plateau. Protected by its location, Kunming has a mild pleasant climate, with an average temperature of 18°C (64°F), making it delightfully spring-like year-round.

The southern atmosphere, and the variety of cultures and customs apparent in the streets of Kunming, can best be enjoyed by strolling through the market streets away from the avenues.

Cui Hu (Green Lake), in the northwest of town, has pleasant promenades, small temples and pavilions, and it is amongst the favorite excursion spots of local residents. At the provincial museum are cultural artifacts from Yunnan's different nationalities.

Southeast of town, two brick pagodas – both square and with thirteen storys – tower over Kunming: **Dongsi Ta** (East Temple Pagoda) and **Xisi Ta** (West Temple Pagoda), the more interesting of the two.

On the southern edge of the town is **Dianchi**, the sixth-largest inland lake in China: 40 kilometers (30 mi) long and eight kilometers (5 mi) wide.

One can take a boat trip and watch the southern-style junks on the lake, with mountains in the background, where a small Daoist temple high up in the rock face is obvious. Climbing up to this temple, **Sanqingge** (Pavilion of the Three Pure Ones), may seem a little precarious – it involves following paths and tunnels carved into the rock. (The three pure ones, by the way, are the three main Daoist deities.)

There are two monasteries worth visiting at these same mountains: **Taihua Si** and **Huating Si**. In the latter monastery, the Luo figures in the Hall of the 500 Luohan are particularly interesting.

To the north, about 15 kilometers (9 mi) away, is **Heilongtan** (Black Dragon

Bai women,
Dali.

Pond), situated in a nice park. Heilonggong (Black Dragon Hall) is the last remaining memorial of a former Daoist temple, which dates from the time of the Yuan dynasty.

Some 10 kilometers (6 mi) in a northwesterly direction is **Qiongzhu Si** (Bamboo Temple), built during the early Ming dynasty and renovated several times since. The temple is particularly interesting because of its either very surrealistic or else realistic Luohan figures. The often brazen, absurd or amusing depiction of the Luohan is in sharp contrast to the otherwise customary, serious and respectful presentation of the Luohan figures in most Buddhist monasteries in China.

The 17th-century **Jindian** (Golden Hall) in the northeastern suburbs is made of bronze – the rafters, columns, tiles, statues and wall decorations. Only the staircases and the balustrade are made of marble. The hall alone weighs more than 200,000 kilograms (440,000 lbs).

The main reason that most travelers come to the Kunming area is **Shilin** (Stone Forest), located 120 kilometers (75 mi) southeast of Kunming and in the autonomous district of **Lunan**, home of the Yi people. The "trees" in this almost 26,000-hectare (64,250-acre) forest consist of narrow, bizarrely-shaped needles of rock, rising from five to 30 meters (15–100 ft) in height.

This karst formation goes back about 200 million years, when the earth's crust rose and the waters from a lake receded. A huge rock carved with the two symbols, *shi* and *lin*, greets visitors at the entrance to the small portion of the formations heavily treaded upon by tourists. Following the marked 1,200-meter-long path leads to all sorts of peculiarly-shaped rock formations.

One of the best-known rocks amongst the locals is Ashma, representing a legend that is popular with the Sani people. The beautiful Ashma had been kidnapped by a rich landowner. Her lover Ahai set off, armed with magic weapons, to free her. Unfortunately, she died through some misfortune during her escape and was transformed into a rock.

Lush Yunnan landscape.

Even to this day, she is still waiting for Ahai. On special days, Sani from the nearby villages gather for their traditional festivals by Ashma.

Xishuangbanna: The tuneful name of Xishuangbanna, a region located to the south near Burma (Myanmar), has a more prosaic meaning in the Dai language: Twelve Administration Units. However, nature provides what the name lacks. The landscape in this tropical region is still the home to many animals long extinct elsewhere: elephants, tigers, pythons, Malay bears, leopards and rare birds.

The lush tropical jungle covers 100,000 hectares (250,000 acres), embellished with kiwi, mangoes, bananas and papayas that grow in abundance in the hilly countryside. In the forests are precious woods, including mahogany, teak, camphor and sandalwood. All is not tropically idyllic, however, as its increasing popularity with Chinese tourists means that, at peak times, there is a constant bus caravan on the roads.

Xishuangbanna is most easily reached by flying from Kunming to **Jinghong**, perched on the Mekong River and the capital of the autonomous district. This Chinese-looking town gets crowded with people from the outlying villages, particularly on Sundays, the traditional market day. They are mostly Dai – related to the Thai and who make up one-third of the population – but there are also Hani, Jinuo and other nationalities.

If tired of temple-hopping, rejoice that there are few temples in the area. The most striking and beautiful pagoda is **Manfeilong** (White Pagoda of Damenglong), built in the thirteenth century about 70 kilometers (40 miles) south of Jinghong, close to the border of Burma (Myanmar). Legend has it that the pagoda, which was built in a distinct Southeast Asian style, shelters a footprint left by the wandering Buddha.

The ochre-colored pagoda of **Manlei**, in Mengzhe, was erected in the shape of a Tibetan stupa. **Jingzhen Baijiaoting** (Octagonal Pavilion of Jingzhen), about 14 kilometers (9 mi) to the west of Menghai, has a striking and unique roof.

Manfeilong.

TIBET

Known as Xizang in Chinese, Tibet is, for the most part, hidden and was historically difficult to reach behind a wall of the highest mountains in the world. For centuries, Tibet was the dream of innumerable explorers and adventurers.

Unfortunately, a journey to Tibet has no longer anything in common with the adventures of the past. Instead of strong nerves, energy and privations, it is now simply an expensive endeavor, and takes about two hours of flying time from Chengdu, in Sichuan.

If looking for adventure, travelers can go overland from Nepal or from Lanzhou via Xining and Golmud, taking the bus or a jeep to Lhasa. There is a highway from Kashi, in the province of Xinjiang, winding through the frontier in the extreme west, in a southerly direction via Xigaze to Lhasa. Expect this route to take about a week.

Geography and people: The Himalaya are the youngest folded mountains in the world. Before the southern Indian land mass began to shift northwards about 40 million years ago, one of the largest oceans in the history of the earth occupied the area. Today, the Tibet-Qinghai Plateau is, at an average altitude of 4,000 meters (13,000 ft), the world's most elevated plateau, covering 25 percent of China. It is closed off on three sides by the highest mountain ranges in the world: to the south, the Himalaya; in the west, the Karakorum; and in the north, the Kunlun and Tanggula ranges.

The Indus and Sutlej rivers have their source in the sparsely-populated west, on the sacred mountain of Kailas; the source of the Brahmaputra (Yralung Zangbo) is to the east. It crosses Tibet in an easterly direction, before flowing through huge gorges southwards into the Gulf of Bengal. Further north, in the province of Qinghai, are sources of the two big Chinese rivers: Huang He (Yellow River) and Chang Jiang (Yangzi).

The Tibetans have been nomads for centuries, crossing the highland pas-

tures in the south with their herds of sheep, goats and yak. (In contrast, the north is an uninhabited desert.)

The Tibetans are thought to be the descendants of Turan and Tangut tribes from Central Asia, who reached Tibet from the north and mixed with the local population. The Tibetans settled in the Yarlung Zangbo valley, where nature was kind and provided everything necessary for successful agriculture. Today, 2.2 million people live in the autonomous region of Tibet, of whom about 1.7 million are Tibetans, who also live in Qinghai, Sichuan and Yunnan provinces, as well as in exile in India and Nepal. The total number of Tibetans is estimated to be six million.

Tibetan history: The 31st king of the Yarlung empire, Namri Songtsen, succeeded in AD 607 in unifying the various Tibetan tribes into the Thufo empire. However, Songtsen Gampo (620–649) is considered historically to have unified the empire, creating a powerful military state, conquering a vast territory and even threatening the Chinese capital. He transferred his residence from the Yarlung valley to Lhasa.

Conflicts with the powerful Chinese neighbor continued well into the ninth century, when Tibet broke up into numerous small vassals. In 866, the western Tibetan kingdom of Guge was founded. In the 1100s, the abbots of the larger monasteries became powerful rulers, challenging the worldly rulers. In 1207, the first Mongol armies invaded Tibet; Kublai Khan gave secular powers to the powerful abbots of the Sakya monastery.

In the 1300s and 1400s, the great reformer Tsongkhapa (1357–1416) revived Buddhism and founded new monasteries that became centers of both religious and secular power. He founded the Gelugpa (Virtue) Sect – still called Yellow Hat Sect, after the color of the monks' hats – which was to become the dominant religious and secular power. Indeed, its highest representatives became the Dalai Lama and the Panchen Lama, incarnations of the highest gods of Tibet. The Great Fifth Dalai Lama founded the theocracy of the Yellow

Church, supported by the Mongol Khan Gusri, who benevolently governed the Tibetan kings and followers of the ancient Tibetan Bon religion.

Chinese rule over Tibet began in the eighteenth century. In 1720, the Qing emperor Kangxi chased the Dsungar invaders out of Tibet and took control. Chinese functionaries, so-called Ambane, headed the local government. Finally, in the late nineteenth century, the British began to penetrate into the heights of Tibet, and the country quickly became a center of big-power conflicts. In addition to the British, the Chinese and Czarist Russians also made claims on the country. China, torn by war and revolution in the early 1900s, lost control of Tibet for quite some time, until barely a year after the foundation of the People's Republic. In 1950, the Chinese army entered Tibet.

The early hopes of Tibetans for a better life and more freedom under the Chinese were quickly crushed. In 1959, a Tibetan uprising was brutally repressed; the Cultural Revolution of the 1960s and 1970s resulted in vigorous suppression of religious life, and in the destruction of Tibet's cultural treasures. After China's limited opening of its economic and political system in the early 1980s, demonstrations and violent clashes followed in the late 1980s. To this day, Tibet remains a thorn in the side of Beijing.

Lhasa: The capital of the province and center of Tibetan Buddhism, Lhasa lies at an altitude of 3,660 meters (12,000 ft) on the banks of the river Kyichu (also called Lhasa River), a tributary of Yarlung Zangbo. Lhasa is reached by plane from Chengdu, Xi'an and Golmud, or via overland routes. The airport is on the southern bank of the Yarlung Zangbo, a two-hour journey from the city.

The gold-clad roofs of the **Potala Palace** greet from afar. A palace built by Songtsen Gampo stood on Marpori, the Red Mountain, in the seventh century. After the completion of the Potala Palace in 1645, the Dalai Lamas resided here as religious and secular rulers. The section called **White Palace** was con-

Monasteries have reopened.

structed first; half a century later, the **Red Palace** was completed. It rises like a huge tower from the sea of white-painted buildings. This is also where the private residence of the Dalai Lama is located. The entire palace covers an area of almost 400 meters (450 yds) from east to west, and 350 meters (380 yds) from north to south. It rises 120 meters (385 ft) above the Lhasa valley. The thirteen floors hold almost 1,000 rooms, whose ceilings are supported by more than 15,000 columns.

In the Red Palace are the great ceremonial halls, 35 small chapels, four meditation halls and eight vaults for deceased Dalai Lamas. The most splendid and valuable one is for the fifth Dalai Lama – it is 15 meters (50 ft) high, and is decorated with four tons of gold, innumerable diamonds, turquoise, corals and pearls. The vault for the 13th Dalai Lama is 14 meters (46 ft) long. In the northeastern part of the palace is the chapel of **Avalokiteshvara**, which is considered the oldest part of the structure and said to have been preserved from the original palace of Songtsen Gampo. The chapel contains a statue of the king Songtsen Gampo with his Chinese wife, Wen Chen, and his Nepalese wife, Bhrikuti.

Look down into the valley and the old city from the roof of the Potala. The holiest temple of all Tibetans is in the city center. The central building, surrounded by buildings of **Tsuglagkhang**, was once the offices of the Tibetan government administration.

Arrive at the temple of **Jokhang** by walking through a prayer hall supported by red columns. The main building of Jokhang, built on a square mandala foundation, dates from the seventh century. The temple was built as a shrine for a Buddha statue that the Chinese princess Wen Cheng brought to Lhasa, as a wedding gift from the Chinese emperor. This Buddha, called Jobo in Tibetan, gave the temple its name: Jokhang, the hall of the Jobo Buddha. The center of the temple is anchored by a courtyard. Four gilded roofs mark the holiest halls: the chapels of the Jobo Buddha,

Jokhang, in old Llasa.

Avalokiteshvara and Maitreya, and the chapel of Songtsen Gampo.

The golden Jobo statue is richly decorated with jewels and usually covered with brocade and silk bands. At the feet of the Buddha, lamps made of heavy silver and filled with yak oil burn continually. It is not quite certain whether the statue really is the original from the seventh century, as other statues and paintings were destroyed during the Cultural Revolution and later replaced with copies.

From the roof of Jokhang is a view of Potala Palace and of the **Barkhor**, the sacred ritual path that surrounds Jokhang and Tsuglagkhang. Numerous pilgrims and traders are crowded on the 800-meter-long path. The pilgrims constantly prostrate themselves in the dust and circle in this manner around the Jokhang temple; others continuously turn their prayer hats. On both sides of the path, traders offer their wares. Traveling monks meditate at the side of the road and will offer special prayers in return for a donation. There used to be a longer ritual path, the seven-kilometer-long Lingkhor, which surrounded the town, but it has today been broken up by new buildings. In those times, the pilgrims had to measure the path with the length of their bodies before they were allowed to enter the city.

At the entrance of the Jokhang temple, along the Barkhor, a willow tree planted in 1985 marks the spot where, in AD 641, a Chinese princess originally planted another willow as a friendship symbol. A floor tile in front of the temple entrance has an inscription of a Tibetan-Chinese friendship treaty, in 821.

About seven kilometers (4 mi) from the city center is **Norbulingkha** (Precious Stone Garden), which was built on the orders of the 7th Dalai Lama in the second half of the eighteenth century. Since then, it has served as a summer residence for the Dalai Lama. The New Summer Palace, which was built for the 14th Dalai Lama and completed in 1956, is the best-preserved of the whole site. On the top floor of the building, which is decorated with numerous wall murals, is an audience hall with paintings from the history of the Tibetan people. Also open are the meditation room and bedroom of the Dalai Lama. There is a throne for the God King in the reception hall, and the wall paintings tell of the various experiences in the life of the 14th Dalai Lama, framed by legends from the lives of the Buddha and Tsongkhapa.

Other buildings in the park include the palaces of the 8th and 13th Dalai Lamas, and the Drunzig Palace, with a library and study.

In the north of the town, near the Barkhor, is **Ramoche**, probably the oldest monastery in Lhasa. It is said to have been constructed in the first half of the seventh century and served as a shrine for a statue brought to Tibet by the Nepalese wife of King Songtsen Gampo. Later, after the arrival of the Chinese princess Wen Cheng, the Jobo Buddha was housed here before it was transferred to Jokhang. The temple was only restored and reopened in 1958, but was later destroyed during the Cultural Revolution and used as a residence. Now, monks reside in it once more.

Three great monasteries near Lhasa are considered as important centers of the Yellow Hat sect, and as pillars of the theocratic state: Sera, Drepung and Ganden. **Sera Monastery** was built in 1419 by a pupil of Tsongkhapa, at a place where his great master had spent many years studying and meditating in a small hut. During its most active period, almost 5,000 monks lived in the monastery, which had a brilliant reputation throughout Tibet because of its famous academy. Today, nearly 300 monks live in the monastery, whose main buildings were saved from the destruction of the Cultural Revolution. Sera is about five kilometers (3 mi) north of Lhasa, at the foot of the mountains dominating the Lhasa valley.

On the way to Drepung Monastery, 10 kilometers (6 mi) west of the town center, is the small **Netschung Monastery**, which used to house the Tibetan state oracle. (Both monks and lay people could become oracle priests.) Before each decision, the oracle was consulted after the priests had put themselves into a trance. The last oracle priest went into exile in India with the Dalai Lama and died there in 1985.

Drepung Monastery, which was built in 1416, also by a pupil of Tsongkhapa, was for a long time the political headquarters of the Yellow Hat sect. Before the Potala Palace was completed, the predecessors of the Great Fifth Dalai Lama resided here before moving to Potala; the tomb stupa of the second, third and fourth Dalai Lama are housed in Drepung Monastery.

Drepung is probably the largest monastery in the world. At the height of its activities, nearly 10,000 monks are said to have lived within its walls. Walking around the cloistered city is somewhat tiring, particularly in the thin air. The lower part of the site is occupied by hermitages for the monks, along with numerous storerooms. Further up are the prayer halls and *dukhang*, which contain valuable statues and Thangka.

The third big monastery of the Gelugpa sect is **Ganden Monastery**, 40 kilometers (25 mi) northeast of Lhasa.

The monastery, which was founded in 1409 by Tsongkhapa, the reformer and founder of the Yellow Hat sect, is one of the most sacred places of Tibetan Buddhism. It was where 5,000 monks once lived, making the almost-total destruction of the site during the Cultural Revolution even more tragic. Hardly any of the monastery's treasures were preserved, and the buildings were torn down to their foundations. Only in 1985 was the rebuilding of the monastery finally completed, and that was limited to the most important buildings, including the mausoleum of Tsongkhapa, recognizable from a distance by its red walls. Meanwhile, some 300 monks have returned to the monastery.

Yarlung Valley: A two-hour bus ride from Lhasa airport in an easterly direction is **Tsetang**. This small country town has a few hotels for tourists; from here, one can undertake excursions to the Yarlung Valley and the Tibetan kings' graves, and to the old Samye and Mindroling monasteries. The town of Tsetang is said to have been built on the

Ornament of amber, silver and coral.

spot where bodhisattva Avalokiteshvara descended from heaven in the shape of a monkey and, with the help of a female demon, produced the first Tibetan.

Seven kilometers (4 mi) south of Tsetang, on the road to the Yarlung Valley, is **Khrabrug Monastery**, one of the first Buddhist monasteries in Tibet and said to have been built under the rule of King Songtsen Gampo. After the Cultural Revolution, the site was used as a farm and the buildings for agricultural storage.

Thirty kilometers (20 mi) from Tsetang lies the **Yarlung Valley**, where the kings of the Yarlung dynasty, who reigned between 627 and 842, were buried. The tombs are only discernible as small mounds of earth. The biggest mound, which has a small temple built upon it, is claimed to be the burial ground of Songtsen Gampo. **Yumbulhakhang** is said to be one of the few early Tibetan buildings; it looks as if it literally grew out of the peak of a hill. The citadel had already been changed into a chapel in early times. The Cultural Revolution

reduced it to a ruin, but the buildings were rebuilt in 1982.

Travelers can visit the oldest monastery of Tibet, **Samye Monastery**, from Tsetang. First cross the Yarlung Zangbo in a ferry, which takes less than a couple of hours. On the opposite bank, a lorry or tractor with a trailer carries travelers to the monastery in about 30 minutes. It is said that Samye was founded by the Indian teacher Padmasambhava, around AD 767. He is considered to be the founder of Tibetan Buddhism who, so it is said, succeeded in winning over the demon gods of the Bon religion. Many of the demon gods in the Tibetan monasteries refer back to such Bon gods. The site has been built on a mandala foundation and reflects the cosmic view of Tibetan religion. The main temple stands in the center and symbolizes Mount Meru. Four smaller chapels were erected on the four cardinal points of the compass. The whole site is surrounded by a wall that is still partly preserved.

About 60 kilometers (40 mi) west of Tsetang is **Mindroling Monastery**,

Left, traveling monk, with drum and bells; right, mask dance at monastery near Xining.

which can also be visited on an excursion to or from Lhasa. Built in 1676, it is a monastery of Nyingma, the oldest order founded by Padmasambhava.

The journey from Lhasa, via Gyantse to Xigaze, is a breathtaking experience. First, the route winds along the banks of the Yarlung Zangbo, up to **Kampa-La Pass** (4,794 m/15,728 ft). Looking back, the valley of Yarlung Zangbo is visible below, and in front, a hundred meters or so further down, are the deep blue-green colors of Yamdrok – the road continues for several kilometers along the shores of the lake. Travelers often stop at the lake for a picnic. From the opposite shore, a hairpin road hewn into the steep mountain face leads up to the next pass, the 5,045-meter-high (16,552-ft) **Karo-La**. One of the glaciers goes down as far as street level.

The way to Gyantse passes small villages, fertile valleys, cattle herds and many yaks, the Tibetan oxen who climb up the steepest slopes with surprising skill to graze. **Gyantse**, which lies by the northern bank of Nyangchu River,

Yamdrok.

265 kilometers (165 mi) southwest of Lhasa, is, after Lhasa and Xigaze, the third-largest of the old Tibetan towns. The exposed location of the town – on the road from Xigaze to Lhasa and on the trading route to India, Sikkim and Bhutan – makes it into one of the most important trading centers.

Dzong, a fortification on a hill, is visible from quite a distance away. This citadel was attacked and destroyed in 1904 by an English military expedition. In 1910, an English diplomat compared the market of Gyantse with Oxford Street in London; apparently, one could buy Scottish whisky and Swiss watches in Gyantse, in addition to silk, brocade, wool and jade. The fortification was opened to visitors in 1985.

The most important structure in Gyantse is **Palkhor Tschöde**. The circle-shaped site, which is enclosed by a wall, used to have several monasteries belonging to different sects. The 32-meter-tall (105-ft) Kumbum dagoba in the center of the monastery site is a unique example of Tibetan architec-

tural skill. The layout of this dagoba is in the shape of a three-dimensional mandala and symbolizes Mount Meru. The central structure at the tip of the dagoba is a chapel for the original Buddha; again, there are four chapels at the four cardinal points of the compass. Other shrines are located on the four floors, and visitors walk along it as if in a trance. The path to the center is thus a symbol of the spiritual path of salvation. The stupa erected in the first half of the 1600s has survived centuries of historical turbulence.

Xigaze, 360 kilometers (225 mi) west of Lhasa on the southern bank of Yarlung Zangbo, is traditionally the seat of the Panchen Lama, the second head of Tibetan Buddhism. In ancient Tibet, the town, which today has less than 50,000 inhabitants, was the provincial capital of Tsang. The Great Fifth Dalai Lama bestowed the title of Panchen Lama on his teacher from Tashi-Lhunpo Monastery. While the Dalai Lama is said to be an incarnation of the Tibetan deity bodhisattva Avalokiteshvara, the Panchen Lama is worshipped as the reincarnation of the Buddha Amithaba, and is therefore higher up in the heavenly hierarchy. This latent conflict of hierarchy was constantly used by the Russians, British and Chinese in their colonial rivalries.

The 10th Panchen Lama died in early 1989, in Beijing. In 1993, the Chinese government invited the Dalai Lama to help in the search for the next Panchen Lama, now claimed by the Chinese government to have been found in 1995.

The residence of the Panchen Lama, **Tashi-Lhunpo Monastery**, was founded in 1447 by a pupil of Tsongkhapa. The monastery site was substantially enlarged during the seventeenth and eighteenth centuries. Nearly 4,000 monks used to live here; today, there are around 600. The most important building is without doubt **Maitreya**, a chapel built by the 9th Panchen Lama in 1914. A 26-meter-tall (86-ft) golden statue of Maitreya, the Buddha of the Future, is housed in the 30-meter-high (100-ft) red-stone building.

Gyantse, with Kumbum in the foreground.

The memorial of the 4th Panchen Lama is also worth seeing. Eleven meters (36 ft) tall and erected in 1662, it is decorated with 3,000 ounces of gold, 15 tons of silver and innumerable precious stones. The gilded roofs of the chapels for the deceased Panchen Lamas tower over the entire site. A high stone wall stands on the slope behind the monastery. On feast days, huge Thangka are revealed there.

To the west of the town, in a large park, is the palace of the 7th Panchen Lama. While it was easy to visit in the early 1980s, when it was still a protected building, this has become more difficult in recent years because the palace had been returned to the 10th Panchen Lama, and the resident monks are not keen on tourist visits.

About 145 kilometers (90 mi) southwest of Xigaze is **Sakya**. The road to Sakya crosses two high mountain passes. On a clear day, one can see the summit of Mount Everest. Sakya Monastery has a special place in Tibetan history. Its foundation in 1073 also saw the crea-

Tashi Lhunpo, seat of Panchen Lama.

tion of a new order, the Sakyapa school. In some ways, the Sakya abbots were the predecessors of the Dalai Lamas. Since 1247, when the Mongol Khan Göden made the abbot Pandita of Sakya vice-king of Tibet, the Sakya Trizin, an incarnation of the bodhisattva Manjusri, ruled over most of the region to the west of Xigaze.

The Sakya monastery buildings are striking because of their dark grey color and the white horizontal stripes under the roof, as well as the red vertical stripes on the corners. While the southern monastery was left alone during the violence of the Cultural Revolution, the northern monastery was almost completely destroyed. Some buildings have since been rebuilt.

On the way back to Lhasa, unless planning to leave overland towards Nepal, consider the northern route. There are many pastures here; consequently, you will come across the nomads. The route heads across a 5,300-meter-high (17,400-ft) mountain pass, past the glacier-covered summit.

INSIGHT GUIDES
Travel Tips

FOR THOSE
WITH MORE THAN
A PASSING INTEREST
IN TIME...

Before you put your name down for a Patek Philippe watch *fig. 1*, there are a few basic things you might like to know, without knowing exactly whom to ask. In addressing such issues as accuracy, reliability and value for money, we would like to demonstrate why the watch we will make for you will be quite unlike any other watch currently produced.

"Punctuality", Louis XVIII was fond of saying, "is the politeness of kings."

We believe that in the matter of punctuality, we can rise to the occasion by making you a mechanical timepiece that will keep its rendezvous with the Gregorian calendar at the end of every century, omitting the leap-years in 2100, 2200 and 2300 and recording them in 2000 and 2400 *fig. 2*. Nevertheless, such a watch does need the occasional adjustment. Every 3333 years and 122 days you should remember to set it forward one day to the true time of the celestial clock. We suspect, however, that you are simply content to observe the politeness of kings. Be assured, therefore, that when you order your watch, we will be exploring for you the physical—if not the metaphysical—limits of precision.

Does everything have to depend on how much?

Consider, if you will, the motives of collectors who set record prices at auction to acquire a Patek Philippe. They may be paying for rarity, for looks or for micromechanical ingenuity. But we believe that behind each $500,000-plus bid is the conviction that a Patek Philippe, even if 50 years old or older, can be expected to work perfectly for future generations.

In case your ambitions to own a Patek Philippe are somewhat discouraged by the scale of the sacrifice involved, may we hasten to point out that the watch we will make for you today will certainly be a technical improvement on the Pateks bought at auction? In keeping with our tradition of inventing new mechanical solutions for greater reliability and better time-keeping, we will bring to your watch innovations *fig. 3* inconceivable to our watchmakers who created the supreme wristwatches of 50 years ago *fig. 4*. At the same time, we will of course do our utmost to avoid placing undue strain on your financial resources.

Can it really be mine?

May we turn your thoughts to the day you take delivery of your watch? Sealed within its case is your watchmaker's tribute to the mysterious process of time. He has decorated each wheel with a chamfer carved into its hub and polished into a shining circle. Delicate ribbing flows over the plates and bridges of gold and rare alloys. Millimetric surfaces are bevelled and burnished to exactitudes measured in microns. Rubies are transformed into jewels that triumph over friction. And after many months—or even years—of work, your watchmaker stamps a small badge into the mainbridge of your watch. The Geneva Seal—the highest possible attestation of fine watchmaking *fig. 5*.

Looks that speak of inner grace *fig. 6*.

When you order your watch, you will no doubt like its outward appearance to reflect the harmony and elegance of the movement within. You may therefore find it helpful to know that we are uniquely able to cater for any special decorative needs you might like to express. For example, our engravers will delight in conjuring a subtle play of light and shadow on the gold case-back of one of our rare pocket-watches *fig. 7*. If you bring us your favourite picture, our enamellers will reproduce it in a brilliant miniature of hair-breadth detail *fig. 8*. The perfect execution of a double hobnail pattern on the bezel of a wristwatch is the pride of our casemakers and the satisfaction of our designers, while our chainsmiths will weave for you a rich brocade in gold *figs. 9 & 10*. May we also recommend the artistry of our goldsmiths and the experience of our lapidaries in the selection and setting of the finest gemstones? *figs. 11 & 12*.

How to enjoy your watch before you own it.

As you will appreciate, the very nature of our watches imposes a limit on the number we can make available. (The four Calibre 89 time-pieces we are now making will take up to nine years to complete). We cannot therefore promise instant gratification, but while you look forward to the day on which you take delivery of your Patek Philippe *fig. 13*, you will have the pleasure of reflecting that time is a universal and everlasting commodity, freely available to be enjoyed by all.

Should you require information on any particular Patek Philippe watch, or even on watchmaking in general, we would be delighted to reply to your letter of enquiry. And if you send us

fig. 1: The classic face of Patek Philippe.

fig. 4: Complicated wristwatches circa 1930 (left) and 1990. The golden age of watchmaking will always be with us.

fig. 9: Harmony of design is executed in a work of simplicity and perfection in a lady's Calatrava wristwatch.

fig. 6: Your pleasure in owning a Patek Philippe is the purpose of those who made it for you.

fig. 10: The chainsmith's hands impart strength and delicacy to a tracery of gold.

fig. 5: The Geneva Seal is awarded only to watches which achieve the standards of horological purity laid down in the laws of Geneva. These rules define the supreme quality of watchmaking.

fig. 7: Arabesques come to life on a gold case-back.

fig. 11: Circles in gold: symbols of perfection in the making.

fig. 2: One of the 33 complications of the Calibre 89 astronomical clock-watch is a satellite wheel that completes one revolution every 400 years.

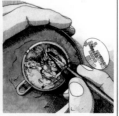

fig. 3: Recognized as the most advanced mechanical regulating device to date, Patek Philippe's Gyromax balance wheel demonstrates the equivalence of simplicity and precision.

fig. 8: An artist working six hours a day takes about four months to complete a miniature in enamel on the case of a pocket-watch.

fig. 12: The test of a master lapidary is his ability to express the splendour of precious gemstones.

PATEK PHILIPPE
GENEVE
fig. 13: The discreet sign of those who value their time.

your card marked "book catalogue" we shall post you a catalogue of our publications. Patek Philippe, 41 rue du Rhône, 1204 Geneva, Switzerland, Tel. +41 22/310 03 66.

Reality check. Call home.

—— *AT&T USADirect® and World Connect®. The fast, easy way to call most anywhere.* ——

Take out AT&T Calling Card or your local calling card.** Lift phone. Dial AT&T Access Number for country you're calling from. Connect to English-speaking operator or voice prompt. Reach the States or over 200 countries. Talk. Say goodbye. Hang up. Resume vacation.

American Samoa 633 2-USA	Korea 009-11	Taiwan* 0080-10288-0
Australia 1800-881-011	Macao ■ 0800-111	Thailand♦ 0019-991-1111
Cambodia ■ 1800-881-001	Malaysia* 800-0011	
China, PRC♦♦♦ 10811	Micronesia ■...............................288	
Cook Islands ■ 09-111	New Zealand 000-911	
Fiji ■ 004-890-1001	Palau ■ 02288	
Guam...018-872	Philippines* 105-11	
Hong Kong 800-1111	Saipan† 235-2872	
India♦ 000-117	Singapore...........................800-0111-111	
Indonesia† 001-801-10	South Africa 0-800-99-0123	
Japan*■ 0039-111	Sri Lanka....................................430-430	

AT&T
Your True Choice

For a free wallet sized card of all AT&T Access Numbers, call: 1-800-241-5555.

Getting Acquainted

The Place

China is the third-largest country in the world after Russia and Canada. Topographically, the country is 35 percent mountains, 27 percent high plateau, 17 percent basin or desert, 8 percent hilly areas, and 13 percent plains. Only about 11 percent of the land area is agriculturally useful. The highest population densities are along the coast.

Local Time

Despite its immense size, there is but one time zone throughout China: GMT +8 hours, adjusted to daylight saving time in summer.

Climate

The largest part of China is in a moderate zone with separate seasons. There are distinctive climatic differences resulting from monsoons, the expanse of the land area, and the considerable differences in altitude. While it is generally warm and humid in southeastern and central China, the north and northeast are relatively dry. The best times for traveling: spring (May) and fall (September/October).

China covers 35 degrees of latitude, resulting in a great variation of regional climates. In many areas, the summer is hot and rainy, with a high level of humidity, while the winter is dry. In northern China, more than 80 percent of rainfall occurs in the summer months, but only 40 percent of the annual rainfall occurs in southern China during the same period.

There are frequent typhoons in southeast China during the rainy season, between July and September. North of the Chang Jiang (Yangzi), the winter can be extremely cold.

The northeast has hot, dry summers and long, cold winters. Summer in the desert regions of Xinjiang and Inner Mongolia is also hot and dry, while winter is cold and dry. In central China, the summers are hot and humid, with a lot of rainfall in the late summer months. In the low lying regions of the Yangzi, winter is somewhat milder than in the central Chinese loess mountain regions or in Sichuan, which is surrounded by mountains. In the regions around Beijing, Xi'an and Zhengzhou, there are occasional sand storms in winter and spring.

On the Tibet-Qinghai Plateau (average altitude: 4,000m/13,100ft), summer is short and moderately warm, while winters can get very cold; there is little rainfall throughout the year, and the differences in day and night temperatures are great. A mild climate with warm summers and cool winters generally prevails on the Yunnan-Guizhou High Plateau, with little rainfall, and very rare frosts.

Southern China has a sub-tropical climate. Rainfall is distributed around the year; the summers are long, humid and hot, and the winters are short with cooler temperatures.

The People

The People's Republic of China is the world's most populous nation. Around 1.2 billion people live in China. About 20 percent of the population live in urban areas. A little over 90 percent of the population are Han Chinese; the remaining percentage, or around 70 million people, includes 55 national minorities who differ fundamentally in their customs, traditions, languages and culture from the Han Chinese. The minorities have been exempted from China's strict population controls.

Culture & Customs

Chinese politeness has always been a formal one that follows strict rules. Chinese people can seem, however, quite impolite by Western norms in public situations. Nevertheless, travelers are advised to remain polite towards their Chinese counterparts, and to refrain from shouting or being insulting. Stay calm in all situations but indicate politely and firmly what your problem or inquiry is about.

Politeness is definitely a foreign word when it comes to public transport. Whether on the underground or the bus, the overcrowded conditions always encourage a struggle. No priority is given to pedestrians on the roads; be careful when crossing the road, as you have no right-of-way.

For Chinese, it is bad to lose face, especially in front of a foreigner. Don't put a Chinese in a position where they might lose face. Any criticism should be done discreetly and tactfully.

It is usually not the custom in China to greet people with a handshake, though it is commonly used with foreigners. Moreover, embracing or kissing when greeting or saying goodbye is highly unusual. Generally, Chinese do not show their emotions and feelings in public. Consequently, it is better not to behave in too carefree a manner in public. Too, it is advisable to be fairly cautious in political discussions.

It is very important for the Chinese to have good connections; someone who has no connections (guanxi) is only half Chinese. It is important for the Chinese to make contacts, and to keep them. This is equally important to foreigners on business. One should expect lots of invitations and gifts. Qingke, the wining and dining of guests, is an old Chinese tradition and is still used today to thank friends for a favor or to make new business contacts. If invited by a Chinese, you are obliged to return the invitation.

It is considered quite normal in China to eat noisily and belch during a meal. This doesn't mean that a foreign guest must do likewise. An increasing number of Chinese, particularly in the big cities, don't find it very pleasant either. In many simple restaurants, bones and other remnants are thrown on the table or the floor. It is also quite common for people to spit, despite official campaigns to try and restrain this and other such habits. It is important for foreign visitors to know that these things are customary and not at all bad manners.

Names: The family name comes first, the given name second. Mao Zedong's family name is Mao, for example, and the given name is Zedong. Only among family and very good friends is it usual to use given names. Therefore, address men or women whom you may meet by their family name, with an honorific following the family name: xiansheng for men, furen for women. The same goes for the form of address referring to the per-

See the World with a different eye.

The world's leading series
of full-colour travel guides

★ More than 300 titles

★ Three distinct formats
tailored for individual needs

★ Spectacular photography
and award-winning writing

FLY SMOOTH AS SILK TO EXOTIC THAILAND ON A ROYAL ORCHID HOLIDAY.

Watching exquisite cotton and silk umbrellas being hand-painted in Chiang Mai. Lazing in the shade in sun-drenched Phuket. This

ROYAL
ORCHID
Holidays

Thai

is what holidaying in Thailand is all about. Book the holiday of your choice now, flying Thai. Smooth as silk.

MALACCA

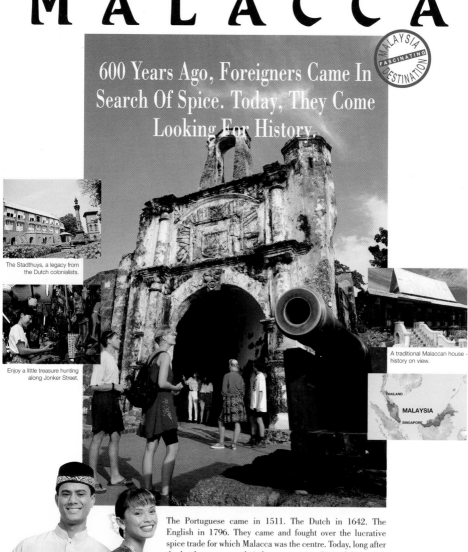

600 Years Ago, Foreigners Came In Search Of Spice. Today, They Come Looking For History.

The Stadthuys, a legacy from the Dutch colonialists.

Enjoy a little treasure hunting along Jonker Street.

A traditional Malaccan house - history on view.

THAILAND

MALAYSIA

SINGAPORE

The Portuguese came in 1511. The Dutch in 1642. The English in 1796. They came and fought over the lucrative spice trade for which Malacca was the centre. Today, long after the battles are over, their legacy remains. Ruined fortresses, old colonial buildings and red-bricked churches stand alongside Chinese clan houses, Muslim mosques and Indian temples. On the streets you'll find an interesting blend of cultures and races, including descendants of the Portuguese who still speak *Cristao* - an ancient language, as well as the *Babas* and *Nyonyas* or Straits Settlement Chinese. A testimony to the living history of Malacca. Isn't it about time you came to take a look?

FASCINATING
MALAYSIA

MTPB HQ:
17th, 24th-27th & 30th Floor, Menara Dato' Onn, Putra World Trade Centre, 45, Jalan Tun Ismail,
50480 Kuala Lumpur, Malaysia. Tel: 03-2935188 Fax: 03-2935884
MTPB Singapore:
10, Collyer Quay, #01-06, Ocean Building, Singapore 0104, Tel: 02-5326321/6351 Fax: 02-5356650

son's position, which is sometimes used in China. For instance, Manager Li in Chinese is Li *jingli*, and Professor Wang is Wang *jiaoshou*.

Government & Economy

The People's Republic of China is, according to its constitution, a socialist state. It was founded on 1 October 1949. The national flag is red with five stars: the large star at the center symbolizes the Chinese Communist Party, while the smaller stars represent the four main social classes that participated in the revolution. The state emblem is Tiananmen (Gate of Heavenly Peace), illuminated by five stars, on a red background. It is surrounded by a corn wreath with a cog-wheel below.

The capital of the country is Beijing. All provinces and autonomous regions are strictly subordinate to the central government. Administratively, China is divided into 23 provinces (including Taiwan, considered by China as a misbehaving province), five autonomous regions (Inner Mongolia, Xinjiang, Tibet, Ningxia and Guangxi), and four locally-governed cities (Beijing, Tianjin, Shanghai and Hong Kong). The provinces and autonomous regions are further subdivided into districts, counties and towns, which are further subdivided into districts.

The **autonomous regions** are mostly populated by members of ethnic minorities who have the right to determine their own affairs – within the framework of a central state policy. They can follow their own customs and traditions and use their own language.

The **National People's Congress** is the highest governing body. Only the people's congresses at the lowest local level are directly elected, though the method of election can be called neither free nor secret, as the party retains the right to propose candidates. The People's Liberation Army, overseas Chinese and the national minorities send their own representatives to the congress.

The **Communist Party** has the leading role within both state and society. It was founded in 1921. Since the Cultural Revolution, increasingly the party has been held in low esteem among the population, because of privileges for high functionaries, misuse of power and bureaucracy.

Mao Zedong led the party from 1935 until 1976; after his death, Hua Guofeng became party leader. By 1978, Deng Xiaoping had virtually consolidated his position. Two potential successors to Deng have come and gone – Hu Yaobang, who took over as general secretary in 1981, and was forced to resign, and his successor, Zhao Ziyang, who was sacked after the 1989 democracy movement. Even after officially retiring from politics in the early 1990s, Deng Xiaoping has held on as China's *de facto* leader. There is no mechanism for an orderly succession of power.

The **Four Modernizations**, which are official party policy, are the modernization of agriculture, industry, science and technology, and defence. China is aiming to transform itself from a backward agricultural country into an industrial nation by the year 2000. This target is to be reached with structural reforms in the economic and political sectors that are intended at loosening the centralized economic and government system. Socialist planning is to be combined with a market economy.

Planning the Trip

What To Bring

As anywhere, it is best to take your usual toilet articles and medicines. Hotel shops will have a good choice of Western goods. Elsewhere, items such as tampons or sanitary napkins are still difficult to find.

Photographic items – film and batteries – are available, but may be cheaper and fresher if bought before arriving. It is worth taking a small flashlight, especially for individual travelers who may stay the night in modest hostels. Chinese-made batteries tend not to last long. An electrical adapter may be useful too; many of the older hotels have sockets which require a three pin plug and the hotel service often only has a limited number of adapters available.

Electricity

Electricity is 220 volts, 50 cycles AC. Plug types span those used in Australia, Europe and North America/Japan. Unless staying in an international-class hotel, obtain adapters before arriving in China. If traveling away from the tourist centers, it is worth taking battery-operated equipment.

What to Wear

Simple and appropriate clothing is advisable for visitors. In the summer months, take light cotton clothes that are easily washed and not too delicate. Something modestly warm is useful, even in the hottest season, as the air conditioning in the hotels is often vigorously used. Footwear should be comfortable and strong.

Most Chinese wear ordinary clothes to evening performances at the Beijing opera, the theater or circus. It is best to follow this custom, especially at some of the venues. In rural areas, the floor is often of compressed mud, making high-heeled shoes foolish. In contrast, urban discos and clubs are the venue for more fancy dress.

Rain gear is useful, especially during the summer months – China's rainy season is from May to August. In the north, winters tend to be very dry and cold. Day temperatures of between –15° to –20°C are common.

Entry Regulations

Visas & Passports

All foreigners need an entry visa. If part of a group, the tour operator will often obtain it; group visas will usually be issued for groups with at least 10, and the guide accompanying your group will keep the visas. Individual travelers can apply at any Chinese embassy, and the procedure is usually straightforward, taking about a week. The duration depends upon current regulations, and upon your own country's regulations for visiting Chinese citizens. Typical is a 30-day single-entry visa. The passport must be valid for six months after the expiration of the entry visa.

Traditionally, it has been easier to obtain visas in Hong Kong, including long-term, multiple-entry visas, than anywhere else. Quicker, too. With the return of Hong Kong to China, the situation will no doubt soon change. Will entry through Hong Kong be the same as through other ports of entry into China, or will there be a limited-entry visa for, say, only Hong Kong and maybe Guangzhou? As of early 1997, China had not announced its future policies. If planning to visit Hong Kong after July 1997, don't assume the same ease of access as before.

If your visa runs out while in China, it can be extended by the local Public Security Bureau – the ubiquitous police (*Gongan Ju*).

There was a time when many areas were off limits to foreigners, or else special travel permits, exceedingly difficult to obtain, were required. Nowadays, most of the country is open to foreigners, except some delicate border areas.

Customs

On arrival, each traveler must complete a form declaring foreign currency and valuables such as cameras, antiques and jewelry. The declaration must be handed in on departure; if required, the listed objects must be shown to verify that they haven't been sold within China.

Tourists can freely import two bottles of alcoholic beverages and 600 cigarettes, as well as foreign currency and valuables for personal use without restrictions. The import of weapons, ammunition, drugs and pornographic literature (broadly interpreted) is prohibited. On departure, antiques such as porcelain, paintings, calligraphy, carvings and old books must carry the red lacquer seal of an official antique shop. Otherwise, they can be confiscated by the customs officials without compensation.

Health

The best prevention is to ensure maximum hygiene while traveling, especially in restaurants and roadside snack bars. Never eat raw, uncooked or partially-cooked food, including salads outside of top-end hotels. Animal or human excrement is still frequently used as fertilizer, so that bacteria on uncooked vegetables can easily be ingested. Also suggested if traveling outside of a tour group: acquire chopsticks and a tin bowl with lid for train

journeys and meals in small roadside restaurants. Drink only boiled or bottled water, even though the tap water is drinkable in some places and hotels. The adjustment to a different climate and different food frequently leads to colds or digestive problems that, although rarely serious, can nevertheless impede one's enjoyment.

Tibet, the northwest, and the tropical province of Yunnan make particularly high demands on the body. Heart disease and high blood pressure can lead to serious problems in Tibet. Along the Silk Road, expect high temperatures and dry conditions.

If planning to visit areas outside of Beijing, Shanghai, Guangzhou and Hong Kong, consider carrying emergency evacuation insurance. If injured in the deserts of western China, for example, medical and transportation costs could leave you indebted into the next decade. Two of the largest emergency evacuation companies are SOS Assistance and Asia Emergency Assistance. They have offices in many major cities throughout the world, or contact them in Hong Kong:

International SOS Assistance, 507 Kai Tak Commercial Bldg, 317 Des Voeux Road, Central, Hong Kong. Tel: 2541 6483, Fax: 2544 1677.
Asia Emergency Assistance (AEA), Allied Resources Bldg 9F, 32-38 Ice House Street, Central, Hong Kong. Tel: 2810 8898, Fax: 2845 0395. In Beijing: 505 5352.

Illnesses

Travelers to East Asia may be exposed to potential illnesses or diseases from a number of sources. The most frequently reported illness, and this should come as no surprise, is traveler's diarrhea.

Other diseases are unique to East Asia or the tropics, transmitted by insects, contaminated food and water, or close contact with infected people. Diseases are not restricted to clearly-defined geographical areas. To reduce the risk of infection:

• reduce exposure to insects
• ensure quality of food and water
• be knowledgeable about potential diseases in the visited region

Insect-Transmitted

Malaria: Transmitted to humans by a mosquito, which bite at night from dusk to dawn. *Symptoms:* Fever and flu-like symptoms, chills, achiness, and tiredness. Up to one year after returning home, travelers should consult a physician for flu-like illness. *Risk:* Little or no risk in urban areas and popular tourist destinations; there is no risk in provinces bordering Mongolia, and in the western provinces of Heilungkiang, Kirin, Ningsia Hui Tibet, and Tsinghai, nor in Hong Kong. Risk exists in rural areas not visited by most travelers. In areas of risk, transmission is highest from May to December; in the south, transmission occurs year-round. Whether taking preventative drugs or not, travelers in risk areas should reduce exposure to malaria-carrying mosquitoes, which bite mainly during the evening, from dusk until dawn.

Taking drugs to prevent malaria is recommended only for travelers to rural areas and who will have outdoor exposure during evening hours. What medication to take is not as easy as it was a decade ago. There is increasing evidence that mosquitoes in many parts of the world, including in parts of northern Thailand and Burma, are developing resistance to traditional preventive drugs such as choloroquine and Mefloquine (Lariam).

Moreover, some individuals have extreme reactions to many of the more recent preventative drugs. Consult medical authorities or a physicians knowledgeable in travel medicine for recommendations.

Dengue fever: Primarily an urban – in or around human habitations – viral infection transmitted by mosquitos. The mosquitoes are most active around dawn and dusk. *Symptoms:* sudden onset of high fever, severe headaches, joint and muscle pain, and a rash, which shows up 3 to 4 days after the fever begins. *Risk:* Occurs in parts of southern China and Taiwan. The risk is minimal for most travelers. Those who have lived several years in high-risk areas are more susceptible than short-term visitors. There is no vaccine or specific treatment available.

Japanese encephalitis: A mosquito-borne viral disease in rural areas, often in rice-growing areas. *Symptoms:*

none, or headache, fever, and other flu-like symptoms. Serious complications can lead to a swelling of the brain (encephalitis). *Risk:* Occurs in rural China and Korea, and occasionally in Hong Kong and Taiwan. The mosquito bites in the late afternoon and early evening. Low or minimal risk for most travelers. Transmission is usually seasonal during the rainy season. There is no specific drug for treatment, but there is a preventative vaccine, which should be considered for persons who plan long-term – 4 weeks or more – visits to rural areas.

Yellow fever: Not in China or Asia.

Contamination

Food and water-borne diseases are the primary cause of illness to travelers, and many travelers to China might expect some degree of discomfort, especially diarrhea, which is caused primarily by viruses or bacteria. Transmission is usually through contaminated food or water.

Hepatitis A: A viral infection of the liver transmitted by ingestion of fecal-contaminated food or drink, or through direct person-to-person contact. *Symptoms:* Fatigue, fever, no appetite, nausea, dark urine and/or jaundice, vomiting, aches. There is no specific treatment, although an effective vaccine is available, especially for those who plan to travel repeatedly or reside in risk areas. Immune globulin is recommended only for short-term protection.

Hepatitis B: All countries in Asia, including China, report high levels of infection. Hepatitis B is a viral infection of the liver transmitted through the exchange of blood or blood-derived fluids, or through sexual activity with an infected person. Unscreened blood and unsterilized needles, or contact with potentially-infected people with open skin lesions, are sources of infection. An effective vaccine is available, which should be started six months prior to travel.

Typhoid fever: A bacterial infection transmitted by contaminated food and/or water, or even directly between people. Travelers to East Asia are susceptible to typhoid fever, particularly in smaller towns or rural areas. *Symptoms:* Fever, headaches, tiredness, no appetite, and constipation (rather than diarrhea). Be cautious in selecting food and water. Bottled or boiled water

and eating only well-cooked food lowers the risk of infection. Typhoid fever is treated with antibiotics. Vaccination is recommended for travelers off the tourist routes, especially if staying for six weeks or more. Available vaccines protect 70–90 percent of users.

Cholera: Although some cases have been occasionally reported in China, the risk is virtually nonexistent. An acute intestinal infection caused by bacteria, most often through contaminated water or food. *Symptoms:* Abrupt onset of watery diarrhea, dehydration, vomiting, and muscle cramps. Medical care must be sought quickly when cholera is suspected. The available vaccine is only 50 percent effective, and is not recommended for the majority of travelers.

Schistosomiasis (bilharzia): An infection from a flatworm larvae that penetrates the skin, including unbroken skin. *Risk:* Schistosomiasis is found in some areas of China, including rivers and lakes of southeastern and eastern China, especially along the Chang Jiang (Yangzi River) and tributaries. The risk comes from bathing, wading, or swimming in contaminated freshwater. There is no easy way to identify infested water. If exposed, immediate and vigorous drying with a towel, or the application of rubbing alcohol to the exposed areas, can reduce risk. Water treated with chlorine or iodine is virtually safe; saltwater poses no risk.

Money Matters

The Chinese currency is called *renminbi* (people's currency) and is often abbreviated RMB. The basic unit is the *yuan*. Ten *jiao* make one yuan, and ten *fen* make one *jiao*. Thus, 100 fen make one yuan. Notes are currently issued for 2, 5, 10, 50 and 100 yuan. Coins include 1 yuan, 5 jiao, and 1, 2 and 5 fen.

Before China abandoned, in 1994, its dual-currency system – RMBs and FECs, or Foreign Exchange Certificates, which foreigners were required to use – there was a reasonably active black market in currency exchange. Since the RMB is not completely convertible on the world markets, a black market still exists, although it is highly illegal and the black-market exchange rates are laughable and not worth the risk of

being short-changed, receiving counterfeit bills or being arrested.

Most of the world's primary currencies are accepted in banks and hotels. Eurocheques, however, are not accepted anywhere, including branches of European banks.

Increasingly, many places frequented by foreigners take the usual **credit cards** such as American Express, Visa, Diners Club, and MasterCard. Don't expect much utility from them outside of the major cities, however. Also, most transportation costs – domestic air and train tickets – must be paid for in cash.

Cash advances may be obtained from major branches of the **Bank of China**, including the head office of the Bank of China, 410 Fuchingmennei Dajie, Tel: 6016688, or the Beijing branch at 19, Dong An Men St, Tel: 5199115/4.

Forget about **wire transfers** of money to China. It'll take about a month and a considerable amount of patience with paperwork.

Public Holidays

In contrast to the traditional festivals, such as the Spring Festival (Lunar New Year), which follow the lunar calendar and thus vary in timing from year to year, important official holidays follow the Gregorian calendar.

1 January: New Year's Day
February: Variable. Lunar New Year (Spring Festival)
8 March: International Women's Day
1 May: International Labor Day
4 May: Youth Day (May 4th Movement)
1 June: Children's Day
1 July: Founding of Communist Party
1 August: Founding of People's Liberation Army
1 October: National Day

Most shops are open on holidays. School holidays in China are between 1 August and 30 September. This also applies to universities.

Don't plan on travel – or border crossings – during holidays, unless reservations have been made and confirmed long before. Especially make no plans during the Spring Festival, which is three days long, when everyone is traveling to hometowns.

By Air

BEIJING

The international airport connects Beijing to all parts of China and to the world's major cities. Beijing's airport is 27km (25 mi), a 25-minute drive, from the center.

Taxis are on the left as you leave the terminal. Air China has a coach service to its offices at Xidan, west of Tiananmen Square and Dongsi, in the northeast of the city. This is recommended only if you have light baggage. Most major hotels offer limousine or bus transfers. Passengers on international arrivals must fill out arrival cards, customs and health declarations. Travelers with tuberculosis and AIDS carriers are barred from entry.

If leaving on a domestic flight from Beijing, check in at least 30 minutes before the flight or you will lose your seat. (29 minutes before the flight is not good enough.) International flight check-in should be done at least one hour before the flight. Foreigners leaving China by air are required to pay a 90 yuan airport tax. Domestic flight tax is 15 yuan.

GUANGZHOU

The major airports are in Guangzhou and Shenzhen. Guangzhou's Baiyun Airport is 10km (6 mi) and a 30-minute drive from the city. The domestic and international terminals are housed in separate buildings. Shenzhen's Fuyong Airport is about 25km (15 mi) from Shekou, at the western end of Shenzhen, and 55km (34 mi) from the center of Shenzhen. Domestic flights operate between Guangzhou and Shenzhen and major cities in China.

Guangzhou is connected via international flights to Bangkok, Hanoi, Ho Chi Minh City, Hong Kong, Jakarta, Kuala Lumpur, Manila, Surabaya, Singapore, Sydney and Vientiane.

With the exception of Singapore Airlines, MAS and Garuda, which have offices selling tickets in Guangzhou, tickets for international flights on Chinese and foreign carriers must be purchased from the CAAC main office. Tickets for domestic flights are sold at the offices of the Chinese carriers and also at the CAAC main office. Bear in mind that buying a return ticket on a domestic route is difficult, except to cities like Beijing and Shanghai.

HONG KONG

Hong Kong is served by more than 30 airlines, plus a dozen other charter and cargo companies. Kai Tak Airport in Kowloon is about 20 minutes by car from most hotels in Kowloon and less than 40 minutes' drive via the Cross-Harbor Tunnel to Hong Kong Island. The new airport at Chek Lap Kok on Lantau island, scheduled for completion in late 1997, will replace Kai Tak.

The terminal building at Kai Tak doesn't win any architectural awards, but recent massive renovation efforts have eased many bottlenecks. Upon arrival, airplanes are parked alongside modern passenger bridges. Immigration, customs and baggage check points are all within a short walking distance, and free baggage carts are available.

By Rail

BEIJING

Beijing has five railway stations with lines running to most major cities throughout China. Beijing's new West Railway Station, the largest station in Asia, opened in 1996, providing badly need relief for the overloaded Beijing Railway Station.

If arriving via the **Trans-Manchurian** or **Trans-Mongolian** railways (often called the Trans-Siberian, which goes to Siberia, not China), all the same health and customs procedures apply as if arriving via an international flight.

There is a choice of two routes. The Chinese train – which is better equipped and maintained – takes 5 days via Ulan Bator through Mongolia, entering China via Erlian. The Russian train, which goes through Manchuria and takes a day longer, enters China at Manzhouli. Both trains leave once a week from Moscow.

Depending upon the type of train, there are two or three classes. Food is not included in the ticket price. Initially, the food on the train is fairly reasonable, but becomes increasingly monotonous as the journey continues.

If you want to interrupt the train journey in Russia for longer than 24 hours, you need a tourist visa and you have to show a hotel booking.

Note: Military installations must not be photographed, in Russia and in China. Film will be confiscated and a few hours of inconvenience enjoyed.

For train tickets from Beijing to other parts of China, go to the foreigners' booking office. One word of caution: train tickets must be bought at the point of departure; return tickets cannot yet be purchased.

GUANGZHOU

There are trains to most large cities in China. Four daily trains link Guangzhou and the Hunghom station on the Kowloon side of Hong Kong, with two extra trains added during special festivals, the Guangzhou Fair and other peak periods. Traveling time is 2 hours. There is also a direct train between Foshan and Hong Kong, with a traveling time of 3 hours.

In Guangzhou, most hotels and the CTS office can help get train tickets. In Hong Kong, tickets can be purchased through travel agents, hotels, CTS offices or at the lobby of the Hunghom railway station (Tel: 8333 0660). If tickets to Guangzhou are sold out, take the Kowloon-Guangzhou Railway (KCR) to the border terminus of Lo Wu (a short 40-minute journey, with three departures an hour from 6am–9pm). The Shenzhen station is right across the border.

There are a dozen trains a day between Shenzhen and Guangzhou. Traveling time is 2 hours. Trains arrive in Guangzhou either at the central station or at Guangzhou East Railway Station (Guangzhou Dong), in Tianhe, a 45-minute taxi ride from the city center. All trains between Kowloon and Guangzhou are air-conditioned, but not all between Shenzhen and Guangzhou. Ask for the air-con class when buying a ticket, a small price to pay when temperatures soar in the heat of summer.

By Sea

HONG KONG

If traveling to China from Hong Kong by boat, the choice of destinations includes Guangzhou, Xiamen, Shantou and Shanghai.

There is an overnight steamer between Hong Kong and Guangzhou, which takes 8 hours; there is also a daytime catamaran service, which takes just over 3 hours. Ferry journeys to Shantou take 14 hours; to Xiamen,

20 hours; and to Shanghai, 60 hours. All have restaurants on board.

Hong Kong is linked by hydrofoil with Guangzhou, Huangpu, Guangzhou's commercial port, and the delta cities of Lianhua Shan, Nansha, Shekou, Shunde, Zhongshan and Zhuhai. There are also services between Macau and Shekou. For information on hydrofoil schedules, call 2833 9300 or 2542 3428 in Hong Kong. Most departures are from the Hong Kong-Macau Ferry Terminal at the Shun Tak Center (200 Connaught Road, Hong Kong) and from the China Ferry Terminal, Guangzhou Road, Tsimshatsui.

By day, the most impressive trip is the one between Kowloon and the Bogue port of Nansha, sited at the entrance of the Pearl River, aboard a huge modern catamaran traveling at 35 knots. From the Nansha terminal, a free bus shuttle takes travelers to the White Swan Hotel in Guangzhou. Three high-speed catamaran hydrofoils operate daily (1-hour) between Nansha and Hong Kong: 8.30am, 9.15am, 2pm from Hong Kong, and 11.20am, 4pm and 5pm from Nansha. Tickets can be purchased from the China Ferry Terminal (Tel: 23750537) in Hong Kong, the Nansha Terminal (Tel: 4988312) or the basement floor of the White Swan Hotel in Guangzhou.

You can also catch a night boat from Hong Kong and Macau to Guangzhou. They run daily except on the last day of each month, leaving either way at dinner time and arriving at sunrise. The departure from Hong Kong sails through the harbor and the view is especially impressive. The *Xinghu*, sailing from Hong Kong, is the most comfortable boat. Departures are from the China Ferry Terminal in Hong Kong and from the Porto Interior in Macau.

There are numerous cruises from Hong Kong along China's coast. They usually stop at Xiamen, Shanghai, Yantai, Nanjing, Qingdao and Dalian.

KOREA

Ferry service is available from Inchon, South Korea, to Weihai, Qingdao and Tianjin. Between Inchon and Weihai takes about 18 hours, departing twice weekly. Between Inchon and Qingdao takes at least a full 24 hours, departing weekly. Between Inchon and Tianjin

takes nearly 30 hours, operating every five days. Fares for all services range from US$100 to US$350, depending upon class.

JAPAN

There is a weekly deluxe cruise ship between Shanghai and Japan, alternating every week between Yokohama and Shanghai. There is also a weekly boat between Kobe and Tianjin/Tanggu. Trips take two days, and fares run from US$300 to $1,500 or more.

By Ground

Several of China's international borders are open for crossing. Other parts, like the frontier with Bhutan, are restricted areas. A border crossing with Burma opened in 1996, but the Burmese authorities go out of their way to discourage foreigners from using the crossing.

NEPAL

Crossing via Nepal by bus or taxi has been possible since 1985, with sporadic periods of closed borders. Procure a Chinese visa anywhere else but Nepal, unless part of a tour.

It's possible to travel by road between Kathmandu and Lhasa, but it requires considerable time, not only for travel, but for bureaucracy, including mandatory tours of Lhasa upon arrival. Independent travelers should note that transport on the Nepal side is good, but scarce on the Tibetan side. Most travelers must plan on a vehicle hire/share to Lhasa.

PAKISTAN

Since 1986, it has been possible to travel the Karakorum Highway between Kashi (Kashgar), in northwest China, and Islamabad. Pakistan requires a visa for most nationalities. Visas are not available at the border for either China or Pakistan.

On both the Pakistani and Chinese side of the border, the roads may be blocked by landslides, and you may have to walk a fair distance, carrying your luggage. Accommodation along the journey is quite modest.

KAZAKHSTAN

There are both a daily bus service and a twice-weekly train service between Urumqi and Almaty, in Kazakhstan.

VIETNAM

In 1995, train service began between Hanoi and Beijing via the Friendship Gate crossing, but it has been plagued by red-tape at the border and has proved to be troublesome, for locals and foreigners alike. From Vietnam to China requires a special visa. One may also cross the border by foot at Hekou (China) and Lao Cai (Vietnam), and at Friendship Gate (Dong Dang, Vietnam/Pingxiang, China).

RUSSIA/MONGOLIA

A journey on the **Trans-Mongolian/Trans-Manchurian railways** between Moscow and Beijing was once one of the world's classic train journeys. Things have changed, and the train now carries a larger number of scoundrels and thieves. Service on the Russian train (both China and Russia run trains on the service) is said to have degraded considerably. Nevertheless, it is an adventure worth considering.

Special Information
Children

The Chinese are fond of children, so traveling with children in China is not difficult. If with toddlers or babies, note that disposable nappies and baby food in jars are not readily available. Children travel at reduced cost on trains and planes. Big hotels offer child-care for a fee.

Disabled

Only in recent years have the needs of disabled people received attention in China. In general, towns, institutions, public transport and sights offer little accessibility for the disabled. Traveling in a group for the disabled certainly reduces these problems considerably. The China National Tourist Offices and CITS have information about whether special trips for the disabled are possible and how they might be organized.

Students

There are no special rules for foreign students in China. International student cards are not recognized in most of China, only the student cards of foreign students studying in China.

Public Security Bureau Offices

Beijing: 85 Beichizi Dajie, Tel: 525 5486, Monday–Friday 8.30am–5pm, Saturday 8.30am–11.30am.

Shanghai: 210 Hankou Lu, Tel: 6321 5380.

Guangzhou: 863 Jiefang Beilu, Tel: 8333 1326.

Visitor Hot Lines:
Shanghai: Tel: 6439 0630
Guangzhou: Tel: 8667 7422
Police: 110
Fire: 119
Local directory assistance: 114
International directory assistance (English): 115

CNTA

China National Tourist Office, London, 4 Glentworth St., London No. 1 UK. Tel: 935 9787, Fax: 487 5842.

Fremdenverkehrsamt der Volksrepublik, China Ilkenhans Strasse 6, D-60433 Frankfurt A.M. Deutschland. Tel: 52 0135, Fax: 52 8490.

Office du Tourisme de China, Paris, 116, Ave des Champs-Elysees, 75008 Paris, France. Tel: 4421 8282, Fax: 4421 8100.

China National Tourist Office, Madrid, Gran Via 88, Grupo 2, Planta 16-8 28013, Madrid, Espana. Tel: 548 0011, Fax: 548 0597.

China National Tourist Office, New York, 350 Fifth Ave, Suite 6413, Empire State Bldg, New York, NY 10118. Tel: 760 9700, Fax: 760 8809.

China National Tourist Office, Los Angeles, 333 West Broadway, Suite 201, Glendale, CA91204 USA. Tel: 545 7505. Fax: 545 7506.

China National Tourist Office, Sydney, Level 19, 44 Market St., Sydney, NSW 2000, Australia. Tel: 299 4057, Fax: 290 1958.

China National Tourist Office, Tokyo, 6F Hachidai Ramamatsu Cho Bldg, 1-27-13 Hamamatsu-cho, Minato-Ku, Tokyo, Japan. Tel: 433 1461, Fax: 433 8653.

Office of China International Travel Service, P.O. Box 3281 Tel-Aviv 61030, Israel. Tel: 524 0891, Fax: 522 6281.

China National Tourist Office, Singapore, 1 Shenton Way, #7-05 Robina House, Singapore 068803. Tel: 211 8681, Fax: 221 9267.

Tour Operators

There are countless travel agencies within and outside of China that handle domestic travel arrangements. Prominent among the agencies is **China International Travel Services** (CITS), formerly and virtually the sole agency handling overseas tourists. It now has branches throughout China, which operate independently. **China Travel Services** (CTS) is a similar organization, originally responsible for domestic tourists and overseas Chinese, but now also catering to foreigners. While the efficiency of both organizations can be brutally lacking in some of their offices, some say CTS is slightly better than CITS.

Agencies may also have business interests extending beyond simply arranging tours and bookings; they may own or partly own hotels. An agency that arranges a tour may do so by contacting agencies in places you will visit, and asking them to deal with local bookings. This means that if you go direct to an agency in the area you are visiting, savings may be possible.

Sometimes, agencies such as CITS may hold tickets for rail journeys, operas, acrobatic performances and concerts even when such tickets are sold out at the stations or venues. Prices will be high, however.

There are also small-scale unlicensed tour operators. Reportedly, some of these use unroadworthy vehicles, take their customers to shops and restaurants that give the guides 'backhanders' (though perhaps this can also happen with licensed operators), and demand mark-ups of 100 percent or more for tickets to tourist sites. Others may be trustworthy, and cheap.

It is also quite possible nowadays – and increasingly common amongst the adventurous – to travel in China without the services of any agency.

Note that within China, agencies – including CITS – have nothing to do with visa extensions or other passport matters. Visit the police for these.

CITS Offices

Beijing, 1 Jian Guo Men Wai Ave, China World Hotel. Tel: 6607 1575, 6608 7124. Open Monday–Saturday 8am–8pm, Sunday 8am–noon.

Chengdu, 65, Sec 2, Remin Rd. S. Tel: 667 9186.

Dalian, 1 Changtong St. Tel: 364 0273.

Guilin, 14 North Ronghu Rd. Tel: 282 2648/283 3905. Open Monday–Sunday 8am–noon, 2.30–5.30pm, 7–9pm; Bing Jiang Nan Rd, Sheraton Hotel. Tel: 282 5588 Ext: 8234. Open Monday–Sunday 8–noon, 1–6pm, 7–10pm.

Guangzhou, No. 1, Shihan Rd. Tel: 8515 2888 Ext. 256. Open Monday–Saturday 8.30am–5pm.

Hangzhou, 1 Shihan Rd. Tel: 515 2888 X 256.

Hong Kong, 6th Fl, Tower 2, South Seas Center 75, Mody Rd, Tsim Sha-Tsui, Kowloon. Tel: 732 5888, Fax: 721 7454.

Kunming, 218 Huan Cheng Rd. S. Tel: 313 4019.

Nanjing, 202-1 N Zhong Shan Rd. Tel: 342 1125. Open Monday–Saturday 9am–5pm.

Ningbo, East Seaport Hotel, No. 52 Caihong North Rd. Tel: 737 5751. Open Monday–Saturday 8.30am–5pm.

Suzhou, Nan Lin Hotel. Tel: 529 1642.

Tianjin, 22 You Yi Rd. Tel: 835 5309. Open Monday–Friday 9am–5pm; Saturday 9am–noon.

Wuhan, Rm 303, 1365 Zhongshan Ave, Hankou. Tel: 284 2331. Open Monday–Friday 8.30–11.30am, 2–5pm.

Wuxi, 7 Xing Sheng Rd. Tel: 20 4420. Open Monday–Saturday 9am–5pm.

Xiamen, No. 2 Zhongshan Rd. Tel: 203 1781 or 202 5277. Open Monday–Sunday 8am–5.30pm.

Xi'an, 32 (N) Changan Rd. Tel: 723 1234/526 2066. Open Monday–Sunday 8am–8pm; Sheraton Hotel, 12 Feng Gao Rd. Tel: 426 1888 Ext 1000. Open Monday–Sunday 8am–8pm.

American Express Travel Service Offices

Beijing, L115D West Wing Bldg., China World Trade Center. Beijing 100004. Tel: 6505 2888. Open Monday–Friday 9am–5pm, Saturday 9am–noon.

Guangzhou, 339 Huan Shi Dong Lu, Guangzhou 510060. Tel: 8331 1771. Open Monday–Friday 9–5pm, Saturday 9am–noon.

Shanghai, 206 Retail Plaza, Shanghai Ctr. 1376 Nanjing Rd West, Shanghai 200040. Tel: 6279 8082. Open Monday–Friday 9am–5pm, Saturday 9am–noon.

Xiamen, Rm 27, 2/F Holiday Inn Crowne Plaza Harbour View, 12-8 Zhen Hai Rd. Xiamen 361001. Tel: 212 0268, Fax: 212 0270.

Embassies & Consulates

BEIJING

Australia, 21 Dongzhimenwai Dajie. Tel: 532 2331, Tlx: 22263 AUSTM CN.

Austria, Jianwaixiushui Nanjie. Tel: 532 2061, Tlx: 22258 OEBPK CN.

Canada, 19 Dongzhimenwai Dajie, Chaoyangqu. Tel: 532 3536, Tlx: 222445 CANAD CN.

France, 3 Dongsanjie, Sanlitun. Tel: 531 1331.

Germany, 5, Dongzhimenwai Dajie, Sanlitun. Tel: 532 2161, Tlx: 22259 AAPEK CN.

Ireland, 3 Ritan Donglu. Tel: 532 2691.

Israel, 405 China World Trade Centre. Tel: 505 2970.

Italy, Dongerjie, Sanlitun. Tel: 532 2131.

Mongolia, 2 Xiushui Bei Jie, Jianguomenwai. Tel: 532 1203.

Nepal, Sanlitunlu, Xiliujie. Tel: 532 1795.

Netherlands, 4 Liangmahe Nanlu. Tel: 532 1131.

New Zealand, Ritanlu Dong erjie. Tel: 532 2731, Tlx: 22124 RATA CN.

Norway, 1 Dongyijie, Sanlitun. Tel: 532 2261.

Pakistan, Dongzhimenwai Dajie. Tel: 532 2504, Tlx: 22673 CMREP CN.

Philippines, 23 Xiushuijie, Jianguomenwai. Tel: 532 2794.

Russia, Dongzhimen Beizhongjie. Tel: 532 2051, (visa section): 532 1267, Tlx: 22247 SOVEN CN.

Singapore, 1 Xiushuibeijie, Jianguomenwai. Tel: 532 3926.

South Korea, 4/F China World Trade Centre. Tel: 505 3171.

Sweden, 3 Dongzhimenwai Dajie. Tel: 532 3331.

Switzerland, 3 Dongwujie, Sanlitun. Tel: 532 2736.

Thailand, 40 Guanghuali. Tel: 532 1903.

United Kingdom, 11 Guanghualu, Jianguomenwai. Tel: 532 1961, Fax: 532 1939 Ext 239, Tlx: 22191 PRDRM CN.

United States, Jianwai Xiushui Beijie No. 3. Tel: 532 3831, Fax: 532 3178, Tlx: 22701 AMEMB CN.

Vietnam, 32 Guanghualu, Jianguomenwai. Tel: 532 1155.

HONG KONG

Australia, 24th Fl, Harbour Ctr, 25 Harbour Rd, Wanchai. Tel: 2827 8881.

Austria, 22nd Fl, Emperor House, 34–37 Connaught Rd, Central. Tel: 2522 8086.

Belgium, 9th Fl, St. John's Bldg, 33 Garden Rd, Central. Tel: 2524 3111.

Canada, 12th Fl, Tower One, Exchange Square, 8 Connaught Place, Central. Tel: 2810 4321.

Denmark, 24th Fl, Great Eagle Ctr, 23 Harbour Rd, Wanchai. Tel: 2827 8101.

France, 26th Fl, Tower Two, Admiralty Ctr, 18 Harcourt Rd, Central. Tel: 2529 4351.

Germany, 21st Fl, United Ctr, 95 Queensway, Central. Tel: 2529 8855.

Great Britain, c/o Hong Kong Immigration Department, Immigration Tower, 7 Gloucester Rd. Tel: 2824 6111.

Israel, 7th Fl, Tower Two, Admiralty Ctr, 18 Harcourt Rd, Central. Tel: 2529 6091.

Italy, 8th Fl, Hutchison House, 10 Harcourt Rd, Central. Tel: 2522 0033.

Japan, 46th Fl, Tower One, Exchange Square, Central. Tel: 2526 1483/0796.

Korea (South), 5th Fl, Far East Finance Ctr, 16 Harcourt Rd, Central. Tel: 2529 4141.

Netherlands, 3rd Fl, China Bldg, 29 Queen's Rd, Central. Tel: 2522 5127.

New Zealand, Rm 2705, Jardine House, Connaught Place, Central. Tel: 2877 4488.

Norway, Rm 1502, Great Eagle Centre, 23 Harbour Rd, Wanchai. Tel: 2587 9953.

Singapore, 9th Fl, Tower One, Admiralty Ctr, 18 Harcourt Rd, Central. Tel: 2527 2212.

South Africa, 27th Fl, Sunning Plaza, 10 Hysan Ave, Causeway Bay. Tel: 2577 3279.

Spain, 8th Fl, Printing House, 18 Ice House St, Central. Tel: 2525 3041.

Sweden, 8th Fl, Hong Kong Club Bldg, 3A Chater Rd, Central. Tel: 2521 1212.

Switzerland, 37th Fl, Gloucester Tower, The Landmark, 11 Pedder St, Central. Tel: 2522 7147.

Thailand, 8th Fl, Fairmont House, 8 Cotton Tree Drive, Central. Tel: 2521 6481.

United States, 26 Garden Rd, Central. Tel: 2523 9011.

Airline Offices

BEIJING

Air China, Aviation Bldg, 15 West Changan Ave. Tel: 601 6667.

Air France, Rm 2716 27F China World Trade Ctr, 1 Jianguomenwai Dajie. Tel: 505 1818.

Alitalia, Rm 139/140 Jianguo Hotel, Jianguomenwai Dajie. Tel: 501 4861.

Asiana, Rm 134 Jianguo Hotel, Jianguomenwai Dajie. Tel: 506 1118, 500 2233 ext 134.

British Airways, Rm 210 SCITE Tower, 22 Jianguomenwai Dajie. Tel: 512 4070/75.

Canadian, Lufthansa Centre. Tel: 463 7901.

China Eastern, Tel: 601 7589.

China Northern, Tel: 602 4078.

China Southern, Tel: 601 6899.

Dragonair, L107 1F China World Trade Ctr, 1 Jianguomenwai Dajie. Tel: 505 4343.

Finnair, 102 SCITE Tower, 22 Jianguomenwai Dajie. Tel: 512 7180.

Garuda Indonesia, GF Unit 116A, West Wing, China World Trade Centre, Jianguomenwai Dajie. Tel: 505 2905.

Korean Air, Rm L115C, First Fl, West Wing, China World Trade Centre. Tel: 505 1047.

Lufthansa, Beijing Lufthansa Ctr. Tel: 465 4488.

Malaysian, Lot 115A/B West Wing Offices, China World Trade Centre, 1 Jianguomenwai Dajie. Tel: 505 2681.

Northwest, Suite 104 China World Trade Ctr, 1 Jianguomenwai Dajie. Tel: 505 3505.

Philippines, 12-53 Jianguomenwai. Tel: 532 3992.

Qantas, Rm 102 Lufthansa Ctr. Tel: 467 4794.

Russian International, Beijing-Toronto Hotel. Tel: 500 2412.

SAS, 1F SCITE Tower, 22 Jianguomenwai Dajie. Tel: 512 0575/6.

Singapore, China World Trade Centre, 1 Jianguomenwai Dajie. Tel: 500 4138/342, 505 2233.

Swissair, 2F SCITE Tower, 22 Jianguomenwai Dajie. Tel: 512 3555.

Thai International, Rm 207-209 SCITE Tower, 22 Jianguomenwai Dajie. Tel: 512 3881.

United, 1F Office Bldg, Lufthansa Ctr. Tel: 463 1111.

HONG KONG

Air Canada, 10F, Wheelock House, 20 Pedder St, Central Tel: 2522 1001 (res & flight info.); 2522 1993 (gen office).

Air France, 21st Fl, Alexandra House, Chater Rd, Central. Tel: 2524 8145 (res.); 2769 6662 (flight info.).

Air New Zealand, 16F, Fairmont House, 8 Cotton Tree Drive, Central. Tel: 2524 9041 (res.); 2769 6046 (flight info.).

Alitalia, Rm 806, Vicwood Plaza, 199 Des Voeux Rd, Central. Tel: 2543 6998 (res. & flight info.); 2769 6448 (recorded flight info.).

Ansett, Unit A, 26F, United Ctr, 95 Queensway, Admiralty. Tel: 2527 7883 (res.); 2769 6046 (flight info.).

British Airways, 30F, Alexandra House, Chater Rd, Central. Tel: 2868 0303 (res.); 2868 0768 (flight info.).

Canadian, 17F, Swire House, Connaught Rd, Central. Tel: 2868 3123 (res.); 2769 7113 (flight info.).

Cathay Pacific, Level 4, Swire House, Connaught Rd. Tel: 2747 1888 (res.); 2747 1234 (flight info.); City Check-In facility, Rm 403 Pacific Place.

China, 3rd Fl, St George's Bldg, 2 Ice House St, Central. Tel: 2868 2299 (res.); 2769 8361 (flight info.).

CNAC, Ground Fl, CNAC Bldg, 10 Queen's Rd, Central. Tel: 2861 0322/ 2973 3733 (res.); 2769 8571 (flight info.).

Delta, 29F, Tower Two, Pacific Place, Queensway, Central. Tel: 2526 5875.

Dragonair, 6F, Wheelock House, 20 Pedder St, Cental. Tel: 2590 1188 (res.); 2769 7728/7017 (flight info.).

KLM Royal Dutch, 22nd Fl, World Trade Ctr, 280 Gloucester Rd, Causeway Bay. Tel: 2808 2111 (res.); 2769 8800 (flight info.).

Lufthansa, 6F, Landmark East, Queen's Rd, Central. Tel: 2868 2313 (res.); 2769 6560 (flight info.).

Northwest, 29F, Alexandra House, Chater Rd, Central. Tel: 2810 4288.

Qantas Airways, 14F, Swire House, Connaught Rd, Central. Tel: 2842 1438 (res.); 2842 1400 (flight info.).

SAS, 14F, Harcourt House, 39 Gloucester Rd, Wanchai. Tel: 2865 1370 (res.); 2769 7017 (flight info.).

Singapore, 17F, United Ctr, 95 Queensway, Admiralty. Tel: 2520 2233 (res.); 2769 6387 (flight info.).

Swissair, 8F, Tower Two, Admiralty Ctr, 18 Harcourt Rd, Central. Tel: 2529 3670 (res.); 2769 6031 (flight info.).

United, 29F, Gloucester Tower, The Landmark, Central. Tel: 2810 4888 (res.); 2769 7279 (flight info.).

Virgin Atlantic, 41F Lippo Tower Lippo Ctr, 89 Queensway. Tel: 2532 6060 (res.); 2769 7017 (flight info.).

Photography

Taking photographs or videos of military installations is prohibited. As in other countries, some museums, palaces or temples will not allow photographs to be taken, or will charge a fee. Other times, photography is allowed, but without using flash.

Cameras must be declared when arriving in China. No special permit is necessary for video or movie cameras, as long as it is clearly not for professional use.

Practical Tips

Emergencies

Security & Crime

There is still less crime in China than in many other countries, but as vigorous crime crackdowns by the government attest – over 1,000 executions in a two-month period in 1996 – crime is increasingly a problem, particularly in urban areas.

Foreigners are not exempt from being victims of crime. Take the same precautions applicable anywhere, on the street and with valuables in hotels and on public transportation. Pickpockets and bag-slashers can be a problem, especially on crowded trains and buses, and stations. Because of large numbers of migrant workers seeking employment, cities like Guangzhou have higher levels of crime than elsewhere. Nevertheless, in most towns and cities, one needn't worry.

The **Public Security Bureau** (Gongan Ju) is the ever-present police force responsible for *everything* – chasing murderers, quenching dissent, issuing visa extensions. They are usually friendly towards foreigners, even if the rules that they are strictly enforcing seem illogical at times. Also, with serious travel-related disputes – for example, with taxi drivers or hotels – they are usually able to resolve the problem. To stay on their friendly side, don't be caught trying to travel in restricted areas or on an expired visa.

Loss or theft of belongings

If you've lost something, do what one would do anywhere else: Notify the hotel, tour group leader or transportation authorities, and the police, who will usually make a serious effort to recover items. Then, most likely, you might start considering how to replace the lost or stolen items.

Public Security Bureau offices:
Beijing: 85 Beichizi Dajie, Tel: 525 5486, Monday–Friday 8.30am–5pm, Saturday 8.30am–11.30am.
Shanghai: 210 Hankou Lu, Tel: 6321 5380.
Guangzhou: 863 Jiefang Beilu, Tel: 8333 1326.

Visitor Hot Lines:
Shanghai: Tel: 6439 0630
Guangzhou: Tel: 8667 7422
Police: 110
Fire: 119

Luggage

Forget designer luggage with fine leather trim, useful only for posturing in a hotel lobby. Likewise with shiny aluminum cases which plead to be stolen. Take sturdy, strong luggage. This is especially recommended if traveling independently or away fro the catered tourist venues. Luggage should be lockable, sometimes a requirement for transport.

Medical Services

There is a big difference in China between urban and rural medical services. If traveling in the countryside, there may be no appropriate medical services beyond primary health care, which is a success story in China. Some hospitals in cities have special sections for foreigners and where English is spoken.

Many of the large hotels have their own doctors. Payment must be made on the spot for treatment, medicine and transport.

If planning to visit areas outside of Beijing, Shanghai, Guangzhou and Hong Kong, consider carrying emergency evacuation insurance.

If injured in the deserts of western China, for example, medical and transportation costs could leave you indebted into the next decade.

Two of the largest emergency

evacuation companies are SOS Assistance and Asia Emergency Assistance. They have offices in many major cities throughout the world, or contact them in Hong Kong:

International SOS Assistance, 507 Kai Tak Commercial Bldg, 317 Des Voeux Road, Central, Hong Kong. Tel: 2541 6483, Fax: 2544 1677.
Asia Emergency Assistance (AEA), Allied Resources Bldg 9F, 32-38 Ice House St, Central, Hong Kong. Tel: 2810 8898, Fax: 2845 0395. In Beijing: 505 5352.

BEIJING

International Medical Center, Beijing Lufthansa Ctr, 50 Liangmaqiau Lu. Tel: 465 1561; Fax: 465 1984. Emergency service 24 hours. Vaccinations and dental services.
Sino-German Polyclinic, Landmark Tower, B-1. Tel: 501 1983.

SHANGHAI

Shanghai Emergency Center, 68 Haining Lu, Tel: 6324 4010.
Huashan Hospital, 12 Wulumuqi Zhonglu, Tel: 6248 9999.

HONG KONG

Adventist Hospital, No. 40 Stubbs Road, Happy Valley, Tel: 2574 6211.
Central Medical Practice, 1501 Prince's Bldg, Central, Tel: 2521 2567.
Hong Kong Central, 1B Lower Albert Rd, Central, Tel: 2522 3141.

GUANGZHOU

Red Cross Hospital, emergencies: Tel: 8444 6411, in English.
Guangzhou No. 1 People's Hospital, 602 Renmin Beilu, Tel: 8333 3090.
Provincial Hospital No. 1, Foreigners' Dept, 123 Huifu Xilu, Tel: 8777 7812.

Weights & Measures

Both the local and international standards for weights and measures are used in China:

feet	chi	meter
3.28	03.00	1.00
1.09	01.00	0.33
1.00	00.91	0.31
acre	**mu**	**hectare**
0.62	15.00	1.00
0.31	01.00	0.51
1.00	03.22	1.61

pound	jin	kilo
2.20	02.00	1.00
1.10	01.00	0.50
1.00	00.91	0.45
gallon	**sheng**	**liter**
0.22	11.00	1.00
1.00	14.55	4.55

Business Hours

Shops are open everyday, including public holidays. Opening hours are usually from 8.30am–9am to 8pm. Government offices and banks are usually open from Monday to Friday, 8.30am to 5.30pm, with a lunch break from noon to 1.30pm. Times are approximate; allow local variations. In western China, for example, offices often open later – they are on Beijing time, but it's before dawn when it's bright daylight in Beijing.

Tipping

Officially, it is still illegal to accept tips in China. Moreover, for a long time, it was considered patronizing. Tourists and visitors in recent years, however, have changed attitudes in areas like Guangzhou and Shanghai. It's also become the custom for travel groups to give a tip to the Chinese travel guides and bus drivers. If you are traveling with a group, ask the guide, who is responsible for the "official" contacts of the group, whether a tip is appropriate and how much.

Tipping is still not common in most restaurants and hotels, although it is accepted in the top-class hotels and restaurants. Note that it is part of the ritual that any gift or tip will, at first, be firmly rejected.

Religious Services

Officially, the People's Republic encourages atheism. However, the dominant religion in China is Buddhism, with Buddhist temples and places of worship throughout the country. Daoist temples can also be found, as are mosques in the Muslim areas and in all large cities, which have regular prayers at the prescribed times. Catholic and Protestant churches can also be found in most big cities.

Media

An English-language newspaper, the *China Daily*, is published in China, daily except on Sundays. It is informative and sometimes even a bit bold, depending upon the climate at the moment. Often obtainable from the big hotels for free, it contains the television schedule and a diary of cultural events in Beijing. The sports section is good and informative. Unfortunately, same-day editions are available only in large cities; elsewhere, it'll be several days late. Overseas editions of the *China Daily* are published in Hong Kong and the United States. Another English-language paper, the *Shanghai Star*, is available in Shanghai.

Most large hotels sell foreign-language newspapers and journals, including the *International Herald Tribune*, *The Times*, *Asian Wall Street Journal*, *Time*, *Newsweek*, *Far Eastern Economic Review*, and many more.

The overseas edition of the party newspaper *Renmin Ribao* (*People's Daily*) is usually available in the hotels.

Postal/Courier Services

Domestic mail delivery is exceedingly fast and cheap, and it puts most Western postal services to shame. Within some cities, there is often same-day delivery; between large cities, delivery is usually overnight. International mail, too, is efficient. Express mail (EMS) is available to most international destinations, as are private international courier services.

Small parcels, have comprehensive mail services. Large parcels must be packed and sealed at the post office. For general delivery or *postal restante*, visit the central post office in each city.

Card members can also use American Express offices for receiving mail.

Courier Services

BEIJING

DHL: Tel: 466 2211, Fax: 467 7826.
TNT: Tel: 465 2227, Fax: 467 7894.
UPS: Tel: 465 1565, Fax: 465 1897.

SHANGHAI

DHL: Tel: 6536 2900.
Federal Express: Tel: 6275 0808.
TNT: Tel: 6419 0000.
UPS: Tel: 6248 6060.

Telephone, Telex & Fax

Telephone: Domestic long-distance calls are cheap, international calls are expensive. Local calls in China, including in the hotels, are usually free of charge. International calls made from hotels typically have high surcharges added to China's ALREADY HIGH IDD rates. Increasingly common in cities are card phones, with cards available in Y20, 50, 100 and 200.

Telex and fax: Most of the big hotels have telex and fax facilities to help business people. Alternatively, central telegraph and post offices offer telex and fax services.

Telegrams: Sending telegrams abroad is relatively expensive. Express telegrams are double the price. There is usually a telegram counter at the hotel; otherwise, go to the central telegraph or post office.

Like many nations expanding their domestic telephone networks, China's telephone numbers can change without too much fanfare. If you hear a funny ringing sound on the line and can't get through, the number may have changed.

Country code for China: 86

Direct-dial international calls: dial 00, then the country code and telephone number.

Home country direct-dial: dial 108, then the country's international area code. For example, to call Britain, dial 108-44, then the domestic area code and number. For the United States and Canada, dial 108-1. (For AT&T, 108-11; MCI, 108-12; Sprint, 108-13.

Domestic area codes: Add 0 to the codes below if dialing from within China:

Beijing	10
Chengde	314
Chengdu	28
Chongqing	811
Dalian	411
Dandong	415
Guangzhou	20
Guilin	773
Hangzhou	571
Hankou	27
Harbin	451
Jilin	432
Kaifeng	378
Kunming	871
Luoyang	379
Nanjing	25
Shanghai	21
Shenyang	24
Suzhou	512
Taiyuan	351
Tianjin	22
Urumqi	991
Wuhan	27
Wuxi	510
Xi'an	29
Xiamen	592
Xinxiang	373
Zhengzhou	371

Getting Around

Orientation

The main means of public transport in the PR of China are the railways, buses and airplanes. In the regions along the big rivers, boats play an important part. All main cities can be reached by plane and train. The road network has been improved in recent years but is still very poor in many areas.

Road names and orientation: Street names are determined by the traditional checkerboard of Chinese urban design. The most important traffic arteries are divided into sectors and laid out in a grid typically based upon the compass points.

Suffixes are added to the primary name to indicate north, south, east or west, and, additionally, to indicate the middle section. The middle section is called *zhong*; *nan* means south; *bei*, north; *dong*, east; and *xi*, west. A main road is *lu*, smaller is *dajie* or *jie*.

On Arrival

You will have to fill in a customs declaration listing all items of value, such as camera, tape recorder, watches and money. Another form asks for details of your health (health declaration). A third requirement is the entry card, on which you fill in details about the length of your stay in China. It will be put with your passport. Keep the customs declaration safe, because you need to hand it in at the end of the trip.

The Chinese customs officers may check, when you hand in your customs declaration, whether you are taking out all the items you declared. The loss of the customs declaration can incur a high fine.

There are exchange bureaus at the arrival halls of the airport, railway station and harbour where you can change money. You can also find taxis to your hotel. The Chinese airlines provide buses which will take travellers from the airport, which is often a long way outside the city, to the airline offices in town. The fare is modest.

Be wary of people offering taxis before you reach taxi ranks. Before setting off in a taxi, agree on a price for the journey, or ensure the driver will use the meter.

Domestic Travel

Also see travel descriptions and options in *Getting There*, pages 268–269.

By Air: The following list shows the time needed for flight connections from Beijing to other domestic destinations.

Flight connections from Beijing to	Travel time hrs/min
Chengdu	2.35
Chongqing	2.30
Dalian	1.10
Guangzhou	2.40
Guilin	2.35
Hangzhou	1.50
Harbin	1.40
Hohhot	1.15
Kunming	2.55
Lanzhou	2.10
Nanjing	1.50
Qingdao	1.15
Shanghai	1.50
Taiyuan	1.35
Ürümqi	3.55
Wuhan	1.45
Xi'an	2.00

By Rail: The distance and time needed to travel from Beijing to other domestic destinations are as below:

From Beijing to	Distance km (miles)	Travel time hrs
Chengdu	1,273 (2,048)	34
Chongqing	1,586 (2,552)	40
Datong	249 (400)	8
Dalian	770 (1,239)	19

Guangzhou	1,437 (2,313)	33
Guilin	1,326 (2,134)	31
Hangzhou	1,026 (1,651)	26
Harbin	862 (1,388)	17
Hohhot	423 (680)	14
Kunming	1,975 (3,179)	59
Lanzhou	1,169 (1,882)	33
Luoyang	509 (819)	12
Nanjing	719 (1,157)	15
Qingdao	551 (887)	17
Shanghai	908 (1,462)	17
Suzhou	855 (1,376)	21
Taiyuan	319 (514)	9
Ürümqi	2,345 (3,774)	73
Wuhan	764 (1,229)	16
Wuxi	829 (1,334)	17
Xi'an	724 (1,165)	17

Water Transport

There are regular ferry and boat connections between the large coastal cities in China. The same is true for some of the big rivers, particularly the *Yangzi* and the *Pearl* River (but not the Yellow River). Both the ocean liners and the inland river boats have several classes. You can find out the exact timetable from travel agents or the shipping agencies.

Public Transport

Railways: The Chinese rail network covers 53,400 km (32,467 mi), of which 2,734 miles (4,400 km) are electrified. Average train speed is not very high, mainly due to poor construction. There is no first or second class on Chinese trains, but four categories or classes: *ruanwo* or soft-sleeper; *ruanzuo* or soft-seat; *yingwo* or hard-sleeper, and *yingzuo* or hard-seat. The soft-seat class is usually only available for short journeys. Long distance trains normally only have soft-sleeper or hard-sleeper facilities. The soft-sleeper class has 4-bed compartments with soft beds. It is to be recommended particularly for long journeys. The hard-sleeper class has open, 6-bed compartments. The beds are not really hard, but are not very comfortable either. While you can reserve a place for the first three classes (you always buy a ticket with a place number), this is not essential for the lowest class.

There is always boiled water available on the trains. There are washrooms in the soft-sleeper and hard-sleeper classes. The toilets, regardless of which class, are usually not very hygienic, and it is a good idea to bring your own toilet paper. There are dining cars on long-distance trains which can vary in quality. Trains are usually fully booked and it is advisable to get a ticket well in advance. This is particularly so during the main travel season. There are special ticket counters for foreigners at railway stations. Fares are higher for foreigners than for the Chinese. The price also depends on both the class and the speed of the train; there are slow trains, fast trains, express trains and inter-city trains. Reservations can be made at ticket offices in the town centre or through travel agencies. Be on time, as trains tend to be punctual.

Buses (*gongongqiche*): Overland buses are the most important means of transport in many parts of China, especially where there is as yet no railway line. In most towns and settlements, there are main bus stations for overland buses. They are certainly the cheapest means of transport, but are also correspondingly slow. There are regular breaks during bus journeys; on journeys lasting several days you will usually find simple restaurants and overnight accommodation near the bus stations. Many overland buses have numbered seats and it is advisable to book a ticket and seat well in advance. Modern buses with air conditioning are frequently available in the tourist centres.

Town Transport

The visitor can choose between taxis, buses or bicycles for transport in the cities. In Beijing, Hong Kong and Shanghai there is also the underground. Taxis are certainly the most comfortable form of transport, and can be hired for excursions.

Buses in Chinese towns are always overcrowded. The fare depends on distance, and should be paid to the conductor. Buses are usually easy to use, and timetables or town maps are available everywhere. In some Chinese cities such as Beijing, there are also minibuses for certain routes. They carry a maximum of 16 people. They are a bit more expensive but will stop at any point you want along the route.

You can hire bicycles in many Chinese towns, either at the hotels or at special hiring shops. It is advisable to park the bicycle at guarded parking spaces for a small fee. China too has bicycle thieves and there is a fine for illegal parking.

On Departure

Before leaving by train or plane, you must first hand in your customs declaration, and, on request from the customs official, show the valuables you declared on entry. You could also be asked to produce all the receipts showing what money or travellers cheques you changed.

There is a departure tax.

Where To Stay

Hotels

China's large cities have seen the sprouting of numerous new hotels, most of them at the high end of the market, including many of world-class caliber. Many belong to international hotel chains, or else to international marketing associations, and their management and staff have been trained abroad. Usually the prices of these better hotels are in line with hotel prices in the West.

Tour groups are usually accommodated in good tourist hotels, which are well-appointed. Except in the first-class hotels, take caution with laundry service, particularly with delicate clothes.

Bookings with hotels in the middle and lower price ranges sometimes can be difficult, particularly during the main summer season in May, September and October, when they are hopelessly booked up. Fortunately, if you have confirmed reservations, your room will be waiting, as hotels rarely overbook.

* Worth mentioning are a few well-preserved hotels built by the colonial powers in some cities. They include the Peace Hotel (*Heping*) in Shanghai, the People's Hotel (*Renmin Dasha*) in Xi'an and the Friendship Hotel (*Youyibinguan*) in Beijing. Although inte-

riors have been modernized, of course.

Luxury hotels abound in the largest cities. Hong Kong is saturated with them. Rates at all but the cheapest hotels are subject to 10 to 15 percent service surcharge. Rates indicated are for standard rooms.

$$$$$	=	US$200 and up
$$$$	=	US$150–US$200
$$$	=	US$100–US$150
$$	=	US$50–US$100
$	=	below US$50

Beijing

$$$$$

China World Hotel, 1 Jianguomenwai Dajie. Tel: 6505 2266. Top of the line service and accommodations, well located for business. Health club with swimming pool, shopping plaza and business center, plus a variety of Western and Asian restaurants. Part of a huge complex that includes the China World Trade Centre.

Palace Hotel, 8 Jinyu Hutong Wangfujing. Tel: 6512 8899, Fax: 512 9050. 5-star hotel managed by the Peninsula group. Centrally located for shopping and Imperial Palace sights, on a lively downtown alleyway. Restaurants and designer shopping.

$$$$

Kempinski Hotel (Beijing Lufthansa Ctr), 50 Liangmaqiao Lu. Tel: 6465 3388, Fax: 465 3366. Shiny new 5-star hotel with the works. Attached to Youyi Shopping City.

Shangri-La Hotel, 29 Zizhuyuan Rd. Tel: 6841 2211. The Shangri-La offers top-notch accommodation with experienced service staff and friendly surroundings. The hotel is located on the western edge of town, but shuttle buses are available to take guests to the center.

$$$

Hilton Hotel, 1 Dongfong Lu, Dongsanhuanbei Lu. Tel: 6466 2288. New 5-star hotel right off the airport expressway. Posh surroundings, good food.

Hotel New Otani, Changfugong 26 Jianguomenwai Dajie. Tel: 6512 5555, Fax: 513 9810. Japanese joint-venture with swimming pool and health club. Well located for business in the eastern part of the city.

Holiday Inn Crowne Plaza, Beijing 48 Wangfujing Dajie Dengshikou. Tel: 6513 3388. Located on a busy shopping street in central Beijing, close to the Imperial Palace and other sights. Health club and swimming pool.

Hotel Beijing-Toronto, 3 Jianguomenwai Dajie. Tel: 6500 2266. Friendly 4-star lodging in eastern Beijing.

Peace Hotel, 3 Jinyu Hutong Wangfujing. Tel: 6512 8833. Unremarkable rooms, centrally located for shopping and the Imperial Palace. Lively nightlife in the neighborhood.

Guang Dong Regency Hotel, 2 Wangfujing Dajie. Tel: 6513 6666. Comfortable atmosphere and deluxe accommodation in a prime location.

Swissotel Beijing (Hong Kong Macau Centre), Dongsi Shitiao, Lijiao Qiao. Tel: 6501 2288. New luxury highrise hotel northwest of business area.

Traders Hotel (China World Trade Centre), 1 Jianguomenwai Dajie. Tel: 6505 2277. Good solid service, food and accommodation. Well located for business in the east section of the city.

$$

Beijing Bamboo Garden Hotel, 24 Xiaoshiqiao Lane, Jiugulou Dajie. Tel: 6403 2229. Modest and clean rooms that open into a classical-style Chinese garden. The hotel is just one block from the Drum Tower.

Fragrant Hills Hotel, Fragrant Hills Park. Tel: 6259 1166. Sunny modern getaway in the lush hills to the northwest of Beijing, near Summer Palace, but far from the city. Swimming pool, Chinese and Western restaurants.

Jianguo Hotel, 5 Jianguomenwai Dajie. Tel: 6500 2233. A favorite for long-term business travelers to the city. Experienced staff and a comfortable atmosphere. Located in eastern Beijing. Good value.

Holiday Inn Lido Hotel, Jiangtai Lu. Tel: 6437 6688, Fax: 437 6237. A village unto itself catering to short- and long-term guests. Indoor/outdoor swimming, tennis courts, business and shopping facilities. Near the airport.

Novotel 88, Dengshikou Dajie. Tel: 6513 8822. Clean, no frills, centrally located. A real bargain for Beijing.

Qianmen Hotel, Beijing 175, Yongan Lu. Tel: 6301 6688. Standard accommodations in old outer city, near Tiantan. Opera performances nightly.

Xin Qiao Hotel, 2 Dong Jiaomin Xiang, Dongcheng District. Tel: 6513 3366.

Elegant old-style hotel located in the former Legation Quarter, close to Tiananmen Square. Peaceful and convenient to transportation.

$

Beijing Friendship Hotel, 3 Baishiqiao Rd. Tel: 6849 8888. An old-style, state-run hotel in the peaceful northwest corner of town. Located near the universities and the Summer Palace.

Ritan Hotel, One Ritan Road, Jianguomenwai. Tel: 6512 5588. Intimate little hotel located inside Ritan Park. Peaceful and reasonably-priced for basic accommodation.

Guangzhou

$$$$

China Hotel, Liuhua Lu, Guangzhou. Tel: 8666 6888; Fax: 8667 7014. Five-star hotel managed by the New World Group of Hong Kong. Restaurants, electronic games arcade and bowling alley. The hotel is across the street from the Canton Trade Fair grounds.

White Swan Hotel, 1 Shamian Nanlu. Tel: 8188 6968; Fax: 8186 1188. One of the finest hotels in China and a member of the Leading Hotels of the World network. The 843-room hotel on Shamian island has stunning views.

$$$

Dongfang Hotel, 120 Liuhua Lu, Guangzhou. Tel: 8666 9900; Fax: 8666 2775. The Dongfang was built in the 1950s by the Soviets and a new wing added in the 1970s. Has managed to retain a lot of charm. Centrally-located and convenient for businessmen, as the China Trade Fair grounds are just opposite. A 5-star hotel.

Garden Hotel, 368 Huangshi Donglu, Guangzhou. Tel: 8333 8989; Fax: 8335 0467. A 5-star hotel located across the street from the largest Friendship Department Store.

Guangdong International Hotel, 336 Huangshi Donglu, Guangzhou. Tel: 8331 1888; Fax: 8331 1666. The newest luxury-class hotel to open in Guangzhou. Has 14 food and beverage outlets and a shopping arcade.

Holiday Inn City Centre Overseas Chinese Village, Huanshi Dong, 28 Guangmin Lu, Guangzhou. Tel: 8776 6999; Fax: 8775 3126. This 430-room hotel, which opened in 1990, is known for its friendly service.

Ramada Pearl Hotel, 9 Mingyue Yilu, Guangzhou. Tel: 8777 2988; Fax: 8776 7481. Part of the Ramada International chain, this 400-room hotel is located in the eastern part of the city.
Forum, 67 Heping Lu, Shenzhen. Tel: 8558 6333; Fax: 8556 1700. Opened in 1990, the Forum is located just west of the railway station. A member of the Inter-Continental hotel and resorts.
Shangri-La, East Side, Railway Station Jianshe Lu, Shenzhen. Tel: 8223 0888; Fax: 8223 9878. Part of the Shangri-La International chain. Luxuriously-appointed 553 rooms with extensive food and beverage outlets.

$$

Equatorial Hotel, 931 Renmin Lu, Guangzhou. Tel: 8667 2888; Fax: 8667 2583. Comprehensive range of food and beverage outlets, business center, health club and discotheque.
Overseas Chinese Hotel, 90 Zhanqian Lu, Guangzhou. Tel: 8666 3488; Fax: 8666 3230. This 400-room hotel has two restaurants, a coffee house and a discotheque.
Century Plaza (Shenzhen), Kinchit Lu, Shenzhen. Tel: 8222 0888; Fax: 8223 4060. Luxury hotel situated in the hub of Shenzhen. Five restaurants, pool, and health and business centers.
Oriental Regent (Shenzhen), Financial Centre Bldg, Shenan Zhonglu, Shenzhen. Tel: 8224 7000; Fax: 8224 7290. Centrally-located, 4-star hotel. Close to nightlife area.
Shenzhen Bay Hotel, Overseas Chinese Town, Shenzhen. Tel: 8660 0111; Fax: 8660 0139. Facing Deep Water Bay and a short walk from attractions like Splendid China, China Folk Culture Village and Windows of the World. This resort-style hotel on the beach offers a full range of recreational facilities.

$

Guangzhou Youth Hostel, 2 Shamian Sijie, Guangzhou. Tel: 8188 4298. Cheap rooms can be found at this hostelry, nicknamed the 'Black Duck', as it faces the luxury White Swan Hotel. A favorite with backpackers.
Victory Hotel, 54 Shamian Sijie, Guangzhou. Tel: 8186 2622; Fax: 8186 2413. Located on the former concession island of Shamian, near the old town. This was one of Guangzhou's top hotels in the 1930s.
Zhongshan Hot Springs Resort, San Xiang, Zhongshan. Tel: 8683 888; Fax: 8683 333. An idyllic retreat from the city. Hotel rooms feature marble baths with hot spring water on tap.
Songtao Hotel, Wan Song Gang, Qixing Crags, Zhaoqing. Tel: 8224 412; Fax: 8224 412. A 3-star hotel situated in the scenic Seven Star Crags area.
Zhuhai Hotel, Jingshan Lu, Zhuhai. Tel: 3833 718; Fax: 8332 339. Luxury hotel with good leisure facilities, including sauna, tennis courts, billiard room, swimming pool, nightclub and mahjong rooms.
Zhuhai Holiday Resort, Shihuashan, Zhuhai. Tel: 8332 038; Fax: 8332 036. Idyllic beachfront 5-star property west of Jiuzhou Harbor. Full range of leisure amenities, including a bowling alley, a roller skating rink, go-cart racing and horse riding.

Hong Kong

$$$$$

Conrad International, Pacific Place, 88 Queensway. Tel: 2521 3838; Fax: 2521 3888. A European-style deluxe boutique hotel. Understated elegance; spacious rooms and good location adjacent to Pacific Place shopping, Admiralty MTR and tramlines.
Grand Hyatt, 1 Harbour Rd, Wanchai. Tel: 2588 1234; Fax: 2802 0677. Probably the most expensive and glitziest hotel in Hong Kong. Luxury on a truly palatial level; overlooking the harbor and only a couple of steps from the HK Convention and Exhibition Centre, the HK Arts Centre.
Island Shangri-La, Pacific Place, Supreme Court Rd, Central. Tel: 2877 3838; Fax: 2521 8742. This gracious oasis lives up to its name. Elegant decor, helpful staff and beautiful, spacious rooms with stunning panoramic views of the harbor or Peak. Great location; adjacent to Hong Kong Park, Pacific Place shopping and Admiralty MTR and tramlines.
Mandarin Oriental, 5 Connaught Rd, Central. Tel: 2522 0111; Fax: 2810 6190. Classy hotel established in 1963 and consistently rated among the world's best. Impeccable service and quality. Full range of facilities including a indoor pool and some of the finest hotel F&B establishments in town. Convenient location.
New World Harbour View, 1 Harbour Rd, Wanchai. Tel: 2802 8888; Fax: 2802 8833. A shade cheaper than the Grand Hyatt but enjoys same prime location overlooking the harbor; with easy access to Kowloon from Wanchai Ferry Pier. Superb recreation facilities.
Ritz-Carlton, 3 Connaught Rd, Central. Tel: 2877 6666; Fax: 2877 6778. Post-modernist exterior gives way to classy traditionalist interior decorated with period art and antiques. Facilities include outdoor pool and good Italian and Japanese restaurants. Convenient location close to Central MTR, Star Ferry, and Admiralty and Central business and commercial districts.
Kowloon Shangri-La, 64 Mody Rd, Tsimshatsui East. Tel: 2721 2111; Fax: 2723 8686. Opulent grandeur and great harbor views. Full range of deluxe facilities including indoor swimming pool and highly rated restaurants. Across from Tsimshatsui East waterfront with easy hoverferry access to Central.
Omni Hong Kong Harbour City, 3 Canton Rd, Tsimshatsui. Tel: 2736 0088; Fax: 2736 0011. Many rooms with magnificent harbor views. Deluxe facilities include an outdoor pool and 5 restaurants. Shopping opportunities are unparalled as it's inside the enormous shopping complex stretching from Ocean Terminal up to the Gateway.
The Peninsula, Salisbury Rd, Tsimshatsui. Tel: 2366 6251; Fax: 2722 4170. Hong Kong's oldest and most prestigious hotel has been a byword for impeccable service and colonial-style grandeur since it opened in 1928. Extensivle refurbished, with a new 30-storey extension tower. Eight top restaurants and superb location in the heart of Kowloon's shopping, restaurant and entertainment area; close to Tsimshatsui MTR.
The Regent, Salisbury Rd, Tsimshatsui. Tel: 2721 1211; Fax: 2739 4546. Elegant with breathtaking views across Victoria Harbour. Full range of facilities, including a poolside spa, the 1930s-style Club Shanghai nightclub and top-notch Lai Ching Heen and Plume restaurants. Superb location on the waterfront; convenient for Star Ferry and Kowloon's prime commercial and entertainment district.
Sheraton Hong Kong Hotel and Towers, 20 Nathan Rd, Tsimshatsui. Tel: 2369 1111; Fax: 2739 8707. Swish hotel on corner of Nathan and Salisbury roads with full range of deluxe

facilities, including an outdoor pool and 5 top-notch restaurants. Good location close to museums, MTR, and Kowloon's prime commercial and entertainment district.

$$$$

Century Hong Kong Hotel, 238 Jaffe Rd, Wanchai. Tel: 2598 8888; Fax: 2598 8866. Modern hotel with good facilities including an outdoor pool, health club and Lao Ching Hing, one of oldest and best Shanghai restaurants in town. Convenient for HK Exhibition and Convention Centre and Wanchai's commercial district.

The Excelsior, 281 Gloucester Rd, Causeway Bay. Tel: 2894 8888; Fax: 2895 6459. Overlooking the colorful Causeway Bay typhoon shelter. Managed by the Mandarin Oriental group, the hotel offers efficient service and a pleasant environment. Close to Causeway Bay's shopping and commercial district and MTR.

Furama Kempinski, 1 Connaught Rd, Central. Tel: 2525 5111; Fax: 2845 9339. Quietly plush business hotel. Good value considering its convenient location to Central MTR, Star Ferry, and Admiralty and the Central district.

Grand Plaza, 2 Kornhill Rd, Quarry Bay. Tel: 2886 0011; Fax: 2886 1738. Modern business hotel with good facilities including golf-putting green, tennis courts, indoor pool and gym. Close to Tai Koo MTR.

Wharney Hotel, 57–73 Lockhart Rd, Wanchai. Tel: 2861 1000; Fax: 2865 6023. Smart modern hotel with good facilities including indoor pool. Located in the heart of Wanchai's commercial and nightlife district, close to HK Convention Centre, MTR and trams.

The Kowloon Hotel, 19–21 Nathan Rd, Tsimshatsui. Tel: 2369 8698; Fax: 2739 9811. Smart, modern business hotel tucked in behind 'The Pen', in the heart of Kowloon's commercial and entertainment district. Close to MTR.

Majestic, 348 Nathan Rd, Yau Ma Tei. Tel: 2781 1333; Fax: 2781 1773. Well-appointed business hotel. Close to Temple Street night market, shops, cinema and Jordan MTR; also well-served by buses.

Nikko, 72 Mody Rd, Tsimshatsui East. Tel: 2739 1111; Fax: 2311 3122. Japanese business hotel with impeccable service and panoramic harbor views. Amenities include an outdoor pool and good Cantonese, French and Japanese restaurants. Just across from Tsimshatsui East waterfront promenade and convenient for HK Science Museum, Coliseum, Kowloon kcr station and the Cross-Harbour Tunnel.

Omni Marco Polo Harbour City, Canton Rd, Tsimshatsui. Tel: 2736 0888; Fax: 2736 0022. Elegant, Continental-style hotel in the middle of enormous Harbour City complex; marginally cheaper than sister-hotel Omni Hong Kong, but lacking views and pool.

Omni Prince Harbour City, Canton Rd, Tsimshatsui. Tel: 2736 1888; Fax: 2736 0066. Similar standard to sister-hotel Omni Marco Polo; with outdoor pool. Very convenient for China Ferry Terminal and Kowloon Park.

$$$

Harbour View International House, 4 Harbour Rd, Wanchai. Tel: 2802 0111; Fax: 2802 9063. Worth paying the extra HK$200 for a harbor view room, but book early at this upscale YMCA, next door to Arts Centre and directly across from the HK Convention and Exhibition Centre.

New Cathay Hotel, 17 Tung Lo Wan Rd, Causeway Bay. Tel: 2577 8211; Fax: 2576 9365. Good option for single travelers, with singles from HK$650. Close to tramlines, Hong Kong Stadium, Victoria Park and Causeway Bay commercial, dining and shopping districts.

New Harbour Hotel, 41–49 Hennessy Rd, Wanchai. Tel: 2861 1166; Fax: 2865 6111. One of the cheapest deals for a centrally-located hotel on Hong Kong Island. Convenient for HK Convention and Exhibition Centre, Wanchai's commercial and entertainment districts, MTR and tramlines.

Concourse, 22 Lai Chi Kok Rd, Mongkok. Tel: 2397 6683; Fax: 2381 3768. Well-appointed modern hotel popular with Asian business travelers. Bargain shopping nearby in Fa Yuen St factory-outlets. Close to MTR.

Imperial Hotel, 30–34 Nathan Rd, Tsimshatsui. Tel: 2366 2201; Fax: 2311 2360. Pleasant rooms. Good value; at the bottom end of this price category. Convenient location on Tsimshatsui's 'Golden Mile', close to shops, restaurants, MTR.

Nathan Hotel, 378 Nathan Rd, Yau Ma Tei. Tel: 2388 5141; Fax: 2770 4262. Close to Temple Street night market, Yue Hwa Chinese merchandise emporium, restaurants and shops, cinema and Jordan MTR.

The Salisbury (YMCA), 41 Salisbury Rd, Tsimshatsui. Tel: 2369 2211; Fax: 2739 9315. Book ahead to be sure of a room at this very upscale YMCA. All rooms are well-equipped and many enjoy panoramic views of the harbor. Amenities include a large indoor pool and an impressive range of sports facilities. As conveniently located as 'The Pen'; but a fraction of the cost.

$$

South China Hotel, 67–75 Java Rd, North Point. Tel: 2503 1168; Fax: 2512 8698. Well-appointed with modern decor. Cantonese restaurant. Close to MTR and ferry piers.

Bangkok Royal, 2–12 Pilkem St, Yau Ma Tei. Tel: 2735 9181; Fax: 2730 2209. Bottom end of this price category. A good option for lone travellers and small groups with 32 singles and extra beds for HK$100 over the standard twin rate. Good Thai restaurant. Jordan MTR is just a few steps away.

Caritas Bianchi Lodge, 4 Cliff Rd, Yau Ma Tei. Tel: 2388 1111; Fax: 2770 6669. Clean, spacious rooms in well-run Roman Catholic hostel between Nathan Road and the Meteorological Station. Close to Temple Street night market, shops, restaurants, and Yau Ma Tei MTR.

Eaton Hotel, 380 Nathan Rd, Yau Ma Tei. Tel: 2782 1818; Fax: 2782 5563. Well-equipped rooms; good value restaurants with regular clientele. Close to Temple Street night market, shops, cinema and Jordan MTR.

Evergreen Hotel, 42–52 Woo Sung St, Yau Ma Tei. Tel: 2780 4222; Fax: 2385 8584. Clean, tidy rooms. Triples and 4-bed rooms are good value for small groups. Steps from Temple Street night market, Yue Hwa Chinese emporium and Jordan MTR.

$

Ma Wui Hall Youth Hostel, Mt Davis Path, Victoria Rd. Tel: 2817 5715. Spartan dormitory accommodation but superb views from mountain-top location above Kennedy Town and Pokfulam. Advance booking advised as these beds fill up quickly.

Anne Black Guest House (YWCA), 5 Man Fuk Rd, Ho Man Tin. Tel: 2713 9211; Fax: 2761 1269. Clean, simple rooms for women and couples. A short walk away from the Ladies' Market, Mongkok KCR and MTR stations.

Chungking House, 4–5 Fl, Block A, Chungking Mansions, 40 Nathan Rd. Tel: 2366 5362; Fax: 2721 3570. There are cheaper deals in the area but Chungking House is the only establishment to win the HKTA's seal of approval. Located on Kowloon's 'Golden Mile'. Steps away from MTR.

Shanghai

LUXURY

Garden Hotel, 58 Maoming Nanlu. Tel: 433 1111, Fax: 433 8866. A 33-story tower that incorporates the former Cercle Sportif Francais, inject a little of the past into the hotel's modern facilities. Surrounded by a garden, the Garden is popular with Japanese, as it is managed by the Hotel Okura, probably Tokyo's finest hotel.

Hilton International, 250 Hua Shan Rd. Tel: 248 0000, Fax: 248 3848. Over 40 stories tall, the Hilton makes an unforgettable first impression with its expansive marble lobby. Popular with both Europeans and Asians. Restaurants include the rooftop Sichuan Court restaurant, with fine views.

Holiday Inn Crowne Plaza, 388 Pan Yu Rd. Tel: 252 8888, Fax: 252-8545. Located near the diplomatic neighborhood, the Crowne Plaza follows the elegant design of the chain's top-end hotels everywhere. With full business and recreational facilities, several respected restaurants offer imaginative East-West menus.

JC Mandarin, 1225 Nanjing Xilu. Tel: 279 1888, Fax: 279 1822. Conveniently located in the heart of Shanghai's shopping district and on its most commercial avenue, the hotel is within walking distance of the Bund and other sights. Facilities include an indoor pool, gym, and two tennis courts.

Pacific Hotel, 104 Nanjing Lu. Tel: 327 6226, Fax: 326 9620. Not one of Shanghai's finer establishments, the hotel is sagging and somewhat Gothic in ambiance. One of Shanghai's older hotels, the granite structure is architecturally interesting: a gold-plated dome with a clock tower crown the roof, and a classically-robust entrance leads into an art-deco lobby.

Peace Hotel, 20 Nanjing Lu. Tel: 321 1244, Fax: 329 0300. Located on the Bund and a classic colonial retreat, one of the city's most famous landmarks. When it opened in the 1920s as the Cathay, it was the hotel in China. Somewhat rundown now, but comfortable, the Peace appeals to those who prefer nostalgia to generic creature comforts. Even if not staying here, drop by the bar in the evening to see the Old Jazz Band, a sextet of men in their late 60s.

Portman Shangri-La, Shanghai Center, 1376 Nanjing Xilu. Tel: 279 8888, Fax: 279 8999. One of Shanghai's finest hotels, known not only for its central location, but also for its style – Chinese works of art, including statues of horses and camels, adorn the lobby. Chamber music in the lobby each afternoon and evening. The hotel is part of the extensive Shanghai Center, a complex with top restaurants, airline offices, and residential apartments.

Chongqing

EXPENSIVE

Holiday Inn Yangtze Chongqing, 15 Nan Ping Bei Rd. Tel: 280 3380, Fax: 280 0884.

MODERATE

Chongqing Guest House, 235 Minsheng Rd. Tel: 35 4491, Fax: 35 0643.

Chongqing Hotel, 41-43 Xinhua Rd. Tel: 34 9301, Fax: 34 3085.

Renmin Hotel, 175 Renmin Rd. Tel: 35 1421, Fax: 35 1387.

Shaping Grand Hotel, 84 Xiaolongkan New St. Tel: 66 3194, Fax: 66 3293.

Guilin

EXPENSIVE

Guilin Plaza, 20 Lijiang Lu. Tel: 581 2488, Fax: 581 3323.

Guilin Royal Garden Hotel, Yuanjiang Rd. Tel: 581 2411, Fax: 581 5051.

Guishan Hotel, Chuan Shan Rd. Tel: 581 3388, Fax: 581 4851.

Holiday Inn Guilin, 14 South Ronghu Rd. Tel: 282 3950, Fax: 282 2101.

Sheraton Guilin Hotel, Bing Jiang Nan Rd. Tel: 282 5588, Fax: 282 5598.

Ürümqi

EXPENSIVE

Holiday Inn Ürümqi, 168 North Xinhua Rd. Tel: 21 8788, Fax: 21 7422.

World Plaza, 2 South Beijing Rd. Tel: 33 6400, Fax: 33 9007.

Xi'an

LUXURY

Sheraton Xi'an, 12 Feng Gao Rd, West Suburb. Tel: 426 1888, Fax: 426 2983.

EXPENSIVE

Dynasty Hotel, 55 Huanchengxi Rd North. Tel: 721 2718, Fax: 721 2728.

Grand New World Hotel, 48 Lian Hu Rd. Tel: 721 6868, Fax: 721 9754.

Hyatt Regency Xi'an, 158 Dongda St. Tel: 723 1234, Fax: 723 6799.

Shangri-La Golden Flower, 8 Chang Le Rd West. Tel: 323 2981, Fax: 323 5477.

Xi'an Garden Hotel, 4 Dongyanyin Rd, Dayanta. Tel: 526 1111.

Guesthouses

Individual travelers may find accommodation in guesthouses in smaller towns off the beaten tourist track. Guesthouses usually have rooms with two or more beds, and often dormitories are available; there are usually shower and washing facilities, as well. They are recommended as cheap accommodation for backpackers.

Some guesthouses or simple hotels refuse to take foreign guests, usually because of the rules of Chinese travel agencies or the local police, who often determine where foreigners may stay.

Others

It is practically impossible for foreigners to find accommodation outside of hotels and guesthouses. Private lodgings are unknown because of crowded living conditions. At times, some universities and institutes have guesthouses where foreign visitors can find good, cheap accommodation. Advance booking is not possible.

If going on a long trip or hike in the countryside, especially in Tibet or in areas around the sacred mountains of China, you will come across various types of "long-distance travelers' lodgings". It is advisable to carry a sleeping bag.

Eating Out

What To Eat

For Westerners, the single identifying symbol of Chinese cuisine is the use of chopsticks, which are practical as the food is cut into small pieces. Due to the short supply of fuel over the centuries, it has been necessary to prepare food using a minimum of fuel – small pieces cook quicker.

Only about 10 percent of China's land area is suitable for agriculture. Thus, beef is not a significant source of food; the need to cultivate intensively means grazing is neither possible nor common, except in the extreme north and northwest. Thus, until recently, milk and dairy products were not widely known. In place of animal protein, soybeans have often been a primary source of protein.

Traditionally, food should not only be filling, but it should also have a healing effect. A Chinese meal is based on balance, even the largest and most extravagant banquets.

There are roughly four main styles of Chinese cuisine (this does not take into account the often completely different cooking and eating traditions of the national minorities):

Northern cuisine, with Beijing at its center. The soil around Beijing is fairly poor, thus the food it produces is unvaried. In contrast to the south, where rice is preferred, noodles dishes predominate here. The main vegetable is Chinese cabbage: boiled, steamed, fried, preserved, with a variety of different spices. Special mention should be made of Peking Duck and the Mongolian hotpot, feasts not to be missed if in Beijing. **Haiyang**, in the eastern coastal areas around Shanghai. The predominant food is fish (particularly freshwater) and shellfish. There is a greater choice of vegetables here than in the north. **Cantonese**, the southern cuisine, is the most familiar to Westerners, and the most common in Chinese restaurants around the world. **Sichuan** is famous for its highly-spiced foods, assuring that diners can warm up even in the often humid and cold winters.

The Chinese tend to eat quite early; lunch is often served in Chinese restaurants from 11am. (Hotels and restaurants for foreigners have, of course, adjusted to their preferences.) In the evenings, you won't easily find a meal after 8pm, though this is different in the south, where social life continues until the late evening.

Where To Eat

Chinese meals are best eaten in a group, with diners sharing a variety of dishes; Chinese restaurants are often not suited to individual diners.

The individual traveler is more likely to frequent one of the typical Chinese roadside eateries. Make sure the restaurant is clean and the food has been freshly-prepared and is hot. Bringing one's own chopsticks isn't considered an insult at all. Chinese restaurants are often not heated even during winter (nor are theaters or concert halls), so it is advisable to dress warmly.

Beijing

Fangshan Canting, Qionghua Dao Beihai Park. Tel: 6401 1889. Garden setting at Beihai Park. $$

Li Family Restaurant, 11 Yongfang Hutong, Denei Dajie. Tel: 6601 1915. Serves four tables of up to 12 each day – two at lunch and two at dinner in the home of the chef, who has a story for each dish. Book ahead. $$

PEKING DUCK RESTAURANTS

Zhengyangmen Quanjude Roast Duck Restaurant, East side of Tiananmen Square, opposite War Heroes Monument. Tel: 6512 2265. Clean and well-run, with more than 300 different duck dishes. $

Qianmen Quanjude Roast Duck Restaurant, 32 Qianmen Dajie. Tel: 6701 1379. Beijing's most famous. The restaurant is arranged so you can watch the duck being prepared. $$

SHANDONG CUISINE

Dishes from neighboring Shandong Province are the main element in what Beijingers refer to as home cooking. The number of restaurants serving this fare outnumber any other kind. Because Shandong is a coastal province, its dishes feature seafood such as jumbo shrimp, eel, sharks' fin and sea cucumber.

Special Flavours Restaurant, 7/F Beijing Hotel, Old West Wing, 33 East Chang'an Ave. Tel: 6513 7766 Ext 374. Dine in a classic Chinese banquet room. $$

Confucian Heritage Restaurant, 3 West Liulichang Jie. Tel: 6303 0689. An inviting two-storey teahouse in the historical Liulichang area. $–$$

SICHUAN CUISINE

The isolated southwestern province of Sichuan is known for its spicy food, which, it is said, matches the temperament of the people. Chicken, pork, freshwater fish and shellfish are favorite ingredients, and noodles or bread is usually served as the staple. Try some wicked dan-dan noodles, a sizzling fish-head soup, or one of their crispy rice dishes.

Sichuan Restaurant, 51 Xi Rongxian Hutong. Tel: 6603 3291. Frequented by some of Beijing's leaders. Located in what was the mansion of a Qing dynasty prince. $

Yuyuan Restaurant, Northeast corner of Ritan Park. Tel: 6502 5985. Indoor and courtyard dining in the Temple of the Sun Park. Reservations are usually needed. $

Yidairen Home Made Food, 181 Xi'anmen Dajie (opposite the Honglou Cinema). Tel: 6601 5097. Cozy and clean, privately-owned restaurant with cooks from Sichuan Province. $

CANTONESE CUISINE

Cantonese food is known for its delicate flavors and fresh ingredients, preferably bought the same day and cooked briskly before serving, using little oil or spicy seasoning. Dim sum are dumplings meant to be a snack food, but there are so many different kinds to try that a dim sum meal often turns into a feast. There are now many excellent Cantonese restaurants in Beijing, but also tend to be more expensive than other restaurants.

Windows On The World, 28/F, CITIC Bldg 19 Jianguomenwai Dajie. Tel: 6500 3335. Excellent dim sum dishes served in a pleasant dining room on the 28th fl, overlooking the city. $$

Four Seasons, 1/F Jianguo Hotel Jianguomenwai Dajie. Tel: 6500 2233, Ext 8041. Quiet, classical setting enhances the fine food. $$
Hong Kong Food City, 18 Dong'anmen Dajie. Tel: 6513 6668. Fresh seafood served in a lively dining hall. $$

OTHER CHINESE RESTAURANTS

Bamboo Garden Hotel Restaurant, 24 Xiaoshiqiao Jiugulou St. Tel: 6403 2229. Hearty Chinese dishes served in a classical garden restaurant. Formerly the home of a shadowy secret security chief, Kang Sheng. $
Kaorouji Restaurant, 14 Qianhai Dongyan. Tel: 6401 2170/445 921. Muslim-style grill on Qianhai Lake. $
Xinjiang Restaurants, Weiguncun Uyghur Village off Baishiqiao Rd. Pick any restaurant in this three-block area for noodles and grilled mutton made by Uighur people. While the food is great, wear old clothes. $
Donglaishun Restaurant (2 branches), 16 Jinyu Hutong and 198 Wangfujing Dajie. Tel: 6552 2092/6550 069/ 6556 465. Mongolian hotpot. $
Duyichu Dumplings, 36 Qianmen Dajie. Tel: 6511 2094. Beijing tradition. $

OTHER ASIAN CUISINES

Omar Khayyam, Asia Pacific Bldg, 8 Yabao Lu. Tel: 6513 9988 Ext 20188. Tasty Indian cuisine in pleasant surroundings. $$
Sakura, 2F Changfugong, New Otani Hotel, Jianguomenwai Dajie. Tel: 6512 5555 Ext 1226. Japanese. Light and sunny atmosphere. $$
Go Nin Nyakushou, 2/F Beijing Hotel, East Chang'an Ave. Tel: 6513 7766 Ext 666. Japanese food and posh ambience. $$$
Liyuan Restaurant, 8 Xi Huang-chenggen. Tel: 6601 5234. Thai and Chinese food. $$

WESTERN

Gone is the time when Western food could only be found in Beijing's hotels. These days every week seems to witness the opening of a new western-style bar or restaurant. Most of these establishments are found in the Sanlitun embassy area, where a stroll in any direction will present a choice of possibilities.

Paulaner Brauhaus, Beijing Lufthansa Ctr, 50 Liangmaqiao Lu. Tel: 6465

3388 Ext 5734. Friendly pub serving tasty German fare. The beer is brewed in-house. $$
Frank's Place, Gongrentiyuguan Donglu (next to Chains City Hotel). Tel: 6507 2617. The best burger and chilli in town. Darts and re-runs of football add to the fun. $
Maxim's, 2 Chongwenmennei Dajie. Tel: 6512 1992. French restaurant, modelled after Maxim's of Paris. Owned by couturier Pierre Cardin. $$$
Metro Cafe, No 6 Gong Ti Xi Lu. Tel: 6591 7828. Mix and match pastas and sauces. $
Peppino's Shangri-La Hotel, 29 Zizhuyuan Lu. Tel: 841 2211. Italian restaurant. Candlelight and a roving guitarist. $$
T.G.I. Friday, No 19 Dongsanhuanbei, Lu Hua Peng Da Sha. Tel: 6595 1386. Chain well known in the States. $

Guangzhou

CANTONESE CUISINE

Guangzhou Restaurant, 2 Wenchang Lu. Tel: 8188 4339. The largest in Canton, serving 10,000 a day, with branches south of the city, and also in Hong Kong and Los Angeles. The restaurant is famous for its sharks' fins soup and abalone sprinkled with 24K gold flakes. $$$
Panxi, 151 Longjin Xilu. Tel: 8181 5718. Established more than a century ago, this is one of the oldest restaurants in Canton. Located on the shore of Liwan Lake, there is an old pavilion where the dining room is entirely wood-panelled and decorated with antique porcelain. Regular concerts of Beijing opera and Chinese classical music are held for diners. $$
Feixia Dasha, 19 Zhongshan Qilu. Tel: 8181 3688. Serves chicken-based Qingyuan cuisine from the north of Guangdong province. $
Fo Si Jie, Niunai Changjie, off Tongfu Zhonglu. Tel: 8444 0726. Located south of the Pearl River near the small Hai Tong Si temple, this is one of the few restaurants in Canton that serves Buddhist vegetarian food. $
She Can Guan, 43 Jianglan Lu. Tel: 8188 3811. For a taste of the exotic. This restaurant has been specialising in snake meat for the past 80 years. Try longhufeng soup, a dish prepared with snake, cat and chicken meat. $
Xin Jia Lu, 383 Renmin Zhonglu. Tel:

8188 7992. Another restaurant serving unusual dishes. The house speciality of country rat meat is delicately called Super Deer. $
Lai Wan Market Garden Hotel, 368 Huangshi Donglu. Tel: 8333 8989. Specialises in dim sum and serves two Cantonese varieties of rice gruel: teng chai chuk made of pork, beef, fish, shrimp, cuttlefish, and kap tai chuk made with fish, beef and pork liver. $$

OTHER CHINESE CUISINES

Chaozhou Garden China Hotel, Liuhua Lu. Tel: 8666 3888. Teochew cuisine, also called Chaozhou or Chiu Chao, is much lighter than Cantonese food. Ask for sharks' fin soup (yu chi), cold marinated goose with vinegar (lou si ngoh), fish with plum sauce and bae-fu noodles. $$
South Sea Fishing Village, 350 Huangshi Donglu. Tel: 8346 1111. Teochew seafood restaurant which offers huge lobsters from Hainan. Famous for its waitresses in dresses slit to the hip with fur stoles slung around their shoulders in winter. Look out for the owner's Rolls-Royce parked at the restaurant entrance. Frequented by the emerging Canton nouveau riche class. $$$
Tong Kong, 337 Zhongshan Xilu. Tel: 8333 5568, 8333 5343. Hakka food from the northeast of Guangdong is often salted down but not spicy. Try the house speciality of chicken baked in salt (yim kuk kai). $
Gourmet Corner, Mezzanine fl, Office Tower, China Hotel, Liuhua Lu. Tel: 8666 3888. Serves hot-pot (siji huoguo), a meal of Mongolian origin. Diners cook fresh meat, seafood and vegetables in a pot of boiling stock. $
Four Seasons China Hotel, Liuhua Lu. Tel: 8666 3888. Excellent Peking duck and seasonal dishes. $$
Northern Province, Mezzanine fl, White Swan Hotel, 1 Shamian Nanlu. Tel: 8188 6968. Specialises in Sichuan food. The well known resident Sichuanese chef used to cook for Deng Xiaoping. $$
Food Street, Ground fl, China Hotel Liuhua Lu. Tel: 8666 3888. Serves a combination of regional foods. Good Shanghainese xiao long bao buns. $
Dai Jia Lu, 3/F Yixing Guesthouse, 728 Dongfeng Donglu. Tel: 8778 2989. Serves food of the Dai minority of Yunnan. $

Matham al-Muslimin, corner of Zhongshan Liulu and Renmin Zhonglu Serves Hui (Chinese Muslim) food, which is basically Chinese food without pork and using halal meat from ritually-killed animals. Try the mutton kebabs, and candied apple fritters. $

Guangzhou Muslimin Fanguan, 2 Sanyun Li. Tel: 8666 1624. Muslim food from Xinjiang (Chinese Turkestan). Ask for shorba, a thick soup, mutton kebab and lahmien, thick fresh noodles with mutton, tomatoes, green pepper and other vegetables. $

OTHER ASIAN CUISINES

Hirata, Mezzanine fl, White Swan Hotel, 1 Shamian Nanlu. Tel: 8188 6968. The only genuine Japanese restaurant in Canton, according to local Japanese residents. Food prepared by well-trained Cantonese cooks and supervised by a Japanese maître d'. $$$

Dong Nam Ya Canting, 105 Haoxian Lu. Tel: 8335 1654. Serves food from Cambodia, Indonesia, Laos, Thailand and Vietnam, prepared by overseas Chinese returnees from Southeast Asia. Located near the Pearl River, not far from the end of Beijing Lu. $

Yue Nan Caiguan, Longjin Xilu. Serves good Vietnamese food, in particular excellent cha gio (spring rolls). $

Hong Kong

Chinese Bodhi Vegetarian, 32–34 Lock Rd, Tsimshatsui. Tel: 2739 2222. A good place to sample mushroom, beancurd and imitation 'meat' dishes which the Cantonese describe as 'Buddhist monk's fare'. Vegetarian dim sum in the afternoon. $–$$

Carrianna Chiu Chow, 151 Gloucester Rd, Wanchai. Tel: 2511 1282 and Hilton Tower, Tsimshatsui East. Tel: 2724 4828. Some of the best value Chiu Chow food in town, except luxury items like shark's fin. Go for staples like fried e-fu noodles and pomfret fish. $$–$$$

Dim Sum, 63 Sing Woo Rd, Happy Valley. Tel: 2834 8893. Wonderful dim sum in a retro-nostalgia setting, away from the tourist circuit. $–$$

Great Shanghai, 26 Prat Ave, Tsimshatsui. Tel: 2366 8158. This massive eatery with a 400-item menu lives up to its name. Tasty traditional home-style cooking from Shanghai and the Yangtze River region. $–$$

Han Lok Yuen Restaurant, 16–17

Hung Shing Ye, Yung Shue Wan, Lamma Island. Tel: 2982 0608/0680. Relaxed family-run restaurant with a terrace overlooking Hung Shing Ye beach. Minced quail in lettuce and roast pigeon are the house specialities but seafood dishes are also good. Closed Monday. $

Jumbo Floating Restaurant Shum Wan, Wong Chuk Hang Aberdeen Harbour. Tel: 2553 9111. A theatrically-decorated palace of twinkling lights in the middle of a junk and yacht-choked waterway. The food's only so-so but the unabashedly kitschy setting is memorable. $–$$

Kung Tak Lam Shanghai Vegetarian Restaurant, 31 Yee Wo St, Causeway Bay. Tel: 2890 3127. Imaginative and, if requested, MSG-free vegetarian fare from a renowned family enterprise established a century ago. $$

Luk Yu Tea House, 24–26 Stanley St, Central. Tel: 2523 5464. A 1930s tea house with an atmosphere that is classic: dark wooden booths, marble-backed chairs, brass spittoons and surly waiters. Some of the best dim sum in town. $$

Man Wah, 25th Fl, Mandarin Oriental Hotel, 5 Connaught Rd, Central. Tel: 2522 0111. Gracious service combined with stunning harbour views and elegant surroundings make this one hard to beat. Mouthwatering Cantonese food complemented by Imperial dishes and a superb wine list. Smart dress, reservations essential. $$$$

One Harbour Road, 8th Fl, Grand Hyatt Hotel, 1 Harbour Rd, Wanchai. Tel: 2588 1234. The classic Cantonese menu, wine list and service are all topnotch. The setting is stunning, complete with trees and lily pond and spectacular harbour views. Smart dress, reservations essential. $$$–$$$$

Peking Garden Alexandra House, 6 Ice House St, Central (and other locations). Tel: 2526 6456. An enjoyable introduction to northern Chinese cuisine, including the famous Peking duck; order beggar's chicken and join in the clay-breaking ceremony. $$–$$$

Steam & Stew Inn, 21–23 Tai Wong St E, Wanchai. Tel: 2529 3913. Tasty casseroles and other homely, MSG-free. Cantonese and Shanghainese fare served with unusual nutty red rice. Frequented by local political luminaries and often packed. $

Red Pepper, 7 Lan Fong Rd, Causeway

Bay. Tel: 2577 3811. The spicy hot Szechuan food is a perennial favourite with expats and tourists but the service can be a bit brusque. $$–$$$

Tai Woo, 17–19 Wellington St, Central. Tel: 2524 5618 (and other locations). Seafood is the forte of this highly-rated Cantonese restaurant. Set menus are a boon to the uninitiated. $$

Tin Tin Seafood Harbour, 4th Fl, Elizabeth House, 250 Gloucester Rd, Causeway Bay. Tel: 2833 6683 (and other locations). Boisterous Cantonese seafood palace where staff communicate by walkie-talkie. Choose from an selection of fish and crustaceans in tanks. $$

Yung Kee, 32–40 Wellington St, Central. Tel: 2523 1624/2343. A local dining institution for over 50 years, this Cantonese restaurant is famous for its speciality roast goose. Its four floors accommodate as many as 1,000 diners at one sitting. $$

OTHER ASIAN

Banana Leaf Curry House, 440 Jaffe Rd, Wanchai. Tel: 2537 8187 (and other locations). Popular Malaysian restaurant serving a delectable medley of Malay, Indian and Straits Chinese favourites on banana leaves instead of plates. $–$$

Gaylord, 1st Fl, Ashley Centre, 23-25 Ashley Rd, Tsimshatsui. Tel: 2376 1001/1991. One of the oldest, plushest Indian restaurants in town. $$

Gu Gu Jang Korean Barbecue, 3rd Fl, Caroline Ctr, 28 Yun Ping Rd, Causeway Bay. Tel: 2577 2021. Nibble on spring onion pancakes while you watch marinated meat and fish sizzle to perfection on a table-top hotplate. $$

Her Thai, Tower 1, China Hong Kong City Canton Rd, Tsimshatsui. Tel: 2735 8898. Excellent Thai food with added attraction of panoramic views. $$

Indochine 1929, California Tower, 30-32 D'Aguilar St, Lan Kwai Fong, Central. Tel: 2869 7399. Designer-chic recreation of yesteryear Vietnam. Excellent food and the verandah-style interior evokes images of bygone French colonial elegance. $$$

Koh-I-Noor, California Entertainment Bldg, 34 D'Aguilar St, Central. Tel: 2877 9706 (and other locations). Delicately spiced Mughlai, tandoori and other delicious fare from northern India. $–$$

Kublai's, 3rd Fl, One Capital Place, 18

Luard Rd, Wanchai. Tel: 2529 9117 (and other locations). All-you-can-eat Mongolian barbecue restaurant. Good value for money. $

Lee Kam Kee Vietnamese Restaurant, 53 Pilkem St, Yaumatei. Tel: 2735 7703 (and other locations). Authentic traditional Vietnamese food at rock bottom prices. Specialities include crispy stuffed pancakes (*bánh xèo*) and meat stew with vermicelli (*bún bò Hué*). $

Nadaman Island Shangri-La Hotel, Pacific Place, 88 Queensway, Admiralty. Tel: 2820 8570. Gracious service and elegant surroundings heighten the gastronomic pleasure of fine Japanese cuisine. $$$$

Rangoon Hoi Kung Building, 265 Gloucester Rd, Causeway Bay. Tel: 2893 2281. Warm, friendly little place offering a rare chance to sample Burmese food outside of Myanmar. $

Tokio Joe, 16 Lan Kwai Fong, Central. Tel: 2525 1889. Pleasantly avant garde sushi bar and Japanese restaurant with good value set lunches. $$$

Woodlands International, Ground Fl, Mirador Tower, 61 Mody Rd, Tsimshatsui Easr. Tel: 2369 3718. Good Indian vegetarian food in a relaxed environment. Try the crispy dosai pancakes and thali appetizers. $

East-West Cafe Deco Bar & Grill, Level 1 & 2, Peak Galleria, 118 Peak Rd, The Peak. Tel: 2849 5111. Eclectic menu strong on pizza, tandoori and Thai. Spectacular city views and live jazz each evening. Dinner reservations advised, especially for one of the window tables. $$–$$$

Peak Cafe, 121 Peak Rd, The Peak. Tel: 2849 7868. Good Mediterranean and pan-Asian fare in a picturesque old colonial building with a vaulted ceiling. The leafy terrace is perfect for romantic dinners. High on charm and very popular so book ahead. $$–$$$

Wyndham Street Thai, 38 Wyndham St, Central. Tel: 2869 2616. Inspired Thai food with an Australian slant in a designer-chic setting. Good wine list. Reservations advised. $$$–$$$$

WESTERN

American Pie California Entertainment Building, 34–36 D'Aguilar St, Central. Tel: 2877 9779. New England eatery famous for its sublime desserts. The Mississippi mud and banana cream pies, and New York

cheesecake are positively sinful; salads and main dishes are good too. $$

Casa Lisboa, 20 Staunton St, Central. Tel: 2869 9631. Traditional Portuguese fare, enthusiastic young staff and a warm, southern European ambience. $$

Dan Ryan's Chicago Grill, 114 The Mall, Pacific Place, 88 Queensway, Admiralty. Tel: 2845 4600 and 200 Ocean Terminal, Harbour City, Tsimshatsui. Tel: 2735 6111. Bustling, 1950s-style American brasserie serving the biggest and best burgers in town. $$–$$$

Gaddi's, 1st Fl, The Peninsula Hotel, Salisbury Rd, Tsimshatsui. Tel: 2366 6251 Ext 3171. Superlatively classy restaurant that deserves every one of the accolades it receives for its classic French cooking, fine wines, impeccable service and elegant setting. Reservations, smart dress essential. $$$$

Grissini, 2nd Fl, The Grand Hyatt Hotel, 1 Harbour Rd, Wanchai. Tel: 2588 1234 Ext 7313. Mouthwateringly delicious Milanese food, charming service, striking modern interior and spectacular harbour views add up to one chic, very classy yet pleasantly relaxed Italian hotel restaurant. $$$–$$$$

Harry Ramsden's, 213 Queen's Rd East, Wanchai. Tel 2832 9626. A cheery retro-nostalgia fish 'n chips restaurant from Yorkshire. Great family-dining with generous portions, and friendly staff. $

Il Mercato California Entertainment Building, 34–36 D'Aguilar St, Central. Tel: 2868 3068. Unpretentious Italian trattoria in the heart of trendy Lan Kwai Fong. $$

Michelle's at the Fringe, 1st Fl, South Block 2, Lower Albert Rd, Central. Tel: 2877 4000. Good Continental menu, well-chosen wine list, pleasant service, lovely arty dining room and an aura of romantic intimacy. $$$

Post 97, 9–11 Lan Kwai Fong, Central. Tel: 2810 9333. Trendy European cafe-restaurant with a welcoming ambience and imaginative menu. Tasty vegetarian options and herb teas for the health-conscious. $$

Shanghai

Dongfeng Restaurant, 3 Zhongshan Lu. Suzhou and Cantonese cuisine.

Gongdeling Sucaiguan, 43 Huanghe Lu. Tel: 327 1532. Vegetarian specialities.

Meilongzhen, 1081 Nanjing Xilu. Tel: 255

1157. Yangzi cuisine, Sichuan cuisine.

Shanghai Lao Fandian, Near Yuyuan. Tel: 328.2782. Shanghai cuisine.

Sichuan Fandian, 457 Nanjing Lu. Tel: 322.2247. Spicy Sichuan cuisine.

Yangzhou Restaurant, Nanjing Donglu. Yangzhou specialities.

Drinking Notes

In most hotel rooms are thermos flasks with hot and cold water, and bags with green or black tea (*hong*, or red). A cup of hot tea, or just "white" tea (hot water), as the Chinese usually drink it, is the most effective way of quenching your thirst. At meal times, Chinese beer, which contain less alcohol than European beer, mineral water or lemonade (often very sweet) are offered in addition to the ubiquitous green tea.

While being in drunk in public is considered unacceptable in China (unlike in Japan, for example), there is a surprisingly large choice of Chinese spirits on offer. The most famous are *maotai jiu*, a 55-percent spirit made of wheat and sorghum that, for centuries, has been produced in Maotai, in Guizhou Province, and *wuliangye jiu*, a spirit made from five different grains. You'll either take to it immediately or not in a lifetime. Chinese wine, both red and white, tend to be very sweet, tasting a bit like sherry. Wine for foreign tastes is also being produced now.

Attractions

Group Travel

The simplest and most comfortable way of travelling to China at a reasonable price is in a group. Participants will have their passage, hotel accommodation and full board, and sightseeing program booked in advance. There are hardly any additional costs apart from drinks and shopping. Sometimes, additional excursions may be on offer once you have arrived, but they are generally not too costly. Some places charge for taking photographs.

The local tour guide is supplied by the Chinese tourist office and is in charge of taking you to the sights.

Specialists will have better knowledge of places of special interest when planning a particular route. Also, the pitfalls of a journey through China have increased rather than diminished in recent years; an experienced tour operator can avoid many difficulties.

Another decisive factor for a successful group trip is the tour guide. While each group with more than ten participants is allocated a permanent Chinese guide in addition to the local guides, their qualifications vary considerably, both in terms of organising the trip and in their knowledge of the country and its sights, and their ability to communicate. The importance of the guide employed by the tour operator shouldn't be underestimated.

A number of tour operaters now offer trips around a theme as well as the traditional routes. A few offer courses in shadow boxing, calligraphy or acupuncture; some even offer language courses.

Individual Travel

There are three ways of travelling in China for the individual traveller. The most comfortable, and of course, most expensive way, is to book a full package tour through an experienced travel agent. Everything is pre-booked, including flights and journeys, accommodation, full board, transfers etc., with the difference that the traveller can choose a route according to their preference. The same is the case for sightseeing: a guide from a China travel agency is available in each town and will help with putting together and arranging a sightseeing program.

The second possibility is booking a mini-package tour. The agent pre-books the flights, accommodation with breakfast, transfers and transport of luggage in China while the traveller is responsible for organising sightseeing. The traveller is met at the airport or railway station of each town and taken to the hotel. Each hotel has a travel agency counter, where you can discuss your plans for sightseeing and have them arranged for a fee.

You can usually have lunch and dinner at your hotel or maybe try a Chinese restaurant while out and about.

The individual tourist may have the most pleasant travel. The most essential bookings have been made (to make them yourself requires a lot of time and strong nerves), and with thorough preparation, you have a good chance of getting to know China beyond the usual tourist routes. You should get a definite booking with an experienced travel agent three months before departure at the latest.

Then, there is also the completely independent travel, without any pre-booking. This form of travelling in China has increased in recent years. The Chinese travel bureaus have partially adapted to it and can help, in the large towns, with buying air and train tickets. You have to arrange your own air and train tickets at each place you visit; unless you speak Chinese, you will probably find it easiest to do this through a travel agency, where it is more likely you will find English-speaking staff. At airports and stations, you will often find that information about destinations is given in Pinyin, or sometimes only in Chinese characters. You shouldn't expect last-minute plans to come through; it can easily happen that you have to wait several days for your railway or air ticket, or abandon your chosen destination and choose a different town for your next visit. You should try and reserve air or rail tickets as soon as you arrive. Tickets cost more for foreigners than for Chinese, and only in rare cases might you succeed (for instance if you have a student card) in getting a ticket at the cost that overseas Chinese pay.

Travel agencies will book hotels for a relatively small fee, though this is typically only the case with hotels in the more expensive range. It is best to approach cheaper hotels or guest houses directly; here, a knowledge of Chinese is an advantage.

Culture

Museums

There are a great variety of museums in China. From the revolution to natural history, everything is captured in exhibitions at various places. Many Chinese museums are not very well administered and not easy for the visitor to appreciate. English labeling is the exception. Recommended below are mainly museums in the field of art and

culture. Opening hours are usually between 9am and 5pm.

BEIJING

Museum of Chinese History (Zhongguo Lishi Bowuguan), Tiananmen Square. Tel: 55 8321. On Tiananmen Square. It is one of the most comprehensive and best museums in China covering the entire Chinese history.
Military Museum, Fuxingmenwai Dajie. Tel: 801 4441.
Museum of the Revolution (Zhongguo Geming Bowuguan), Tiananmen Square. Tel: 55 8321.
Palace Museum in the Imperial Palace (Gugong Bowuguan). Tel: 513 2255. The Imperial Palace is one huge museum; occasionally it has special exhibitions.
Lu Xun Museum, Fuchengmennei Dajie. Tel: 603 7617.
Xu Beihong Memorial Hall, Xinjiekou Beidajie. Tel: 66 1592.
Museum of Chinese Art (Beijing Meishu Zhanlanguan), 1 Wusi Dajie, Chaoyangmennei. Tel: 401 7076.
The Beijing Agricultural Exhibition Hall (Nongye Zhanlanguan), Sanlitun. Tel: 58 2331.

CHANGSHA

Hunan Provincial Museum. The museum mainly contains objects which were discovered in a Han tomb near Man-wangdui, 3 km (˘ mi) east of the museum. They include the perfectly preserved corpse of a 50-year-old woman.

NANJING

Nanjing Museum. 321, Zhongshan Donglu. The most precious exhibit, in addition to pottery, porcelain (including some from the Ming Dynasty), bronzes, tortoise shells and jewellery from various dynasties, is a 2,000-year-old shroud made of 26,000 jade pieces.

SHANGHAI

Shanghai Museum of Art (Yan'an Lu). West of Xizang Lu. It houses one of the best collections of Chinese art history. It has bronzes, pottery, stone figures, weapons as well as an excellent collection of Chinese painting from the Tang dynasty to the end of the Qing dynasty.

ÜRÜMQI

Xinjiang Provincial Museum (Xinjiang Bowuguan). It contains an archaeological exhibition about the Silk Road as well as an exhibition about the minorities in Xinjiang.

WUHAN

Hubei Provincial Museum. It is located on the western shore of Lake Donghu and has finds from a tomb of a prince from the 5th century BC. They include unique bronze chimes with 65 well perserved bronze bells which can still be sounded. Other bronzes and musical instruments were also found in the tomb.

XI'AN

Shaanxi Provincial Museum. The museum is located in the former Confucian temple found in the south of the town. It has three departments: the history of Xi'an and its surroundings to the end of the Tang Dynasty, Stele forest, and stone sculptures. It also regularly holds special exhibitions.
Museum of the Terracotta Soldiers of the First Qin Emperor. In Lintong county near the tomb of Emperor Qin Shi Huangdi.

Concerts

There are regular concerts of Western classical or traditional Chinese music in various cities. Indigenous or foreign songs and musical performances are often part of the program. Dance performances are also common. In many areas – particularly in those of the national minorities – you can admire performances of local dances and songs on the stage. Ballet is also performed. Young people – though not only them – are very keen on concerts by various pop stars, whether from the PR of China, Hong Kong or even Taiwan. You can find out about time and place of performances in each town from the hotel or through travel agencies.

Operas

There are more than 300 types of opera in China. You can attend performances of traditional opera in virtually every town. The most famous one is the Beijing Opera. The address of the opera and theatre is available from the hotel or from travel agencies. A visit to the Chinese opera is a relaxed affair and occasionally quite noisy. You can leave your evening dress and tie at home; normal day clothes are fine.

BEIJING OPERA

Liyuan Theater, Qianmen Hotel, Yong'an Lu. Daily performances in a large theater.
Gong Wangfu Huayuan. Small theater in the former residence of Prince Gong, just north of Beihai Gongyuan (Park). Performances daily at 7.30pm.

Acrobatics

Acrobatics is popular throughout China. Almost every large town has its own troupe of acrobats. Many of the troupes tour the country. You can get details of time and place of performances locally. In big cities such as Beijing, Shanghai and Guangzhou, there are permanent performances. In China, acrobatics means a mixture of proper acrobatics, magic and animal acts, and of course clowns. Circus performances are similar.

Nightlife
Pubs & Bars

Nightlife is not particularly widespread in China, except in Hong Kong and perhaps Guangzhou. Most restaurants close early, and theaters and concerts generally finish before 10pm. In southern Chinese towns, there is more life at night, with restaurants, bars, and cafes open till midnight or even later. *China Daily* has a good listing of cultural life, particularly in cities like Beijing and Shanghai.

There are, of course, bars in hotels, offering both Chinese and foreign drinks. Also, in the larger cities, some places resembling pubs have opened, meeting places for affluent youths.

Far more common than these 'pubs' are karaoke bars. The Japanese-style singalong bars have swept China, increasing the planet's off-key harmonies considerably. Most are easily recognised by the letters 'OK' amongst the characters for their names. Some are relatively pricey – members of China's *nouveau riche* are happy to show off by paying amounts that would seem wildly extravagant to most of the country's workers. Also, some of these bars are fronts for prostitution; such hostess-style bars are illegal, and can fleece customers.

Discos

Discotheques are popular throughout China and can be found in a number

of towns. Many hotels have their own discos, which are frequented by well-off local youths. The most fashionable dances are as well-known here as anywhere else in the world. Many discos – particularly in the hotels – are often open until after midnight.

Festivals
General

Holidays such as National Day and International Labour Day are fixed on the modern calendar, but most traditional festivals and events are determined by the lunar calendar, which means the date varies a little from year to year.

January / February

The most important festival time is the Lunar New Year, or **Spring Festival**, which falls in late January or early February. Public buildings are festooned with colored lights, people from all over China travel to reunite with families, debts are settled, and there is food consumed – lots of it. On the first days of the lunar year, Chinese visit family and friends. In recent years, a more relaxed atmosphere has brought the revival of old Spring Festival traditions, such as giving *hongbao* – small, red envelopes containing money – to children and young adults. Temple fairs feature martial arts demonstrations, stand-up comic sketches, homemade toys and, of course, food.

Northerners, who have amazing resilience to the bitterly cold winters, partake with gusto in ice-sculpting competitions and winter swimming. The time and duration of the festivals depends on the weather.

Both Beijing and Harbin are noted for their ice-sculpting festivals.

April

On the 12th day of the third lunar month, in the beginning of April, the

Chinese honor their deceased ancestors by observing **Qingming**, sometimes referred to as the 'grave-sweeping' day. It is much less impressive nowadays, as people are cremated instead of being buried. Qingming is a time for remembering ancestors, but also for reveling on a warm spring day.

May / June

International Labor Day is a one-day public holiday. Following hot on its heels is **Youth Day**, a commemoration of the May 4th Movement of 1919, reflected by large editorials and government hoopla in the official press. **International Children's Day** is celebrated in earnest on June 1, by letting classes out early and treating children to outings at public parks.

July / August

July 1 is the **Anniversary of the Communist Party**, which was founded in Shanghai in 1921. This means very little to the average citizen but plenty of fun for high-level party members.

The fifth day of the fifth lunar month – usually late July – brings the **Dragon Boat Festival**, marked by dragon boat races in many cities, sometimes involving teams from around the world. It commemorates the memory of Qu Yuan (340–278BC), a poet in the days of the Kingdom of Chu, who, rather than submit to political pressure, drowned himself in the Miluo river, in Hunan. To prevent the fishes from eating his body, the people threw glutinous rice cakes into the river. Nowadays, these *zongzi* are simply eaten to mark the occasion.

August 1 is the **Anniversary of the People's Liberation Army**. Inaugurated in 1927 and formerly marked by enormous parades, it is now noted mainly in the media.

September / October

The **Mid-Autumn Festival** again depends on when the moon reaches its fullest, usually around mid-September. The shops do great business in 'moon cakes' – pastries filled with gooey sesame paste, red-bean and walnut filling. *Tang yuan*, glutinous rice flour balls with sweet fillings in sugar syrup, and *yue bing*, a cake baked specifically for this occasion, are eaten. In the tradition of poets, this is the time to drink a bit of wine and toast the moon.

Late September is normally the time when Chinese communities celebrate the memory of Confucius.

October 1 is the PRC's birthday, **National Day**, celebrated with a two-day public holiday. Government buildings, road intersections and hotels are decked out in lights, and flower arrangements and Sun Yatsen's portrait is displayed in Tiananmen Square. Tens of thousands turn out on the square for picture-taking and general merry-making.

November / December

November and December are quiet months in China, but **Christmas** is gaining momentum as a consumer's celebration. Christian churches hold special services that draw thousands of spectators. In Beijing, for example, it is trendy to exchange greeting cards and presents, while Santa Claus makes the odd shop appearance.

Shopping

What To Buy

Typically "Chinese" goods such as silk, jade and porcelain are still cheaper and of a better quality in Hong Kong than in the People's Republic of China. The choice varies – if you are lucky, the shelves are well stocked and you can find excellent and well-cut silk articles being sold cheaply; if the supply has dried up, you will only find meagre remnants even in Hangzhou, the centre of silk production. You will usually find good quality goods which are produced for export. These are mostly sold in the "Friendship Stores" (*Youyi Shangdian*) and in the hotel shops.

Until recently, it was not usual to bargain and it is still not advisable in the state-owned shops and warehouses. But at the many souvenir stands, it is a good idea to bargain because of the greatly overpriced goods on offer. It is also worth comparing prices in the free markets (if you can read them) and watch how much Chinese customers pay.

When buying antiques, it is essential to check that the official red seal of the shop is on the product. Buying and exporting of antiques is only permitted with this official stamp, otherwise you could meet with great difficulties when leaving the country.

It is worth looking for local products in the smaller towns or in the places where ethnic minorities live. These will be difficult to find anywhere else in China. The most usual articles are craft objects for everyday use or specially worked or embroidered garments.

Import & Export

Antiques that date from before 1795 may not be legally exported. Those that can be taken out of China must carry a small red seal or have one affixed by the Cultural Relics Bureau. All other antiques are the property of the Peoples' Republic of China and, without the seal, will be confiscated without compensation. Beware of fakes; producing new 'antiques' (and the seal) is a thriving industry.

Foreign currency can be imported and exported without restrictions. You may not export more foreign currency than you imported, except with a special permit.

You should not export, nor even buy in the first place, objects made from wild animals, especially from ivory. Most Western countries ban the import of ivory objects, and will confiscate them without compensation.

Shopping Areas

Forget any notions about an austere workers' paradise. Consumerism is the only meaningful 'ism' around China these days.

The number of *dakuan* – the fat cats with portable phones – is increasing. New markets and stores are sprouting up everywhere.

It's advisable to check prices first at state-operated stores, such as the Friendship Store, before buying a similar item in a hotel shop or on the free market. And in the free market, bargain, and be stubborn – but friendly – if interested in an item. Avoid drawn out dickering just for the sport.

Bargaining usually begins with the shopkeeper suggesting a price and the buyer responding with a lower one. In Beijing, the starting price is generally 30 to 50 percent higher than the price shopkeepers will eventually accept. Be persistent, look for missing buttons, stains and other flaws, keep smiling, and walk away if you find the price unacceptable.

Department stores: In every town is a department store selling products for everyday use, from toothpaste to a bicycle. However, the quality of clothing fabric (artificial), the cut and the sizes are usually not up to expectation.

The big department store are state-owned institutions, but many small shops and street stalls – privately owned – have sprung up as well. Here you will often find products from Hong Kong, including higher-quality clothing.

Friendship stores: A visit to the Friendship Store (*Youyi Shangdian*) is an essential part of the program of all tour groups. These stores usually offer a good selection of wares for export: silk fabric, craft articles, electronic devices, clothing and books. Often, there is a whole department offering both traditional and modern medical products and equipment. Individual travelers, too, should take the opportunity to look round these stores from time to time. The Friendship Store in Beijing, for instance, has an excellent food department. A visit to the antiques department in the Friendship Store in Shanghai is also worthwhile.

Some large Friendship Store and warehouses have a delivery section that will send purchases to one's home country. Shops and department stores generally open around 9am and close at 6pm or 7pm.

Markets: Food items such as fruit, vegetables, fish and meat are sold at markets. In the free markets, where prices are more flexible, and sometimes more expensive (off-setting higher quality and availability), there are often additional items, such as wicker baskets, metal and iron bits, and clothes; tailors are sometimes found. In the big towns, numerous street traders offer their wares well into the evening; one can often find jeans or silk blouses from Hong Kong at such places.

Watch how much the Chinese themselves pay. All too often, traders in free markets will happily fleece unwary – foreign – customers.

Beijing

SPECIALTY MARKETS

Silk Alley (Xiushui Shichang) – on Xiushiu Jie and intersecting with Chang'an Lu about 800 m east of the Friendship Store, has been growing in the past few years. As the name implies, vendors flog silk in all shapes and sizes – ties and boxer shorts, dresses and slinky nightgowns – at prices about half of that found in Hong Kong. Just a few blocks away is **Yabaolu Market**, commonly known as the Russian market (open daily 9am–6pm) and on Ritan Lu, opposite Ritan Park. It is a huge clothing market specializing in cotton and wool garments, and also goose-down jackets.

A few blocks straight north of Yabaolu Market is the **Chaowai Flea Market** (open daily 10am–6pm), a favorite shopping ground for resident diplomats and journalists. The front building is filled with antique and classical-style furniture. In the rear building are curios: snuff bottles, ceramics and Mao memorabilia. **Hongqiao Farmers' Market**, on Tiantan Lu (open daily 7am–5.30pm), has the best collection of antique clocks and Mao statues, as well as freshwater pearls.

For traditional Chinese paintings, calligraphy supplies and rare books, poke around at **Liulichang** (open daily 9am–5.30pm), just west of Qianmen district. A bit further afield, but considered to be the most reliable source of antique porcelain in Beijing, is **Jingsong Market** (open daily 9am–6pm) located at East Third Ring Road at the Jingsong east intersection.

Tucked under the southeast corner of the Xizhimen overpass, the **Bird Market** (open daily 7.30am–sunset) is hardly an extension of nature, but it has a wonderful array of feathered creatures. At least as important are the elegant handmade cages, ceramic feeders and other avian paraphernalia sold here.

There are three lively shopping streets in the city center that cater to local customers. **Wangfujing**, **Xidan** and **Dongdan**, which run perpendicular to Chang'an Lu, have mostly inexpensive local goods, with bargains on leather and furs.

At 192 Wangfujing Dajie, check out the **Jianhua Leather Goods Company** (open daily 8am–8.30pm). It has leather jackets for as little as 250 yuan and full-length mink coats running up to 18,000 yuan. Available are suede backpacks, belts and fox pelts.

Further north, along the east side of Wangfujing, is the **Foreign Languages Bookstore**, run by the China News Agency. The first floor has a wide range of books on China. The upper floors have everything from Chinese art and language tapes to computers and a music store.

All three streets are undergoing radical transformation, with more and more boutiques, watch stores and ice-cream shops replacing the old standbys. Xidan and Wangfujing are both undergoing massive rebuilding, which will expand the shopping greatly.

Among the most popular department stores for Chinese products is **Longfu Dasha** (No 95 Longfusi Jie, Chaoyang District; open daily 8.30am–8.30pm). This is the spot to buy China's most famous brands of household products – Flying Pigeon bicycles and Butterfly sewing machines.

ONE-STOP SHOPPING

Capitalism's answer for one-stop shoppers is the glossy, new joint-venture shopping centers that draw China's *nouveau riche*, as well as tourists and mobs of window shoppers. Directly across the street from the Friendship Store is the CIVIC-Yaohan (No 22 Jianguomenwai Dajie, open daily 9am–9pm), a Japanese department store full of luxury, trendy imports.

The **Youyi Shopping City** in the Beijing Lufthansa Center (No 52 Liangmaqiao Lu, Chaoyang District; open daily 9am–9pm) carries products with a broader price range. The city's best silk selection – sold by the yard – is offered at reasonable prices.

Stock up on all the beautiful things that China produces – traditional paper cuttings (cheap and easy to pack), jade carvings, kites and chopsticks – at the state-run **Friendship Store** (No 17 Jianguomenwai Dajie; open daily 9am–9pm). The store is also good for getting an estimate of what things outside should cost, and for any last-minute gifts.

Guangzhou

Don't expect the glitz and variety of goods available in Hong Kong. Still, Guangzhou offers interesting shopping and good bargains. Among Chinese cities, Guangzhou is considered to have the widest range of goods, many of which are imported from other parts of the country.

ANTIQUES

The largest private market for antiques is the **Daihe Lu Market**, which sprawls over several lanes. Access the market by the first lane on the right after entering Daihe Lu from Changshou Xilu. There are smaller antique markets nearby; one at the middle lane of the Qingping Market and the other at the Jade Market. Do not buy antiques that the vendor claims are over 100 years old. Even if not trying to rip you off (and most are), a genuine antique that is over a century old cannot be exported if it doesn't carry an official red-wax seal.

Beware of fakes, as new 'antiques' with the official seal is a thriving industry in China. Despite the difficulties, there is still much to buy: *kam muk* (gilded sculptured wood panels), vintage watches, tiny embroidered shoes for Chinese women with bound feet, and beautiful Shiwan porcelain.

If a serious collector, antiques with authentic red-wax seals authorizing export can be bought from government shops. Try the **Guangzhou Antique Shop** (146/162/170 Wende Beilu, Tel: 8333 0175, Fax: 8335 0085) for *kam muk*, calligraphy works, jewelry boxes, paintings, porcelain and silver jewelry.

CLOTHING AND TEXTILES

Guangdong province is a major production center for ready-to-wear clothes and shoes. The biggest variety is to be found at the government-owned **Friendship Stores**. These stores are your best bet for down jackets (one-fifth the price you would pay elsewhere) and cashmere sweaters and scarves. The **Bingfen Fashion Market** on Haizhu Square, the **Gong Lu Fashion Market** on Zhongshan Erlu in Dongshan District, the night market under the Quzhuang Overbridge, and the Xihu Lu night market are also good hunting grounds for apparel.

Of special interest is Guangdong black-mud silk, which is painstakingly hand-made and dyed as many as 30 times, using the red extract of the gambier root and the iron-rich river mud from the Pearl River. The material stays cool and dry in humid weather. The silk is available from the **Xin Da Xin department store**, at the corner of Beijing Lu and Zhongshan Wulu.

HANDICRAFTS

Paper Cuts: The Renshou Temple in Foshan, previously famous for its paper cuts of scenes from the Cultural Revolution, has remained the major production center for this delicate craft. However, its production nowadays focuses on farm scenes.

Bird cages: The Chinese love songbirds and show them off in splendidly-decorated cages at public parks. Antique cages cost from 100 to 700 yuan; newer ones can be bought at the **Bird Market**, located at the Dongfeng Lu entrance of Liuhua Park.

Seals: You can have your name engraved in Chinese characters on a seal, called a chop in colonial English, at the basement floor of the White Swan Hotel. When selecting your Chinese name, choose auspicious characters and limit yourself to two or three. If you need assistance, the staff at the shop will help you to choose the right combination. The material used can be hard wood, soapstone, crystal or agate. The shop will also sell you the special red ink (*hong yau*) that goes with the seal. Do not buy from side street sellers, as the seals they sell are made of bakelite and colored resin imitations of stone.

JADE AND PEARLS

Jade holds a greater fascination for the Chinese than any other stone. Traditionally, it is worn for good luck, as a protection against sickness and as an amulet for travelers. There are several types of jade: nephrite, tomb jade, jadeite, Imperial jade, and a local variety, *nanyu* jade. Do not buy from open-air private markets, as there are plenty of imitations in the market. Buy from established shops like the **Jade Shop** (12–14 Zhongshan Wulu), **Baoli Yuqi Hang** (220 Zhongshan Silu), **Guangzhou Antique Shop** (696 Wende

Lu), and the jewelry shops of the China, Garden and White Swan hotels.

For centuries, pearls have been the indispensable ornament of the nobility, especially emperors. Most of the pearls on sale in Guangzhou are salt-water southern pearls called *hepu*, cultured in silver-lipped oysters. The largest of these lustrous pearls can have a diameter of 1.2–1.6 cm. Recommended shops are: Guangzhou Gold and Silver Jewelry Center (109 Dade Lu) and Sun Moon Hall (Equatorial Hotel, Renmin Beilu).

MAO MEMORABILIA

In celebration of Mao's 100th birthday in 1993, centennial souvenirs appeared, such as commemorative watches and musical cigarette lighters playing revolutionary ditties. The Daihe Lu antique market has a reasonable variety of Mao artifacts, while the Friendship Stores sell 24K, diamond-studded medals. For badges, the stamp market in People's Park has the best pieces. Prices can be steep.

Where to Buy

The main shopping areas in Guangzhou are Zhongshan Wulu, Beijing Lu, Renmin Nanlu, Zhongshan Silu and Xiajiu Lu-Shangjiu Lu. The main open-air market is at Qingping Lu, near Shamian Island.

There are several large department stores in Guangzhou worth a visit for their wide array of foreign merchandise, at prices lower than in Hong Kong. **Nanfang Dasha** (49 Yanjiang Xilu) offers a good choice of local products. **Xihu Lu Baihuo Dasha**, on Xihu Lu, has a huge choice, especially foreign goods, at amazing prices. **Xin Da Xin**, at the corner of Beijing Lu and Zhongshan Wulu, offers a good range of Chinese goods, including silk (and the rare Guangdong black-mud silk), and a large musical instrument department. The **Guangzhou Foreign Trade Center** at the Guangzhou Fair Building, on Renmin Beilu, has a large arts and crafts department and a good choice of silk merchandise.

The government-owned **Friendship Store**, on the ground floor of the China Hotel, and the Kwangchow Friendship Store, at 369 Huanshi Donglu, opposite the Garden Hotel, offer a wide selection of goods.

Outside of Guangzhou, **Shenzhen** is considered by the Chinese as the best city in China for shopping. However, the stress is more on consumer goods than on handicrafts or art. There are several shopping centers, of which the largest is the World Trade Center. The main attraction in Shenzhen is Zhongying Lu (Anglo-Chinese Street).

Hong Kong

The Economist recently found Hong Kong to offer the best value for luxury goods among leading cities in the world.

Before browsing, pick up a copy of the HKTA's *Official Shopping Guide* – available at the HKTA Information Centres in Central and Tsimshatsui – an invaluable free booklet with many useful tips. An important thing to note about shopping in Hong Kong is that goods purchased are not normally returnable or refundable; don't make expensive purchases if not certain.

Tourists have clout in Hong Kong. If you run into significant problems with merchants that you cannot resolve, call the **HKTA's multilingual hotline**: 2807 6177. If the offending shop is a HKTA member, the tourist board will try to resolve the matter. Otherwise, it can recommend cases to the Hong Kong Consumer Council (tel: 2929 2222).

FASHION

Hong Kong tailors are as skilled as ever, at both classic tailoring and copying existing garments. Prices vary according to the work involved, as well as the quality and quantity of cloth and trimmings. A good custom-tailored shirt starts at around US$35, and a suit from about US$350. Quality tailors prefer several fittings; the so-called 24-hour suit, at rock-bottom prices, is rarely the bargain it sounds. **Tailor Kwan** (314, Worldwide Plaza, Central), **Sam's Tailor** (Burlington Arcade K, 92–94 Nathan Road, Tsimshatsui), **Yuen's Tailors** (233, Escalator Link Alley, Central Market) and **William Cheng & Son** (8th Floor, 38 Hankow Road, Tsimshatsui) are recommended.

Designer boutiques invaded Hong Kong during the 1980s, primarily to serve locals and Japanese tourists. All the big names are here – Armani, Chanel, DKNY, Issey Miyake and dozens more. They cluster in **The Land-**mark, **Pacific Place**, **Prince's Building**, **Swire House** and **Times Square Galleria** on Hong Kong-side; the topflight hotel arcades – **New World Centre** and **Harbour City** complex – and along **Canton Road** in Tsimshatsui. Don't expect lower prices than in Europe or US.

Inspiring work by up-and-coming Hong Kong designers can be found in the TDC's **Design Gallery** (Level 1, Convention Plaza, Harbour Road, Wanchai). More unusual still are quintessential Chinese *cheongsam*, Mao suits and Tang jackets available off-the-peg, or custom-tailored, from **Shanghai Tang** (Pedder Building).

For real bargains, head for the street markets and factory outlets. For a fraction of the price back home, these sell over-runs and slightly damaged 'seconds' of locally-manufactured clothes designed for the export market. As a general guide, bargain-priced women's wear, men's wear, T-shirts and jeans, and children's clothes can be found in the factory outlets along Haiphong and Granville roads, in Tsimshatsui; Spring Garden Lane and Johnston Road in Wanchai; Stanley Market and Jardine's Bazaar in Causeway Bay; and Tung Choi Street Ladies' Market and Fa Yuen Street in Mongkok. The shops in Pedder Building, Central, are good places for quality women's wear, and Temple Street Night Market has cheap men's wear.

ELECTRONICS & PHOTOGRAPHIC

If prepared to shop around, this is another area where cut-rate prices can still be found. Shops selling televisions, video cameras and recorders, laser-disc players, stereo systems, and portable tape and CD players cluster in Causeway Bay and Tsimshatsui, especially along Nathan, Peking, Mody and Carnarvon roads. Merchants can spot a sucker at fifty paces, so bargain hard; the fixed-price retail chains **Broadway Photo Supply** and **Fortress** are good alternatives.

Computer equipment can be found at the **Computer Mall** in Windsor House, Causeway Bay; **Star Computer City** in Star House and the **Silvercord Centre** in Tsimshatsui; **Mongkok Computer Centre**; **New Capital Computer Plaza** and **Golden Shopping Centre** in Sham Shui Po (the latter is renowned for pirated software). Prices for genu-ine PCs and programs are about the same as in Europe and North America.

The streets around Nathan Road are also full of camera shops. But most local professional photographers buy their film and equipment on Hong Kong-side, at **Photo Scientific Appliances** (6 Stanley Street, Central).

ART, ANTIQUES & CRAFTS

Hong Kong is a center for Asian arts and crafts, with museum-quality antique furniture, ceramics, sculptures, textiles and traditional paintings from China, Tibet, Japan, and Southeast Asia. More affordable are modern Chinese and Vietnamese paintings, Oriental rugs, reproduction Korean chests, 'antique' Chinese furniture and ceramics, Thai Buddha figurines, Balinese woodwork, Chinese folk paintings and other ethnic handicrafts.

The greatest concentration of antique and carpet dealers is along Hollywood Road and Wyndham Street in Central, but there are also a number of top-quality shops in Pacific Place, and at Harbour City and New World Centre on Kowloon-side. Fine-art galleries are considerably spread out, so it's best to check under exhibition listings in the newspapers, the free HK and BC magazines or HKTA's diary pages.

The Chinese Arts & Crafts (HK) Ltd and other PRC department stores are great places to look for Chinese arts and crafts. Shops like **Amazing Grace Elephant Co** (Harbour City, Tsimshatsui), **The Banyan Tree** (Prince's Building, Central and Harbour City), **Tequila Kola** (Prince's Building and United Centre, Admiralty), **Vincent Sum Collection** (Lyndhurst Terrace, Central) and **Mountain Folkcraft** (Wo On Lane, Central) stock furniture and craft items from elsewhere in Asia. **Welfare Handicrafts** in Jardine House and the HK Museum of Art shop are good places to pick up smaller gift items and cards.

Wanchai is the best place for customized rattan and reproduction rosewood furniture, but **Luk's Furniture** warehouse in Aberdeen is also good for reproduction 'antiques' and Korean chests. Your best bet for Chinese ceramics is a local factory, like **Wah Tung China** in Aberdeen (which also has a small outlet on Hollywood Road) and **Overjoy Porcelain Factory** in Kwai Chung, New Territories.

JEWELRY, WATCHES & GEMSTONES

Hong Kong is the world's largest jade market, the third-largest diamond trading center (after New York and Antwerp), one of the largest gold brokers, and a magnet for precious stones from all over Asia and pearls from the Pacific Rim. Many finished items are manufactured in Hong Kong, ranging from simple gold bangles to exquisite diamond necklaces.

A lot of people think they get the best buys on gold and jewelry at factory outlets in Hung Hom. But these have been flooded with bus loads of Japanese tourists in recent years and prices have risen accordingly. Better bargains, in fact, can be found in the jewelry and gold shops along Queen's Road Central. **Chinese Arts & Crafts** and other PRC department stores offer good deals on gold and jade, with a written guarantee. Top-flight hotel shopping arcades are another place to find quality jewelers. It's a good idea to get a professional gemologist to certify diamonds or other gemstones. Contact the HK **Gemological Society** at tel: 2366 6006.

Designer watch shops selling the top brands cluster along the lower end of Nathan Road in Kowloon – which is equally famous for 'copy-watch' salesmen – and in the malls of Central. **City Chain** is a reasonably-priced watch retailer, with more than 40 branches in Hong Kong. Lots of watches are for sale at the **Temple Street Market**. Be warned: they are fakes.

DEPARTMENT STORES

Hong Kong's oldest department store, **Lane Crawford**, and the upmarket Japanese store **Seibu**, in **Pacific Place**, are the local equivalents of Bloomingdale's or Harrods – classy and very expensive. For more down-to-earth prices, try long-established local department stores like **Sincere** and **Wing On**, where local people shop.

The Japanese department stores in Causeway Bay – **Sogo**, **Mitsukoshi**, **Daimaru**, **Matsuzakaya** and **Loft** – are popular with both locals as well as the Japanese expatriate community. Likewise, the several branches of **Marks & Spencer** are a little piece of England in the tropics, although considerably pricier than in the UK.

However, it's the mainland Chinese department stores that are most wor-thy of exploration, even if you don't intend to buy. **Chinese Arts & Crafts** is the most upmarket of all and concentrates on high-quality handicrafts, antiques, clothing and jewelry. **Yue Hwa and Chung Kiu Chinese Products Emporiums** stock arts and crafts, and a whole range of consumer items produced across the border. CRC **department stores** sell Chinese foodstuffs as well as inexpensive household items, ceramics and handicrafts. And finally, don't miss out on the Hong Kong-owned designer-chic 1930s-style **Shanghai Tang** department store (Pedder Building, Central), which has great retro-nostalgia Chinese fashions and gift items.

Language

General

English is increasingly being used in the People's Republic of China, but on the whole, you will still find it difficult to meet people away from the big hotels and business and tourist centres who speak English, not to mention German or French. It is therefore advisable – especially for individual travellers – to learn some Chinese. Some people joke that, apart from *meiyou* ("it doesn't exist"), the most common words in China are "change money?".

More than a billion people in China, and many other Chinese in Southeast Asia and the United States, speak Chinese. In the People's Republic of China, other languages in addition to Chinese – the language of the Han people, the original Chinese – are spoken in the regions where the national minorities are settled, including Tibetan, Mongolian, Zhuang or Uygur. But everywhere in the People's Republic today, standard Chinese, also called Mandarin, is more or less understood or spoken. Regardless of whether you are in Guangzhou or in Heilongjiang, in Tibet or in Xinjiang, you can get through with standard Chinese.

The Chinese language is divided into several groups of dialect. For instance, a native of Guangzhou or Hong Kong cannot understand someone from Beijing or vice versa, unless both speak standard Chinese. The different dialects have, however, the same grammar and vocabulary; but above all, the writing is the same. The pronunciation may differ, but the written symbols can be understood by all literate Chinese. Thus, a native of Guangzhou and a Beijing citizen can understand each other by simply writing down the symbols.

Since the 1950s, all schools in the People's Republic of China teach standard Chinese or Mandarin – also called Putonghua or common language. It is also used on radio and television. Young Chinese people, particularly, know standard Chinese. Consequently, one can manage throughout the People's Republic – including in Guangzhou – by using standard Chinese. You will immediately notice the difference when you go from Guangzhou to Hong Kong: in Hong Kong, the official language amongst the Chinese is Cantonese.

The transcription of Chinese symbols: Standard Chinese is based on the pronunciation of the northern dialects, particularly the Beijing dialect. There is an officially approved roman writing of standard Chinese, called Hanyu Pinyin (the phonetic transcription of the language of the Han people). Pinyin is used throughout the People's Republic; many public transportation facilities show name places and street names both in symbols and in the romanized transcription.

Most modern dictionaries use the pinyin system. (Taiwan, however, usually uses the older Wade-Giles transliteration system.) This transcription may at first appear confusing if one doesn't see the words as they are pronounced. The city of Qingdao, for example, is pronounced *chingdow*. It would definitely be useful, particularly for individual travellers, to familiarize yourself a little with the pronunciation of pinyin. Even when asking for a place or street name, you need to know how it is pronounced, otherwise you won't be understood. This guide uses the pinyin system throughout for Chinese names and expressions.

The pronunciation of Chinese: The

pronunciation of the consonants is similar to those in English. b, p, d, t, g, k are all voiceless. p, t, k are aspirated, b, d, g are not aspirated. The i after the consonants ch, c, r, sh, s, z, zh is not pronounced, it indicates that the preceding sound is lengthened.

Pinyin/English transcript/Sound

a/a/f**a**r
an /un/r**un**
ang/ung /l**ung**
ao/ou/l**ou**d
b/b/**b**ath
c/ts/ra**ts**
ch/ch/**ch**ange
d/d/**d**ay
e/er/d**ir**t
ie (after i,u,y)/a/tr**a**m
ei/ay/m**ay**
en/en/wh**en**
eng/eong/**ng** has a nasal sound
er/or/hon**or**
f/f/**f**ast
g/g/**g**o
h/ch/lo**ch**
i/ee/k**ee**n
j/j/**j**eep
k/k/**c**ake
l/l/**l**ittle
m/m/**m**onth
n/n/**n**ame
o/o/b**o**nd
p/p/tra**pp**ed
q/ch/**ch**eer
r/r/**r**ight
s/s/me**ss**
sh/sh/**sh**ade
t/t/**t**on
u/oo/sh**oo**t
ü (after j,q,x,y)/as German u+/m**u+de**
w/w/**w**ater
x/**ch**/as in Scottish lo**ch**, followed by s
y/y/**y**ogi
z/ds/re**ds**
zh/dj/**j**ungle

It is often said that the Chinese language is monosyllabic. At first sight this may seem the case since, generally, each symbol is one word. However, in modern Chinese, most words are made up of two or three syllable symbols, sometimes more.

Chinese generally lacks syllables, there are only 420 in Mandarin to represent all symbols in sounds or tones. The tones are used to differentiate – a specifically Chinese practice which often makes it very difficult for foreigners when first learning the Chinese lan-guage. Each syllable has a specific sound. These sounds often represent different meanings. For instance, if one pronounces the syllable *mai* with a falling fourth sound (mài) it means to sell; if it is pronounced with a falling-rising third sound, mai, it means to buy. When one reads the symbols carefully this is always clearly shown. To show this again with the simple syllable ma:

First sound *ma* mother
second sound *má* hemp
third sound *ma* horse
fourth sound *mà* to complain

The Chinese language has four tones and a fifth, 'soundless' sound: The first tone is spoken high pitched and even, the second rising, the third falling and then rising, and the fourth sound falling. The individual tones are marked above the vowel in the syllable in the following way: First tone -, second tone ´, third tone ˇ, fourth tone `.

The Chinese sentence structure is simple: subject, predicate, object. The simplest way of forming a question is to add the question particle 'ma' to a sentence in ordinary word sequence. It is usually not possible to note from a Chinese word whether it is a noun, adjective or another form, singular or plural. This depends on the context.

The Chinese language is a language of symbols or pictures. Each symbol represents a one-syllable word. There are in total more than 47,000 symbols, though modern Chinese only use a part of these. For a daily paper, between 3,000 and 4,000 symbols are sufficient. Scholars know between 5,000 and 6,000. Many symbols used to be quite complicated. After 1949, several reforms in the written language were introduced in the People's Republic in order to simplify the written language. Today, the simplified symbols are used throughout the People's Republic, though in Hong Kong and Taiwan, the complex ones are still used.

Many Chinese words are composed of two or more symbols or single-syllable words. For instance, the Chinese word for film is *dian-ying*, and is made up of the two words: *dian* for electricity and *ying* for shadow. To make reading easier, the pinyin system joins syllables which, together, form words. Group travellers generally have translators with them to whom they can turn in case of communication problems. But if you are travelling on your own, it is worth taking a dictionary with you.

Further Reading
Other Insight Guides

Looking for more on China? More detailed information on Beijing? Descriptive, entertaining walking itineraries for Guangzhou (Canton)? In-depth information on Hong Kong? Consider, then, these other Apa Publications guides:

USEFUL PHRASES

Greetings

How are you?	Nǐ hǎo	你好
How are you?	Nǐ hǎo mǎ?	你好吗?
Thank you	Xièxìe	谢谢
Good bye	Zài jiàn	再见
My name is…	wǒ jiào….	我叫…
My last name is…	wǒ xìng…	我姓…
What is your name?	Nín jiào shénme míngzì?	您叫什么名字?
What is your last name?	Nín guìxìng?	您贵姓?
I am very happy…	Wǒ hěn gāoxìng …	我很高兴…
All right	Hǎo	好
Not all right	Bù hǎo	不好
Can you speak English?	Nín huì shūo yīngyǔ mǎ?	您会说英语吗?
Can you speak Chinese?	Nín huì shuō hànyù mǎ?	您会说汉语吗?
I cannot speak Chinese	Wǒ bú huì Hànyǔ.	我不会汉语。
I do not understand	Wǒ bùdǒng.	我不懂。
Do you understand?	Nín dǒng mǎ?	您懂吗?
Please speak a little slower	Qīng nín shuō màn yìdiǎnr.	请您说慢一点儿!
What is this called?	Zhègè jiào shénme?	这个叫什么?
How do you say…	…..zěnmè shuō?	…怎么说?
Please/Thank you	Qǐng/Xièxiè	请/谢谢
Never mind	Méi Guānxì	没关系
Sorry	Duìbùqǐ	对不起

Pronouns

Who/Who is it?	Shéi?	谁
My/mine	wo/wode	我/我的
You/yours (singular)	nǐ/nǐdè	你/你的
He/his	tā/tādè	他/他的
We/ours	wǒmén/wǒméndè	我们/我们的
You/yours (plural)	nǐmen/nǐméndě	你们/你们的
They/theirs	tāmèn/tāmènde	他们/他们的
You/yours (respectful term when addressing seniors)	Nín/Nínde	您/您的

Travel

Where is it?	…zài nǎr?	…在哪儿?
Do you have it here?	Zhèr yǒu …. mǎ?	这儿有…吗?
Hotel	fàndiàn	饭店
Restaurant	fànguǎn	饭馆
Bank	yìnháng	银行
Post Office	yóujú	邮局
Toilet	cèsuǒ	厕所
Railway Station	huǒchēzhàn	火车站
Bus Station	(gōnggòngqì) chēzhàn	公共汽车站
Embassy	dàshíguǎn	大使馆
Consulate	lǐngshìguǎn	领事馆
Passport	hùzhaò	护照

Visa	qiānzhèng	签证
Medicine shop	yàodiàn	药店
Hospital	yīyuàn	医院
Doctor	yīshēng	医生
Translate	fānyì	翻译
Bar	jǐubā	酒吧
Rented car	chūzqìzhē	出租汽车
Do you have…?	Nín yōu…. mǎ?	您有…吗?
I want/I think I want	Wǒ yào/wǒ xǐang yào	我要/我想要
I want to buy…	Wǒ xǐang mǎi …… .	我想买……
Can I buy it there?	Nǎr néng mǎi ….. mà?	哪能买…吗?
This/that	zhège/nèige	这个/那个
Green tea/red tea	lǜchá/hóngchá	绿茶/红茶
Coffee	kāfēi	咖啡
Cigarette	xiāngyān	香烟
Films	jiāojuǎnr	胶卷儿
Ticket	piào	票
Post card	míngxìnpiàn	明信片
A letter	yì fēng xìn	一封信
Air mail	yì fēng hángkōngxìn	一封航空信
Postage stamp	yóupiào	邮票

Shopping

How much…?	Duōshǎo?	多少?
How much does this cost/ What is the price…	Zhègē duōshǎo qían?	这个多少钱?
Too expensive, thank you	Tài gùile, xièxiè.	太贵了，谢谢。
Very expensive	Hěn gùi.	很贵。
A little (bit)	Yìdiǎnr.	一点儿。
Too much	tài duōle	太多了
A lot	dūo	多
Few	shǎo	少

Money Matters

Cash/money	qián	钱
Chinese currency	Rénmínbì	人民币
One dollar	yì yuán	一元
Ten cents	yì jiǎo	一角
One cent	yì fēn	一分
Traveller's cheques	lǚxíngzhīpiào	旅行支票
Credit card	xìnyòngkǎ	信用卡
Foreign currency	wàihuìquàn	外汇卷
Where can one change money?	Zài nár kěyī huànqián?	在哪可以换钱?
I want to change money	Wǒ yào huàn qián.	我要换钱
What is the conversion rate?	bǐ jìa shì duō shǎo?	比价是多少?
We want to rent a car for one/two/three persons	Wǒmén yào zhù yì (liǎng, sān …) tiān.	我们要住一 (俩，叁…)天。
What is the room rates for a day?	Fángjīan duōshǎo qián yì tiān?	房间多少钱一天?
Hotel	fàndiàn	饭店
Room	fángjīan	房间
Single room/double room	dānrén fángjīan/shúangrén fángjīan	单人房间/双人房间

393

Airport	fēijīchǎng	飞机场
Bus	gōngoǹqìchē	公共汽车
Rented car	chūzhūqìchē	出租汽车
Telephone	diànhùa	电话
Long distance call	chángtú diànhùa	长途电话
Telephone number	diànhùa haòmǎ	电话号码
Reception	fúwútai	服务台
Telegram	diànbào	电极
Telex	diànchúan	电传
Key	yàoshì	钥匙
Clothes	yīfù	衣服
Luggage	xínglì	行李

Restaurants

Waiter	fúwúyuán	服务员
Miss/Madam	xǐaojǐe	小姐
Breakfast	zǎofàn	早饭
Lunch	wǔfàn	午饭
Dinner	wǎnfàn	晚饭
Chopsticks	kùaizi	筷子
Fork	chāzi	叉子
Soup ladle	sháozi	勺子
I want	Wǒ yào …	我要…
I do not want	Wǒ bú yào ….	我不要…
I did not reserve	Zhègè wǒ meí dìng.	这个我没订。
Beer	píjiǔ	啤酒
Eat	chīfàn	吃饭
Coca-cola	kěkóu kělè	可口可乐
Mineral water	kúangqúanshǔi	矿泉水
Menu	càidān	菜单
Rice	mǐfàn	米饭
Noodles	miàntiáo	面条
Tea	chá	茶
Soup	tāng	汤
Dishes (food dishes)	(fàn)cài	(饭)菜
Beef/pork/lamb	níuròu/zhūroù/yángroù	牛肉/猪肉/羊肉
Fish	yú	鱼
Vegetables	shūcài	蔬菜
Fruit/fruits	shúigǔo	水果
Bread	miànbāo	面包
Toast	kaǒmiànbāo	烤面包
Butter	húangyóu	黄油
Egg	jīdaǹ	鸡旦
Cup	bēizi	杯子
Glass cup	bōlì bēizi	玻璃杯子
Hot (spicy))/sweet/sour/salty	là/tián/suān/xián	辣/甜/酸/咸
White wine/red wine	bǎi pútàojiǔ/hóng pútàojiǔ	白葡萄酒/红葡萄酒
Can we have the bill?	Qǐng sùanzhàng bǎ.	请算帐吧。

Time

| When? | Shénmè shíhòu? | 什么时候? |

What time is it?	Jǐ diǎnzhōng?	几点钟?
How long?	Duōcháng shíjiān?	多长时间?
one/two/three	Yī/liǎng/sān diǎnzhōng	一/俩/三点钟
morning/early afternnon/ late afternoon	zǎoshàng/shàngwǔ/zhōngwǔ/	早上/上午/中午
Afternoon/night	xiàwǔ/wǎnshàng	下午/晚上
Monday	xīngqīyī	星期一
Tuesday	xīngqīèr	星期二
Wednesday	xīngqīsān	星期三
Thursday	xīngqīsì	星期四
Friday	xīngqīwǔ	星期五
Saturday	xīngqīliù	星期六
Sunday	xīngqītiān	星期天
Weekend	zhōumò	周末
Yesterday/today/tomorrow	zuótiān/jīntiān/míngtiān	昨天/今天/明天
This week/last week/ next week	zhège/sháng/xiàxīngqī	这个/上/下星期
Hour/day/week/month	xiǎoshí/tiān/xīngqī/yuè	小时/天/星期/月
January, February, March, April, May	yīyuè/éryuè/sānyuè/sìyuè/wǔyuè	一月,二月,三月,四月,五月,
June, July, August, September	liùyuè/qīyuè/bāyuè/jǐuyuè	六月,七月,八月,九月,
October, November, December	shíyuè/shíyīyuè/shíèryuè	十月,十一月,十二月,

Numbers

One	yī	一
Two	ér	二
Three	sān	三
Four	sì	四
Five	wǔ	五
Six	liù	六
Seven	qī	七
Eight	bā	八
Nine	jiǔ	九
Ten	shí	十
Eleven	shíyī	十一
Twelve	shíèr	十二
Twenty	érshī	二十
Thirty	sānshī	三十
Forty	sìshī	四十
Fifty	wǔshī	五十
Sixty	liushī	六十
Seventy	qīshī	七十
Eighty	bāshī	八十
Ninety	jiǔshī	九十
One hundred	yìbǎi	一百
One hundred and one	yìbǎilíngyī	一百零一
Two hundred	èrbǎi	二百
Three hundred	sānbǎi	三百
Four hundred	sìbǎi	四百
Five hundred	wǔbǎi	五百
Six hundred	liùbǎi	六百

Index

The Insight Approach

The book you are holding is part of the world's largest range of guidebooks. Its purpose is to help you have the most valuable travel experience possible, and we try to achieve this by providing not only information about countries, regions and cities but also genuine insight into their history, culture, institutions and people.

Since the first Insight Guide – to Bali – was published in 1970, the series has been dedicated to the proposition that, with insight into a country's people and culture, visitors can both enhance their own experience and be accepted more easily by their hosts. Now, in a world where ethnic hostilities and nationalist conflicts are all too common, such attempts to increase understanding between peoples are more important than ever.

Insight Guides:
Essentials for understanding

Because a nation's past holds the key to its present, each Insight Guide kicks off with lively history chapters. These are followed by magazine-style essays on culture and daily life. This essential background information gives readers the necessary context for using the main Places section, with its comprehensive run-down on things worth seeing and doing. Finally, a listings section contains all the information you'll need on travel, hotels, restaurants and opening times.

As far as possible, we rely on local writers and specialists to ensure that the information is authoritative. The pictures, for which Insight Guides have become so celebrated, are just as important. Our photojournalistic approach aims not only to illustrate a destination but also to communicate visually and directly to readers life as it is lived by the locals.

Compact Guides
The "great little guides"

As invaluable as such background information is, it isn't always fun to carry an Insight Guide through a crowded souk or up a church tower. Could we, readers asked, distil the key reference material into a slim volume for on-the-spot use?

Our response was to design Compact Guides as an entirely new series, with original text carefully cross-referenced to detailed maps and more than 200 photographs. In essence, they're miniature encyclopedias, concise and comprehensive, displaying reliable and up-to-date information in an accessible way.

Pocket Guides:
A local host in book form

However wide-ranging the information in a book, human beings still value the personal touch. Our editors are often asked the same questions. Where do *you* go to eat? What do *you* think is the best beach? What would you recommend if I have only three days? We invited our local correspondents to act as "substitute hosts" by revealing their preferred walks and trips, listing the restaurants they go to and structuring a visit into a series of timed itineraries.

The result is our Pocket Guides, complete with full-size fold-out maps. These 100-plus titles help readers plan a trip precisely, particularly if their time is short.

Exploring with Insight:
A valuable travel experience

In conjunction with co-publishers all over the world, we print in up to 10 languages, from German to Chinese, from Danish to Russian. But our aim remains simple: to enhance your travel experience by combining our expertise in guidebook publishing with the on-the-spot knowledge of our correspondents.